Law, Violence and Constituent Power

This book challenges traditional theories of constitution-making to advance an alternative view of constitutions as being founded on power which rests on violence.

The work argues that rather than the idea of a constitution being the result of political participation and deliberation, all power instead is based on violence. Hence the creation of a constitution is actually an act of coercion, where, through violence, one social group is able to impose itself over others. The book advocates that the presence of violence be used as an assessment of whether genuine constitutional transformation has taken place, and that the legitimacy of a constitutional order should be dependent upon the absence of killing.

The book will be essential reading for academics and researchers working in the areas of constitutional law and politics, legal and political theory, and constitutional history.

Hèctor López Bofill is Associate Professor in Constitutional Law at Pompeu Fabra University. He has written eight books and more than 20 articles in the field of constitutional theory, fundamental rights, federalism, secessionism, and judicial review of legislation. He is also a writer in Catalan language. He has published five poetry books and five novels which have received several awards.

Comparative Constitutional Change

Comparative Constitutional Change has developed into a distinct field of constitutional law. It encompasses the study of constitutions through the way they change and covers a wide scope of topics and methodologies. Books in this series include work on developments in the functions of the constitution, the organization of powers, and the protection of rights, as well as research that focuses on formal amendment rules and the relationship between constituent and constituted power. The series includes comparative approaches along with books that focus on single jurisdictions and brings together research monographs and edited collections which allow the expression of different schools of thought. While the focus is primarily on law, where relevant the series may also include political science, historical, philosophical, and empirical approaches that explore constitutional change.

Series editors

Xenophon Contiades is Professor of Public Law at Panteion University, Athens, Greece and Managing Director at the Centre for European Constitutional Law, Athens, Greece.

Thomas Fleiner is Emeritus Professor of Law at the University of Fribourg, Switzerland. He teaches and researches in the areas of Federalism; Rule of Law; Multicultural State; Comparative Administrative and Constitutional Law; Political Theory and Philosophy; Swiss Constitutional and Administrative Law; and Legislative Drafting. He has published widely in these and related areas.

Alkmene Fotiadou is Research Associate at the Centre for European Constitutional Law, Athens.

Richard Albert is Professor of Law at the University of Texas in Austin.

Also in the series

Peace, Discontent and Constitutional Law
Challenges to Constitutional Order and Democracy
Edited by Martin Belov

Populist Challenges to Constitutional Interpretation in Europe and Beyond
Edited by Fruzsina Gárdos-Orosz, and Zoltán Szente

Constitutional Change and Popular Sovereignty
Populism, Politics and the Law in Ireland
Edited by Maria Cahill, Colm Ó Cinnéide, Seán Ó Conaill, and Conor O'Mahony

For more information about this series, please visit:
www.routledge.com/Comparative-Constitutional-Change/book-series/COMPCO NST

Law, Violence and Constituent Power

The Law, Politics and History of Constitution Making

Hèctor López Bofill

Routledge
Taylor & Francis Group
LONDON AND NEW YORK

First published 2021
by Routledge
2 Park Square, Milton Park, Abingdon, Oxon OX14 4RN

and by Routledge
605 Third Avenue, New York, NY 10158

Routledge is an imprint of the Taylor & Francis Group, an informa business

British Library Cataloguing-in-Publication Data
A catalogue record for this book is available from the British Library

Library of Congress Cataloging-in-Publication Data
Names: López Bofill, Hèctor, author.
Title: Law, violence and constituent power : the law, politics and history of constitution making / Hèctor López Bofill.
Description: Milton Park, Abingdon, Oxon ; New York, NY : Routledge, 2021. | Series: Comparative constitutional change | Includes bibliographical references and index.
Identifiers: LCCN 2020055256 (print) | LCCN 2020055257 (ebook) | ISBN 9780367516710 (hardback) | ISBN 9781003054801 (ebook)
Subjects: LCSH: Constituent power. | Political violence. | Constitution (Philosophy). | Constitutional history.
Classification: LCC K3289.5 .L67 2021 (print) | LCC K3289.5 (ebook) | DDC 342.02--dc23
LC record available at https://lccn.loc.gov/2020055256
LC ebook record available at https://lccn.loc.gov/2020055257

ISBN: 978-0-367-51671-0 (hbk)
ISBN: 978-0-367-51673-4 (pbk)
ISBN: 978-1-003-05480-1 (ebk)

Typeset in Galliard
by Deanta Global Publishing Servies, Chennai, India

This book is for Prof. Dr. Dr. h.c. mult. Peter Häberle, with humility and admiration, hoping that this dedication shall compensate my theoretical deviation from his teachings.

Contents

Acknowledgements

This is an ambitious book. I began to write about what in continental Europe is known as the "constituent power" from an orthodox constitutional legal scholarly perspective and I suddenly found myself writing on the origins of public power in constitutional democracies: a comprehensive investigation. Indeed, in pursuing the topic on constitutional creation I have mainly followed the contributions provided by authors trained in the legal tradition, but my analysis also draws on information and insights from a wide range of scholarly disciplines, most notably: history, historical sociology, economics, and political philosophy. I have, in fact, tried to imitate the approaches of such constitutional legal theorists that I find more appealing and that I admire most, true giants of my discipline such as Bruce Ackerman, Peter Häberle, and Joseph Weiler, to whom I shall be eternally in debt.

I have constructed this book in the institution in which I have taught and researched for most of my academic life: the Pompeu Fabra University in Barcelona. Even though I am not very old, I still belong to that generation of legal scholars that had the fortune to get a position in earlier stages of their career, who have spent more time locked in their office reading and writing than travelling around the world in search of a postdoc or applying for a research project. Accordingly, I have to thank my law department for providing me the stability to develop my theoretical inquiries. I should here follow by thanking the many mentors, professors, and colleagues that I have had the great pleasure to meet within the frame of the Pompeu Fabra: Marc Carrillo, Carles Viver, Alejandro Sáiz Arnáiz, Víctor Ferreres, Josep Joan Moreso, Josep Lluís Martí, Jorge Malem, Ricardo Caracciolo, Ferran Requejo, Fernando Guirao, Pau Salvador Coderch, Josep Maria Vilajosana, Tomás de Montagut, Pau Bossacoma, Albert Lamarca, Aïda Torres, Neus Torbisco, Francesca Maria Pou, Marc Sanjaume, Maribel Pascual, Rosa Lucas, Luis Javier Mieres, Marisa Iglesias, Josep Capdeferro, Alfons Aragoneses, Josep Pich, Iván Carlo, Nico Krisch, Jaime Lluch, Armin von Bogdandy, and Roberto Gargarella. My sedentary professional life (my personal life is another matter) has not deprived me of attending several international congresses, particularly those organized by the International Society of Public Law, in which I presented some ideas that I have introduced in the following pages. I had the opportunity there to discuss with prominent specialists on the issue of constitutional foundations and their transformations such as Antoni Abad Ninet, Vito Breda, Joel Colón-Rios, Oran Doyle, Zoran Oklopcic, Yaniv Roznai, Nikos Skoutaris, Sergio Verdugo, and Rivka Weill. I'm especially grateful to Oran Doyle and his comments on recent Irish constitutional developments that I have included in Chapter 5 and the same I would say to Sergio Verdugo concerning the epigraph devoted to the Chilean case. I am, however, the only one to blame for any gaps or flaws in those sections. I'm also in debt to Professor Jose Luis Caballero Ochoa whose invitation in Spring 2016 to the Universidad Iberoamericana in Mexico City was an inspiration for the development of my considerations on the contemporary constitution-making processes that can be found in the following pages. In a different vein, I will be eternally grateful to professor Häberle's disciples (who have now become very important professors) Lothar Michael and Markus Kotzur, for their help during my research stages in Bayreuth. My special thanks to Richard Albert, who always believed in my task as a researcher and whose support was essential for this book to see the light. Such an outcome would have not been possible either without the staggering work of my publishers in Routledge. Also essential was the support of Mathew Barton for his enduring help, reviewing my English. I wish also to thank my friends Àlex Perera, Ana Hernández, Felip Martí, and Jaume Renyer (the latter is also my brother-in-law) who, coming from quite different disciplines, crucially inspired me in composing the ideas of this contribution.

I reserve the biggest thanks for my family, which, being not so numerous, I would like to mention in its entirety: my father, Josep López Martí, my mother, *in memoriam*, Maria Rosa Bofill, my grandmother, Maria Martí, my brother, Raül López Bofill, my wife, Hye Young Yu, and my son, Marcel López Yu. Thanks to all of them for their love.

Introduction

Violence and foundation

The origins of constitutional democracy

A political community not founded on violence has probably never existed. In the beginning was violence and then appeared the word that ensured the order emerged from the original breach. First comes the force and then comes the myth. In such considerations are included authoritarian patterns of government but also (herein the main concern of this text) States organized under the set of political and legal practices identified with the concept of constitutional democracy.

The basic idea of this text is that even the founding of a system grounded on the rule of law, the separation of powers, fundamental rights, and political participation is originally rooted in some form of coercion, such as wars, exploitation, ethnic cleansing, or domination through armed force, and not in a public, fair, and rational deliberation developed within a space of freedom and equality. Accordingly, constitutional limitations, including the idea of constitutional supremacy and its safeguards, such as judicial review of legislation, besides the task of protecting liberties within day-to-day democratic developments also help to maintain the powers erected during the creation of the political regime.

Constitutional settlements that supposedly serve liberalism and democracy, in short, that have been drafted and adopted in the shadow of the gun,[1] or similar circumstances, have consequences that reemerge in the present. Modern scholars who have approached the question of constituent power tend to admit that "(almost all) actual beginnings are linked to dictating violence and can have no normative justification" (Arato, 2016, p. 1). To put it in Nietzsche's words (an author that through Foucault's genealogical analysis shall be crucial in my analysis) legal and moral concepts "in their beginning, as all that is great in the earth have been watered by blood" (Nietzsche, 1892, p. 51). Any research into constituent power is a research on the origins *par excellence*, an inquiry on the formation of political order and the drafting of the rules that organize it. The constitutional State has this "original sin." The liberal and democratic State has found in constitutionalism a way to rationalize (and to forget) the original violence, the centrality of sacrifice (of killing and being killed) in the construction of the political entity (Kahn, 2011, p. 28).

The veil that helps partly to cover the trace of the corpses is related to the concept of "popular sovereignty," and more precisely, to the narratives developed around the participation of the public in the approval of the constitutional settlement (Balkin, 2011, pp. 31–32; Torres and Guinier, 2012, p. 1057). Under the constitutionalist paradigm the justification of constitutional supremacy hinges on the "We the People,"[2] the political entity that, as a sovereign nation, conscious of its unity and supposedly as an act of free will, gives itself the framework of the basic rules that will organize the community in the future. Current enquiries on constituent power are centred in tracing a normative theory on people's participation while creating a constitution (see, among many others, Agne, 2012; Banks, 2008; Colón-Ríos, 2012; Eisenstadt et al., 2017; Elster, 1994, 1995, 2000a, 2000b; Habermas, 2001; Lindahl, 2015; Loughlin, 2014; Rubenfeld, 2001; Rua Wall, 2012). But another point of this book handles violence as a decisive factor involved in every constitution-making process.

In spite of the fact that some prominent scholars who had turned their interest to the question of how constitutions are created admit the decisive role of coercion in drafting and passing constitutions (Patberg, 2017, p. 55; Loughlin, 2014, p. 229; Kumm, 2016a, p. 920; Walker, 2016, p. 908) they tend to elude any further consideration on that issue in order to look at the empirical forms of democratic practices and public participation that may be registered in some constituent experiences (so Jacobsohn and Roznai, 2020, p. 224). Unsurprisingly, violence barely plays a role in their theoretical analysis of the constituent power.[3]

Instead, my approach is concerned about *the empirical practice of violence* in constitution-making processes arguing that any of the violations perpetrated during the founding cannot be compensated by narratives on popular participation.[4] In other words, the mere presence of violence cancels any justification of constitutions grounded on the supposed democratic character of the process that created them. Since the real world offers a general connection between violence and the building of constitutional order, I consider it secondary to explore in detail which condition should be fulfilled in order to determine if a constitution is, or is not, a product of popular will.

Narratives on public mobilization and participation

However, and in spite of stubborn reality showing itself over and over again, the crucial link between turbulent revolutions and the creation of new constitutional orders, modern and classical theories on constitution, constitutionalism, and constituent power insist on the promise of an inclusive founding process among free and equal individuals, both from the perspective of describing constituent experiences of the past and from the perspective of formulating prescriptive statements.

Constituent power, in this fashion, is seen as an act of collective and self-conscious mobilization able to redirect decisively a nation's governing principles and practices (Jacobsohn, 2014, p. 2). Constitutions of democracies are thought to supply democratic and self-contained standards of legitimacy that express people's fundamental and enduring values (Fox-Decent, 2016, p. 119).

Constraints imposed by a constitution would somehow be constraints agreed by the people itself (or *rectius*, by the "electorate" acting as if it were the "people." See Colón-Ríos, 2020, p. 280). Consequently, considering that the constitution is the highest level of lawmaking and provides the ultimate rule of recognition for lawmaking processes, it requires the greatest possible level of legitimation in democratic theory (Ginsburg, Elkins, and Blount, 2009, p. 206). It is commonly assumed, thus, that the constituent process has to be itself democratic in a strong sense (Arato, 1995–1996, p. 191). Conceptualizations of constituent power in this fashion often coincide with conceptualizations of the people (Contiades and Fotiadou, 2017, p. 9): who is the bearer of the power to create constitutions has become in modern political theory a particular expression of a theory on the people's sovereignty and, therefore, on the reconstruction and imagination of what a people is (Oklopcic, 2018, p. 1).

The idea on constituent power has, in fact, attempted to simplify the question of the people's sovereignty by limiting its analysis to the body of people from whom the constitutional authority emanates (Saunders, 2012, p. 3; Tushnet, 2013, pp. 1985–1986). Some of these traces of a relationship between a popular body and the formation of a constitutional framework might be inferred, for instance, from the very beginning of the United States Federal Constitution, which famously proclaims that "We the People ... do ordain and establish this Constitution," and the same justification lies behind the reasoning of the United States Supreme Court in *Marbury versus Madison* when exposing the premise that:

> the people have an original right to establish, for their future government, such principles as, in their opinion, shall most conduce to their own happiness.[5]

The concept of the constituent power has been from its origins associated with a constitutional theory on democracy (Böckenförde, 1992a, p. 93; Kalyvas, 2008, p. 99; Roznai, 2017, p. 125; Schmitt, 1993, p. 238). As Antonio Negri stated, talking about the constituent power is talking about democracy (2002, p. 11). But what popular mobilization and participation is there, theoretically surrounding the foundation of each constitutional order? To what degree and under which procedural conditions should the action of the citizenry be expressed in order to affirm that constitutional decisions correspond to the people's will? Beyond the normative premise according to which constitutions should be the result of a democratic decision-making process in a way that all those subjected to the collective binding decisions of the State that is being created and regulated are entitled to determine the form and the competences of its political institutions. (Patberg, 2017, p. 51) the aforementioned questions fall into a well of vagueness, confusion, and contradiction. As we shall see, there has been a shift in modern constitutional design towards more inclusive and participatory mechanisms whereby the people can assume their constituent role (see Jacobsohn and Roznai, 2020, p. 257) but there are no clear avenues neither in the doctrine nor in the institutional practice for assessing that the exercise of constituent power approximately manifests the popular view. Referenda, for instance, are usually seen as carrying a higher degree of popular legitimacy but, conversely, it is stated that people's involvement need not be limited to mere ratification via referendum (see Abad Ninet, 2013, p. 14) since such a conception lacks any rational deliberation. Ratification via referendum has been, however, a usual path taken by a relevant part of constituent experiences to confer democratic legitimacy to the constitutional product, to the degree that among current constitutions, more than 40 per cent were publicly ratified by referenda (see Jabsohn and Roznai, 2020, pp. 256–257 and Versteeg, 2014, p. 1142). In short, we do not exactly know what it means, nor which specific normative and institutional implications have to state that a constitution-making process ought to be "inclusive," "participatory," "time consuming," or "deliberative."

In the context of transitions from authoritarian regimes to liberal ones, in another sense, contemporary discussions highlight that the more the public are involved in the constitution-making process (in terms of electing a constitution-making body, participating in its debates, or approving the final constitutional draft by referendum), the more the citizens will internalize constitutional norms to the extent of defending the constitution from any authoritarian abuse and, consequently, the more the stability of the system will be safeguarded (Mendez and Wheatley, 2013, p. 13; Weingast, 1997, p. 251). But real experiences of constitution-making show that constitutional discussion is displayed in closed *fora*, through an exchange provided by the interaction among elites, in which the citizenry, at most, is invited to agree or not by the means of a referendum with the whole package of decisions already adopted. And, in fact, deciding such arrangements within closed circles beyond the pressure of the population has frequently represented the stage in which transitions in profoundly divided societies have gained some opportunity to succeed. Still, appealing to the will of the people has rather emerged as the favourite resource of modern autocrats to circumvent the representative bodies and impose their particular constitutional model (Colón-Ríos, 2020, p. 1 and p. 14; Partlett, 2012, p. 96; Scheuerman, 1997, p. 151) and as such, there is a wide range of authors (from Sieyès to Arato, see 2016, pp. 19–74) who are reluctant to couple the idea of the constituent power with forms of direct popular democracy. Such a strand of thought is not worried about the deficits of participation or the deficits of fairness that might arise during the constitutional drafting. It seems, rather, that they are concerned by *the excesses that the people may commit* (Duong, 2017) or, more precisely, by *the excesses that someone may commit in the name of the people* (Chryssogonos, p. 1305).

The people is the indisputable source of political legitimacy in modern constitutional thought but is also, as is well known by the German constitutional tradition, a source of fear (Möllers, 2007; Preuss, 1995). It is at least curious to confirm the extent to which the constitutional system among those in the

Western tradition, that is most remarkable in its resistance of the present siege of populist trends, is precisely the regime of the German Basic Law, that was passed with a lack of popular participation both in 1949 and in the process towards German reunification in 1990. Maybe all the scholars concerned in the narratives of public involvement should ask themselves why the German constitutional system has done remarkably well for more than 70 years by marginalizing any form of popular direct participation (such as federal referenda) in the debate on the constitutional foundation and by refusing to contemplate a constituent assembly directly elected by the citizenry.

The legitimacy grounds of constitutional supremacy

The involvement of the people in deciding the core issues of government has been, from the eighteenth century, related to the modern trust in the human ability to transform reality (Klein and Sajó, 2012, p. 420; Krish, 2016, p. 659; Colón-Ríos, 2015, p. 568). If, before modernity, the source of legitimacy of a political order's foundation was located beyond human-made law (in God, in the Holy Scripture, in Nature), from the Enlightenment era onwards such a source of legitimacy is monopolized by the people (Benhabib, 1994, p. 9), and the emergence of the democratic revolution was precisely possible as long as absolutes evaporated from the grounding of societies (Lefort, 1988, p. 19). Few ideas in the political sphere express so sharply the potency of human will in deciding human fate, instead of being subjected to the avatars provided by divinity, as that related to constituent power.[6] As Habermas declared, the democratic procedure for the production of law (in our case the production of fundamental laws) forms the only source of legitimacy for our "postmetaphysical" age (Habermas, 1996, p. 448).

Even today, and mainly as a consequence of the attractiveness of such a radically democratic promise for citizens to change the reality and their polity if they so desire, the concept of a democratic constituent power continues to play a major role in liberal constitutional orders. It provides a justification for the superiority of the constitution in the hierarchy of norms, and a basis of legitimacy for constitutional review over parliamentary legislation (Krish, 2016, p. 661).

Bruce Ackerman, with his notion of "dualism," distinguishes between times when politics enjoy "constitutional moments" (during which, according to his vision, the public is more engaged with political affairs) and "ordinary politics" mainly conducted through representatives within a frame of less public interest. Ackerman's basic insight consists in associating the periods of "higher lawmaking" with a high deliberative citizenry mobilization.[7] Exceptional constitutional politics are developed in periods in which "mobilizational forms of mass engagement … dominate the constitutional stage." In Ackerman's theory such expressions of people's constitutional will, since they require clear, strong, sustained, and committed majorities, are represented by time-extended courses of political events.[8] The Ackermanian higher lawmaking track imposes special rigorous tests upon the political movements that hope to earn the heightened sense of democratic legitimacy awarded to spokespersons for the people. The supreme character of constitutional developments, thus, would be justified by such acute exceptional political episodes triggered by wide majorities in favour of major constitutional changes.

As I mentioned, besides Ackerman's work, we may currently find a broad consensus in the literature about the importance of public participation and deliberation while constitution-making. Scholars and practitioners have come to view a high level of popular engagement as necessary for a constitution to be regarded as legitimate and relevant by the citizenry (among many others see Banks, 2008, 1046; Ginsburg, Blount, and Elkins, 2008, p. 381; Klein and Sajó, 2012, p. 434; Blokker, 2017, pp. 40–42; Blount, 2011, p. 1046; Näsström, 2007; Samuels, 2006, p. 668). Joel Colón-Ríos (2012, p. 5) has also developed his theory on constitutionalism and democracy under the idea that ordinary citizens must be allowed to propose, deliberate, and decide upon important constitutional transformations through the most participatory methods possible (a conception that Colón-Ríos wraps under the category of "weak constitutionalism"). So, under that perspective, any barrier on public participation at the level of the creation of fundamental law should be viewed with suspicion. Such a view of constitutional democracy claims that democracy should enshrine a more direct and substantive participation of citizens in the democratic process, including constitutional politics (also Blokker, 2017, p. 41; Tekin, 2016, p. 4).

As we shall see, some recent experiences on constitutional change in liberal democracies have been strongly influenced by the "weak constitutionalist" vision of public involvement in debating on the foundations of a constitutional order. However, I might already advance that if the success in practice of such ideals has been meagre, that has been due to the fact that *constitutions are precisely made to put barriers to citizenry participation* on changing the legal basic principles. Constitution-making operations are more related with the struggle of the founders to armour to the future the particular constellation of powers held by them in the constituent moment than by the intention of opening channels of discussion on the basic principles that define said constitutional order. In that vein it might be stated that the paradox of most liberal democracies is that the outcome of their ordinary legislation *is more democratic than the context of their founding.*

While scholars of constitutional law have maintained comparative silence on the issue of the foundational processes of constitutions, those of political philosophy have produced a plethora of contributions dealing with the objection to the lack of democracy that have characterized political and constitutional formation (Honig, 2007; Olson, 2007; Tekin, 2016; Zurn, 2010). Frank Michelman's criticisms are remarkable (1996) on Habermas' theory regarding the supposed mutual interaction between democracy and legality in relation to human rights in the origins of constitutional democracy (Habermas, 1996, see on that point also Cronin, 2006). Michelman pointed out the bootstrapping paradox concerning the application of democratic procedures to assess the legitimacy of constitutional grounds. According to Michelman, the foundational task of a democracy requires a set of procedures that have to fulfil democratic requirements as well, which would lead us to an infinite regression of procedures of democratic legitimacy presupposing procedures (Michelman, 1996). Although such a line of reasoning has had many followers, who have analyzed in detail the terms of the democratic paradoxes lying behind the foundation of a constitutional democracy (see Honig, 2007; Olson, 2007) it is not easy to find among them an examination of the role of historical events as distorting factors of such democratic procedures.

From my perspective, nonetheless, the foundation of a constitutional democracy is explainable because the aforementioned unlimited chain of procedures on regulating the democratic conditions of a democratic founding *is broken up by an historical event.* Descriptively, constitutional appearance shows a suspension of the democratic circumstances of validity, provided by *the facts* (see also Atria, 2020, p. 51). In my opinion, thus, when in Michelman's legal theory it is stressed that a liberal democratic constitutional order cannot be democratically founded in a procedurally legitimate sense, it is meant that the act of the founding depends on someone's unilateral, procedurally unregulated will (Keenan, 2003, pp. 41–54), as an outcome of a historical experience. And that experience is usually (if not always) supported by the use of force. The sentence, of religious echoes, according to which "the event of the foundation of an order is not a part of the founded order" (Arato, 2016, p. 20) has from the methodological point of view, accordingly, to be applied to a constitutional democracy in order to state that either liberalism or democracy is part of the structure that establishes both of them.

In a different direction from the political one presented, another philosophical tradition, focused on ontological and linguistic analysis, has perceived the importance of coercion in creating a homogeneous social body as an agent of constitutional founding. Such a path has been explored in the writings of Jacques Derrida, in his considerations on the 1776 American Declaration of Independence (Derrida, 1986) and on the origins of authority (Derrida, 1990) as well as the linguistic analysis of republicanism developed by Jean-François Lyotard in his essay "Le Différend" (1983). However, beyond the (quite inexplicable) loss of influence of the so-called "postmodernist" approaches in legal thought and, particularly, concerning their ideas on constitutional origins, in my opinion, Lyotard or Derrida's treatment of violence as an ultimately meta-political and meta-legal question is only tangentially exposed. The ascertainment of sheer power in the enquiries on the creation of a constitutional framework is rather more precisely captured in the writings of Seyla Benhabib, in stressing that every act of foundation and every act of constitution of a polity may conceal a moment of exclusionary violence (Benhabib, 1994, p. 10).

Already David Hume (Hume, 1963, p. 460) announced a similar idea pointing out the basic questions that I am going to develop in this contribution:

> Almost all the governments which exist at present, or of which there remains any record in history, have been founded originally, either on usurpation or conquest, or both, without any pretense of a fair consent of voluntary subjection of the people.

> The face of the Earth is continually changing, by the increase of small kingdoms into great empires, by the dissolution of great empires into smaller kingdoms, by the planting of colonies, by the migration of tribes. Is there anything discoverable in all these events but force and violence? Where is the mutual agreement or voluntary association so much talked of?
> I maintain that human affairs will never admit of this consent, seldom of the appearance of it; but that conquest or usurpation, that is, in plain terms, force, by dissolving the ancient governments, is the origin of almost all the new ones which were ever established in the world. And that in the few cases where consent may seem to have taken place, it was commonly so irregular, so confined, or so much intermixed either with fraud or violence, that it cannot have any great authority.

Certainly, the case in which a constitutional transformation has been joined by an inclusive political process of constitution-making leading to a document approved by the vast majority of the population without any individual or collective rights violation is not only rare (Oklopcic, 2014, p. 203), it is almost completely absent from the human experience. Constitution-making is often undertaken in situations in which existing political institutions have broken down and abuses and arbitrariness are unleashed.

Eluding the objection of the historical role of violence has been, however, quite common in social studies. As was remarked by political theorists such as Stathis Kalyvas, Ian Shapiro, and Tarek Masoud, disciplinary and sub-disciplinary barriers have long separated the various ways of studying the influence of violence in creating and maintaining an order (Kalyvas et al., 2008, p. 1). As the mentioned authors observe, researchers on violence and conflict tend to focus on places and periods in which order has collapsed and they rarely consider *how violence is used to create the subsequent order that appears.* Regarding my point, more precisely, the traditional silence of political philosophers, historians, sociologists, anthropologists, economists, or constitutional law scholars diminishes when determining the influence of violence in constitutional processes *that succeeded* in building constitutional democracies.

My hypothesis, in that sense, is that *violence is an essential element in explaining the idea of constituent power in constitutional democracies* and that the study of the historical constitutional origins of liberal democracies leads to a general reconsideration of the political legitimacy grounds of constitutionalism. In my approach, and precisely given the scarce implication of the people in the historical experiences of constitution-making in supposed liberal democracies, the problem is *previous* to the democratic legitimacy of the constitution-making processes. Thus, the problem is asking not about popular involvement in the different stages of constitution approval *but asking about whether there was violence or not.* When in his contribution on revolutionary constitutionalism Bruce Ackerman (2019, p. 4) almost casually mentions that insurgencies that led to constitutional creations were accompanied by mortal victims, this author is likely to tackle the relationship between violence and the formation of constitutional democracies almost as a neglectable fatality, a collateral damage in the process of establishing later legal constraints on top decision-makers under a system defined by the rule of law, human rights, and the regular calling of free elections. But to me, where Ackerman sees the contingency of history with scarce interest in explaining the grounds of constitutionalism,˙I see precisely the main problem of the liberal democracies. It is probably on the disruptions experienced during the creation of the system where there lie the causes of the present instabilities that plague such political structures.

Under my perspective, thus, the darkness comes not when we ask ourselves about what lies behind the constituent power in the People's Republic of China or any other authoritarian State, the main concern of the following lines is the involvement of violence in the creation of States and in the configuration of their constitutional order central to the tradition constitutionalism, such as the United States or the Federal Republic of Germany. This book is, in sum, a *critic of constitutionalism within liberal democracies through the notion of constituent power.*

Precisely because my interest is mainly focused on the most prominent patterns of liberal constitutionalism I will not get into the discussion (in another way crucial for contemporary constitutionalism) regarding the fuzzy zone between authoritarian constitutionalism and liberal constitutionalism (Tushnet, 2015a) considering, furthermore, that some of the problems that present liberal democracies have to deal with are related to the descent of their government into different types of authoritarianism. The point is that almost no liberal democracy (or perhaps *none* of them) fulfils a liberal democratic standard in the creation of its fundamental rules and perhaps, as I shall argue, it is because of such non-democratic backgrounds' origins that the current authoritarian turn in supposed liberal democracies can be explained.

As such, populism and radicalism, in many ways expressed through extreme conservativism, would not be anything else but a return to the origins, in times when there is the perception that the fundamentals of a given political system are in danger.

My point would be rather that in highlighting the shortfalls of the liberal constitutionalist mainstays of the Western tradition, in pointing out that *liberal constitutionalism would not be so distant to authoritarian constitutionalism as one* prima facie *may think* if we turn our view to the original position from which both constitutional democracies and authoritarian regimes originated. The question would not be to what extent the American Revolution, for instance, differs to any other revolution, even a cruel one, arisen during recent times in Africa, in the Middle East or in Asia that has driven to a constitutional transformation. The question is, rather, what *they have in common*, and if these factors in common concerning violence are consubstantial in exercising constituent power.

The definition of violence

Violence is crucial in my investigation on the constitutional foundations. But what do I understand "violence" to be? Violence is used in my analysis as an essential category and is not handled as a metaphor but as a fact. I may here mention the distinguishing between different notions of violence provided by Žižek when he recognizes in the first term a "subjective violence" (a direct and visible violence), in the second term a "symbolical violence" (related to the language), and in a third term an "objective violence" [what Žižek calls "systemic" violence which is, according to him, inherent to our political and economic orders (Žižek, 2008, pp. 1–2)]. The violence to which I refer in these inquires on the constituent power is straightforwardly the one referred to by Žižek as the "subjective violence:" *direct, rough, and undisguised violence*. What makes measurable my discourse on the involvement of violence in the emergence of a constitutional system is the strict limitation of this phenomenon to physical force and, still more particularly (and thus more defined and able to be counted) to the physical force that *has a death as a result*. It is in that sense that my exploration on the ontology of violence does not allude to an abstraction or to a comprehensive assessment of a social system (as Žižek is likely to do when he defines his notion of "systemic" violence) but to *the concrete death of a human being*. Death, political death, is the essential category in which the struggle of the forces for domination may be identified and is, in that way, the material root of further ideal constructions, as a constitution, from which the mortal fight is a reverberation. Maybe it would not be accurate to talk about analysis on the constituent power from the ontological perspective, as long as it would be defined as the science of being. I'm rather setting up, in a kind of Heideggerian or Sartrian turn, a study grounded on the extinction of the being, on the elimination of those who were human beings and are not anymore, an analysis on "the nothing." However, a killing *is* something, *the deaths are real*, not an illusion or a narrative but a specific event in the physical world inhabited by humans.

The revival of the discussion on constituent power (and some possible reasons for its previous abandonment)

Aside from the relatively recent revival of the issue,[9] political philosophy and legal thought had been scarcely concerned in the second half of the twentieth century by the question of constitutional foundation (see Van Middelaar, 2013, p. 36). Such a lack of interest can be seen in spite of, or precisely because of, the fact that most of the constitutional documents in the Western tradition still in force in the twenty-first century were produced during the decades that followed the end of the Second World War.

The theoretical indifference to self-assessment about the origins of Western constitutional democracies in places such as Germany, Italy, or France may be assessed as a political strategy to entrench the legitimacy of such regimes from the ashes of war and given a context in which the Communist bloc could have spread its power to the whole continent. In my opinion, the circumstance that the history of the creation of constitutional orders in the Western tradition and, particularly, in the European tradition, owes something to the developments experienced in the interwar period, during the Second World War and in its immediate aftermath, is what explains the lasting abandonment of the question. In other words, *the violence of that time*, as my research on the present German constitutional system shall remark, had something to do with the configuration of the present constitutional structures, including the taboo on undertaking a serious critique of the constitutional foundations in Europe.

Besides that, the point was that constitutional regimes designed in the postwar decades were stable, stable enough to the degree that they were triumphant in contrast with the collapse of the Soviet bloc from 1989. Nobody was likely to care about the coercions and abuses involved while designing those European political systems that, at the end of the day, *worked*. Even in Germany, as we shall see, the lack of profound constitutional transformations during the process of national reunification in 1990 and the circumstance that East Germany was absorbed by the West German constitutional system, in a move conceived by the Western German political elites, did not provoke relevant protest in Eastern Germany nor among the Western German opposition (Ackerman, 2019, p. 20). German scholars, who maybe in 1990 had been the most active in campaigning for a new German constitution for a unified Germany, soon renounced their proposals.

The European integration process provided instead an opportunity to debate again on the constituencies, but such discussions did not challenge the constitutional pillars of member States nor the condition of the latter of the "masters of the treaties,"[10] in the words of the German Federal Constitutional Court, that is, of their condition as sovereign entities.

An alternative crisis would be necessary in order to provoke any meaningful discussion on constituent processes in Europe. As a consequence of the 2008 global economic crash, everything began to be questioned, particularly in the 2010s when the Western tradition of political thought dealt with the political consequences of the previous economic disaster (Tooze, 2018, p. 13). It is in that vein that some attempts to pass brand new constitutions were undertaken in those political systems that had been sharply affected by the economic devastation (as happened both in Iceland and in Ireland) and that the moves for a new constitutional framework caused a total reconsideration on the theory of political participation regarding the approval of fundamental laws.

Curiously, in those places where a complete constituent operation has been perpetrated were places, like in Hungary, in which constitutional democracies, pressed by the so-called illiberal drift, suffered the questioning of some of their most fundamental principles. They were also places in which the constitutional change *was* effectively culminated with the approval of a new constitution and that happened without instruments of popular direct political participation, not to say any of such innovative figures of public involvement (random citizenry assemblies, partial referenda ...) proposed by theoreticians concerned with the relationship between democracy and the creation of a constitution. Experiences such as the Hungarian one show, to some degree, that a new constitution is likely to be passed precisely *when public involvement is curtailed*.

Apart from the political developments in Western Europe, the conclusions of which are still very uncertain, the question of constituent power had created some interest in other parts of the globe much before the convulsions in the liberal order that the 2008 crisis represented. The aforementioned dismantling of the Communist world, including its consequences in Eastern Europe and the split of some Eastern European States (the Soviet Union, Yugoslavia, and Czechoslovakia), marked another point of increasing theoretical elaboration on constitutional design. The struggles of constitution-making in Latin America were another scenario that brought the topic of constitutional creation to the core of academic concern and, more recently, anti-authoritarian revolutions in the Middle East, already occurring in a moment defined by global economic turmoil, opened other paths for debate on constituent power. But leaving aside the fact that the episodes experienced in Eastern Europe, in Latin America, or in the Middle East were clearly tainted by bursts of violence (which in fact made evident some of the claims expressed in my analysis), the events developed in these areas, far from calling for a reconsideration of constitutional theory, expressed the struggles of some political orders to adapt themselves to the paradigm of constitutionalism as exhibited by liberal democracies in Western Europe and North America.

Only in some Latin American experiences were there substantial reviews of the constitutional foundations of the State as such (and, particularly, as an exercise able to consider the involvement of the citizenry in the creation of fundamental laws). However, the arguable product of the mentioned constitutional experiments developed in places like Venezuela or Bolivia, surrounded by serious social conflicts and authoritarian turns, have had no other effect than casting all sort of doubts on any radical critique of the basic elements of the foundations of their constitutional democracies.

To sum up, the issue of the creation of constitutional democracies (and collaterally the issue of the constitution-making processes) has not been preeminent in theoretical discussion because the central constitutional tradition, depicted by the Western liberal democracies, has not had to deal with the prospect of new beginnings, following a major crisis, in decades. Some convulsions recently detected, such as the rise of populisms, the threats to the supranational integration processes, or the demands of secession in Western Europe, may force a revival of the debate around the creation of political orders and their legal translation.

At the time of writing these lines, it is still too soon to state if the illiberal wave engulfing some long-standing Western liberal democracies will have any impact in rethinking the legitimacy around constitutional foundation. It is also too soon to assess the constitutional consequences of the health, social, and economic crises unleashed by the Covid-19 pandemic in 2020. Either way, with some exceptions, current debates on the erosion of liberal democracy by the day-to-day developments of the constituted power will play a secondary role in my research. They shall only be examined as long as they are related, as I suspect that mostly they are, with the violence that originally blueprinted the constitutional system.

Rethinking democratic theories on constitution-making under the shadow of violence

I will begin my approach with methodological considerations which will encompass the first part of the book. At this stage I will develop my theoretical preference to focus on the description of the historical and social circumstances involved in constituent processes, which I will call henceforth the "genealogical model" inspired by Michel Foucault's social and political terminology (on Foucault's concept of genealogy see Couzens Hoy, 1998, pp. 18–32). This theoretical insight will be presented contesting the models provided by positivist theories and social contract theories which, under my perspective, are not able to give a satisfactory account on the question of the constituent power, even though, as happens in the case of the social contract theories, they introduce some pretended historical descriptions with the intention of supporting their normative assertions. The positivist approach shall be criticized, since in my opinion it does not provide any explanation on what lies behind the normative supremacy, but I will follow some of its premises regarding the idea of "effectiveness" as a crucial notion to grasp the foundation of a constitutional order and its preservation. Effectiveness is, in my analysis, attached to the question of authority and, in a nutshell, to the mere existence of a constitutional legal system.

The main strands of the discussion about the constituent power in liberal democratic constitutional regimes shall be introduced in the central, and second, part of this book.

I will begin by expounding the classic theories on constituent foundations emphasizing the approach of the thinker that, according to some versions, created the concept of constituent power: Emmanuel Sieyès (Sieyès, 1988, p. 137). In introducing Sieyès' ideas on the *pouvoir constituant* and its reinterpretation provided by Carl Schmitt (Schmitt, 1993, p. 75) and particularly given the boundless normative character of the constituent power as traced by both Sieyès and Schmitt, I will go profoundly into my description of the constitution-making processes *as the legal translations of the coercions given in the foundations of the system*. For that I shall distinguish and analyse the historical scenarios of State-building, the drafting of a constitution, and the enforcement of the fundamental rules and the violent clashes respectively experienced in the three of them, as sources of creation of constitutional normativity. The latter will lead me to define a concept of constitution essentially marked by *a decision on the allocation of power gained by force*, and I shall subsequently present a theory on constitutional transformations linked with the previously developed ideas about what a constitution is. At that point we shall turn our attention to some considerations arising from the work of the author who, possibly, has most acutely explored from the perspective of political philosophy the relationship between violence and the foundations of political systems: Giorgio Agamben (2000, 2003, 2005). Differently from Agamben's seminal work, nevertheless, my contribution rather than being centred on a general theory of sovereign power, distinguishes between stages involved in the creation of a constitutional order:

1. the formation of the political community.
2. the specific constitution-making process.
3. the reaffirmation of the constitutional system through the effectiveness of states of emergency.
4. constitutional transformation when the previous order is superseded.

On the other hand, while Agamben's work exposes what may be considered *another* narrative (a different kind of narrative compared with that of the public involvement but a narrative after all), my intention lies in the struggle of providing a conceptual framework to generate empirically accountable research from historical facts and, more precisely, from the restricted notion of violence that I have mentioned above in referring to Žižek's "subjective violence" (on violence as a contested concept see De Haan, 2009, 27–40).

An attempt to demonstrate the empirical research through the analysis of the historical circumstances is delivered through the experience of two prominent constitutional democracies: the United States of America under the 1787 Federal Constitution, and the German Federal Republic under the 1949 German Basic Law. The analysis on the creation of such constitutional systems is enshrined in Chapters 3 and 4 of the book. In those chapters I will invoke the classic pattern in which the emerging of a constitutional framework is supposed to come from the people's will (the United States) and a pattern of a modern constitutional democracy which is mainly imposed by foreign powers (although the latter point is contested by some German historians and political thinkers). Notwithstanding these fundamental differences regarding constitution-making, both constitutional narratives, the American and the German, ground their legitimacy on the idea that constitutional provisions somehow reveal the expression of an extraordinary and democratic power. Examining the historical circumstances closer I will suggest, however, that the web of coercions that envelops a constitution presumably passed "in the name of the people," as the American one, do not broadly differ *from an imposed constitution* such as the German one. Throughout the research I will always have in mind the aforementioned perception: similarities between the American and the German pattern might not only be traced on the outcome (both systems are currently recognized as democracies and federations in which human rights are more or less protected) but on the foundations as well. I will extend my considerations on the German Basic Law to the foundations of the European integration process and the importance of a background of violence to understand the present situation of constitutional structures.

It might be claimed that in my detailed historical analysis should be included, not only the United States and the German Federal Republic cases, but also the French constitutional developments. However, aside from the fact that I shall deal with some French historical events with constitutional relevance while commenting on Sieyès' theory on constituent power, I must emphasize that I have centred my enquiry in constitutional systems which, while founded in the remote past as happens with the United States Federal Constitution, *are still in force* and decisively determine the tradition of current liberal democratic constitutionalism [and leaving aside the considerations expressed by some American authors according to which the United States Constitution has, from a material point of view, radically transformed the original document (see for instance, and in comparison to the French constitutional system, Ackerman, 2019, p. 395)]. Even though the influence of the French constitutional tradition is undeniable both for liberal democratic constitutionalism, in general, and for the theory of constituent power, in particular, I think that a study of the circumstances that led to the approval of the current French Constitution in force, the Constitution of the Fifth Republic adopted on October 4, 1958, would not add any significant point to my thesis. Rather, its adoption in the midst of a political crisis marked by violence, the decolonization wars, and, particularly, the bloody experience of Algerian independence, would do nothing but confirm my intuition (Gildea, 2002, pp. 50–60). Such an appreciation would also emerge if we consider French constitutional history as a whole, since the constitutional replacement has classically taken place through revolutions and coups (Hauriou, 1923, p. 281). In a different sense, the French constitutional experience from 1958 has not been so defining in understanding the dynamic of constitutional development in European integration as the German model has been (Halberstam, 2020, pp. 262–263) an issue on which I shall centre my attention and my critique.

A final part of this work, Chapter 5, will be devoted to the analysis of recent examples of constituent developments in stable liberal democracies which I associate with the term of "new constitutionalism." As we shall see, such struggles of creating a new constitutional settlement have been oriented under the premise of displaying a constituent action with a background of citizenship participation and deliberation, and without any vestige of violence. However, it is symptomatic to confirm the extent to which most of such experiences regarding constituent revisions developed in completely peaceful and deliberative frameworks have historically failed (or did not entail a real constitutional transformation). The recent developments will enable me to show some contradictions inherent to the constitutional founding experience, namely, the paradox of a normative product grounded on an idealized popular unity which is historically created during episodes of radical social and national confrontation.

Hypothesis and empirical challenges

This is a book made of intuitions. Any statement, let's say, on the oligarchies involved in the establishment of a constitutional framework and the violence undertaken to build the legal order (or the understanding of a constitutional decision as a basic decision on the allocation of power resulting from a grave conflict) would need endless empirical research. I have only envisaged the concurrence of the mentioned circumstances in a more elaborated way in the cases of the United States and the German Federal Republic which, due to their weight in the configuration of the constitutionalist tradition, both count with an oceanic background of literature (even though, in my opinion, the critical literature considering the violent strains of both systems and their influence in the determination of constitutional institutions is, particularly in the German case, much scarcer).

If the episodes related to describe the factual, historical, and sociological conditions that lie behind the struggle of creating a constitution, or transforming it, are necessarily incomplete in dealing with both the U.S. and the German precedents, they might be more meagre in alluding to the scenarios in which constitutional transformations have been experienced during the last decades. Furthermore, every constitutional system should be subjected to the test on examining if the involvement of violence has been decisive in the configuration of its constitutional principles.

My initial position is that no constitutional system escapes from this dark side; that when examining the history of creation of public authority, it is easy to find deaths and all sorts of bloodbaths and, in the same way, constitutional supremacy is a device to ensure (and to remember) those deaths, coercions, and bloodbaths that occurred as events of genesis of the new political order.

My contribution would be only limited at least in determining the conceptual frame in which ulterior analysis might be developed. As such, I will be concerned with defining the time and the space of the constitution-making and thus the gap in which the eruption of violence should be considered. In other words, my research would offer some steps forward for future research if it would enable scholars to have some certainties about *what* to count.

Every constitutional democracy, thus, would need at least a book written wearing the glasses of the "genealogical" model in order to ascertain if my hypothesis is correct. Hence a profound quantitative analysis of that sort is still pending, which could be developed by political scientists with exhaustive statistics (which for the mainstream, also in social sciences, is the only way for passing off a research activity as "science"). However, the information currently available will suffice, in lieu of more patient scientific efforts in the future focused on the reconstruction of particular historical, sociological, and economic conditions of the founding moments; while respecting those already developed in the past, such as the noble and advanced works for their time written by Charles Beard (1964) concerning the case of the U.S. Constitution.

My aim will be achieved, if I place the question of violence and its relationship with the legitimacy of constitutionalism in liberal democracies, at the centre of debate.

Notes

1 Such an idea is mentioned by Noah Feldman (Feldman, 2004–2005, p. 858) concerning his research on the Constitutions imposed from outside after a military conflict but he suggests that the statement can be extended even to constituent process grounded on a supposed collective self-determination. On the role of force in the emergence of the State see generally Azar Gat, 2008, pp. 231–322. On the violent foundations during State-building in the case of liberal democracies see, among many others, Istvan Hont, 1994; Michael Mann, 1986 and 2005, and Charles Tilly, 1975 and 1990. For the connection between violence and the elaboration on the ideas of constitutionalism see Bates, 2007.

2 On the conception of a constitution as a product of popular sovereignty able to justify constitutional supremacy see, for instance, Waldron, 2016, pp. 39–41; Klein and Sajó, 2012, p. 427; or Hahm and Kim, 2010, at 800.

3 Such a lack of interest in the relationship between violence and constitution-making processes is appreciated at least among constitutional law scholars. Another vision is available from political philosophers, sociologists, or historians. We shall mention the works of Giorgio Agamben, (Agamben, 2005) who, from philosophy, has built a general theory on violence and the origins of political power including constitution-making. Among the authors that have dealt with the question of violence and constitutional foundations within the framework of studies of constitutional law, see Bates, 2007; Elster, 2012[a], and Samahon, 2011–2012.

4 On the normative value of the narratives concerning the constitutional founding see Kuo, 2019.

5 *Marbury v.Madison*, 5 U.S. 137 (1803), at 176. On Chief Justice Marshall's narrative of the founding, resting on the people's participation see Gilhooley, 2019, pp. 100–104.

6 The idea that the people lies behind the generation of constitutional arrangements has ancestral roots in political thought but it is after the revolutionary experiences in France and North America by the end of the eighteenth century that the political will of the people as the only source of constitutional authority began to expand in justifying the foundation of a new political entity until becoming almost hegemonic (even regarding authoritarian regimes) in the contemporary era. Daniel Lee, for instance, showed how the conception of the people as constituent agent already has vestiges in medieval and early modern civilian thought (Lee, 2016, p. 318) and also Bodin, for instance, in the sixteenth century, distinguished between sovereignty, the locus of authority, and the government, which was described as the instituted form through which the sovereign rules. In this vein, whereas *majestas personalis* or "the personal sovereignty" was placed on the the ruler (usually the Monarch) the *majestas realis* or "the real sovereignty" was held by the people and was superior to the former (on Bodin's characterization of popular sovereignty in creating constitutional rules see Loughlin, 2010, p. 58 and pp. 70–72 and Roznai, 2017, p. 107).

7 Among the large work of Bruce Ackerman, a synthesis on his idea of constitutional dualism might be found in Ackerman, 1993, pp. 3–33 and Ackerman, 1998, pp. 3–31 On the idea of exceptional political moment at the level of creat-

ing fundamental laws see also the works of Sh. Wolin, for instance, Wolin, 2004, p. 602 and Wolin, 1996, p. 34.

8 See Michelman's considerations on Ackerman's account (Michelman, 1998, p. 76).

9 Yaniv Roznai (2016) relates the increasing interest in the question of the constituent power with the wave of constitutional drafting triggered by political changes across North-Africa and the Middle East See "We the Limited People," conference paper presented at the 2016 Annual Meeting of ICON-S, The International Society of Public Law, Humboldt University Berlin, June 18, 2016. One should also mention experiences of constitution-making in Latin America and within stable European liberal democracies such as in Iceland or Ireland as inspiring processes for the deluge of theoretical approaches that have appeared in the last decade.

10 See for instance *Maastricht* Judgment *BVerfG*, 2 *BvE* 2134, 2159/92 of October 12, 1993.

1 Methodological considerations

A description on the origins

The discussion on constitutional founding often eludes the description of the specific historical conditions and the concrete relations of power that interacted during the approval of a constitution. This silence on the previous set of coercions involved in the constitution-making process plays a role in conferring authority to the constitutional framework, especially within such constitutional contexts in which legitimacy has been erected on the ideas of popular sovereignty and the protection of fundamental rights.

Rights and democratic procedures could be reasonably respected according to constitutional provisions in force, but they were usually absent to some extent in the definition of the political framework that gave birth to the basic rules. They are rather connected to the conflicts and domination structures that made some social groups prevalent upon others (see, for instance, Mann, 1986, pp. 416–449 or Tilly, 1975).

As might be inferred from the remarks already expressed, my analysis of constituent power shall be centred in discerning the historical avatars that lead to the foundation of the constitutional settlement. It will be, thus, eminently, a *descriptive* approach, a description not related to the norms and their function (as would be developed from a positivist analysis) but to the facts (on the constituent power as *de facto* residuary power of changing and replacing a constitution, see also Friedrich, 1968, p. 134 and p. 138).

I will not be, in principle, concerned with normative propositions on the constituent power. Such a statement might be understood with a double sense: on the one hand, I will not deal with the phenomenon of the constituent power as a set of rules since, as it has been pointed out, I am reluctant to display any approach to the question through legal categories as presupposing that actions of the constituent drafters are bound to other rules or might be described as bound by other rules. On the other hand, I will not set out any normative theory on constituent power grounded in democratic theory. I will not offer, consequently, any ideal on how the constituent power ought to be expressed within a liberal and democratic framework. Such considerations do not mean that providing historical descriptions on constituent processes under what I call "the genealogical method" are not lacking consequences regarding the legitimacy of the constituent power and, specially, regarding the legitimacy of the liberal and democratic political orders developed within the limits traced by the action of the *pouvoir constituant*. The description of the circumstances involved in the founding might obviously call for a reinterpretation of the constitutional systems in force, as it has been well assumed by the "social contract theories" devoted to strengthening the justification of the present through the assessment of the past, but, generally, my normative approach (reduced, as we shall see, to only one proposition) will depart from assessments regarding the participation of citizenry, or the quality of such popular involvement.

My approach, thus, might be qualified as empirical, but not in the sense displayed by some authors inspired by some political science techniques of analysis according to which the point would be to depict the conditions involved in constitutional-making processes in order to predict some stability of the constitutional outcome (Ginsburg, Blount, and Elkins, 2009, p. 219; see Ackerman critics on the mentioned analysis, 2019, pp. 39–40). My enquiry, rather, would be concerned, firstly, in observing the influence of violence as a fact given in history during most constitutional transformations (if not all of them) and, secondly, in associating specific expressions of violence historically detected to the exercise of the constituent power that produced some constitutional rules of current liberal democracies.

As has been pointed out, the normative blindness of the research shall have an exception. An absolute normative exception as follows: the legitimacy of an episode of constitutional creation or transformation requires no violence understanding "violence" as a "subjective one" according to the definition provided by Žižek. The problem, thus, would be how to determine that there had not been such coercion and, in order to answer such a question, I shall propose a kind of categorical imperative: during the formation of the constitutional system, there shall not have been the loss of *any* human life. No victims at all of political violence. This is what I shall call the "No victims rule.". Consequently, instead of centring the analysis on an infinite of democratic variables (participation, mobilization, deliberation …) I will focus on a normative horizon only marked by a simple, binary pattern: the presence or the lack of at least one human death.

Before proceeding to sketch the main characteristics of the genealogical approach, I will refer to the two main competing theoretical frameworks which, in my view, have had the most profound impact in the explanation of the constituent supremacy and the possible agency that lies behind the creation of the highest norm. I will thus focus my concerns on elaborating a critique on both positivism, and social contract theories.

Legal positivist theories

The legal positivist analysis on constitutional issues is mainly concerned with the identification of the supreme norm that confers validity to the rest of the norms that compose a legal system. In spite of the vagueness on the use of the term "legal positivism" (Sebok, 1997; Schauer, 1993) it might be possible to identify this doctrine with any theorist willing to insist on distinguishing the category of "law" or "the legal" from that of "morals" or "the moral" (or "reason" and "reasonable," Michelman, 1998, p. 69; Schauer, 1993, p. 800). Concerning the questions on the constitution, thus, whereas positivist thought might provide answers to the conflicts between the constitution understood as the supreme rule of the system and the inferior norms of the legal structure, it does not inquire about the justification of constitutional supremacy. That explains why, for instance, according to the positivist insight, the notion of sovereignty can be just related to a norm. Within the legal world the idea of an original, supreme, and independent power is only attributable to a rule, the one that confers validity to the whole system.

According to one of the most sophisticated versions of legal positivism, that is, the one elaborated by Hans Kelsen (Kelsen, 2005, pp. 193–224), the ultimate legal authority is empowered by the basic norm (*die Grundnorm*) that is not strictly speaking legal but presupposed in legal thinking. As is well known, Kelsen built his legal theory on the idea of a hierarchical legal structure and a strictly procedural relationship.[1] The validity of a legal norm was inferred from a higher-order norm, whose own validity, in turn, was established by an appeal to its higher-order norm, and so on. The highest norm in the hierarchical legal system derived its own validity from a direct appeal to the constitution, but the validity of the constitution could not be derived from another positive norm. Thus:

> [s]o far as the constitution-establishing authority is looked upon as the highest authority that cannot be regarded as authorized by the norm of a higher authority.
>
> (Kelsen, 2005, p. 199)

The validity of the constitution was derived from such *Grundnorm* conceived as a hypothetical norm, a logical assumption, the existence and validity of which was needed in order to explain the normative character of the entire legal system, a transcendental-logical condition in which some writers have seen the echoes of theological and metaphysical thought (see, for instance, Batnitzky, 2016, pp. 14–16). Since Kelsen aspired to create a legal science free from moral considerations and to clean legal norms of any traces and influences of social developments, the questions around the origins of the validity of the basic norm itself (the issue of legitimacy) were dismissed in his analysis (or at least in Kelsen's early writings, see Kalyvas, 2008, p. 104 and Dyzenhaus, 2012, p. 244). He basically argued that discourses on legitimacy were ideological by nature and, thus, irrelevant for statements on the validity of the legal system (Kelsen, 1992, pp. 18–19).

In further developments of his work, Kelsen gave more details on the construction of the ultimate source of validity and, in spite of his struggle to insulate the legal system from politics and power, the facticity of the grounds of the legal system reemerged. Kelsen explained that, at the highest level of the hierarchical structures of norms, the validity was founded by the historically "first constitution2 enacted by an assembly or individual (on this point see Lindhal, 2015, p. 168, Raz, 1974, p. 97, and Roznai, 2017, p. 116). The basic norm would then command "one ought to obey the prescriptions of the historically first constitution." But which facts brought about the creation of the historically "first constitution"? Kelsen detailed that the historically first constitution was the outcome of replacing a positivist constitution with another positivist constitution without following the conditions of validity prescribed by the former constitution. Kelsen remarked, furthermore, that from the point of view of his insight, the conditions within political life that brought about the replacement of a constitution by another are irrelevant. Facts are only relevant in Kelsen's positivist theory in order to show if the new constitution is "effective" in the sense that the norms of the legal order are created in conformity with the constitution emerged from the revolution and are by and large applied and obeyed. But, at the end of the day, as Kelsen's theory critics in the time of the Weimar Republic, such as Schmitt or Heller, suggested,[2] facticity was reintroduced into legal theory by the back door and even with a more pressing difficulty: Kelsen's theory did not provide any criteria in order to assess such facts beyond observing the efficacy of certain actors to impose the basic norm. In other words, what counted was the effectiveness of the coercion able to oblige citizens to obey the legal system. Final statements on rules were, thus, referred to facts of social practice. As Frank Michelman (1998, p. 70) observed in his explanation on the legal positivism approach to constitutionalism, Kelsen's account (in the same vein as Hart's) has no other way out but admitting that the normative system's ultimate foundation can only be a social fact that is not itself a norm.

As is well known, many other authors have at the end of their enquiries concluded that the source of the legal quality of a constitution must be found in some phenomenon other than law (see for instance, Kay, 1984, p. 116 and 1987, p. 58). The latter had been the path taken, for instance, by Wade (1955, p. 196) when describing the validity of a constitution as a matter of political fact or by Hart himself (1994, pp. 103–106) in postulating a legal system's rule of recognition which provides the ultimate criteria for identifying valid law without being validated by prior positive law (for a more recent version on the positivist analysis concerning the constitutional founding grounded on Hartian terms see Barczentewicz, 2019, p. 77)

Confronted by the facts that are involved in the normative analysis, the theory traced by Kelsen was likely to fall into a contradiction: facts are expelled from the normative analysis but, at the same time, are invoked in order to evaluate the effectiveness of a positive constitution (if it is obeyed or not) and thus identifying the validity of the ultimate normative authority. There is, nonetheless, a silence about the question of why a positive constitution is obeyed within the social realm, not to mention the silence around the question on who dictated the constitution and under which legitimacy it was dictated.

While facts on the empirical experience that show the obedience to a positive constitution in a given society are relevant, facts concerning the question of why this positive constitution is obeyed are not relevant. Kelsen's approach does not deal with the reasons and experiences that give force to a positive constitution, it declines to explain, for instance, why a positivist constitution was replaced by another or under which circumstances a positivist constitution was issued. In fact, a legal revolution and its specific social, political, and historical circumstances (thus, for example, if the normative change and the higher lawmaking were motivated by a popular mobilization or by a military coup d'état) are irrelevant in order to explore the validity of the constitution. There being no difference between a democratic revolution and a reactionary coup d'état (since there is no discrimination between legitimated and non-legitimated higher laws) the criteria to determine the validity of a constitution just depend on the ability of a group to impose a new constitution, and the people's compliance with that norm (see on this point Kalyvas, 2008, p. 111).

As it has been advanced, as far as Kelsen's theory alludes to the facts that reveal the effectiveness of a positivist constitution it can be argued that the idea of the use of force is not completely absent from the positivist analysis. Rather the idea of coercion seems central to this approach and this consideration would be coherent with Kelsen's theory of norm, according to which norms are prescriptions that include a sanction. Legitimacy conditions in the constitutional founding are not mentioned by Kelsen because he counts that only effectiveness, that is, the ability to enforce a norm through violence, is relevant in order to identify norm's supremacy.[3] In the same strand, nevertheless, centring the debate on the validity conditions of a norm, and referring to the ultimate legal authority to a presupposed norm beyond the historical facts, Kelsen's positivism declines to enter into the question of the specific relations of power that lie behind the constitutional founding and, thus, he doesn't give account either of the positivist constitution origins or of the role of coercion in the definition of a norm's supremacy.

Similar remarks can be mentioned around positivist contributions coming from the common law tradition such as the theory of H.L.A. Hart about the rule of recognition and the foundations of a legal system (1994, pp. 100–110). The rule of recognition would be, according to Hart, a secondary rule accepted and used for the identification of primary rules of obligation and, thus, it would provide the criteria by which the validity of other rules of the system is assessed. As long as the rule of recognition establishes the supreme criterion of validity it could be described as the ultimate rule of the legal system.

Unlike Kelsen's basic norm, characterized as a presupposed norm whose validity cannot be demonstrated, but "assumed" or "postulated," Hart's rule of recognition is intertwined with the fact that a social group normally identifies the law by reference to certain criteria.[4] As Hart asserts, whether as an external statement given by an observer of a social group's behaviour or as an internal statement coming from a member of the system, the existence of the rule of recognition is a matter of fact (1994, p. 110). What is outside the scope of Hart's analysis, in a similar strand to Kelsen's basic norm theory, are, nevertheless, the *causes* of the fact that allow the existence of the rule of recognition to be ascertained: why, in other words, the rule of recognition is followed by a social group to identify the primary rules of obligation.

As we see, then, most prominent positivist theories are concerned with the facts only in order to confirm the effectiveness of the positivist constitution and the presupposed basic norm that confers validity to the former (as in Kelsen's theory) or to identify the criteria of validity that are followed by the members of a social community (as in Hart's theory on the determination of the existence of the rule of recognition). Even though the idea of coercion underlies the explanation of the basic norm's effectiveness or the rule of recognition's existence, both Kelsen and Hart refuse to explore the particular facts that are brought about the foundation of the legal system and that support the general obedience of the primary rules. Coercion factors that emerged in the construction of the constitutional framework are not considered although the stipulation of a sanction (as an expression of the physical force) is at the core of Kelsen's and Hart's theories on the primary rules and in their profound insight on the question of why a rule is obeyed. Both Kelsen's and Hart's approaches, on the other hand, reject any connection with moral or any other values in explaining the effectiveness of a legal system within a social group.[5]

Positivism, in summary, does not provide any information on the facts that lie behind the supremacy of the norm that confers validity to the legal system (see Arato, 1995–1996, p. 191). Both Kelsen's version and Hart's one, renounce any depiction of the factual conditions that construct the norm's supremacy. Since positivism is mainly committed to analyzing the norms and their dynamic it consciously departs from any inquiry in which the language on norms is not involved. Coherently thus, positivism seems to remain indifferent towards the origins of the basic norm or the rule of recognition but remains also indifferent to the reasons for their effectiveness and their capacity to promote obedience. Distinctions, such as the one traced by Raz (1995, p. 211) between "legitimate authority" and "*de facto* authority" (that related to power and entailed in every legal system which is in force anywhere), seem not to have echoed in the mentioned orthodox positivist tradition.

Social contract theories

The social contract theory, from a different viewpoint, focuses its attention on describing the ideal conditions by which the basic rules that organize a society could be justified. As is well known, the different versions of contractualism (such approaches traced by Locke, Rousseau, Kant, or, in the twentieth century, by political philosophers such as Rawls) inquire into the principles of justice that would be agreed in a hypothetical original position where participants would meet in equal conditions.

The idea of an agreement adopted by individuals in an original position might be put closer to the foundation of the political community than to the stage of drafting a constitution. However, since the appearance of constitutionalism during the eighteenth century through the American and French revolutions was associated to a new beginning, in which the approval of a constitution sought to establish an entire system of both new rules and a new basis of legitimacy, a constitution might be perceived, according to such traditions, as the necessary instrument to create the effect of a social contract (see Krisch, 2010, p. 49). A constitutional legal framework would be thus conceived as the prime tool to translate the moral principles adopted in the contract into institutional practice. Constitutions today, as a result of the aforementioned theoretical evolution, are generally conceived as contracts drawn up by "the People" (see Loughlin, 2010, p. 275).

The narrative of the social contract and the adoption of a constitution are intertwined by constitutional theory to the extent that constitutional supremacy had been usually justified seeing the constitution as the representation of the social agreement, the particular terms in which the contract (among the people that have participated and have consented to the rules within a context of special mobilization) is written (see in the context of the United States formation Rakove, 1997, pp. 96–102 and Wood, 1998, pp. 282–291).

My critical approach towards the social contract theories is related to my critique of an account on constituent power centred in analyzing citizenry participation, mobilization, and deliberation. Generally, my main objection, as I will develop, is the difficulty to determine, ontologically and epistemologically, the structure of the decision-making process attributed to the action of individuals. In my opinion, the theoretical approach to the phenomenon of creating a constitutional framework is more fruitful, both from ontological and epistemological perspectives, when we attend to the historical struggles that are expressed in facts and, particularly, in violence.

Even an author aware of the relevance of coercions in maintaining the system, such as Thomes Hobbes, intended nonetheless to explain the origins of the State through covenants. Hobbes stated that only force allowed the covenants to be respected but remained ambiguous on the mechanisms that led to the conclusion of the foundational agreement. Though, on the one hand, he admitted that "he which is made Sovereign made no Covenant with his subjects before-hand" (1965, p. 134) he also pointed out that the Commonwealth, the Civitas, was generated by the covenants concluded between men "one with another" (1965, p. 132) a consideration that justifies why Hobbes was incardinated, in spite of his scepticism and realism, in the social contract tradition (on this point see Schmitt, 2003, pp. 104–105). It is true that Hobbes distinguished between the Commonwealth created from *Institution* (that was grounded on an agreement among men) and the Commonwealth by *Acquisition* [that was established by the force of arms (Hobbes, 1965, p. 132)] but instead of exploring, as the historical experience suggests, if *all* the Commonwealths are in reality founded by acquisition, Hobbes delves into the Commonwealth established by consent focusing his thoughts regarding violence on the enforcement of the covenant but eluding the problem of the lack of fundamental agreement given the original imposition of the sovereign's will.

Contractualist accounts on constituent founding are subjected to several problems long observed by political theorists. Here I might underline three main objections. I shall mention briefly the first and the second (bearing in mind the huge literature that both have generated) while tackling in a bit more detail the third (also abundant in references) related to the difficult dialectic between the ideal conditions of a theoretical contract in the struggle of providing legitimacy to the constitutional founding and the empirical circumstances in which such foundations take place.

Firstly, I should remark that the building of a contractual theory on constitutional foundations is subjected to the same paradox already appreciated concerning the democratic foundation of a constitutional democracy. The requirement of individual consent as a source of legitimacy in the adoption of a specific constitution presupposes an agreement by the group of individuals that are called to give their consent to the constitutional rules. But no group of persons could be authorized to consent to a particular constitutional framework without a previous constitutional rule which, by the same token, requires a consent rendered by someone involved in the operation of creating a new constitutional framework, and so on, into a paradox of infinite regress (see, for instance, Zurn, 2010, pp. 193–195 and Barnett, 2004, pp. 11–31).

Secondly, contractualist theories on political foundations are usually identified with democratic theory since they are focused on the involvement of individuals and their will in adopting a particular constitutional regime. But contractualism is not necessarily attached to democracy. The agreement of the principles of justice that have to rule a society (which, in constitutional terms, have to be translated into a constitutional framework) may well not be adopted by the individuals because they decide to do it but because such principles *are objectively the best principles* to organize a society. In that way, individuals do not, strictly speaking, *consent* to such rules but they assume them since there are no alternatives to rule a society properly. In fact, the establishment of legitimacy conditions grounded on individual consent or in the democratic endorsement is *procedural* tests for legitimacy (Zurn, 2010, p. 203) different from a *substantive* assessment which may be respected or infringed independently of democratic conditions.

Such an observation might be inferred in analyzing the most famous contemporary theory on the contractual foundations of a political community, that of John Rawls' *Theory of Justice*. In Rawls' theory, individuals, free from social, historical, or personal contingencies, conclude a social agreement that would be rational and fair (Rawls, 1971, pp. 118–123), a range of principles that from the founding moment onwards would establish the normative framework by which the political community would be ruled. But if such principles of justice must be adopted because they are *objectively fair*, then both the will of the individuals and their participation in the decision of adopting the principles, in spite of Rawls' procedural descriptions, *are irrelevant*. If there is a moral truth in organizing a society in its basic terms, such truth has to be established aside from whether individuals consent or not. The argument might be taken under another version which guides us to the main objection that burdens social contract theories regarding the *décalage* between the idea of moral objectivity and disagreements on values that are given in a real political framework. In this way, authors such as Jeremy Waldron (1999, p. 111) in noticing that in political contexts, disagreements burst out disregarding the existence or not of moral certainties and are prone to conclude that moral objectivity is unhelpful in the situation of a need for political decision and, thus, is *politically irrelevant.*

In summary, if there are objective principles of justice in organizing a political consociation, democratic procedures established in order to ascertain them are superfluous. But if the important thing is the democratic procedure per se to approach moral objectivity, then what is irrelevant is the moral objectivity itself.

The latter leads us to my third objection, which would be the classic objection to the social contract theory (posed not only towards Rawls' approach but also towards the versions of Locke, Kant, or Rousseau, which had a decisive impact on the configuration of constitutionalism). If there is not moral objectivity, that is in part because moral decisions are embedded by a particular historic and social context. In other words, what is criticized of social contract theories struggling with defining the universal conditions to ascertain the morality of the social agreement is, precisely, the *lack of links between the theory and the reality*, the lack of links between the performance of such universal agreement based on a supposed correct reasoning and any background shown by history or culture. Both modern communitarian traditions and authors close to what has been called "cultural liberalism" have centred their objections to contractualism under the mentioned perspective, pinpointing the detachment between the ideal and the real world (see, among many others, Taylor, 1992; Kymlicka, 2001b; Tamir, 1993; or Tully, 1995).

The influence of factual, historical, and existential circumstances in political processes poses the doubt around whether the reconstruction of a hypothetical agreement has any sense at all. Or worse, the abstraction of hypothetical agreement always carries the risk of excluding voices (Chambers, 2004, p. 155) to the extent that the entrenchment of general ideas such as Rawls' overlapping consensus may be deemed as a medium to undermine differences (Mouffe, 2009). General principles of political liberalism in Rawls' fashion would represent only abstractions oriented to impose the vision of the victorious groups upon the groups that have been defeated by history.

Regarding the relationship between Rawls' ideas and constitution-making, one might question to what extent the description of the original position and the principles of justice stemmed from it, may be related to the constituent moment and the normative conditions to evaluate the process of drafting and passing a constitution. Even according to the Rawlsian perspective, the "veil of ignorance" is said only to encompass interests, opinions, and personal circumstances of the individuals involved in the original position and not the circumstances of a given society (the veil of ignorance would be, thus, "partially lifted" in the expression provided by Arato, 1995–1996, p. 222, on interpreting Rawls' theory). The abstraction of Rawls' procedure in deciding the principles of justice is not likely to be applicable in assessing a product, a constitution, essentially linked to the particular historical, cultural, and social circumstances of a human community. For instance, when Rawls and other liberals held that in spite of the concurrence of conflicting political views in a given society, it is possible to reach a consensus on the essentials since all the individuals may agree to such principles and their pluralism may be reasonably handled, it is likely to be missed that discrepancies on constitutional matters might be *existential* and not subjected to any reasonable negotiation, to begin with, the foundation of the constitutional State itself and the determination *of the political identity* of the members of the founding community.

Somehow surprisingly, if we take into account the idealistic preconception that embeds Rawls' theory on the possibility of elucidating the principles of justice, Rawls argued that ontological claims, that is, presuppositions about the constitution of agents and the social world, needed to be avoided in political thought (Rawls, 1996, 2001; see on this point Rosenthal, 2019, pp. 238–245). On the one hand, the principles of justice resulting from consensus are beyond the historical circumstances but, on the other hand, in Rawls' account such principles are not ontologically defined, since under an ontological grounding of society it would be impossible to reach a stable consensus on justice in liberal political communities (Rawls, 1996, p. 387). In this way, Rawls' conception of justice would not be grounded on citizens' ontological claims that may confront them, but on principles able to leave to the individuals an ample space to make their coexistence in society compatible with their own ontological doctrines (Rawls, 1996, p. 375). But the question, particularly if we turn to a "genealogical approach" as I shall introduce in the next section, is if the principles of justice in a liberal society such as the ones outlined by Rawls are not themselves *an ontological claim* even though there is the attempt to represent them as freestanding and even-handed political values resulting from consensus. The principles of justice are either partisan outcomes of historical contingencies or ontologically founded. There is nonetheless another possibility relying on the fact, as Rosenthal derived from her lecture of Rawls through Foucault's critique on liberalism (2019) that if the principles of justice, as the foundations of liberalism themselves, are not anything but the outcome of the political struggles for power displayed along the history legitimized through a narrative of even-handed political values. In other words, Rawls' principles of justice would not have done anything different than the solutions provided by the metaphysical and religious systems, which is to conceal through an idealization, that what is the result of a strategy of domination given by the historical events.

Contractualism and history

In spite of the difficulty to adjust the normative requirements of social contract theories to real historical experiences, the struggle to associate a social compact ideal to particular founding episodes has been present in the representative authors of the strand from the beginning of the tradition. Christian Wolff, Emer de Vattel,[6] John Locke, and Jean-Jacques Rousseau may be considered ancestors of contemporary scholars intending to find pathways to establish normative premises about constitutional creation grounded on individual participation, deliberation, and consent.

Indeed, the predominance of the social contract theory in the seventeenth and the eighteenth centuries could only be understood as the effect of thinking about the States as independent actors on the world stage (see David Bates, 2007, p. 18 and Richard Tuck, 1999, pp. 84–85). But the appearance of such States, their consolidation as sovereign entities vested with internal and external supreme power, was the result of a cycle of repeated violence both between the social, religious, and ethnic groups at the internal level, and between other powers at the external level (Mann, 1986; Tully, 1975). Thus, according to Tuck, the "autonomous" agent described by the theory of the social contract was an analogy between the individual and the State only possible to be conceived as a mirror of the sovereign condition to which the States acceded after bloody conflicts. Behind the thinking of figures such as Locke or Rousseau, in sculpting the idea of free and equal individuals agreeing on the fundamental regulation of the society, violence was presupposed in preparing the frame in which the contract would take place in a similar vein that had previously happened to the internal order created by the sovereign States in the Modern Age after defeating rival powers.

In analyzing the process of colonization in North America under the parameter of the social contract theory, John Locke, for instance, had to deal with the apparent incompatibility of his theory on the consent of the governed, with the appropriation of land by European settlers despite the opposition of native peoples (on this criticism of Locke's theory see Tully, 1995, pp. 72–80; Simmons, 2001, pp. 158–178). The answer provided by Locke suggests the kind of strategy adopted by a contractual vision which, though focused within a historical context, makes abstraction of cultural and national particularities: the a priori exclusion of a group from the contract. According to Locke, thus, the appropriation "with any express Compact of all the commoners" (Locke, 2015, Sec.25, p. 286) was justified in the case of the Europeans occupying America's indigenous peoples' lands since, even admitting that natives were human, they belonged to the earliest and most primitive stage of the human evolution and they had not even created any political jurisdiction (among other passages, Locke, 2015, Sec. 30, pp. 289–290 and Sec.108, pp. 339–340). They represented "the perfect State of Nature" (Sec. 87, p. 324) which was called to be regulated by those nations provided of laws, jurisdiction, and sovereignty. In other words, Aborigines ought to be subjected to those who already had concluded the social contract.

Once the social contract theory is compared with a historical circumstance, as the specific historic situation of the European settlers regarding the Aboriginal peoples of North America, the agreement between the supposed free and equal individuals is converted into a structure of the domination of a group (the insiders of the contract) upon others (the outsiders or those that have not given any consent to the rules agreed because they have been, from the beginning, marginalized or destroyed).

The problem that Locke already envisaged and that has been fully developed by those streams of political thought critical of social contract theories relies on determining *the membership of the group* called to conclude the social compact (Preuss, 1992–1993, pp. 656–660; Benhabib, 1994, p. 10). Membership in some human community is the primary good that we distribute to one another and the one on which we ground our other distributive choices: it determines from whom we require obedience and collect taxes or to whom we allocate goods and services (Walzer, 1983, p. 31). The configuration of the membership is, however, the result of ancestral conflicts marked by wars and violence. Historical experience points out to what extent the members met in creating the social agreement integrate a group (mostly defined under ethnic premises) which have been able to impose their power upon other groups. Such dominated groups have been precisely the ones that even subjected to the rules agreed by the participants of the social contract were in the origins of the political community excluded, damaged, and even eliminated (Taylor, 1992, p. 25). Also, Giorgio Agamben, for instance, develops his theory on the creation of the People in a political sense as the outcome of an incessant civil war among the different classes and ethnic groups (2000, pp. 31–32).

Aside from the context of the colonization of the Americas, in a sequence of thoughts that would impinge on the assessment of the revolutionary events that occurred in Great Britain by the end of the seventeenth century, the other historical scenario in which the normative propositions erected around the idea of social contract had a determining influence was the American Revolution.

The independence of the American States and the subsequent constitutional developments there recorded as contexts in which the logic of violence was replaced by the logic of consent, had been explored not only by people politically and intellectually involved in the events, but also by modern scholars, such as Hanna Arendt and Bruce Ackerman, who used an interpretation of the American Revolution in order to provide historical resorts for their political and constitutional theories grounded in the metaphor of the contract. In this strand, even admitting that "social contract" approaches developed by political writers during the seventeenth and eighteenth centuries were referring to "fictions," Arendt aimed to demonstrate that such fictitious explanations of existing relationships between the members of a community had historical and factual translations. Even Habermas estimated that in Arendt's reconstruction of the American founding she placed an excessive emphasis on "the venerable figure of the contract" (1977, p. 24) rather than on her own concept of praxis which would have required major attention to the historical developments that allowed the creation of a new legal order. Arendt's narratives would represent, nonetheless, one of the most prominent endeavours to apply a contractualist political theory to real political conditions and, as such, a magnificent proposal to explore a concept of politics grounded only in an associative bond established through free and public deliberation, supposedly unstained by traces of violence (see Marchart, 2007, p. 159; Topf, 2019, p. 54). Arendt's theory on power associated with the episode of the creation of the American Republic and the notion of constitution as an agreement of free men, such extraordinary commitment of a large number of people to political debate, discussion, and participation directed towards the creation of free institutions, might be summarized in the following and famous passage:

> In distinction to strength, which is the gift and the possession of every man in his isolation against other men, power comes into being only if and when men join themselves together for the purpose of action, and it will disappear when, for whatever reason, they disperse and desert one another. Hence, binding and promising, combining and covenanting are the means by which power is kept in existence; where and when men succeed in keeping intact the power which sprang up between them during the course of any particular act or deed, they are already in the process of foundation, of constituting a stable worldly structure to house, as it were, their combined power of action.
>
> (Arendt, 1963, p. 174)

However, the undeniable attractiveness of Arendt's interpretation of America's Revolution exposed in her book *On Revolution*, with all her praises to the value of public life, the power of collective action, or the construction of a political order linked with the struggle and the participation of free men, does not diminish the background of specific coercions, military conflicts, and social exclusions that were not unknown in the origins of the United States as we shall see in Chapter 3. Putting the stress on such conflicts reveals to what extent the "value of the common action" or "the political consciousness of free citizens" (Ackerman, 1993, p. 206) was a matter of a minority that can hardly be identified with "the People" and that, in another sense, did not constitute the factors capable of bringing the Revolution to fruition, and the constitutional order to be established.

On his commentaries on Arendt's work, Antonio Negri admitted the fascination engendered by Arendt's characterization of the constituent power as an absolute foundation of the political public space but, shortly afterwards, Negri criticizes the transformation of Arendt's theory from a radical idea of freedom associated with the new beginning, to a more modest conception of the agreement and consensus among men. And, finally, in presenting the American Revolution as the scenario in which took place such foundations of the political space through free participants that agree among themselves, Negri qualifies Arendt's move as "historical cynicism" (Negri, 2002, p. 33).

A more detailed historical approach may certainly show that in concrete foundational episodes, power is gained so far as *there is capacity to organize means of coercion*. The power appears and disappears not because of the joining or the dispersion of participants but because of their ability to impose their order through violence and repressing future discrepancies in the same way. "Action," to use Arendt's term, has grounding, in the real world, not only in the coming together of people and the declarations they make. It is accompanied with a weapon or, at least, the threat of using the weapon. It has been plausibly argued that maybe there is some religious or metaphysical belief in the background of Arendt's formulation about "the power," which has been "phenomenological essentialism" conceptually overdrawn and politically unrealistic (Benhabib, 1996, pp. 70–71). The effectiveness of promises and covenants exists only as long as said promises and covenants are enforced by the use of physical might. The legitimacy of a new order, and so it is still appreciated by international public law in the case of the formation of a new State, depends on the capacity of exercising "the monopoly of the use of physical force within a given territory." And such legitimacy is lost when rulers are unable to enforce through coercion the law that they generate. Promises and covenants concluded among men have been irrelevant both to history and to other agents that had to recognize the new political order.

In spite of her discourse on the promises, covenants, and agreements related to the grounds of political foundation, Arendt was perfectly aware of the concurrence of violence during the transformation of a constitutional framework. Such a problem, nevertheless, seemed to be relegated to a secondary position, considering it both in the remote past (as in the comments on the Bible and the foundation of Rome reveal in *On Revolution*, 1963, p. 31) or as a consequence of a wide social inequality, a factor which, according to Arendt in a sublimated lecture on the American Revolution, would mark the difference between the latter, and the French or Russian regime changes (1963, pp. 53–110; on this point see Arato, 2020, pp. 92–93). As we shall see in translating the theory here developed on constituent power in the case of the American States, Arendt's selective portrayal of the American foundation in contrast with the horrors of the abject poverty in France or Russia gives little attention to the barbarism of American slavery (Arendt, 1963, pp. 71–72), while the question of the occupation of indigenous people's lands, and their extermination, does not deserve any comment at all (for criticism of such omissions in Arendt's narrative of the American founding see Scheuerman, 1997, p. 156 and Wolin, 1983).

Social contract theories, from Locke to Rawls, are prone to be presented in an abstract fashion – something difficult to make compatible with research centred on society and history. However, authors such as Locke himself, and Arendt, do not relinquish a presentation of their conceptions on the legitimate social organization and, consequently, on the foundations of a legal order, under the coverage of particular historical developments such as the American colonization by the European settlers, in Locke, or the American Revolution, in Arendt. In my opinion, nevertheless, such accounts blind the eye to the physical coercions that took place in these historical episodes which, among other things, permitted the definition of the group (through both the exclusion and the destruction of other groups) that was called to adopt the fundamental decisions on its future ruling.

The analysis of the historical circumstances surrounding State-building and its legal translation in constitution-making processes are, precisely, the object of the approach that shall emerge as the main theoretical support of my disquisition: the genealogical model.

Genealogical model

In a lecture delivered in January 1976, Michel Foucault (1994a, pp. 160–174) summarized the two theories which analyze the building of power that had been developed from the eighteenth century. The first one was the idea of the contract as a matrix of the formation of political power, the agreement in which free and equal participants transfer their original power in a constituent act of sovereignty. The second one was the idea of political power as the continuity of a war, politics as the confirmation and the preservation of the unbalanced forces expressed in war.

I have already remarked on the difficulties that arise in identifying the historical conditions of social agreement and the concurrence of the free will of participants. Since Foucault was precisely concerned with history and with delving into the historical facts that surrounded political foundations, he chose to abandon any metaphor regarding the contract and straightforwardly described the relations of power that rule a particular society as the clash of forces historically established through violence.

According to Foucault's particular ontology, human existence is defined by power relations (1994b; see on Foucault's view Rosenthal, 2019, p. 246). Identity, morality, and knowledge are the product of a dramatic quest for domination, a process in which is also included the quintessential form of attempting to confer stability to a social system: the law and, for the question that concerns us, the fundamental law. A constitutional framework, viewed from the "genealogical" lens, would be partisan outcomes of social-historical power struggles devoted to marginalizing and to obliterating other notions of identity and justice.

Constitutionalism, as we have seen, was inspired from the very beginning by contractualist theories since both, in the general project of modernity, were devoted to overcoming the accidents of power and history. But the formation of a political entity and the drafting of the constitution that established the legal framework of such entities were themselves a consequence of power, history, and chance. If constitutionalism refers both to power's limitation and foundation, the point is that foundation, which is per se historical, devoured the merits of the limitation of power. The ideal vision of both contractualism and constitutionalism has, moreover, a more sinister side: the creation of a common framework of values and rules oriented by the virtues of reason, order, and collective decision-making within a supposedly neutral framing was, in fact, a way to legitimate exclusion and imposition (Benhabib, 1994, p. 10). As Tully observed, the integrationist, universalizing tendencies of constitutionalism sit uneasily with the diverse identities of individuals in divided societies (Tully, 1995, pp. 58–98). If we turn our attention to the past, it is not hard to notice that such overarching political regulation provided by constitutionalism and the homogeneous agent that gave itself the constitutional framework (the People, the Nation ...) was anything but the outcome of nation-building policies in which measures of forced assimilation and grave violations of human rights were involved.

History shows us, on the one hand, the weakness of a position integrated by free and equal participants as had been imagined by the social contract theory and, on the other hand, the need to analyze constitutional phenomena through the relations of forces that converged in the creation of the political system, as Foucault does in his "genealogical" approach and I try to export to constitutional analysis focusing on the social forces and the historical intricacies involved in constitutional design.

Such a methodological approach centred on the memory of a traumatic event (Foucault, 1994b, pp. 136–156; on this point see also Oklopcic, 2018, p. 28) would allow us to explore the constitution-making process as a practice whereby the structures of coercion shaped in the previous constitutional period under no democratic conditions find their consolidation and their legitimacy. Since the research on the constituent power refers to a research on the origins of the political order, a method devoted to following the details and the randomness of the beginnings seems especially appropriate. As I have suggested, traditional constitutional theories have dealt with the issue of the constitutional foundation either as an inapprehensible metaphysical entity (as positivism offers) or as an idealization of the circumstances regarding the individual's participation and consent (as suggested from the social contract theories).

The genealogist approach is, however, focused *on describing the specific historical avatars that surrounded the creation of a constitutional framework* without providing any normative assessment. In this sense, in Foucault's words, genealogy, "rejects the meta-historical deployment of ideal significations and indefinite teleologies" (1994b, pp. 136–137).

The ontology of violence

The centre of the empirical phenomenon that history shows is, according to the "genealogical approach," violence. This is, without a doubt, a more tangible benchmark by which to understand the foundation of a constitutional order than any narrative linked to popular mobilization and the consent of the governed. The birth of a legal order is also, in Foucault's view, the paradigm of a place whereby abstractions have been used in order to cover the detailed structures of domination. Moreover, as Foucault's remarks, the rules drafted in the beginnings entail the remembrance of the original violence and are effective as long as they update the same framework of coercions while they are applied in the supposed peaceful or stable times (the "constituted moment" or the "ordinary politics," to use the terms of constitutional theory). So:

> Following traditional beliefs, it would be false to think that total war exhausts itself in its own contradictions and ends by renouncing violence and submitting to civil laws. On the contrary, the law is a calculated and relentless pleasure, delight in promised blood, which permits the perpetual instigation of new dominations and the staging of meticulously repeated scenes of violence.
>
> (1994b, p. 145)

The theory of constitutional supremacy would be crippled in its axiological grounds if the supposed social contract that is reflected in the constitutional founding is not inferred through the free will of the participants but shadowed by different sources of submission. Translating the constitutional theory into the terms of the contract theory under the parameters of the civil law, most participants' consent would be pressed by an external force that would distort the real will of the parts and thus the agreement might be null and void.

In a different vein, the genealogical approach would confront the formal vision of the positivist theories, centring its discourse not in the analysis of the norms and the functioning of the legal system but on *the facts* that lie behind the approval of the norms and, regarding the approval of a constitution, the cluster of power relations from which the constitutional framework emerged. Even from other traditions of political philosophy, some authors would share with the "genealogist" approach the idea according to which questions concerning the character of an existing pre-constitutional rule, as well as the probability or propriety of a change to it, necessarily demand reference to the social organizations, the customs and practices, and the history of that group of human beings who are to live under the system of law which that rule is to define (see for instance Kay, 1998, p. 61). The genealogist project would, accordingly, explore the space silenced by positivism since the constituent power would encompass the place which positivist knowledge does not enter. After all, for a genealogist, positivism would belong to the group of idealizations devoted to eluding the explanation of the confrontation of powers developed under the mantle of legal concepts. As Foucault remarked in an observation which would be applicable to such a critique of positivism:

> The history of power struggles, that is the actual conditions of its exercise and its maintenance, remains almost entirely submerged. Knowledge does not touch it: it shall not be known.
>
> (1994c, pp. 224–225)

Outlining such specific power struggles may allow us to challenge some of the deficiencies that afflict the positivist analysis as the explanation on the effectiveness of the ultimate rules and the obedience of the social body. To reformulate the methodological concerns in Foucault's terms one might say that the premise would consist in eluding the central position of the constitution and its attributes (such as supremacy) in the configuration of power. On the contrary, the genealogist method would insist on describing the constitutional framework as the formal receptacle of the existing network of coercions and relations of domination and, at the same time, the veil which covers the violent competition for the power among the national, social, military, and economical groups. From this point of view, *in the constitutional framing the historical hegemony consolidated by some elites upon its competitors through different ways of coercion would crystallize.* In fact, as Foucault himself describes in his famous book *La volonté de savoir* (the first contribution to his history of sexuality) the building of the European Modern State upon the theory of the sovereignty of the king, represented the first attempt to condense, in legal terms, the plurality of forces that had clashed in violent convulsions from the Middle Ages. The idea of sovereignty was a device to encompass such a network of coercions in order to consolidate and reproduce them (Foucault, 1976, pp. 114–115). The scheme alluded to would, thus, gain in abstraction when the theory of the King's sovereignty was replaced through the liberal and the democratic revolutions by the theory of the people's sovereignty and the legitimacy of the basic norms rooted in the consent of the *demos*. The regime had formally changed by changing the holders, but the web of coercions would persist or even, as long as the industrial revolution improved the techniques of domination, would be reinforced.

The genealogical mode of analysis, thus, would be interested in the distillation of the lines of continuity of the specific structures of domination through acts of violence, exploitation, and promotion of economic inequalities that had been prevailing despite the change of regime. In the same way that the building of the King's sovereignty did not mute the effects of the fragmentation of power that featured in the Middle Ages, constitutional supremacy did not displace the network of domination apparatuses developed in the previous centuries but incorporated it in its aim of organizing the political power of the State in comprehensive terms. Is not uncommon, thus, that even from the times of the first liberal revolutions, a substantial part of the European tradition of political thinkers was concerned in underlining these lines of continuity that pre-existed to the constitutional State and found their sources deep under the *Ancient Régime* or even before the centralization of public power in the hands of the King. Such ideas were embraced by philosophers that lived within a context of transition to modern constitutionalism, as prominently represented in the figure of Edmund Burke regarding the evolution of British constitutionalism but would be also recognized in the writings of thinkers that depict the coming of constitutional regimes from a revolutionary process, as notably is shown by Alexis de Tocqueville (1955) and his remarks on the background of some French revolutionary processes.

As I announced in the introduction of this book the concept of violence that I handle in my analysis on the constituent power conducted by the genealogical approach is eminently *factual*. It is related to the one referred by Žižek as the "subjective violence" (2008, pp. 1–2): direct violence that has death as a result. The methodological advantage of using that narrow idea of violence is that it constrains the measurability of its influence in the creation of constitutional orders.

Counting the deaths

Jean-François Lyotard, in a very famous essay which in fact gave name to the philosophical movement, *La Condition Postmoderne* (1979), wrote a report on epistemology which was an enquiry on the forms of conferring legitimacy to knowledge. According to Lyotard, while scientific knowledge is grounded in empirical evidence and data accumulation, the ways of approaching reality displayed by humanities and social sciences are subjected to narrative archetypes. Following such ideas regarding our concerns, any description of a constitutional order's foundation and the justifications of institutions such as, let's say, constitutional supremacy, would be inextricably involved with a narrative. Hence different theories on the constitution would be nothing but a competition between tales in order to ascertain which is the most convincing in order to claim for legitimacy.

Ackerman himself, when displaying his theory on constitutional dualism and the description of the constituent moments by contrast with ordinary politics admits that his vision of North America's constitutional history (and its consequences for legal interpretation) is a "narrative" more or less convincing if we compare it with the other constitutional narratives proposed by other authors (1993, p. 36). Constitutional issues might be specially concerned by Lyotard's insights since "narrative" is not only a function in conferring legitimacy to knowledge on constitutional rules but, as a discourse on constitution-founding, it is involved in the operation of conferring legitimacy to the constitution itself and to assert its role in the credibility of a given political system.

The narrative knowledge regarding constitutionalism, and particularly concerning the question of constituent power, places itself far from scientific pragmatics, since the description of the facts is always intertwined with discourses on values, either the values supposedly involved within the context of passing a constitution or the prescriptive judgements that according to each author must be taken into account in a constituent process, assuming a normative theory on political participation in order to assess the democratic and the inclusive character of a constitution.

In other words, the discourse on the origins of a constitution is blurred by the pretensions of justice that, either to justify the system in force or to criticize it, the author of the judgement is committed to. Certainly, it is difficult to evaluate, for instance, to what extent popular sovereignty gave itself a constitutional framework, or which historical facts might allow us to state that individuals concurred in a more or less equal condition to deliberate and reach an agreement on a constitution. Such circumstances only might be pointed out by a subject previously endorsed by a set of values and oriented by an ideal. The determination of political participation, fair and equal treatment among participants, or consent during constitution-making processes is also a matter of an intersubjective story more or less shared by the individuals of a particular community. The discourse on democracy and its capacity to confer legitimacy or not to a legal product as a constitution depends on a meaning created among people through a common network of stories. It is, in the same way that Oakeshott (1999, p. 131) qualified another classic of constitutionalism, namely, "the rule of law" a

> human invention that purports to declare the conditions of a human relationship.

However, my approach would be closer to scientific pragmatism than to narrative since it might be grounded in verifiable and indisputable fact: human death caused by human political action. Far from evaluating a constitutional process in supposed liberal democracies on the parameters of popular participation, deliberation, and consent, my research would be guided by a simpler remark: *how many died while creating a constitution?* How many died not only in drafting the constitution but in forming the political entity that the constitutional rules regulate? How many gave their lives when constitutional rules, once approved, were enforced?

Violence and counting the death have their methodological advantages, since they are more linked with concrete facts than discourses on democracy and people's sovereignty. Counting the death would indeed represent my particular ontology as an essential truth from which to build the accumulative scientific knowledge. Such data would represent the "quantities of information" in Lyotard's terms, which allow knowledge to become operational. Human death, thus, would emerge as "primary evidence," as a fundamental principle in order to recognize the conditions of the truth.

Constitutional language would be a paradigm of the construction of narratives which aim to have some kind of scientific validity. In fact, the pragmatic success or the defeat of a constitutional regime (or at least the validation of such success in terms of endurance or stability) depends mostly on the ability to create narratives that link generations over time (Jackson, 2008, p. 1280). The mere idea of authority attached to a set of rules named as a constitution results from an interaction of current values and the current perception of historical events (Kay, 2011, p. 716). In other words, the statements around the authority of a constitution and its validity are imbricated with a story that is believed.

Yet with the "counting the death" approach that I propose in analyzing constitution-making processes we are moving closer to an "objective reality" than to an "intersubjective" story, although the two have something in common. Deaths are also involved in the narrative of the creation of human political and legal entities such as constitutions. And, furthermore, a narrative is needed to attribute a human death caused by another human to a political motivation. But isolating the fact of what we may call some "narrative interferences," the point is that human death *is an objective reality* that does not depend on personal beliefs and feelings nor depend on a history shared by different individuals either.

All in all, the objective realm is more intense when the approach focuses *on the ones that have lost their lives* in the process of creating a constitutional order than when the approach is mainly concerned with individual political participation; basically because in order to define the normative conditions of the constitution-making you need to rely on a great deal of narratives concerning democracy, liberalism, human rights, political equality, human dignity, etcetera. Instead, the "counting the death" approach, let alone the easier factual determination of the human death, is committed with less intersubjective stories: only the intersubjective understanding of linking such death to the process of founding the political entity. Killing a person is indisputable as an empirical fact (in the realm of facts other things may be more arguable, such as, for instance, if the person was killed or if he instead had died from natural reasons, but the point here is that the fact of a person being murdered by another could be empirically established).

Counting, gathering information, and managing data, have become the main sources of obtaining legitimate knowledge both in the life sciences *and in social sciences.* Oklopcic, in the political theory field, for instance, speaks about "algorithms" in developing discourse on popular sovereignty and constituent power, self-determination, or constitutional self-government (2018, p. 26). But while data processing in describing the decision-making structures that relate to the people's involvement and decision with the constitution-making lead to contradictory conclusions (see Ginsburg, Blount, and Elkins, 2008, p. 382); the "counting the death" perspective suits better with the purpose of tracing objective causalities by simplifying the data in motion. It is interesting to note how much constitutional changes occurring around the world have provided impressive databases[7] and some of such databases have been used for the literature both to examine and to assess public involvement in constitutional development. However, the factual circumstances that surround such constitutional changes are hardly included in the mentioned databases. The relationship between constitution creation and violence or, to put it another way, the costs that constitutional transformation have provided in terms of deaths are likely to be eluded in such struggles, eager to compute every constitutional movement.

Constitutionalism and forgotten time

Perhaps the victory of the constitutional democracies over their adversaries such as, over time, absolute monarchies, fascist dictatorships, or Communist States consisted mainly in the ability of the former *to conceal* the victims of the violence that led to the erection of the constitutional system. In fact, some theories regarding the struggle to confer legitimacy to liberal democratic orders insist on the idea of looking forward to the developments of the constitutional system in order to calibrate if the evolution of the constitutional structure has become more inclusive in spite of the circumstance that the origins were marked by unacceptable discriminations and convulsions.

Data processing centred on violence may lead to the dissolution of the intersubjective stories around democracy that are told in order to justify constitutional supremacy of constitutional systems in force. Thus, the authority of such systems would not be provided by the original participation of the individuals in agreeing on the basic constitutional arrangements but rather on the capacity of the constitutional rules to ensure a space of peace and security in which the original acts of violence are reproduced. Similar to the conclusions envisaged by Hobbes, according to which covenants "being but words and breath have no force to oblige, contain or constrain any man … but what it has from the publique Sword" (1965, p. 135) we might infer that constitutional democracies do not find their authority in democratic variables but rather in their capacity of ending with internal destructive conflicts. The latter would mean, nevertheless, that the supposed frame of communication among free and equal individuals established by the constitutional rules is not really fair since *the communication is shortcut by the terror* that had burst out in the beginning. Such terror also distorts the communication among the members of the political community during ordinary politics, explains the stability of the system, and is being remembered in any act of constitutional enforcement. The remembrance of the ones that were sacrificed in the beginning, which arises from the depth of any constitutional controversy, would be, according to the genealogical approach, the point from which constitutional authority is derived.

Notes

1 A good (and a brief) account on Kelsen's legal theory in English might be found in the writings of Andreas Kalyvas (Kalyvas, 2006 and 2008, pp. 100–126).
2 Carl Schmitt claimed that Kelsen's supposed derivation of the validity of the legal system from the *Grundnorm* was a "tautology of raw factuality" ("*die Tautologie einer rohen Tatsächlichkeit*"). See Schmitt, 1993, p. 9. See also Heller, 1992, pp. 23–24.
3 E.W. Böckenförde observes that Kelsen's approach "formulates only the legitimacy question but a blank is left regarding the answer." See Böckenförde, 1992a, p. 93.
4 On the differences between Hart's rule of recognition and Kelsen's basic norm see, among many others, Dyzenhaus, 2016, p. 9.
5 On Hart's rejection of the moralizing myths accumulated around the law see Raz, 1995, p. 210. On positivism and the question of constitutional moral legitimacy see, generally, Fallon, 2005, and Barczentewicz, 2019, pp. 76–77.
6 Emer de Vattel, in glossing Christian Wolff's ideas entailed in his *Jus naturae*, remarked: *Populus ipse cum rege quacumque in republica leges fundamentales mutare non potest sine consensus unanimi totius nationis* [The People itself with the king cannot change any basic law of the commonwealth but with the unanimous consent of the whole nation]. In mentioning the "commonwealth's basic laws" such "unanimous consent," however, seems to refer to the erection of a government rather than to the social contract's conclusion. On this point see De Vega, 1995, p. 55.
7 See for instance de database CONSTITUTE (www.constituteproject.org).

2 The concept of constituent power and the concept of constitution

Introduction

My idea is that violence is the crucial factor that enables us both to examine the operation of designing a new constitutional order from a descriptive point of view and to offer a normative parameter in order to assess the constitutional product. The involvement of violence in the founding of a political entity is a pressing circumstance in which to rethink the concept of a constitution itself.

Since the real world offers a general connection between violence and the building of a constitutional order, I find it therefore secondary to explore in detail which conditions should be fulfilled in order to determine if a constitution is or is not a product of popular will. The vexing question of which democratic requirements should surround the creation of the constitutional framework that has disturbed the theory on constitutional democracies is likely to appear less relevant in light of the historical evidence. The mere presence of violence, I argue, cancels out any justification of constitutions grounded on the supposed democratic character of the process that created them. We are faced with the question posed by Simone Chambers (2004, p. 153): how do we know when a constitution really speaks for the people? I answer that never in contemporary experience or history has a constitution truly spoken for the People if violence is involved. In my opinion, thus, the analysis should be transferred from the issue of popular sovereignty to the issue of domination expressed by the struggles to occupy political power that produces countable deaths in the process.

Under my perspective coercion is present in the foundation of both authoritarian States and liberal democracies and, in spite of efforts dedicated to emphasizing the popular origins of constitutional regulations, a historical overview easily reveals to what extent high levels of conflict were present in the political movements that led to the creation of the fundamental laws of constitutional democracies. Tenets such as the citizenry's political participation, the division of powers, or the respect for human rights, may be appreciated, at best, in the working of a constituted State, but when we analyze more profoundly in discovering how the basic decisions on that political community were taken (the ones that, on the other hand, are imposed on the ordinary politics developed in the legislatures), it is inevitable that we find a wide range of abuses, arbitrariness, and horrifying crimes.

The basic ideas here developed on the relationship between constitution-making processes and violence would bring me to a theory of the constitution that, in short, may be described as follows:

1. instead of being an action by which a people gives itself a set of rules that will regulate the political community in the future, a constitution is rather the outcome of violence.
2. it is so because a constitution, according to my vision, is a decision on the allocation of power and such a decision was the consequence of a conflict in which some groups defeated other groups by the worst possible means (wars, killings, ethnic cleansing, and economic spoliation).
3. following this pattern, a constitution may be considered as a device held by the groups that won the previous conflict to freeze the established structure of domination during the ordinary democratic times of the constituted power.
4. given the passing of a set of rules which are the legal translation of such domination there would not likely be a constitutional transformation without a radical change in such relations of domination.

The latter remark would help us to understand, on the one hand, the difference between the emergence of the constituent power, when the previous constellation of powers is contested, and a mere amendment to the system. A consideration such as the one just mentioned makes why violence is likely to occur when there is a constitutional transformation more comprehensible: because it attacks the core decision on power previously adopted. Violence, thus, would be in that fashion not only inherent in the constituent power but, from the analytical point of view, would help to identify when a constitutional transformation is provided. If "violence is the constituent power," we only must ask ourselves about the moment in which violence erupts in order to recognize when the constituent power reappears.

Emmanuel Sieyès, Carl Schmitt, and the legal boundlessness of the *pouvoir constituant*

Let me begin by introducing the main characters of the notion of the constituent power as defined by the author that invented it, Emmanual Sieyès[1] and by one of Sieyès' main commentators: Carl Schmitt (1993, pp. 77–82). I believe that it is important to assume the remarks of both writers concerning the act of constitutional foundation because their approaches are relevant in the concept concerning the constituent power that I am going to outline in the following pages.

According to Sieyès (and according to Schmitt as well), the *pouvoir constituant* as the agency of higher lawmaking is marked, essentially, by its legally boundless character (see on this point Cristi, 1997, p. 198 and Roznai, 2017, p. 106). Sieyès underlies the position of the constituent power as an element located outside the scope of the positive law not limited by previous rules, substantive or procedural. On the contrary, the erection of a constitutional framework relies entirely on political and social circumstances that surround the legal operation.[2] Whereas constituted powers are inseparable from a pre-established constitutional order, constituent power is external to a constitutional order and exists without it (see Jacobsohn and Roznai, 2020, p. 227). Constituent power forms freely (in Sieyès' version) based solely on the nation's will, the framework of the organization, and function of the State power. As Sieyès famously wrote:

> the constituent power can do everything in relationship to constitutional making. It is not subordinated to a previous constitution. The nation that exercises the greatest, the most important of its powers, must be, while carrying this function, free from all constraints, from any form, except the one that it deems better to adopt.
>
> (Sieyès, 2014, p. 127)[3]

Although some recent accounts of Sieyès' thought emphasize his concern in separating the theory of sovereignty from the theory of constituent power (Rubinelli, 2019, 2020, p. 56) the notion of constituent power in Sieyès has been traditionally, and in my opinion correctly, associated to that of sovereignty. In fact, as Colón-Ríos observed (2016, 2020, p. 29; see on this point also Tuck, 2016, p. 2) in most of the political writers that have dealt with the notion of sovereignty (including not only Sieyès or Schmitt but also, for instance, Rousseau), the exercise of sovereign power has been connected to that of adopting fundamental laws.

According to Sieyès and Schmitt, both sovereignty and constituent power are not subjected to a previously existing legal boundary (see Pasquino, 1998, p. 9): both refer to an original, internally supreme and externally independent power; and both the constituent power as described by Sieyès and the sovereign power as described by Carl Schmitt[4] rejected that such attributes belonged to the realm of the norms but to the realm of the facts. It has been argued that according to Carl Schmitt's approach, the constituent power is seen as the locus where sovereignty is ascribed to a subject beyond any legal rule (see Cristi, 1997, p. 193). The genesis of the constitution would be in this fashion deemed as the channel through which sovereignty finds its manifestation.

Sieyès' *pouvoir constituant*, in another way, signals the historicity of the constitution (see Somek, 2012, p. 34) and also for Carl Schmitt historicity is the hallmark of the notion of constituent power (Loughlin, 2014, p. 224) since there is something preceding the establishment of the legal order: the State and the political unity conformed within its frame, a unity that is not a matter of a contract in Sieyès' theory (see Hont, 1994, p. 193, n. 46) and that is conceived as the decision of the sovereign will in Schmitt's.

Even without mentioning the question of violence, the intuition of its involvement in the foundation of a constitutional order lies behind the statements of both Sieyès and Schmitt (Patberg, 2017, p. 52; on Schmitt see Scheuerman, 1997, p. 145). The *pouvoir constituant* was not attached to the mandates of the old regime, because the creation of a new political entity required a quantum break with the previous set of rules that only violence may provide.

Nevertheless, as is well known, Sieyès' approach still depends on some sort of normative statement regarding the need of the political community's consent to the rules that will organize the society in the future. He believed in the possibility of founding a political entity by the free association of men (1988, p. 123) and reasoned that the body formed by such a move, the nation, had to be represented in an assembly called to draft and to pass the Constitution. Sieyès inaugurated, thus, in the European continental tradition, the concern with the legitimacy of the constitutional creation centred on the constituent agent somehow derived from the popular sovereignty but expressed by the indirect means of a system of representation. Although Sieyès' intellectual and political effort went into distinguishing his "nation" as the embodiment of indirect popular sovereignty from its democratic alternatives that, in his perspective, may lead to the despotism of the masses (Hont, 1994, p. 210), the techniques of representation had still to be linked to some sort of popular will.

Also, for Carl Schmitt, who in fact denied democratic tenets of Sieyès' theory,[5] the acceptance of the basic rules by the governed, and to some extent the involvement of democracy during the foundation of the political unity, was crucial (see Dyzenhaus, 2019, p. 498). Schmitt was not concerned by the particular procedures of representation and deliberation reflecting the will of the represented, but for him the ideal was encapsulated in the act of the acclamation, the moment of the total identification between the people and the governed, in which the essence of the political body, the existential decision that both conforms it and justifies it, is revealed (a decision, on the other hand, not deprived of *de facto* measures beyond the uproar of the masses, as Arato observed, 1995–1996, p. 203; on the acclamation see Burchard, 2006, p. 13).

In summary, even for the most anti-positivistic theoreticians on the constitution-making processes, Sieyès and Schmitt, not all the founding relations that lead to the creation of a constitution were grounded on the "state of war" (Agamben, for instance, 2003 p. 46, observes that even for Schmitt the constituent power is not merely a question of raw force but that some legal attachments are nonetheless still involved). They also backed a normative theory based on popular participation (through an agency of representation in Sieyès) and, thus, the normative boundlessness of the force able to design a new constitutional structure was not complete. It should be remarked that, in the case of Sieyès, his reliance on a theory on the justification of the power through will somehow linked to the community and minimizing the force of arms is surprising, given his experience as a member of the 1789–1791 French Constituent Assembly and, afterwards, his leading role in establishing the 1795 Constitution and, particularly, his involvement in the coup of 18 Brumaire which would invest him both as a Consul besides Bonaparte and as a father of the 1799 Constitution (Doyle, 1989, p. 375).

All in all, the stage at which the need for coercive forces is likely to be more relevant in Sieyès' universe is while building the political entity called to give itself a normative framework: the creation of the nation. Although Sieyès covered his theory on the origins of the nation with the fiction of an "association of free individuals living under the laws of nature" (Sieyès, 1988, pp. 123–127) he was very conscious that the unity of the nation required a political homogenization of its entire membership through more tangible mechanisms than "natural law"(see Agne, 2012, p. 837; Hont, 1994, p. 194; for a more inclusive interpretation of Sieyès' "nation" in contrast to the organic, cultural, linguistic, or racial community conceived by Carl Schmitt see Scheuerman, 1997, pp. 148–149).

The concern with the territorial unification of France in order to become the nation as the highest agency of normative production may be appreciated in Sieyès' staunch refusal of federalism, provincialism, or any other form of territorial fragmentation. As he wrote:

> France must not be an assemblage of little nations, governing themselves separately as democracies; it is not a collection of states; it is a single whole, composed of integral parts; these parts must not enjoy separately a complete existence, because they are not merely united wholes, but parts forming but one whole.
>
> (Sieyès, 1985, p. 234)

Sieyès' theory on the constituent power relying on a unitary representative system was only possible if a process of political unification embodied in a single entity had previously taken place, a process that had been conducted through violence while leading to the monarchist despotism from the sixteenth century, but which also played a decisive role in entrenching the revolution across France after 1789 under the idea of civil egalitarianism. Political unification through violence, nevertheless, would reach its paroxysm in revolutionary France when coupling the idea of national sovereignty with a regime of direct popular democracy as the Jacobins did by the means of terror and ethnic cleansing perpetrated in the name of republican virtue (Hont, 1994, pp. 201, 205).

Sieyès' contribution and Schmitt's ulterior interpretation of Sieyès' work are, in short, relevant for our analysis since:

1. they identify the emergence of constituent power as a process not subjected by the previous rules. The constituent power would be "in the state of nature" limited by no law or norms of any kind (see Arato, 2020, p. 105).
2. in doing so, they admit the influence of political and social facts in defining the new constitutional order even mentioning, albeit tangentially, the factor of violence (as in Schmitt when he recognizes the sovereign as the person able to decide during the state of emergency, Schmitt, 2004, p. 1).
3. they link the idea of constituent power to history and, thus, somehow to the violent developments that explain the configuration of political unities (as Sieyès' nation) and their transformations.

4. they are also the fathers of a normative theory on popular involvement as a structure to legitimate the outcome of the constitution-making process (being representative in Sieyès' conception and with more direct attributes in Schmitt's). The latter contrasts with the historical awareness that arises from both authors' thought and their experience in the contexts that dominate the passing of new regime constitutions. However, considering that the lacks in both Sieyès and Schmitt's theories on the democratic character of the constituent agent are still projected in contemporary understandings on the exercise of the *pouvoir constituant*, such deficits will allow us to ground our criticism in approaches which tackle the question from the perspective of democratic theory.

We shall begin our analysis with critique on the struggle to build a normative theory on constituent power grounded on a democratic ideal or, as Sheldon Wolin (1989, p. 5) called it, grounded on "the obscure things around participation."

The paradoxes of democratic theory and founding

The definition of the conditions that, according to democratic theory, a constitution-making process should fulfil in order to be legitimated has countless problems, to begin with the already mentioned paradox pointed out by authors such as Michelman (1996) according to which the conditions of the founding cannot be defined democratically. As we have seen, since the idea of self-legislation has to be realized in a framework of (democratically legitimate) laws such a juris-generative event has itself to be the product of a prior (democratically legitimate) procedural event opening, thus, an infinite regression of validity conditions which are likely incompatible with the practices developed in the real world.

The problem of democratic founding is, indeed, "one of the most intractable issues in political theory" (Kohn and McBride, 2011, p. 153). The sharpest evidence of this observation concerns the definition of the constituent agent, the subject whose participation in the form of deliberation and consent is required by the democratic theory to draft and to pass a constitution. The paradox of the need of a well-formed people to found a political order which, at the same time, has to be defined by someone else was already pointed out by Rousseau in the *Social Contract*:

> In order for a nascent people to appreciate sound political maxims and follow the fundamental rules of statecraft, the effect would have to become the cause; the social spirit, which should be the product of the way in which the country was founded would have to preside over the founding itself; and before the creation of the laws, men would have to be what they should become by means of those same laws.
>
> (Rousseau, 1966, p. 67)

In mentioning such "social spirit," Rousseau is likely to allude to some pre-existing rules, a sort of civic ethos, that ought to be shared by the members of the society called to give itself a basic legislation, including the definition of the attributes that explain and justify their belonging to the community which is going to decide on constitutional issues (see on this point Colón-Ríos, 2020, pp. 46–50; Honig, 2007, pp. 3–4; and Schweber, 2012, p. 49).

The disagreement on the agent that has to exercise the constitutional founding and to give itself a set of rules has been steadily highlighted also from Sieyès and all those concerned with the question of the *pouvoir constituant*. As I have pointed out, according to Sieyès, who was well aware of the problem regarding which are the institutional and procedural presuppositions of the founding, the power to organize the structure in which politics are going to develop relies on the relationship between the one that decides on such fundamental arrangements and the agent in which the common will is encapsulated:

> It is impossible to create a body for an end without giving it the organization, forms and laws it needs in order to fulfill the functions for which it has been established. This is what is meant by the constitution of that body. It is obvious that it could not exist without one ... The body of representatives entrusted with the legislative power, or the exercise of the common will, exists only by the way of the mode of being which the nation decided to give it. It is nothing without its constitutive forms; it acts, proceeds, or commands only by way of those forms.
>
> (Sieyès, 1988, p. 126)

As advanced, my thesis, plainly, is *that the definition of the constituent agent is provided by violence*, that the determination of what is the nation or who belongs to a people or if some people exercises the right (or not) to self-determination depends on historical disruptions traced by massive human rights violations.

The impossibility of defining democratically the constituent agent, the difficulty to think of the people as a corporate body capable of speaking in one voice, opens thus the door to self-arrogate the representation of such will in creating the fundamental norms by anyone, including a power scarcely attached to any form of popular participation which is able to impose its order, not through deliberative persuasion, but rather through savage means.

Different strategies have been displayed in order to surmount the inability of describing and justifying the foundation of a democratic order in democratic terms and, at the same time, diverting the objections related to violence. I gather them into three main groups:

1. those concerned with the virtues of deliberation to justify the adoption of constitutional rules.
2. those centred in describing the constituent power as an ex-post reconstruction.
3. those, somehow linked to the two previous, devoted to minimizing the factor of coercion in the origins of the constitutional system in order to highlight the benefits of the constituted power in terms of stability and inclusiveness.

Besides the three mentioned strategies I will also mention a fourth one related to some attempts developed by international law scholars focused on surmounting the problem of violence in building national constitutional democracies through a cosmopolitan conception of constituent power.

Deliberation in constitution-making processes as a strategy to diminish the influence of violence

One way of containing the problem of violence in the creation of a constitutional order relies on focusing on the episodes of the constitutional discussion. A democratic theory on constitutional settings would not only be provided by political participation and mobilization, but also by deliberation among the different participants in the constitutional drafting. One of the major theorists regarding the idea of deliberative democracy, Jon Elster, has also turned his interest towards deliberation in the creation of a constitutional framework (Elster, 1994, 1995, 1998, 2000b). Elster defines a deliberative setting as a context in which, since speakers have to justify their proposals according to public interest, outcomes may be shaped independently of the motives of the participants (1998, p. 104). Deliberative models of democracy, to present them broadly, see as a necessary condition for attaining legitimacy and rationality with regard to collective decision-making processes in a polity, that the institutions of this polity are so arranged that what is considered the common interest of all results from a deliberation conducted rationally and fairly among free and equal individuals (Benhabib, 1996, p. 69). The antonym of deliberation would be, thus, the imposition of outcomes by self-interested and politically powerful groups (Sunstein, 1988, p. 1550).

The application of the deliberative models of democracy to the constituent processes, the application of a decision-making process conceived as a "well-conducted conversation" (Banks, 2008, p. 1047), clashes with the same challenges that such models have to contend with in general, namely, that supposed rational and fair discussion on the common good among individuals is developed within a horizon of suppositions, assumptions, and power relations which are able to distort both the process and the outcome of the deliberation. Put in another way, deliberation is not developed out of the avatars of the world, ***deliberation is attached to history*** and is a product of it, a frame made of battles, resistances, and defeats, composed by classes, genders, groups, and nations (Benhabib, 1996, pp. 78–79).

The latter may explain why an analysis devoted to handling constituent process from the position of rational and fair discourse, such as the one discussed by Elster himself, is likely to be unsatisfactory. In spite of Elster's struggles to characterize some historical developments regarding constitutional assemblies as the proposed deliberative setting, he admits that force-based threats (which he judges as inadmissible within a deliberative context, 1998, p. 103) concurred with the aforementioned episodes (1998, pp. 112–113). An ambient force was created during the debates of 1789 regarding the drafting of the 1791 French Constitution, or during the discussion regarding the 1848 French Constitution, in both cases with a decisive influence on the outcome of these constitutional processes. On the other hand, although the delegates drafting the U.S. Constitution in Philadelphia never went beyond the threat of force (which might be doubtful as we shall see) Elster also recognizes the flaws in the United States constitutional process from the deliberative and democratic point of view, considering the absolute exclusion of women, slaves, Native Americans, and many property-less individuals (1998, p. 98). The small group of wealthy, property-holding white males that gathered in Philadelphia to draft a written constitution for the United States did it in secrecy, excluding public participation (see Elster, 1994, p.77 and also Ginsburg, Blount, and Elkins, 2008, pp. 361–362). Regarding the drafting of the United States Federal Constitution, we may ask ourselves, how could it be possible to attribute the constitutional outcome to the will of "the People" if its elaboration was conscientiously developed in a context of conspiracy, without permitting the public to know what was being discussed at the Philadelphia meeting, beginning with the decision to abandon the Articles of the Confederation that ruled the relationship between the American States. As Ackerman underlined (2019, p. 366), Madison, Hamilton, and Jay only wrote the *Federalist Papers* addressed to their fellow citizens *after* the Philadelphia Convention took place and when the main decisions on the American Federal constitutional structure had already been taken.

Elster, nevertheless, tries to surmount the objections grounded in the real context of drafting the United States Federal Constitution by defending that is possible to see in some constitution-making processes a deliberative setting by understanding "democracy" and "deliberation" in a minimal sense (1998, p. 98). But the examples provided by the 1787 Philadelphia Convention, or by the 1789 or 1848 French processes, reveal that any deliberative structure recognized in them cannot be detached from the abuses that embedded the elaboration of the constitutional rules finally approved. It is difficult from the outset to see if the deliberative and democratic constitutional processes in which Elster affirms that he is interested, even assuming the words deliberative and democracy in their minimal sense, have in fact taken place somewhere. In an article written later, Elster (2012a) prefers straightforwardly to examine the role of violence in both the making of the U.S. Federal Constitution and the 1791 French Constitution instead of centring the analysis in the deliberative tenets of both experiences. Previously, Elster had already recognized the shortcomings of his earlier approach on deliberation on constitution-making processes by arguing that "constitution-makers are more likely to be vulnerable to impulsive passions than those whose behavior they are trying to regulate" (Elster, 2000a, p. 173). Somehow, this author took a more realistic path and outlined, in a strand closer to the ideas on constituent power described in this book, a characterization of constitutions as structures by which the drafters enacted a fundamental law to bind others rather to bind themselves in the future (see on this point Gargarella, 2020, pp. 68–69).

It is certainly difficult to focus on the deliberative setting regarding the constitution-making process since, as Schmitt rightly detected (1993, pp. 3–11), in the founding moment, existential questions of the political community are at stake. It is not a matter of reaching an outcome through bargaining, it is a matter of all or nothing. Bargaining and deliberation might occur in secondary aspects of the organization of States, but not in the fundamental pillars of the political order, in what Schmitt called the absolute concept of constitution (*der absolute Verfassungsbegriff*) which precisely make fundamental constitutional discussions so easily sway into raw confrontations. This topic is also recognized by Elster (1998, pp. 117–118; 2012a, p. 7) when he remembers that the calm and undisturbed conditions in which a constitution ought to be adopted, according to the deliberative pattern, contrast with the dramatic and turbulent circumstances in which constitutions are drafted in the real world. In fact, Elster himself (1995, p. 370) noticed that the activation of the constituent power is sociologically and historically associated with strong conflicts which are not particularly conducive to deliberation. So:

> new constitutions almost always are written in the wake of a crisis or exceptional circumstances of some sort … . By and large … the link between crisis and constitution-making is quite robust.

Also, Russell (1993, p. 103) admitted that:

> No liberal democratic State has accomplished comprehensive constitutional change outside the context of some cataclysmic situation such as revolution, world war, the withdrawal of empire, civil war, or the threat of imminent breakup.

Furthermore, even while nowadays deliberation is at the centre of normative ideas about democracy (Gutmann and Thompson, 2004, p. VII), there is no agreement in the literature about to what extent deliberative standards are accomplished while discussing and approving a constitution (Ginsburg, Blount, and Elkins, 2008, pp. 367–368). The faith in deliberation is puzzling since scholars have not clarified how deliberation really works (Barabas, 2004, p. 687), and even the normative premises regarding institutions in which deliberation is supposedly to be held, are fuzzy.

The same disagreements that any theory on deliberative democracy has to face when it is confronted with any level of governance are reproduced (and amplified) in the case of constitution-making. As some recent processes of citizen-led constitutional change have shown, participatory and deliberative trends set in motion several factors that might lead to contradictory outcomes. Deliberation is argued to promote rationality by encouraging a real and sustained dialogue (Carolan, 2015, p. 736) but, as suggested, massive political mobilization and participation is likely to cancel scenarios in which rational and deliberative dialogue can be developed.

In fact, it may be doubtful if deliberation, defined as an enlightened and open-minded search for consensus in which participants cast their personal interests aside, is related to political discussion (Barabas, 2004, p. 699). Yet, political discussion is not, or not only, the research of the truth beyond ideologies. Politics is not science. If we have ideologies, it is because the conditions, the procedures, and the outcomes foreseen by deliberative theories are imperfectly given in the real world. A general objection to deliberative analysis and decision-making procedures highlights the problem about the political character of the procedure chosen: procedure might be itself a political decision, able to influence the outcome. The conclusion of the debate would thus not be a rational and consensual solution adopted by free and equal participants, but the answer that those who designed the procedure, motivated by political interests, sought to reach.

A constitution-making is, in addition, a procedure marked by the imperfections, inequalities, and lack of information of the participants, as well as by historical circumstances, prejudices, short-term ambition, the desire for material wealth and political power, and therefore, intimidations and coercions. The literature is full of examples of short-term political interests that impinge on fundamental legal configurations (see, for instance, Ackerman, 2019, pp. 12–13).

The binomial, deliberation/constitution-making has, besides that, to surmount another shortcoming: even while admitting that deliberation may offer a fair frame in which individuals may discuss in equal conditions the experiences that have been developed during the last decades in the form of deliberative citizens' *fora* such as randomly chosen assemblies and juries, consensus conferences, or deliberative polls have been more likely to succeed regarding one particular issue. A discussion on whether a sixth nuclear power plant should be built in Finland is one thing (Setälä et al., 2010) and another is deliberating about an overarching regulation of the public power which is entailed in constitutions (Kong and Levy, 2018). Confronted interests, contradictions, technical ignorance, and atavistic resentment are usual while drafting a constitution. Still, if we focus the definition of a deliberative model on the arrangements conducive to conducting a rational and fair discussion on the common good, the debate on constitutional rules is precisely the debate on those arrangements which enable deliberation. Constitutional matters are matters of the preconditions of deliberation, and such preconditions are not attained in their turn through deliberative processes.

Related to deliberative theory, one particular institution involved in constitution-making procedures tends to generate controversy and reflects the lack of agreement among experts: the referendum. Ratification through a referendum involving direct vote by citizens has been seen as an expression of popular participation necessary for a constitution to be regarded as legitimate (Ginsburg et al., 2008, p. 362; Ackerman, 1992, p. 53). It has been seen, at the same time, however, as an instrument with which all sorts of populist rulers may mislead their citizens. As evidence of the relevance of the referendum in modern constitution-making, it should be highlighted that of 49 new constitutions promulgated in the twenty-first century (until 2020) 26 have been approved in referenda.[6] But it has been suggested that ratification is probably an insufficient instrument to engage the public in the constitutional process. Authors such as Gastil (2000, pp. 69–71), while admitting that referenda may provide a complement for representative government in order to reinvigorate the public sphere, deem that this form of direct political participation may suffer from similar maladies to those that plague elections for public office. Tierney (2012, p. 23, and 2014) for instance, detects three major inherent problems associated with the use of referenda: "elite manipulation" (a problem which, as we shall see, is inherent to the constitution-making process itself), "deliberation deficit," since the voters may have insufficient information to base their vote upon, and "majoritarian danger," since the adoption of a new constitution by referendum with the support of an overwhelming majority does not preclude the violation of the rights of the minority.

Supporters of referenda, on the other hand, are reluctant to limit the constitution-making process to only one final referendum of ratification (see Eisenstadt et al., 2015). A "yes" and "no" vote to the whole draft is not, under this perspective, likely to provide the proper deliberative atmosphere that would require a discussion on the different institutions through which the relationship between the people and the power is designed (See Colón-Ríos, 2012, p. 154; Tully, 2002, p. 213).

If the ratification through a final referendum has been deemed as a device used by the elites to ensure popular consent to the decisions on the governmental system that they have already adopted (Morel, 2012, p. 505; Suteu, 2015, p. 273), in the darkest fashion the *apellatio ad populum* that a referendum entails has been associated with authoritarian government (Kay, 2011, p. 747). In conflictive transitions, charismatic leaders have used referenda to trigger a constituent process suitable with their aspirations to strengthen their power in respect to other representative institutions (Partlett, 2012, pp. 223–233; Arato, 2020, p. 91). The mandate of hearing the voice of the People has sometimes covered up infringements of legality or dismantling of democratically elected bodies.

Generally, recent participatory constitution-making processes, such as the ones triggered in Iceland or Ireland, have highlighted the tension between participation and deliberation, expressing uncertainties as well around representativeness of citizen-led assemblies and their relationship with institutions. It is not clear to what extent direct engagement of the citizenship in participatory forums provides a more qualified deliberation than that developed in the political instances through elected representatives. In that sense, sceptics on the direct engagement of the public in a constituent process have even suggested that citizens are, to a greater degree than the elites, motivated more by self-interest than by ideals of community and good governance (Cusack, 2003, pp. 91–93). From this point of view, thus, might be accepted a limitation on public participation in constitution-making in order to avoid the creation of a governmental system captured by a mass desire for immediate benefit.

In short, even though the idea of deliberation in order to assess public participation has been exhaustively analyzed in historical processes of constitution-making (and even though it still represents the normative keystone in approaching the more recent constituent episodes, see Eisenstadt et al., 2017, pp. 25–54) there is no consensus among the scholars about what deliberation is, or ought to be, in the different phases of passing a constitution. The unleashing of streams of violence that surround deliberative *fora* in real experiences of founding new constitutional regimes jeopardize, in my view, any consideration on the supposed democratic virtues of rational and inclusive dialogues developed in contexts of public participation and mobilization. In another way, as we shall see, where a special effort has been made to engage the citizenry in a brand-new constitution-drafting, what eventually happens is that the constitutional product is usually (if not always) not finally approved.

Constituent power as a permanent reconstruction

Recent theories on constituent power, such as the ones presented by Lindahl (2003, 2007, 2015) or Loughlin (2014) describe constitution-founding through the ontology whereby individuals retroactively identify themselves as the members of a polity in constituent action by exercising the powers granted to them by a constitution. Thus, the act of collective self-attribution would not have taken place in the historical point related to the constitution's approval, but in the timeframe ruled by the constituted power which, in obeying the constitution, would reaffirm the "We" of the original moment. In a similar vein, as some German scholars do in their struggles to rebuild the constituent power through the democratic processes foreseen by the German Basic Law (see Möllers, 2007, pp. 98–99; Kumm, 2016b; Patberg, 2017), for Lindhal or Loughlin constituent power would be therefore discerned through the processes developed *under the constitutional regime*. In fact, some authors have noticed that it is the constitution itself, *after* its enactment, the device called to develop a sense of mutual belongingness among the citizenry. As Joseph Weiler (2003, p. 9) has observed, the demos able to act as the maker of the fundamental rules is constituted, legally, by the very constitution, and often the acceptance of the constitutional framework is among the first steps towards a thicker social and political notion of constitutional demos. Echoing Loughlin's works, Nootens (2015, p. 138) also described the role of the constitution as a factor of building the collective ruled by it:

> constituent power is a symbolic reconstruction of a multitude as a collective political agent that is crystallized a posteriori in distinctive representations of "the people" (in a kind of "back-to-the-future" move) that build on the empirical and discursive significance of specific interests, yet whose function is to represent the *whole* body politics.

Such approaches coincide in underlining the paradox *of giving normative value to something that cannot be confronted with historicity*. This ontology, nevertheless, handles a historical product which is extracted from historical developments. The truth about the facts is consciously lifted in order to create authority. As Lindhal admits (2007, p. 20):

> the characterization of collective selfhood relies on a past that never has been present and a future that never will become a present, hence on a past and a future eliding its control.

Certainly, the "past" to which the exercise of constituted powers by the individuals is referred imagines an action of the People that never was. Lindhal depicts the constituent moment through a retroactive ontology precisely because of the democratic deficits of the *real* constituent moments provided by history. Since we have serious problems characterizing constitution-founding as a collective action based on cohesion, democracy, and deliberation, and completely outside of repressive factors, authors like Lindhal and Loughlin *move the democratic elements of legitimacy to the future.*

To such a strand would also belong the sociological and functionalistic approach developed by Thornhill (2012, p. 389) who, precisely by observing the historical weakness of the foundational experiences as ways of conferring an external legitimacy to the constitutional system, suggests a notion of constituent power fixed through institutions and practices developed within the political system.

In my perspective, nevertheless, evoking a real situation made of conflicts and divisions might precisely provide an explanation *about the current deficits* in the day-to-day functioning of liberal democracy. The "reconstructive" theories see both the reaffirmation of the constitutional foundation and the "We" in the democratic present, in the exercise of fundamental rights and the constraints on government through the division of powers. But the question is do the past flaws *reappear in the present* and distort current developments within the constitutional State? Unavoidable circularities, furthermore, affect the reconstructive approach: we do not have in the present either the confirmation of the "We" because it didn't exist in the past and, when we struggle to solve the conflict in the present, we have to look backwards into a past that has never existed: a past that has motivated the present division.

More criticisms and observations can be added to the reconstructive vision: an individual consent pronounced through the constituted power that confers, retroactively, an entity to the constituent power and the foundation is not rooted in the effectiveness of the constitutional rights or the constitutional framework. In my account, the individual consent that can be inferred from the effectiveness of the constituted power is not retroactively applied in order to revive the presence of the People but *it signalizes the violence and the turbulences that surrounded the original moment.* The constitutional language on the present maybe depends, as Lindhal suggests, on a retroactive ontology, but not in that of remembering "We the People," but in that marked by the fears of the forces that clashed before the approval of the constitution or that fostered the inauguration of the constitutional order. In summary, the "We" is more defined through the remnants of violence in the present than through an idealization of an original consent.

Such retroaction centred on blood and death instead of on the supposed will of the living participants gives a precise account of the ex post facto character of the constituent power. *The acceptance of the order might only be given to a violence that succeeded.* If a constitution, for example, defines a People in national terms (and considering the paradox mentioned, according to which the constituent power cannot be placed upon said "We the People" since it is created by the constitutional rule itself) what the constitutional mention in reality envisages is *the national group which won the original conflict against other nations and ethnic minorities*: the rule creates the People since the facts established the relation of domination. The constitutional determination of the People in national terms would be, in this way, nothing but a certification of *who won the confrontation.*

Observing the issue through the prism of violence in such national clashes enables us to appreciate, firstly, that a subject in the form of a national or ethnic group imposed its coercion upon minorities and created a political community; and secondly, that said subject can only be outlined retroactively since the point from which the winner is perceived is the constitutional determination of the national People and the effectiveness of the constitutional order; thirdly, that constitutional language confers legitimacy to such a retroactive operation; and fourthly, that legitimacy does not come from an authority inferred from the constitutional rule regarding some principles of morality or fairness, but from the sign of the knife with which the prevalent group asserted its dominance upon the others.

Thus, constituent power wouldn't be understood through a reconstruction regarding the virtues of the constituted power as, let's say, the protection of human rights, democracy, or the welfare State; but on the confirmation of the effectiveness of the constitutional order in threatening the population with repetition of the original acts of oppression, in the case of collapse of the current framework.

Again, it is not a matter of the mobilization that surrounded the act of constitution-founding, but a matter of the People's passivity once the system is established, fearing another descent into the hell of war, mass murders, or ethnic cleansing. The constitutional system is, thus, in force, as long as the remembrance of the original founding is able to be imposed and used as a threat when other violence arises strong enough to challenge the repressive mechanisms of the system and to cancel the memory of the clash that underpinned the previous regime.

The constituent power, thus, would not be a reconstruction regarding a democratic past that never had been, but a violent past that, on the contrary, was enough present in the collective and the individual memories to sustain the established constitutional system.

Looking to the future in order to avoid the view of the past

Another way to focus on deliberative and discursive factors in deciding on constitutional issues might be well represented by Jürgen Habermas' theory on the foundations of a constitutional democracy (1996, 2001). In a different way to the theories of the ex post facto reconstruction, Habermas is fully concerned with an exploration of the features of the constituent moment. His struggle is also centred in establishing the normative conditions of the founding even though some defective externalities regarding the empirical conditions on the constitution-making operation might be obvious. Thus,

> Rather than appeal to a moral realism that would be hard to defend, I propose that we understand the regress itself as the understandable expression of the future-oriented character, or openness, of the democratic constitution: in my view, a constitution that is democratic not just in its content but also according to its source of legitimation is a tradition-building project with a clearly marked beginning in time.
>
> (Habermas, 2001, p. 774)

Since the constitution-making practice is oriented to the future, Habermas would assert, shortcomings which alter the constituent moment might be corrected through the deliberation on constitutional issues displayed while the constitutional regime is in force. Thus, a democratic constitution devoted to ensuring liberal basic rights and rights of political participation and communication would enable an inclusive process of opinion- and will-formation on the part of the citizens functioning as a self-correcting process in discussing constitutional issues.

> To be sure, this fallible continuation of the founding event can break out of the circle of a polity's groundless discursive self-constitution only if this process, which is not immune to contingent interruptions and historical regressions, can be understood in the long run as a self-correcting learning process.
>
> (Habermas, 2001, p. 774)

Yet, the problem of Habermas' "self-correcting learning process" of constitutional practices is, in my opinion, that *he is still requiring strong normative conditions for the citizens' participation in the founding, which are not given in reality* (mainly because they are distorted by the involvement of physical force). The latter seems to be recognized by Habermas as well (2001, p. 778), in spite of the fact that he avoids exploring the problem of violence in the foundational moment in its entirety, when said violence might cause *the invalidation of the whole creational endeavour*.

We can see it in more detail: Habermas claims for a co-original formation between the citizen's democratic participation and the basic liberal rights (Habermas, 1996). Such integration between public autonomy and private autonomy, that makes democracy possible, when legally incarnated, would crystallize in the constitutional agreement. Hence, the constitutional agreement would be signed by participants able to fulfil different conditions, the first of which is that they form a *voluntary association* of individuals considered free and equal and committed to regulate their future life together by means of positive law.

> we understand the normative bases of constitutional democracy as the result of a deliberative decision-making process that the founders (motivated by whatever historical contingencies) undertook with the intention of creating a voluntary, self-determining association of free and equal citizens.
>
> (Habermas, 2001, p. 772)

Our objection, of course, is that such association *is never voluntary under the empirical and historical contingencies* to which Habermas alludes and that, rather, the foundational moment has been dominated by coercions and exclusions. Those *"historical contingencies" are precisely what empirically makes the association not free* and avoids the fulfilment of the "normative bases" of the constitutional agreement. Nevertheless, being aware of such circumstances, Habermas insists on the constitution-making practice as a necessary commitment in ensuring the deliberative practice and the inclusiveness in that practice of the *future* members of the association counted as bearers of individual rights:

> the normative expectation of complete inclusion and mutual recognition, as well as the expectation of equal opportunities for utilizing equal rights.
>
> (Habermas, 2001, p. 775)

If the constitution-making moment is legitimate as long as it foresees the expansion of the discursive and deliberative practices under the law through the inclusion of new members covered by both participative and liberal basic rights, it is because in the original agreement *not all the members were historically included.*

The thesis that seems to emerge from Habermas' approach would be that rather than the exclusions and the arbitrariness crossing the constituent moment, the important thing to assess the legitimacy of a constitutional system under democratic parameters would be its ability to establish the pillars to expand the constituent agreement *in the future.* In order to simplify Habermas' proposal with the example of the United States Constitution-foundation, it would not be as relevant if the foundational moment were led by a handful of landowners and slave traders which excluded slaves, indigenous people, or women, if the operation that began in Philadelphia allowed, in the future, the inclusion of those marginalized groups. The important issue is if the established constitutional system would entail a moral basis relating to democratic openness, discursive practices, and safeguards for both democratic and liberal rights that would be sufficient to permit self-correction of the original deficiencies, in the long run. But, again, the mere need to focus on the ability of the constitutional regime, once established, to promote inclusion in the future somehow supposes an admission of paucity, both in democratic and in liberal terms, of the original arrangement (on this point see Olson, 2007, p. 340).

Habermas' characterization of constitutional democracy is rather *a promise* of equal political agency and, in that sense, his idea for evaluating the legitimacy conditions of a constitutional democracy does not differ substantially from other kinds of political regimes (after all, for instance, communist regimes were also grounded in a promise of full political inclusiveness even though it was recognized that before reaching a horizon of equality it was needed to suffer chapters of violence, exclusion, and marginalization, such as the disruption of a revolution and the dictatorship of the proletariat).

Habermas' theoretical developments, in spite of the fact that he deals with the past (as he does in presupposing at least a minimum of deliberative practice in the founders' performance) are likely to stress the future-oriented character of the constitutional project in order to elude the exploration of that problematic background. But, under my perspective, precisely the abuses of the past, and particularly those involved in the creation of the constitutional framework, are the factors *that make the correction of the system in the present impossible.* The problems of the past are dragged into the present and make the future turbid (see Agne, 2012, p. 848). It is not only a matter regarding the shortcomings of the deliberative and inclusive practices developed within the founding act (in most constituent experiences such practices were not given *at all*) but also that the democratic and liberal paucities of the origins are the grounds on which the constitutional regime is sustained in the present.

In my vision, a constitution is the legal way to convey foundational abuses through time, these only ceasing when the basic existential decisions concerning the structure of dominance of that society change, and are replaced by others, which would mean that the system is replaced by a new constitutional settlement.

Political systems and their constitutional regulation, as in fact Habermas' theory is likely to suggest, are partially founded in amnesia. The creation of a constitution requires a quantum of suppressed memories to ensure its effectiveness. A constitution is, somehow, a tool to forget the dark past through the appearance of the law. The French historian, Ernest Renan, acutely described the relationship between the building of a political community and the operation of forgetting historical wrongs:

> The essence of a nation is that all the individuals share a great many things in common and also they have forgotten some things … . Every French citizen should have forgotten the Saint-Bartholomew [the massive killing of French Huguenots by the Catholics in 1572].
>
> (Renan, 1961, p. 892)

If the injustices committed during the founding persist in the memory, the constitutional drafting is more likely to be perceived as a product of a faction. The more buried the deeds, the more impartially the constitutional covenant might be interpreted. Such has been, for instance, the strategy coherently adopted by the social contract theories: individuals concur to agree the contract naked of regrets, under the "veil of ignorance" (to say it in Rawls' terms) or able "to pardon past offenses" (to say it in Hobbes' terms).

A genealogical approach on the formation of political entities and the analysis of the constitution-making that vest such entities with a legal framework is rooted in the opposite position from this selective amnesia. *What matters essentially is what happened*: the description of the abuses that a group committed against others. In the case of the liberal democracies, the genealogical approach is centred on exploring the fissures opened before the time that such entities might call themselves "liberal democracies," or the moments in which, once established, liberal democracies suspend the handling of challenges in a democratic fashion by dedicating themselves to the destruction of opponents.

Memories have an ambivalent character in my interpretation of constitutional supremacy. On the one hand, they contribute to weaken the effectiveness of the constitutional system since they insist on describing the constitutional draft as a legal translation of an injustice (in that sense as an opposite operation to the one provided by amnesia, which tends to strengthen the system). But, on the other hand, as I remarked, the evocation of violence is a device attached to the enforcement of the constitutional order and its prevalence, since the memory of civil confrontation dissuades the losers from pressing for an utter change of the regime, as they fear a subsequent defeat.

Here would come my reading of the positivist model that I have presented in the previous chapter concerning the "effectiveness" of promoting obedience as a character of constitutional rule. More precisely, in my opinion "effectiveness" as a capacity to promote obedience makes the positivist analysis cling to a normative ontology which may be summarized in the statement according to which "effective rule (namely, constitutional rule), able to impose general obedience, is a rule that *exists*."

If we examine how such a rule is obeyed (and thus exists) the answer would be that is because of the violence irradiated from the original moment to the present: obedience relies on the terror that the remembrance of the founding crimes is still able to inspire, or that it reemerges in a moment of crisis in the system.

Saying that effectiveness explains the being of the constitutional norm, as a positivist approach does, may be equivalent to saying, as the genealogical approach may hold, that *violence is the being of the constitution* and that such an essential quality is something that a more or less inclusive development of the constitution, once the constitutional system is established, cannot repair.

Surmounting the debate on constituent power through post-national constitutionalism?

The final strategy that we are going to present regarding the challenge of superseding the lack of democratic attributes in the creation of a constitutional democracy is related to the theories invoked in describing the formation of constitutionalism beyond the State (see Krisch, 2010, 2016; Kumm, 2008, 2016b; Walker, 2008). David Dyzenhaus, for instance, has examined to what extent the issue of international law's constitutionalization has boosted the discussion around the question of constituent power (2012, p. 231). How much might constitutional language be applied to international law practices or specific international regimes? Are the founding categories managed by constitutionalism regarding sovereign States able both to explain and to justify the arrogation of power by international and transnational bodies? Might the foundations of international law, based on constitutional categories, generate the same problems that we see in the legitimacy of the sovereign State itself?

Such issues have been envisaged in recent decades in countless contributions from both constitutional law and international public law scholars which might be gathered under the label of "cosmopolitan constitutionalism" (Fox-Decent, 2016, pp. 125–137) or "post-national constitutionalism"(Krisch, 2010, p. 16; Shaw, 1999). From the "cosmopolitan" perspective, in summary, it is possible to build a justification of a global public authority without connection to the self-governing practices of a people and, nevertheless, call this international phenomenon "constitutionalism." On the other hand, authors such as Nico Krisch, supporters of a post-national conception of the law, go beyond. They even are critical of the idea of translating constitutional language to the global arena, arguing that the continuity between the domestic constitutionalist tradition and the cosmopolitan one by ensuring democratic participation in decision-making processes and the electoral accountability of the resolutions of global governance is "neither practically possible nor normatively desirable" (2010, p. 17). Thus, legal globalization and the interaction between States in the "post-national" space would not be necessarily organized under the ideas of self-government and the ultimate legal authority focused on the form of a written constitution in the service of the "We the people," but in a more ambiguous coordination between plural legal systems, parallel to the considerations on the democratic legitimacy of the domestic orders. The post-national proposal would also reject any idea of a supreme norm to which the whole system might be subordinated. Lacking a global demos able to ground the democratic legitimacy of a supreme norm, the very notion of normative supremacy (crucial to constitutionalism) might be expelled both from the descriptive and the normative analysis of regulatory responses in an interdependent world.

A similar debate has played a central role within the framework of the European Union integration process since, in said scenario, there was perceived a need to build a concept of legal authority beyond the idea of the ultimate authority placed in a demos. Discussions on these issues have been reactivated during recent years, marked by economic crises in which decisions adopted at the European level regarding the returning of debts, the budget balance mandate, or the undermining of the welfare States that compose the Union needed to find some legitimacy beyond democracy. To some extent, nonetheless, the ideas around cosmopolitan constitutionalism and its conclusions, including the ideas provided by the European Union experience, substantially coincide with the approach here developed on the domestic level: by remarking the real lack of popular involvement in the founding. To put it in another way, cosmopolitan constitutionalism and "State constitutionalism" present some analogies regarding the real participation of the people during the foundation of their respective orders. This is also suggested by Mattias Kumm (2008, p. 319) when he observes that:

> When questioning international law it is important not to ignore these features of domestic practice, idealizing constitutional conventions notwithstanding.

> There is a widespread tendency, directly attributable to the prejudices associated with the statist tradition, to adopt idealizing prose when thinking about domestic constitutional practice while insisting on a hard-nosed realist vocabulary when describing the world of international affairs.

According to my vision, in short, translating the discussion on constituent power to the international arena does not erase the problems that democratic theories have both in describing the constituent moment at the domestic level and in conceiving normative theories about it. In fact, international discourse only makes the narratives on popular participation and mobilization in creating State constitutions more unsustainable. The latter, in addition, would be in our opinion, marked by two objections, the first from a normative perspective and the second formulated from a descriptive one:

Firstly, any attempt to reduce the idea of constituent power in the global order, by minimizing popular involvement in the global sphere might be considered a back-door way to justify the current state of things in the international order: that is, a global sphere in which authoritarian States are *in the same position* as liberal democracies, both to create a global legal order and to claim the highest authority for such international rules. Absence of a democratic origin of the public power is precisely the point that enables an author like Dieter Grimm to state that the essential conditions to reconstruct the idea of constitutionalism beyond the nation-State are still not given (2010, p. 22) and, related to this, one might recall that the democratic principle does not belong to the set of principles concerning general international public law. Notice that in the international scenario we find at the end of the day *the proximity between constitutional democracies and authoritarian States* that we already remarked that was appreciated during the founding of both domestic systems.

Secondly, the basic point of our observations regarding the violent origins of State constitutions might be also translated to the configuration of the "international community" and its global rules. So understood, even admitting as Kumm (2016b, p. 699) struggles to show, that the legitimacy of the State in a world of sovereign States depends on its integration into an appropriately structured international legal system and such an international legal system might be considered a "global *pouvoir constituant*" the origins of the present order would be rooted in the most recent global shock: the Second World War. So, in the cosmopolitan constitutional order (both the global, with organizations such as United Nations, and the regional, with examples such as the European Union) the basic premise according to which "constituent power is violence" would be valid as well, or, at least, as valid as it is for State constitutional democracies. When, for example, Bardo Fassbender (2008, pp. 286–291) attempts to portray the United Nations (UN) Charter as a constitution, and "the peoples" of the world as the constituent power behind it, he could not escape from the fact that the creation of the Charter in San Francisco took place in the last throes of the Second World War and was led and conceived by the sovereign States that won the war. Such evidence showing to what extent the legal framework of the

UN Charter depends on the victorious forces in the last global confrontation is provided by the veto bestowed to the Second World War Western Allied Powers, the former Soviet Union (now Russia), and (later) the People's Republic of China as permanent members of the Security Council both in admitting new members of the organization (Article 5.2 of the UN Charter regarding the system of voting in the Security Council provided by Article 27.3 of the UN Charter) and in amending the Charter (Articles 109.1 and 109.2 of the UN Charter).

Provisional conclusions

I have revisited the different proposals conceived to provide both a descriptive and a normative theory on the constituent power from the perspective of democratic theory. My criticism of such approaches, from the deliberative vision of the constitution-making processes to cosmopolitan constitutionalism going through the "back-to-the-future" reconstructive struggles, is centred on the minimization of the role of violence that all of them express.

As has already been outlined, high-scale conflicts are in my opinion crucial to understanding the movement of erecting a constitutional framework even if we depart from some ontologies provided by the theories analyzed, as happened in the case of the reconstructive operations to endorse the ex post facto creation of the constituent agent. I will further expose how far the presence of violence to explain the creation of a constitutional order depends on the concept of constitution itself. But first it is time to describe the different phases in which violence irrupts in a relevant form for constitutional developments and in what way it defines the elements involved in constituent decisions.

Violence and the different phases of constitutional formation

One thing is the creation of the State and another thing is the drafting of a constitution (Schmitt, 1993, pp. 61–62; Wood, p. 286) but both processes are intertwined and so it is in both that violence is revealed. Even if no physical coercions constrain the concrete process of drafting and passing a constitution (which may be arguable regarding many constituent processes) all sorts of abuses have been committed in the formation of the political community through the consolidation of the State.

The constitution, including modern constitutions shaped under the patterns of liberalism, are the reflection of the violence perpetrated during the State-building. The distance between the State-building (and the conflicts arisen with it) and the exercise of the constituent power may be temporarily short, as happens, for instance, between secessions derived from an independence war and the drafting of the new independent State's constitution (Chryssogonos, 2008, p. 1300) or may occupy a longer period, such as the time elapsed between the formation of Europe's modern States and the advent of constitutionalism. But violence, and particularly war among different human groups, is in the beginning of all such processes. As the sociologist Charles Tilly summarized reviewing the rise of the modern European State: "War made the State, and the State made war" (1975, p. 42; see also Gat, 2008, p. 358). Each State's emergence as a defined territory, with a subject people and a ruling authority was a result of multifarious ominous events such as conquests, rebellions, secessions, murders of heirs, surrenders of rights to commercial exploitation (see Oakeshott, 1975, pp. 185–186 and Loughlin, 2010, p. 238) or, in the less convulsive fashion, as a consequence of intermarriage between ruling families (a phenomenon that did not exclude confrontations and bloodbaths throughout the history of the union of kingdoms).

Before the constitutional State could attribute its constitutional regulation to the People such People had to be created with the destruction, assimilation, and subjugation of other peoples and defended from exterior enemies. Constitutional regulation is not only a representation of the network of forces derived from such conflicts and the confirmation of a particular group's hegemony upon others but develops also a narrative of legitimacy through abstract principles (popular sovereignty, rule of law, human rights) devoted to cover the blood stains of the past.

Constitutionalism, from the eighteenth century, provided such a legitimacy that sought to cement the cohesion of political communities beyond the bayonets. But ideas related to constitutionalism presupposed the concentration of power represented by the violence that embedded the creation of the modern State in Europe during the sixteenth, the seventeenth, and the eighteenth centuries. As well as some classic approaches such as Tocqueville's in *The Old Régime and the Revolution*, in which the need of a previous concentration of despotic power in order to make possible the emergence of the liberal State was already noticed, some modern scholars, as Istvan Hont (1994) and David Bates (2007) have established precise connections between the warfare dominating the European landscape of that time and the ideas about constitutional limitations developed in the Enlightenment.

Certainly, if there was a concern about the division of power and the protection of individual rights at the end of the eighteenth century, it was because strong and centralized forms of political administration and organization had been built through the practice of war both at the domestic level and at the level of the confrontation with other States (Tilly, 1975, p. 15). The previous stage of constitutionalism and the sovereignty of the nation, that of so-called "absolutism," provided the build-up of a standardized machinery of government administering the "fiscal-military State" able both to eliminate internal diversity and compete with other powers engaged in the same process of centralization and domination (Hont, 1994, p. 181).

Constitutionalism was possible once political unity and the supreme authority within each independent State had been established. Thus, the limitation of power was conceived after the hurricane of the supreme and absolute power to which the concept of sovereignty was associated. Constitutionalism was a theory about the importance of controlling, limiting, and restraining the power of the

State in a substantive way (McIlwain, 2007, p. 21) but before limiting the power, such power *had to exist*. Consequently, whereas constitutionalism contributes to ordering political life once its legal frame has been decided, it does not take into account the unrestrained violence that accompanied the formation of the State itself. Moreover, the limitation of government provided by the rules of the constitution was only possible after the arbitrariness and killings that occurred before the establishment of such government.

But violence may be present also in the process of drafting, passing, and ratifying a Constitution. Beyond the violence exercised during the creation of the political community that would have a decisive influence in the legal translation represented by a constitution, such an instrument may be associated directly with a previous (and violent) revolutionary event and a violent atmosphere may surround the process of discussion and adoption of the new constitutional framework.

Finally, violence may occur while enforcing the constitutional regime. As we shall see, although the use of physical force is displayed through the application of the criminal code in the ordinary developments of the constitutional State, our approach shall be limited to the enforcement of the constitutional rules that arise in moments of emergency which might be read as a resurrection of the original violence that underlies the system.

Violence and the formation of the political community

The emergence of the State throughout human history has always been accompanied by the organization of armed forces. No effective State power has been able to maintain control, defend its territory against outsiders, or safeguard against usurpation without a substantial underpinning of physical coercion. That happened in the different waves of State-creation, whether in the transition from tribal societies to empires in antiquity, or from feudalism to national States in Europe's Modern Age. Azar Gat, one of the most valued theorists on the history of warfare, gives an excellent account about how such processes, that led to the State, were put in motion (2008, p. 235):

> This process involved accumulation and concentration of power to the point where it could be institutionalized and upgraded to a new level. This seems to have been mostly achieved by individual leaders and their followers who succeeded in gaining ascendancy over their contenders within the elite, but sometimes in a more collective elite form. Wherever such foci of state power emerged, an upward leap in the effectiveness of power was gained, feeding on itself in a positive loop mechanism. Private retinues were turned into state household troops and the nucleus of a standing army. Freely assembled tribal and local militias became subject to compulsory levy and call-ups. Military leadership could enforce discipline on the armed hosts. "Gifts" and services to chiefs and "big men" were being turned into regular taxes and corvée labour. In turn, conquered land and increasing spoils of war gained by all

> these means mainly flowed into the hands of the rulers, further enhancing their power. In this way, independent foci of power within segmentary society could be driven to subordination, disparate tribal units within the same *ethnos* could be welded together and amalgamated, an outside tribes and *ethnies* could be assimilated. A process of "state building" took place.

As Carl Schmitt noticed (1974, pp. 112–119), from the repeated upheavals and carnages that devastated a constellation of territories in Europe during the Modern Age emerged the institution of an inter-State legal order grounded in political units which had the ability to restore order and security within their own borders, maintaining order within Europe as a whole, since they recognized each other as legitimate counterparts. Political unity around the State was possible, in short, after bloody conflicts among the internal powers as well as conflicts between entities which recognized each other as sovereigns. Constitutionalism understood as the regulation of the State, gave legal account to an entity forged within a context of unchained violence and also aimed to organize the system of coercions that would reappear in the case of existential threats against such political unity. The latter explains, for instance, why an ideology of limits, as constitutionalism is, let itself decline in cases where political unity was at stake, blurring such limits to the extent of admitting the suspension of individual rights or subjection to military authority in order to deal with the threat of internal sedition or external aggression. To put it in ontological terms, without existence (the sovereign State) there could not be essence (a State regulated by a Constitution under the form of a liberal democracy) and when the existence is besieged, constitutional law itself may also be suspended.

Under my perception of constitutionalism, as I will emphasize, constitutional limitations are not only *not* applicable to the violence involved during the building of the State and the consolidation of the political unity but are the legal certification of the structure of domination that emerged in the midst of that foundational violence.

During the creation of the political community, warfare was given within the political space that was being consolidated [war among "internal" enemies][7] and between unities already formed (war among "external" enemies) and within the second group of conflicts, disputes arose between authoritarian States, between authoritarian States and incipient democracies, and, in a contrary way to the extended perception, *between democracies as well.* Despite the statement, that had gained some fortune among social scientists according to which "there have not been wars among constitutional democracies" (Babst, 1972; Doyle, 1983; Weart, 1998), such views have deserved a great deal of modulations and criticisms (see, for instance, Gat, 2008, p. 574). First, it has been observed that the absence of violence is at least equally related to modernization and to economic affluence than to democracy [in fact, some conflicts between poor democracies might be appreciated (see Mousseau, 2000)]. Second, we should detail what we understand as a democracy: if we take a broad sense of that in a particular time of the history, perhaps it should be suggested that supposed differences between liberal democracies and what are sometimes considered authoritarian States were not really very relevant. For instance, it is true that in the Germany of the Second Reich the executive was not elected by the citizens nor needed the trust of an elected parliament to rule [as happened in the Third French Republic or in the United Kingdom (see Babst, 1972, pp. 55 and 57)] but in the legislatives of the three States, Germany, France, and the United Kingdom (or at least one chamber of them) all adult males were entitled to vote. Such democratic affinities between France, Great Britain, and Imperial Germany at the beginning of the twentieth century did not restrain them, nevertheless, to get into the destructive fight of the First World War[8]. The First World War, in turn, had its reverberations in subsequent prolonged conflicts contributing to the emergence of new States, in Eastern Europe or as in the case of Ireland.

The Irish case precisely allows us to centre the question on the relationship between violence and democracy. Even assuming that within liberal and democratic contexts violent conflicts tend to diminish, violence has been, up to a certain point, involved in *the creation of a new State*, including the formation of new sovereign and liberal democratic entities from what, at the time of such independences, were considered democratic central States as well. In other words, even concluding that within and between consolidated democracies violent conflicts might be rare, high-intensity conflict generally appears *during the foundation* of such new liberal democracies. War and the foundations would, in this sense, again be closely linked.

Although democracy might decrease the likelihood of war, the *initial* process of democratization, the democratic *transition*, had the opposite effect (see Mansfield and Snyder, 1995; Snyder, 2000; Mann, 2001). Violent conflicts might involve the creation of a democracy in the face of opposition from an authoritarian central State (as it may be argued happened in the Soviet Union disintegration process) but also in the face of opposition from democracies (as the Irish example confirms). And, furthermore, once new democracies are created, as happened within the framework of the fall of communism in Eastern Europe during the last decade of the twentieth century (the former Yugoslavia and the former Soviet Union can be held as examples) the violence bursting out between the new republics transforms a civil conflict into an international conflict in which two or more new democracies are fighting. What is a civil conflict or an international one depends on the ability of the rebels to succeed in controlling a given territory through violent means in the first stages of the war.

From the State's internal perspective, the split of Yugoslavia showed, for instance, that it was precisely democratization that boosted violence. It was not the removal of an authoritarian State that required a convulsion, as had happened in many transitions since the 1789 French Revolution, but the calling for free elections that strengthened the nationalist movements and the claim for statehood in places such as Slovenia, Croatia, Bosnia-Herzegovina, and Macedonia, not to mention States such as Slovenia and Croatia, which in spite of their turbulent origins in the 1990s, are currently members of the European Union, a homologated club of liberal democracies that required conditions on the respect of the rule of law, human rights, and political participation for the candidates for EU adhesion *in the ordinary function* of their constitutional framework. No European Union authority questioned their access to the organization by asking them which was the context of their independence and their constitutional drafting.

The example of the former Yugoslavia also underlines the likelihood of war that accompanies the formation of a new State due to the actions of a secession movement, whether the independence is declared challenging an authoritarian State, or challenging also a democracy. In fact, the American War of Independence against eighteenth-century liberal Britain might be considered a violent conflict among the most advanced constitutional systems of that time. The American constitution-making process, at least in the first phase, may be considered a case of secession (Buchanan, 1991) in confrontation with an incipient liberal State. On the other hand, a constitutional democracy might appear or be consolidated precisely by frustrating a secessionist movement (a case that counts as a "civil war") even though political communities at conflict with each other within the State's borders may enjoy some degree of liberal democratic standards. The American Civil War is, in fact, an example of the latter.

The conclusions of the new trends in the anthropology of war coincide, thus, with the intuitions expressed in the first lines of this book: liberal democracies cannot escape from the killing and the destruction in their foundations. Even empirically accepting that human violence has in the last decades globally decreased (both in liberal democracies and in authoritarian States) it is still particularly rare to find a State beginning and a regime transformation, including those leading to the consolidation of a liberal democratic space, completely absent of violence. And, if the rate of deaths caused by human violence in liberal democratic spaces such as those in Europe are extremely low [between 2004 and 2011 the average in Europe was one murder a year per 100,000 people (Harari, 2014, p. 412) still much lower in the case of deaths caused by political motivations], one may cite the hypothesis according to which such almost negligible impact of political deaths within Western liberal democracies are also explained *by the absence of deep political reconfigurations during the last decades.*

In summary, even if we surmount the problem of violence within existing liberal democracies, it does not follow that such a problem might not persist in the human experience *during the creation* of new political entities, including in constitutional democracies. What will be our threshold to determine that in the aforementioned processes of founding a constitutional democracy someone has suffered the experience of an infringement in his or her personal integrity as a consequence of a political decision? Just one mortal victim, just one sacrificed life, will be enough in order to state that in such constitution-making, violence has been involved. Popular involvement is a central value in assessing the legitimacy of a constitutional democracy, but human life is the absolute moral value in civilization to which constitutional democracy gives coverage.

Violence during the constitution-making

Although the basic question of our approach might cause us to follow the traces of the violence in the foundation of the political community, it is possible to distinguish the particular violence that involves the constitution-making in constitutional democracies as well. In fact, as I have suggested, distinguishing between violence during State-building and violence during constitutional drafting has some analogy with the difference appreciated by the theorists of the social contract between the contract concluded by individual persons which supposedly gives birth to society and that concluded by the people and its ruler which establishes government (see Arendt, 1963, p. 169). I, however, am focused more on the particular set of coercions involved in both stages, while social contract thinkers are centred on the theoretical description of the different situations.

In the stage of the constitution-making process, we may have attacks by outsiders to the constitutional process, as well as violence instigated by groups who are insiders of the drafting process. We might highlight also the examples of a constitution imposed by an alien power (as in Germany or Japan) or the threat of a violent reaction by factual powers in case of not adopting a particular constitutional solution (as has happened in those systems whose constitutional order was designed after a transition from a military dictatorship).

In any event, the distinction between the violence displayed during the State-building and the violence detected during the constitution-making might be minimal. In spite of the fact that no blast of violence can be clearly appreciated during the constitution-drafting, violence might also be present in the constituent moment as the continuity of the State-building violence. In other words, original State-building violence *persists* during the constitution-making since the constitution may be precisely deemed as the *legalization of the violence displayed during the creation of the State.* Constitutionalism is somehow the way to translate into legal language the factual (and brutal) circumstances arisen in a previous moment.

On the other hand, different phases are also distinguished within the constitution-making drama. Thus, it has been remarked that the general idea of a constitutional process includes at least a drafting, a consultation, a deliberation, an adoption, and a ratification (Ginsburg et al., 2008, pp. 363–364; Widner, 2008, p. 1522). Such categories are invoked under democratic theory in order to assess to what extent the normative conditions regarding popular participation are in every moment fulfilled. Under my perspective, however, the distinguishing of the aforementioned scenarios might be useful in order to detect the influence of any specific coercion regarding each episode. Detailing the instances of the constitution-making allows us to identify with precision the violent conditions that surround it throughout its development.

If violence is involved in the constitution-making process, that is because before establishing the new constitutional framework, a negative act of dismantling the previous legal regime has taken place. In this sense, some authors remark that the creation of a new order is preceded by a decision to abolish the existing order, "the negative moment of the constituent power" as Beaud characterizes it (Beaud, 1994, pp. 263–266). The decision to *undo* would, thus, belong also to the analysis of the constituent power. Constituent power would entail, according to such approaches, not only creation *but also destruction.*

The great constitutional tradition from the eighteenth century has indeed been inspired by constitutions established in total rupture with the former constitutional regime. Such a pattern might be appreciated in the case of the independence of the American States, and the making of the State constitutions after 1776, spreading their influence on State-building processes in other cases of liberation from colonial rule. But the decision to reject the preexisting order also arises in processes whereby the State is already built, as in the constitutional developments that accompanied the different French revolutionary waves in the eighteenth and nineteenth centuries or in any regime change from an authoritarian regime to a democratic one.

Such "de-constituent" decisions are crucial to define the agent engaged in the constituent operation. The latter is clearly perceived in State-building processes from national emancipation: the definition of the people, the community of individuals called to participate in the constituent process, might be formed in this moment. In situations of emancipation from colonial rule and in national self-determination processes, for instance, the national-based inclusion or exclusion may be established by significant violent disturbances (we might think, for instance, of tragedies such as the partition of India in 1947). Other more regulated processes of defining the constituent agent in existing States, such as the ones developed in France or in Italy after the Second World War, in creating the 1946 Constitution of the Fourth Republic in France, or the 1948 Italian Constitution, respectively, could not escape from the fact of emerging from big confrontations in which, beyond the global war, the citizenship of many States had been strongly divided (see Ackerman, 2019, pp. 116–156). In sum, founding moments occur at tumultuous times in a country's history, in an anti-colonial conflict, in a civil war, in a legitimation crisis, in a power struggle, or in a contest for consolidation (Albert and Gururswamy, 2019, p. 1).

But coercions, political murders, and all sorts of insurrections and hideous incidents might be given in the specific episodes of discussing, passing, and ratifying constitutions such as the French revolutionary constituent processes at the end of the eighteenth century well testify, with their constituent assemblies or Conventions permanently pressed by upheavals, terror, counterrevolutionary activities, and wars against foreign powers (Elster, 2012a, pp. 21–33). Without leaving France, even the current French Constitution was adopted in 1958 in the midst of the trauma caused by the Algerian Independence War and the threat of a military *putsch* supported by far-right elements inserted within the French army and the police (Ackerman, 2019, pp. 169–198).

Constitution-making processes dominated by appeals to popular mobilization (from the French Revolution to some constituent experiences in the Arab Spring, see Abat Ninet and Tushnet, 2015) have usually been associated with social catastrophes that run in parallel to the constitutional developments decided in a constituent assembly or in a broader public arena. But coercions, as we will see in the following chapter, might be mentioned even regarding processes considered more peaceful, such as the passing of the United States Federal Constitution: we may begin with what is known as the Shays' Rebellion in Massachusetts, that according to some historians made the American elites aware of the need for a strong central power, and fostered the Philadelphia Convention (Fritz, 2008, pp. 80–116; Johnson, 1997, p. 91; McDonald, 1968, pp. 103–107; Szatmary, 1980). Elster (2012a, p. 9) suggested that the memory of the Shays' Rebellion explained the desire of the American framers to have a more robust repressive machinery at their disposal and so was reflected in some of the 1787 Constitution clauses. We can then go on to cite the pressure exercised by George Washington and the new federal instances towards Rhode Island in order to force the authorities of this State to ratify the Federal Constitution in 1788 [threatening Rhode Island with both an internal secession and a trade embargo if the Constitution was not ratified (Beard, 1964, pp. 235–237].

Violence and the enforcing of the constitutional regime

And, thirdly and lastly, we have the violence displayed while enforcing the constitutional framework. We have, in this sense, the example of the different ways to impose the constitutional system on those who did not participate in the drafting, as happens in territorial annexations or forced integrations of peoples originally not recognized as members of the constitutional agreement, or as happens with the answer given to the challenges against a constitutional regulation which cannot be faced by ordinary means (including those challenges posed by a democratic vindication that can only be suppressed by force). Since the State regulated by a constitution is an entity that, in Max Weber's terms (1972, pp. 821–824) "successfully claims the monopoly of the legitimate use of physical force within a given territory" its mere existence is in fact established by its capacity of enforcing basic rules in ordinary times (physical coercion which, on the other hand, is still considered an attribute retained by States as sovereign entities and not transferred in its execution to supranational organizations). A constitutional regime relies per se on violence in repressing illegalities as, for instance, providing imprisonment for those common criminals who infringe the criminal law. But paradoxically, as Carl Schmitt (2004), Walter Benjamin (1986, 1989), and Giorgio Agamben (2003) noticed in their theories on sovereignty, something deeper concerning the essence of the constitutional order seems to be involved in repressing exceptional challenges to such regimes by exceptional means (that is, by the violence displayed beyond the scope of the constitutional provisions) the moment in which, to say it in Benjamin's words,

> the state, whether from impotence or because of the immanent connections within any legal system, can no longer guarantee through the legal system the empirical ends that it desires at any price to attain.
>
> (Benjamin, 1986, p. 287)

The violence displayed during the state of emergency, in which the sovereign is recognized, according to Carl Schmitt's famous statement, would be nothing more than the remembrance of the violence perpetrated in the original moment. By suspending the norm, the state of exception "reveals with absolute purity a specifically juridical formal element: the decision" (Schmitt, 2004, p. 13; see also Agamben, 2019, p. 458) which, as we shall see, might be interpreted as the movement to determine a particular allocation of power resulting from a conflict. If, according to Schmitt's vision, the constituent power never becomes exhausted and remains present alongside and above every constitution (see on this point, Roznai, 2017, p. 127; Scheuerman, 1997, p. 146), the crossroad that the state of emergency represents in terms of violence may be well considered as the *resurrection* of the original (and normatively unbound) power within the life of the constitutional order. Notice that differently from Schmitt, who still associates the constituent power with some democratic tenet such as the people's ability to override the legal order through the popular will (the resurrection of the constituent power would be in this vein close to the reappearance of the popular sovereignty) my theory focuses rather on the reemergence of the coercive means that had been expressed in the foundation of the legal system. The constitutional system would be, thus, reaffirmed if the State's violence is successful in repressing the existential challenge or would derive in another political regime if it fails to maintain the status quo (see Atria, 2020, p. 53). The latter might be expressed as a revolution that leads to another allocation of power and, thus, to another political system able to destroy the entire matrix of pre-existing institutions (as has been experienced in Europe from the French Revolution to the Russian Revolution) or as a constitutional transformation within apparently the same constitutional regime, which is how Bruce Ackerman (1998, pp. 11–13) understands the evolution of American Constitutional Law. Such American constituent episodes, nevertheless, even differentiated from European revolutionary counterparts by being developed within the same existing institutions, had not been deprived, in the same fashion as the European ones, of crimes, wars, or massive human rights violations.

The constitution as a legal translation of a structure of power

Constitutionalism has been traditionally focused on describing the role of constitutions as devices to limit power. But a constitution may be conceived as a mechanism to create and consolidate power (Wolin, 1989, pp. 3–4). My concept of constitution is fuelled by such an idea: a constitution would be, thus, *the legal translation of a decision on the allocation of power resulting from violence.* After the violent act carried out by one social group, this group would seek to consolidate its dominance through a constitution and legal supremacy. Fundamental laws would appear as the medium to entrench in the future the particular relations of power that have emerged through a harsh conflict by designing the rules that shall allow the working of politicians and officials, and particularly judges, to *normalize* the domination (see Gargarella, 2020, p. 68). The stability of the decision about the allocation of power entailed in a constitutional regulation means that such decisions are out of the reach of the majorities formed in ordinary elections in the day-to-day governance.

Several traditions of political and constitutional legal thought might be, of course, involved in depicting such a concept of constitution.

An initial reference would be represented by Carl Schmitt's offspring theory on constitution, which in my view is still valuable to explore the link between constitutionalism and violence. In defining a constitution as the fundamental decisions of the political community in an existential sense (Schmitt, 1993, pp. 3–11 and pp. 75–76; see also Kalyvas, 2008, pp. 129–138; Roznai, 2017; pp. 116–117; Schupmann, 2017, pp. 135–152), Schmitt would allude to the material conditions upon which the positive rules are supported. Which are the decisions reflected in the constitutional text? What would be the "being" of the political community that precedes the form of a legal document? Throughout his work, Schmitt suggests some answers to this question, all of them related to an actual or a potential violent conflict.

He stated, for instance, that politics are founded in the capacity of distinguishing friends from enemies (Schmitt, 2018). Far from being a mere fiction, the *pouvoir constituant* gained density and concretion when it was associated with the concept of the political that Schmitt held: the "foe" was defined in opposition to the People (to a unified and homogeneous *Volk*) in the capacity of the latter to dispatch a violent action against the challenges to its collective identity (see on this point, Dyzenhaus, 2019, pp. 497–499 and Scheuerman, 1997, p. 144).

The specificity regarding what an "existential decision" meant to Schmitt, and its immersion within violent contexts was also perceived when he referred to the scope of a constitutional amendment. Schmitt insisted on the point that even through a formal constitutional amendment procedure, the Weimar Constitution would not regulate the same constitutional order if it would establish a Bolshevik regime (Schmitt, 1993, p. 26). The abolition of a liberal democracy and its conversion into a communist system would represent a break up in the continuity of the constitutional identity no matter how it would be expressed in an amendment scrupulously following the established amendment rules. Such disruption, in another sense, would probably result from a social cataclysm disregarding the circumstance of whether the change had been reflected in a constitutional operation or not.

Yet, Schmitt's existential decisions from which a constitutional order is created *are decisions on power*, decisions that entitle some groups of the society to dominate the others, to dominate the "internal enemies," such as minority ethnic groups or social classes (whether it be capital owners submitting the dispossessed, in a liberal capitalist political order, or the workers and the farmers abolishing private property, as in a Bolshevik regime). Decisions that lead to a constitutional reconfiguration would, thus, represent the outcome of a bloody clash in which there were winners and losers, and the winners would use constitutionalism as a mechanism to perpetuate their privileged situation. For Schmitt, however, the change of decision has not necessarily to be coined in a formal constitutional change. In his later writings (1978), he insisted that constitutional transformations might be carried out in full accordance with the formal law. In modern times the coup d'état and the process for transforming material constitutions might be legalized (see on this point, Agamben, 2019, p. 463). Fundamental norms, at any rate, *would be the legal translation of the decision concerning which groups detain the power of a political entity in a stable manner.*[9]

After all, such a concept does not depart far beyond from the ideas on constitution already outlined in antiquity, such as the one described by Aristotle, who somehow conceded that a constitution was rather than a norm the description of the network of forces operating in a given society (Aristotle, 2005, pp. 19 and 68–71; on Aristotle's concept of constitution see also Schmitt, 1993, p. 4 and Wolin, 1996, p. 38) and, particularly, the expression of the values and interests of a ruling class defined by noble birth, wealth, military prowess, and certain forms of arcane knowledge. To be sure, focusing the concept of constitution on the constellation of forces called to dominate a human collective blurs the differences between liberal democratic constitutions and other ideas on constitution derived from authoritarian regimes which do not fulfil (or they do so only formally) the conditions proclaimed in Article 16 of the 1789 Declaration of the Rights of Man and of the Citizen, wherein it was stated that "any society in which the guarantee of rights is not secured, or the separation of powers not determined, has no constitution at all."

A constitution as a framework of power does not differ much from the vision expressed by Johan Christian Majer (1799, quoted by Preuss, 1995, p. 62) according to whom (alluding to the existing form of rules in the German monarchies and princedoms) the "constitution" was nothing else but the "status quo." Rather than being a progressive, transformative, and liberal concept, the idea of constitution would be embedded by conservative and authoritarian influences in the sense of maintaining the relations of domination grounded in an original carnage.

The concept of a constitution as the legal translation of the allocation of power given in a society and the links between constitutional transformations with a radical change in the allocation of power is not obviously far from the Marxist analysis. Marx distinguished between the ideas of constitutional revolution and social revolution, arguing that a constitutional revolution does not entail a fundamental alteration of property rights and political order as a social revolution does (Marx, 1975, p. 176). Hence, Marx developed the idea that a social revolution renders a constitutional revolution superfluous because the constitutional guarantees are merely an expression of circumstances in society which can and must be overcome by a social revolution (see on that point Preuss, 1995, p. 86). Leaving aside that Marx may qualify the American Revolution (and the movements that led to the United States Federal Constitution) as a constitutional revolution, while in my interpretation the events developed in America at the end of the eighteenth century may be as well related to a social revolution, Marx's terminology would maintain some analogies with my perception on constitutional transformations (a radical alteration of the political order involving a change in the allocation of power) and constitutional amendment (described by Marx as constitutional revolutions wherein no real reallocation of power would take place).

The other tradition of constitutional thinking that would be directly related to the concept of constitution that I depict here would appeal to the variant that we could call the "social democrat" version of the previous approach, which would have one of its most prominent figures in the sociological concept of constitution exposed by Ferdinand Lassalle in a famous conference entitled *Über Verfassungswesen* ("On Constitution's essence"). In Lassalle's approach a constitution is the combination of the real power factors existing in a society in a way according to which the constitutional provisions would be doomed to failure if they do not reflect the correlative of forces present within the social body (1993). Lassalle juxtaposed the formal to the "real" constitution with the intention of "unmasking" the role of the former as a legitimating cover for the undergirding relations of power and domination (see Goldoni, 2019, p. 73). He thought, in sum, that "constitutional questions are not primordially legal questions, but a matter of relations of force." The proposal of Lassalle had a strong influence in the left-oriented constitutionalism that aspired to a reform of the State through democratization. Such ideas evolved in the ***material concept of the constitution*** described by authors such as Hermann Heller (1983, p. 315) and Constantino Mortati (1998, pp. 115–200; on both Heller and Mortati's approaches to the material constitution see Colón-Ríos, 2020, pp. 209–223).

The analysis here developed is also swayed by the tradition of political realism (see Rossi and Sleat, 2014; Rossi, 2016; and Sanjaume-Calvet, 2019). From such a perspective of thought, the autonomy of the political would replace that of morality and, consequently, would take seriously the peculiarities of the historical and institutional context. Indeed, a political realist research agenda would not be focused on the construction of grand theories but, as we shall remark, this does not mean that from a realist point of view, it is not possible to propose a normative theory (Sanjaume-Calvet, 2019, p. 10). In fact, we shall conclude by using what we might call "a minimal notion of empirical legitimacy."

The statements here revealed on the concept of constitution would require further considerations at different levels of philosophical and historical thinking (more precisely, further considerations concerning a particular vision of a philosophy on history) that we may here only pinpoint. The primary digression might refer to an ontological theory on the relations between facts and norms (the facts and the nature of constitutional rules) regarding to which I might set out some perceptions:

I support an absolute factual concept of constitution. The latter was somehow the way opened by Carl Schmitt in distinguishing between the existential decision of creating a political unity (the absolute concept of constitution) and the particular legal regulation into which such a decision is translated (what in Schmitt's terms would be identified with the particular constitution of each State mostly expressed in written rules, what he called the relative concept of constitution). I would, nevertheless, go a step beyond Schmitt, in the factual characterization of the "existential decision" from which the constitutional order emanates.

The absolute concept of constitution would, thus, not be related, as Schmitt is likely to suggest, with a narrative concerning a "decision" adopted by a human group but rather with a fact. Legal language expressed in written constitutions is an abstract object created by human intersubjective discourse in a similar way to how Schmitt's ideas on "existential decisions" are created. But my proposal gets closer to the empirical conditions related to the creation of constitutional rules: violence may, in that sense, appear as a prominent candidate to play both an ontological role (since it is given in the physical reality) and an epistemological one (since it is able to be universally perceived and processed by human knowledge). In that case, violence would be analyzed as the empirical support that relies on the foundation of a constitutional order (including, as we have insisted, constitutional orders developed in the framework of States organized under liberal and democratic parameters). In such an absolute factual concept of constitution, understood in its most radical fashion, *violence* (the violence displayed in the creation of the political unity and during its transformations) *would be the constitutional rule.*

A wide array of analytical consequences (both ontological and epistemological) may be inferred from the statement "constitution is violence."

The first one would be that the apprehension of the nature of a constitutional order would require an approach prone to focus on the violent facts given within a historical context.

Secondly, it should be considered that "violence" is a general category and that, consequently, the analysis of the facts from which the constitutional order emerges would have to scan the whole gamut of coercions and forces experienced in the historical movements that led to the creation of a constitution.

And thirdly, that the analysis of violence is not completely deprived of intersubjective narratives (though those narratives are present to a much lesser degree in some discourses such as the ones related to public involvement). To begin, an interpretation expressed in narrative terms is needed to be built in order to demonstrate *causality* between violence and political motivation. The murders, for instance, that occur in the midst of a regime change, are the fact that has to be established in the first instance in order to ascertain the elements of what I call the "absolute factual concept of constitution." Human death caused by human action may be considered as the typical empirical fact, something able to be verified by human awareness and, thus, epistemologically valuable. Again, statements on public involvement while creating a constitutional regime are much more vaporous than determining how many deaths were perpetrated in the convulsions that led to the passing of a new constitutional frame. As we shall see, thus, the question would be to what extent the appreciation of one single death is enough to invalidate any assertion on public participation in constitution-making processes that supposedly establish a liberal democracy.

From a normative point of view, even in a scenario in which all the individuals had participated, deliberated, and consented in equal terms in all the provisions of a constitution, a single death resulting from a single act of violence would be able to stain all the constitutional developments.

It should be thought, thus, how real experiences might be assessed in which both the participation does not encompass all the individuals in the same terms and where there have been multiple crimes. If the influence of violence during constituent processes leads us into a cul-de-sac in normative matters, at least it may provide a more accurate descriptive frame on the constitution-making experiences in liberal democracies (and, by the same token, it may provide a more realistic perception of the liberal democracies themselves through the analysis of their origins).

If a constitution is a decision on the allocation of power resulting from violence caused by humans (which is able to be captured by human sensitiveness as well), it is time now to focus on outlining the features of that agent that lies behind the material force impinging on constitutional regulation.

Elite coercion as a prime mover of the constituent experience

Throughout this work so far, I have alluded many times to the concept of elite. I'm not the only one. Also, the authors demanding democratic procedures in creating and re-creating fundamental laws take account of the elites' predominance in constitution-making. This is described by Richard Kay (2011, p. 750) when he observes that:

> so many effective modern constitutions have been enacted as a result of a process of elite negotiation among important interests in a given society.

Certainly, politics is an elite-driven affair (Albertus and Menaldo, 2018, p. 28). However, while there is a long tradition that sees the creation of a constitution as a (particular kind) of elite pact (Mendez and Wheatley, 2013, p. 13), an opposite branch of legal and political thought (that would include authors from Carl Schmitt to Colón-Ríos) envisages scenarios in which political agents would not be able to constrain popular fundamental decisions. If the involvement of the elites has been a recurrent issue invoked by the critics of day-to-day democratic procedures, it is still more acute in dealing with the creation of a constitutional framework.

Even though at the normative level, public involvement during the constitution-making had to be more intense, what the historical descriptions show is its character as an apotheosis of imposition of power by the elite. Defenders of constitutions as the product of an elite agreement may be closer to real historical experiences. However, to be more precise, the constituent movement would be the confirmation of a particular elite domination upon other groups rather than an agreement among different elites. When the elites bargaining model in a federal context is mentioned (Riker, 1964), understood as the bargaining among territorial elites that agree to establish a federal centre of government (such as happened with the creation of the United States), what happens, rather than a negotiation among the different groups, is the discovering by such territorial leaders of the mutual belonging to the same social and economic stratum and, thus, their commitment to the same interests of domination.

As I pointed out, we may trace the act of creating a constitution *as the legal translation that certificates a power already gained by a particular elite.* From that observation I may elucidate my particular concept of elite following the path traced by authors such as Wright Mills (2000) and Mosca (1939): the elite is *a social group that has reached power through force.* Notice that I use a concept of elite attached to a theory of the constitution and, thus, such a concept may be considered a special category of the notion invoked by sociologists or political scientists in countless studies on the issue. Given a considerable consensus in the social sciences for defining elites *as persons with power to influence strategic decisions in a society on a regular basis* (see, for instance, Hoffmann-Lange, 1991, p. 81), my approach would be consequently centred in the idea of the elite involvement in the procedure to create a constitution. “Elites,” in my sense, would be therefore able to display their influence in decisively *adopting strategic decisions on creating the fundamental rules that would regulate the political community in the future.* My thesis would be that the privileged position held by the agents in the decision-making process that leads to the adoption of a constitution would be conferred by the violence that had marked the events that occurred before the adoption of the legal frame.[10] Under the perspective here described, constitutions might be regarded as a ceasefire agreement or a peace treaty between social forces struggling for power in which the triumphant forces lay out their principles of how society should be ordered (see also Preuss, 2006–2007, pp. 469–470). Developments during the creation of constitutional democracies would not, despite the historical distance, differ excessively from those dynamics concerning the elites and the appearance of the State or large empires from antiquity, that in the economic analysis have contributed to explain the entrenchment of inequality among individuals (Scheidel, 2017, pp. 53–61). Rulers achieved the political unification of a given territory and population through military success and allocated lands and wealth among their key associates as a reward. Once the system was consolidated, legal structures protected central authorities’ allies by ensuring their participation in the collection of the State revenue and, generally, by giving them freer rein in the pursuit of personal gain.

Such elites may exercise the power within a constitutional democracy as well once the constitution is established through democratic means. The elite may, certainly, be elected. But the point would precisely be that a liberal democratic constitution has been passed in order to ensure *that the elite which previously has gained the power through the force maintains its power through ordinary elections.* In other words, the constitution is the space conceived to confer democratic legitimacy to groups that have used violence to reach political hegemony. As I have remarked, the latter explains why the particular drafting of a constitution, as also Carl Schmitt thought, may perfectly be an act of ordinary politics because the existential decision on the allocation of power benefiting a social group has already been taken (that is precisely what defines the concept of constitution in my vision and, somehow in Schmitt's when referring to the idea of the absolute concept of constitution).

Constitutionalism, on the other hand, would be nothing more than the general trend analyzed by some schools of sociology, political science, and political philosophy according to which elites develop instruments to escape from popular control and to ensure the domination upon wide strata of the society (see, for instance, Miliband, 1983, p. 238). Constitutionalism would not express a concern for the common interest but the only concern by which elites' behaviour is guided: to preserve their privileged status for as long as possible (Hoffmann-Lange, 1991, p. 96). Generally, such perceptions are not far from the approaches developed by Critical Legal Studies in their struggle to show that legal and political institutions adopt rules which serve the dominant interests of groups in society (see Gordon and Nelson, 1988, p. 161).

Such trends match with the ideas more recently outlined by Michael Albertus and Victor Menaldo (2018, p. 13) when they describe the action of constitution-makers more focused on preserving the elites' self-interest rather than on the common welfare of future generations. Albertus and Menaldo's analysis is centred on describing to what extent the elites coming from an authoritarian regime use constitution-making processes developed during the transition to a democratic regime as mechanisms to protect their rights and vital interests in the new political framework (2018, p. 14). However, leaving aside the question on whether such "transitions" from dictatorships to liberal democratic regimes represent "constitutional transformations" or not, the point here is that both in the case of an authoritarian elite that seeks to maintain its privileges in a democratic regime, and in the case of a new elite that has emerged in the midst of a revolution, the particular social group that controls the constituent process won the conflict through violence.

Ackerman's recent contribution on the paths in which constitutionalism develops (Ackerman, 2019, pp. 3–7) also refers to the question of the elites in two of the three types of constitutional establishments that he distinguishes. According to him, constitutionalism would be the outcome of three kinds of experiences: the first one would be that of "revolutionary constitutionalism," in which revolutionary insurgents manage to finish with the constitutional order of the old regime and replace it with a new "constitutional beginning;" the second type, the so-called insider constitutionalism, would rely on an order built by pragmatic insiders who, in facing up to popular movements for change, reach an agreement with moderate outsiders in order to reinvigorate the establishment's claims to legitimate authority. And finally, the third scenario would be defined as an elite construction in which previously existing elites create a new formal constitution given the crises of the old order or a power vacuum. At any rate, in that third type, the general population stays passive on the sidelines of the constitutional arrangements.

Considering Ackerman's description, my claim would be that the analysis of the elites as a prime mover of constitutional creation would not be only centred on the "insider constitutionalism model" or in the "elite construction model" *but in the "revolutionary constitutionalism" as well.* In fact, revolutionary constitutionalism is the scenario in which the elite as a constituent agent is better appreciated, since the destruction of the previous order and the replacement with a new one can be described *as the destruction of an elite and its replacement by another* or, in my terminology, the obliteration by violent means of a given allocation of power by outsiders which establish a new allocation of power reflected in a new constitution.

As we shall see, the "constitutional transformation" would only take place in that type of revolutionary constitutionalism which would entail the replacement of the older elite with the new one. Once the power of the new elite has been consolidated through wars and all sorts of attacks derived from political coups, it would be involved in the task of making a constitution able to perpetuate them in power.

Under the interpretation that I suggest of a constitution as the legal translation of the violent taking of power exercised by the elites (and against Ackerman's opinion), the passing of the 13th and 14th Amendments to the U.S. Constitution, for instance, though some historical nuances shall be added to the following statements, would be a mere execution of a constitutional transformation previously adopted. The real constitutional move in that case was the consolidation of the elites in the North that led and won the war against the Southern elites. Such a thought might lead to another more turbulent sequence of statements: the war in which a social group has smashed other groups *is* the constitution.

The history of constitutionalism, as is the case with all political history, is one of different groups fighting to obtain power. Constitutional revolutions at the end of the eighteenth century, for instance, were not done with the intention of establishing human rights or the rule of law but to foster the substitution of one ruling class for another. Human rights, rule of law, and democracy emerged as *incidental outcomes* of what was a raw battle for power. The substance of those political processes was not to establish limits to State action, but to invest the elite with a monopoly on the legitimate use of force. In a similar way, social function comes under a democratic regime dominated by competing powers among the elites through the electoral process, as Schumpeter (2010, p. 250) brilliantly remarked. The fight for power among different classes and the appearance of tenets traditionally related to constitutionalism defined the English civil wars and revolutions of the seventeenth century, culminating with the Glorious Revolution in 1688 and the subsequent constitutional developments expressed in the 1689 *Bill of Rights*, or in the 1701 *Act of Settlement* (see on this point Hayek, 1999, p. 162). The establishment of these institutions was not based in any consensus nor in any approval by the general population (or at least by a part of it through its representatives) but, rather, was the result of intense conflict as different groups competed for power, contesting the authority of others by violent means and attempting to structure institutions in their own favour (see Acemoglu and Robinson, 2012, p. 102).

The same observations might be applied to the French Revolution in 1789 and the 1791 Constitution. The French Revolution, marked by violent events, was instigated by a class which already dominated some parts of the economy even though their achievements had been frustrated by the *ancient régime* (Preuss, 1995, p. 10). Their appearance as a political agent and their revolutionary struggle, at least until 1792, was mainly aimed at creating a constitutional framework (the 1791 French Constitution) that would certify their interests grounded in property rights, a free market economy, and political recognition through liberal rights. In other words, power had already been gained by the class represented in the Third Estate, including the assignment of property rights, which needed a violent revolution to be consolidated and a constituent process to be legalized. The French Constitution drafted in 1793 demonstrated the emergence of the popular masses through the rule of the Jacobins against both the bourgeois and the nobility [as well as the use of violence in the experience of the founding, see Duong, 2017)]. These regimes were not concerned per se with democratization or ensuring spaces of individual freedom: the constitutional documents derived from those events provided constitutional safeguards or devices of political participation *as long as they benefited the new rulers over the old, displaced cadres.* At any rate, as is well known, the emergency situation which the Jacobin rule had to face allowed Robespierre to suspend the popularly ratified Constitution of 1793 (Arato, 2020, p. 96) and thus liberated his government from the constitutional constraints that the Jacobins had themselves designed with some popular support.

Following Schumpeter's statements, through which he defined democracy as a competitive struggle among the elites to gain votes (2010, p. 241), I might readapt his vision to the foundations of the constitutional democracy themselves. Thus, under my analysis, the questions posed would be centred in determining *where* did such elites involved in the ordinary democratic process come from, and how much the formation of the procedural conditions of such democracy designed by constitutional rules was a matter of their action. The basic structure of the power system (such as for instance, the attribution of property rights under a liberal and free market constitutional State) was already determined *before* the decision on the constitutional rules and, in fact, defined the agents endowed with the capacity of participating in the constituent process and the main features of the constitutional regime alike.

The description of the concrete elite involved in each model in State-building and the drafting of the constitution would require an empirical, historical, and qualitative analysis beyond the scope of this book. My aim would be satisfied enough if I were able to offer some reasonable suggestions in order to boost further research that might define the specific groups that in each system have gained power through violence and have used constitutionalism to translate their supremacy into legal language. I have only explained the participation of the elites in the constitution-making in the cases of the United States and the Federal Republic of Germany, but even in such constitutionally solid traditional models a detailed genealogical reconstruction is, and will be, pending. Still, if it is difficult to link a concrete act of violence to a constitutional creation or to a constitutional transformation, a more ambitious quantitative analysis would be required to make statements about the authorship of such violence and to conclude that coercions have been instigated by single individuals *within the frame of a group.* In fact, establishing who are the elite, may be almost as vague as fixing what the people or the nation is. We may turn to sociological approaches and struggling to identify the origins of the people or the nation through social and ethnic cleavages that have been fighting each other until the point at which one of the groups have gained hegemony over others. But the definition of the elite would be, as well as the definition of the people, closer to a matter of narrative than to a question of "objective" reality. Saying that violence perpetrated by specific groups allowed them to occupy power may be more detailed than saying that a people has given itself a constitution, but it is also related to a representation in an intersubjective discourse. In my structure the deed of the political killing would be the closest to the "objective reality," then, in a superior level of abstraction, we would have the establishment of links between a previously defined elite and such political violence while we would find a higher level of an intersubjective story creation (and, thus, far from the empirical ground) the constitution-making through citizenry participation, deliberation, and consent.

To summarize my proposal, I am still far from providing the historical reconstruction that would enable me to determine of whom I speak when I use the term "elite" and the nexus of causality that would bring me from the social group to power through the use of violence and from such a movement to the drafting of a constitution. However, I find important the mere suggestion of these associations in order to explain the phenomenon of constituent power, opening a path through the confusing jungle in which facts and norms appear mixed.

Constitutional transformation vis-à-vis constitutional amendment

If a Constitution is defined by a basic decision on the allocation of power which is related to the domination exercised by an elite, real constitutional change necessarily concerns the above-mentioned decision. Two dimensions might be here distinguished: on the one hand, constitutional fates might move themselves on the "existential" track (in Schmitt's definition), the dimension of decisions of power, the outcome of which may be identified with total revision of the constituent pillars of a society, a politically radical change of regime which may be called a "constitutional transformation" (Ackerman, 1998), or a "constitutional revolution" (Ackerman, 2019; Jacobson, 2014; Tushnet, 2015b).

On the other hand, the movements may be developed on the track of a constitution understood, as Schmitt did, as a positivistic rule which would not entail a change in the allocation of power. The latter would be associated with the idea of a "constitutional amendment" usually expressed (though not always) through a constitutional change following the previous constitutional rules.

A similar distinction has been proposed by Richard Albert (2018; 2019, pp. 76–82) to which the terms "constitutional transformation/revolution" vis-à-vis "constitutional amendment" would basically suit, even in more precise terms. Albert talks about "constitutional dismemberment," emphasizing that under such a category would be included constitutional changes that are "self-conscious efforts to repudiate the essential characteristics of the constitution and to destroy its foundations" (2018, pp. 2–3) dismantling the basic structure of the constitution while fostering a new foundation grounded on principles contrary to the old constitution. Essentially, "constitutional dismemberments," in Albert's sense, would not be "constitutional amendments" at all, since under such a concept would be implicit the idea of perfecting the constitution. A constitutional amendment, thus, would be associated with the aim of making corrections "to better achieve the purpose of the existing constitution." From the distinguishing between the constitutional transformation/revolution track ("constitutional dismemberment" in Albert's terminology) and the "constitutional amendment" track, different combinations may be traced among the paramount of constitutional experiences.

As we have seen, Ackerman realized that formal constitutional changes in the American Federal Constitution as happened in the Civil War Amendments (apparently passed under the previous positivistic constitutional rules) may entail an upside-down constitutional change of regime (Ackerman, 1998; see also Marshall, 1987, p. 1340; Balkin and Levinson, 2001, p. 1097). In such cases, within the envelope of a "constitutional amendment" a "constitutional transformation/revolution" had taken place.

American experience, according to Ackerman, also shows episodes, such as the New Deal, or the Civil Rights revolution (Ackerman, 1998, 2014, 2019, pp. 395–397), in which existential decisions on the distribution of power appear without formal constitutional amendment.

Some American scholars, as we shall see, consider that the *Bill of Rights* included in the ten amendments to the Constitution ratified in 1791 would be a mere extension of the founding (see, for instance, Tushnet, 2009, p. 17) having thus an example within American experience of a formal constitutional amendment that follows the previous amendment procedures and does not affect the core of the existential decisions.

Not far from the account given by the introduction of the American *Bill of Rights* in 1791 may be mentioned the examples of a brand-new constitution which does not allude to an "existential" constitutional change at all. The latter may be considered to have happened with the total revision of Switzerland's Constitution in 1999–2000. In spite of the fact that the 1999 Swiss constitution-making process led to a new formal constitution, it did not represent a constitutional transformation/revolution, nor a product of the appearance of the constituent power, but a simple "constitutional amendment.". In fact, the Swiss constitutional change did not provide any major change aside from a mere revision of the editing and wording of the constitution and the giving of some new powers to the federation [while providing a new organ of the cantonal governments to participate in the decision-making process at the federal level (see Fleiner, 2013)]. The different allocation of power between the federation and the cantons provided by the new constitution should not be confused with the reallocation of powers in the existential sense which would signalize the emergence of a constitutional transformation/revolution. One thing is a mere administrative reconfiguration of tasks even provided by constitutional rules, and another thing is the outcome of a clash among different groups from which the constitutional provisions testify to the victory of one group over another.

Something similar to the observations offered on the 1999–2000 Swiss constitution might be stated on the revision of the Finnish constitution which entered into force on March 1, 2000. This constitution entailed some changes concerning the allocation of powers between the Parliament-Government axis and the President but was essentially an operation devoted to unifying the document in a modern and concise fashion (see Ojanen, 2013). Since no structural regime change derived from the 2000 Finnish total revision, we might consider such an experience as a pure constitutional amendment in spite of its apparently comprehensive character. Still, the decision on the body that, for instance, holds the main competencies on foreign policy (whether the Parliament or the Presidency) has no relationship with the basic decision on the allocation of power that defines a constitution in its existential sense.

The point we would like to stress here is that historical experience demonstrates that constitutional transformations (or constitutional dismemberments, according to Albert) *are always given in the midst of violent circumstances.* Authors such as Mark Tushnet have argued that it is possible to conceive "constitutional revolutions" through the forms of legality and without direct exercise of physical power. According to Tushnet, when an unamendable provision of a constitutional system (under my perspective: a decision on power adopted in the foundation of the constitutional system) is amended, such amendment:

> is the trace left by a *pro tanto* constitutional revolution, though one can be accomplished without the violence we often associate with events described as revolutions in politics.
>
> (Tushnet, 2015b, pp. 642–643)

Indeed, as Schmitt himself recognized (1978), it is possible to foster a constitutional transformation without a formal constitutional breach. However, it is likely to be difficult to elude the mediation of violence in some part of the process. From Tushnet's approach it is not clear if such a possibility of promoting a constitutional transformation without violence is grounded in some real-world experience or is a normative desideratum. Tushnet, on the other hand, does not provide any historical episode of involvement of the constituent power not accompanied by brute physical violence (on this point see Roznai, 2017, pp. 130–131).

In Ackerman's book on revolutionary constitutions (2019) among the historical experiences analyzed there, *none of them* is developed in peaceful circumstances. In all of them (a list which includes the experiences of India, South-Africa, France, Italy, Poland, Israel, Burma, Iran, and the United States) the constituent moment was preceded or accompanied by wars, big slaughters, confrontations, or, at least, serious troubles in which several people were killed. There would only be the arguable example of Poland (in the case of not assuming the martial law declared by the authoritarian communist government to crush the opposition between December 1981 and July 1983 an act of extreme violence) but Ackerman (2019, pp. 227–281) precisely took the Polish experience as an example of failure of revolutionary constitutionalism.

According to my perspective, in fact, and despite the circular appearance of the following statement, the violence occurring in a scenario of constitutional developments *is the factor that allows us to distinguish the constitutional transformation/revolution from the constitutional amendment*, that is the distinction between an existential constitutional change (a "self-conscious effort to repudiate the essential characteristics of the previous constitution") and a mere correction of the constitutional principles in force.

Put in more classical terms, violence is what really allows us to appreciate when the constituent power emerges which is not, as always has been noticed by the European scholarship (see, for instance, Carré de Malberg, 2004, pp. 496–497), a constitutional amendment under the rules established within the constituted power. In that sense, in the French tradition and in other legal cultures in continental Europe, for instance, the power of amending a constitution according to the constitutional rules is differentiated from other ordinary attributions of the legislative, the executive, or the judiciary by defining it as a "derived constituent power" *pouvoir constituant dérivé* or "instituted constituent power" *pouvoir constituant institué* (see Bonnard, 1942, p. 36; Colón-Ríos, 2020, pp. 8–17; Gözler, 1999, pp. 10–28; Klein, 1996, p. 5; Roznai, 2017, pp. 113–117). Following my account, notwithstanding, the scenario of constitutional transformation/revolution or "constitutional dismemberment" expresses totally different features from that of the *pouvoir constituant institué*. It is no wonder that we find the involvement of violence when a constitutional dismemberment takes place since it presupposes a radical reconfiguration of the distribution of power that is only likely to be displayed breaking up the previous constitutional order. The concept of constitution is thus related to the concept of constitutional change and the concept of constituent power, and in all of them violence inhabits.

Constitutional transformation and the rule of law

In line with the reasoning exposed above, the concept of constitutional transformation (or constitutional dismemberment) is hardly compatible with that of the "rule of law" (see Sánchez Agesta, 1959, p. 382).

If a constitutional transformation seeks a thoughtful reconfiguration of power, such a move is difficult to be developed within a frame of previously existing rules which had served the previous decision on the allocation of power.

Putting it differently, the new decision on power requires a breakup with the existing rules. As Ackerman also remarked (1998, p. 14): "by breaking the law we will find a higher law," a statement which also entails changes apparently respectful with the previous constitutional framework or even with the procedures established to pass constitutional amendments (as the example of the American Civil War amendments again confirms). The latter observations clash with some theoretical proposals such as the ones developed by Andrew Arato (2016, p. 11), Christopher Möllers (2007), Ulrich Preuss (1995), and William Partlett (2012) in arguing for the necessity to tame the disruption inherent to a constitutional creation boosted by popular participation in a revolutionary mode through some legal brakes provided by the previous constitutional framework or by interim constitutional rules. The idea of these authors, if I understand them correctly, would be, putting it simply, to submit a constitutional transformation also to the principle of the rule of law, but such a manner of self-restraint would represent the cancellation of the idea of a constitutional transformation as I have defined here and its replacement by a mere constitutional amendment. The figure would characterize episodes of transition in which, even in the instance of a formal change of regime, no significant reallocation of powers might be detected.

It is important to be aware of the circumstance that a constitution-making process, as I have already underscored, requires a moment of demolishing the principles of the previous regime, and it is in such a "destructive moment" (in such "destituent power" as Oklopcic calls it, 2018, p. 30 and Atria, 2020, p. 53) inherent to the fact of exercising the constituent power, whereby violence is likely both to spread and to mark the core conditions of the following "constructive moment" expressed by the drafting and the passing of a new constitutional structure.

The "no victims rule"

The absolute factual concept of constitution is a *descriptive* concept. It encompasses the historical intricacies across the founding of a constitutional order which enables us to explain, in the field of facts, the functioning of the system and its transformations. As I have pointed out, such an approach, that I have also called "genealogical," provides an empirically verifiable structure with which to analyze the constitutional phenomenon also regarding liberal democracies.

Violence in the origins of all kinds of political power was already described by Giorgio Agamben in introducing his ideas on the concept of sovereignty. Agamben argued that the sovereign power is a power of death expressed in the sovereign's capacity of disposing of *homo sacer*'s life. *Homo sacer*'s life, called by Agamben the "naked life" (in English sometimes translated as the "bare life") is the human life that can be killed without being a murder, since the deed happens while fundamental rules are suspended, because they are being created or transformed (on the concept see Brogan, 2011).

> the sovereign is the point of indifference between violence and law, the threshold at which violence becomes law and law becomes violence.
>
> (Agamben, 2005, p. 38)

In that sense, my approach regarding the absolute factual concept of constitution has been centred in translating Agamben's ideas on sovereignty and the *homo sacer*'s original death to the foundations of constitutional systems in liberal democracies.

Of course, my suggestions, from this descriptive point of view, might require additional empirical research to be applied to every particular constitutional experience. But, under the theoretical parameters that I have presented, the developments of the mentioned empirical research might be oriented by the following statement: search for the violence, or still more specifically, search for *the death*, and you will find the decision on the allocation of power and thus, the constitutional principles of that particular system (rightly according to my previous observations: search for the death and you will find the constitution).

Paradoxically, maybe resulting rather from an almost religious trust against resignation, from the (descriptive) absolute factual concept of constitution might arise an absolute normative principle notwithstanding the evidence that such a normative principle might be placed beyond the human political experience of creating constitutional orders. The absolute normative principle, that I call the "no victims rule," might state as follows:

> No human shall be killed for political reasons during the creation of a constitutional order, in none of its stages.

It would be necessary, thus, to observe only *one* death perpetrated in the origins to assess that a given constitutional system is more related to violence than to democracy (it may be objected, why should we focus on death and not on other forms of violence from which death does not result, but we find it more clear analytically to speak about deaths since they are empirically easier to verify and, either way they encompass most, if not all, the episodes of constitutional founding).

The no victims rule, similar to a Kantian categorical imperative, brings idealism to its peak (and thus, a lack of touch with reality) but at least entails analytical advantages in order to minimize the impact of evaluations focused on the democratic theory on the constituent power.

As I have suggested, determining the legitimacy and practice of constitutional founding through the participation, the deliberation, and the consent of the People (as the bulk of the constitutional legal theorists are devoted to do) seems historically chimerical and theoretically labyrinthine. Under which conditions, thus, may it be appreciated that participation, deliberation, and consent have been given? Which historical processes fulfilled such conditions? Are the current democratic developments within an established constitutional framework enough to confirm, for instance and beyond all the underlined aporias, the democratic character of the constituent power? Under my insight, instead, I require a simpler condition: no mortal victims, no sacrifice of a human life.

In fact, some theories on secession, which is a form of revolutionary act leading to a constitutional foundation (Bossacoma, 2020, p. XIV) have already explored a kind of minimal moral constraint even though they depart from a political realist theoretical background (see, for instance, Pavković's proposal of a "no irreparable harm principle" regarding any secessionist or anti-secessionist claim, Pavković, 2011, p. 451).

The topic should be rather focused on determining if there was any coercion, at least to the sacrifice of a single human life, in the creation of the political body and the configuration of its basic legal framework. Such remarks would be applicable to the construction of any normative theory devoted to the assessment of the legitimacy of future constituent processes, which instead of asking primarily about the value of citizen participation, or other values such as pluralism, inclusion, publicity, fairness, or compromise, should at least wonder if someone has died to make such a constitutional state of things possible. Under a normative perspective the no victims rule, nevertheless, would not be incompatible with assessing a constitution-making process through judgements grounded on political participation, mobilization, democracy, equality, and inclusiveness. In my account, the zero deaths mandate, while founding a constitutional order, would be enshrined *as a necessary condition* that would have to be fulfilled before examining the other parameters of evaluation.

But it is time now to be a little more precise in the historical exploration and, thus, I must turn my attention again to the experiences of the past, centring my concerns on the origins of the two most influential pillars of the current vision of constitutionalism: the United States Federal Constitution and the German Basic Law.

Notes

1 Already in Sieyès' time the authorship of the concept was discussed. While Sieyès himself claimed in 1795 to be the one who coined the term *pouvoir constituant* (in both his 1789 published pamphlets: *Qu'est-ce que le Tiers État?* and the *Préliminaire de la Constitution: reconnaissance et exposition raisonnée des droits de l'homme et du citoyen*), a famous passage of Lafayette's *Mémoires* (1838, volume IV, p. 36) pointed out that the American experience developed from 1776 (encompassing both the American States' Constitution drafts and the United States Federal Constitution) was evidence revealing that the idea of dividing the constituent power from the institutional framework organized by the Constitution was previous to any French contribution, including that of Sieyès. On the origins of the term *pouvoir constituant* see Klein, 1996, pp. 8–9; Laboulaye, 1993, p. 397; and Zweig, 1909, p. 1. At any rate, the term "constituent power" was not used in the American political and legal thought and even today, as Tushnet remarks (2015b, p. 644, note 24), such a term is rarely used in U.S. constitutional theory.

2 On Sieyès' previous precedents of an idea referring to a power able to create a constitutional settlement appreciated in Althusius, Bodin, Defoe, Hobbes, Lawson, Locke, or Cromwell's 1653 *Instrument of government* see Klein, 1996, p. 7; Loughlin, 2014, pp. 219–220; and Roznai, 2017, pp. 106–108. On the precedence provided by the secularization of the theological *potestas constituens* attributed to God see Schmitt, 1993, p. 77 alluding to the works of Althusius (1995, Chapter XVIII, pp. 88–102). On the analogies between the Sieyès' *pouvoir constituant* to *pouvoir constitués* relationship and Spinoza's metaphysical *natura naturans* towards *natura naturata* structure see also Schmitt, 1993, pp. 79–80. On the ideas of Lawson and Locke closer to the modern theory of constituent power see Colón-Ríos, 2014, pp. 307–308, who remarks that Lawson's and Locke's notion gave account for the historical moments of genuine rupture and transformation related to the right of people to resist an oppressive regime. On Lawson's contributions entailed in his 1657 *Politica Sacra et Civilis* see also Kalyvas, 2005, p. 223 and Roznai, 2017, p. 107. Pasquale Pasquino also remarks on the precedent of Fillipo Mazzei who spoke about the "*pouvoir constitutionnel*" commenting on the legal and political developments in the American States one year before Sieyès' contribution, Mazzei, *Recherques: Historiques et Politiques sur les Etats-Unis*, 1788, pp. 43–44, quoted by Pasquino, 2013, p. 1004, note 25. Holding that Rousseau already advanced a distinction between the constituent and the constituted powers even though he did not use that terminology see Colón-Ríos, 2016 and 2020, p. 56.

3 On Sieyès' *pouvoir constituent* not bound by any normative constraint see critically Arendt, 1963, p. 162; Arato, 1995–1996, p. 207; and Arato, 2000, pp. 250–252.

4 On such links between the theory of the constituent power and the theory of sovereignty in Carl Schmitt see Dyzenhaus, 2007, p. 130 and Kalyvas, 2005, p. 226.

5 "[W]ith the democratic doctrine of the constitutional power of the people (which was directed against the existing absolute monarchy), Sieyès connected the anti-democratic doctrine of the representation of the popular will through the constituent National Assembly" Schmitt, 1993, p. 80.

6 Constitutions promulgated with referendum are Burundi (2005 and 2018), Central African Republic (2004), Comoros (2001), Cuba (2019), Democratic Republic of Congo (2001), Cote d'Ivoire (2000), Bolivia (2009), Ecuador (2008), Egypt (2012 and 2014), Guinea (2010), Iraq (2005), Kenya (2010), Kyrgyzstan (2010), Madagascar (2010), Morocco (2011), Myanmar (2008), Niger (2010), Qatar (2003), Rwanda (2003), Senegal (2001), Serbia (2006), Syria (2012), Thailand (2007), and Zimbabwe (2013). The Constitutions promulgated without referendum are Afghanistan (2004), Angola (2010), Bahrain (2002), Bhutan (2008), Chad (2018), Dominican Republic (2015), East Timor (2002), Fiji (2013), Finland (2000), Kosovo (2008), Libya (2011), Maldives (2008), Montenegro (2007), Mozambique (2004), Nepal (2007 and 2015), Somalia (2012), Sudan (2005), South Sudan (2011), Swaziland (2005), Tunisia (2014), and Turkmenistan (2008).

7 Among the rich literature on the empirical sources of civil war provided from the fields of political and economic sciences may be highlighted the works of Boix, 2008; Fearon and Laitin 2003; Horowitz, 1985; and Kalyvas, 2006.

8 Azar Gat mentions other examples of wars among States that might be qualified as liberal democracies at least for the standards of the time in which the war was fought. So, the Boer republics fighting Britain in 1899–1902, the USA fighting Spain in 1898 and leading to Cuban and the Philippines independence, the conflict between "the arguably liberal Britain" and the "variably democratic and liberal" revolutionary France in 1793–1802. See Gat, 2008, p. 578

9 Political sciences have developed a rich literature, in contexts of transitions from authoritarian regimes to liberal democracies, which sees a constitution as, fundamentally, a decision on the allocation of power (see, for instance, Karl, 1990; Karl and Schmitter, 1991; or O'Donnell and Schmitter, 1986).

10 On predation as a source of political power and the consolidation of legal orders for the benefit of extractive elites see, generally, Scheidel, 2017, particularly pp. 48–53.

3 Violence and constituent power in the creation of the American Republic

The American experience and the theory of the constitution

Both the independence of the American States and the foundation of the United States provide an example that fits with the theory on violence and constituent power that I have presented in the previous pages. If that adjustment between theory and practice is perceived in one of the first experiences of modern constitutionalism (and to be sure one of the most prominent given the political dimension that the United States still play in the world of the twenty-first century), maybe that means that my approach concerning the origins of constitutional orders is not misguided and that something relevant in epistemological terms may be inferred from all the analysis.

The American constitutional struggles by the second half of the eighteenth century needed a war of secession to be consolidated and were followed by other convulsions in the process that went from the independence of the American States to the entering into force of the Federal Constitution. Still, as explained before in some abstract terms, but quite clearly reflected in the American foundational episode, the creation of the American Constitution was a decision on the allocation of power triggered by the elite in order to consolidate its hegemony. As the historian Robert Middlekauff highlighted (2007, p. 669), along with many other scholars before him, the centralization of power that the Federal Constitution entailed was a conservative response to a move towards democracy that the Revolution had stimulated. Said Revolution, nevertheless, had already been a matter of conflict between elites developed both by displacing the elite representing the British Crown during the war, and by entrenching the position of the European settlers' descendants towards the indigenous peoples (a fight that had taken place from the very beginning of the colonization of North America and that would continue westwards under the United States constitutional regime).

According to the parameters displayed in Chapter 2 of this book, the American experience would show the violence latent in the background of a constitutional system in two stages, corresponding first to the creation of the 13 States of the Confederation, and second to the violence experienced during the constitution-making. As we shall see, there would also be violence during the life of the

American constitutional order that shall be associated with the transformations of the system, as the American Civil War might well illustrate.

It is in that vein that the paradigm of the free consent of all participants in the basic decision-making of the American political structure cannot be appreciated *at any level* of the American constitutional development. Even Bruce Ackerman (1993, p. 315), the most prominent defendant of the legitimacy of the Constitution's supremacy on the grounds that democracy and popular mobilization were involved during the American constituent moment, admits that

> The Founders established an oligarchy. While they spoke for the People, they only tried to win the mobilized consent of white men.

The lack of democratic foundations of a constitutional artefact have not, nonetheless, discouraged Ackerman and those influenced by his teachings to present the historical events surrounding the U.S. constitutional creation as a political action marked by the mobilization of the citizenry, the deliberation among the different actors, and the majoritarian support expressed within the community on the fundamental decisions adopted. Ackerman's entire enterprise of extracting a general theory of higher lawmaking focuses, in sum, on analyzing the circumstances that allow it to be claimed that someone is speaking in the name of the People and, thus, to justify the break from the previous constitutional framework or to reshape the meaning of the constitutional identity.

Ackerman's writings on such moments of mobilized popular renewal and political consciousness in the history of American constitutional developments have, certainly, many advantages. One of them is helping to isolate the idea of constitutional commitments within their historical context and, thus, helping to simplify the analysis of the influence of violence in each episode. Maybe violence, political violence, is *continuous* throughout American history (as in all human histories), but the theory of moments in which higher laws have been created allows us to detect the time in which violence is a generalized social phenomenon and, even indirectly, a source of legitimacy for the constitutional framework that emerges from it. The division between the higher political moments (from which constitutional changes are inferred) and the ordinary political life would be the division between those moments in which political violence *is more perceptible* in epistemological terms, and those in which violence is more punctual or concealed.

I will take thus the American constitutional moments that Ackerman identifies as crucial to understand the evolution of that order, but I will instead associate them with my approach on the phenomenon of the constituent power in the following terms:

1. I will emphasize the appearance of violence in *all* episodes attached to what in Ackerman is described as a constitutional moment. At any rate, manifestations of violence will show their prevalence in historical terms (that

is, in *the objective causality*) upon the democratic factors in the configuration of the final constitutional product.

2. I will describe the struggles that lead towards the approval of a constitutional framework as the triumph of one human group upon the others and, consequently, I will identify the material sense of the constitutional document by focusing on the decision on the allocation of power that the assault of power by the victorious group has represented.
3. I will tackle the progress associated with constitutionalism that is usually derived from a liberal revolution such as the one that took place in the America of the eighteenth century (namely, rule of law, fundamental rights, or democracy) as *incidental* outcomes on the path of the elite to entrench its hegemony. In short, the recognition of such principles or spheres of liberty relied, according to my vision, on the pure interest of the elites to perpetuate themselves in a leading position within the system.

My basic thesis, the "no victims rule," would state that any act of violence invalidates any democratic consideration about the production of higher lawmaking. And the American experience was, on the contrary, a chain of moments stained by blood. The blood not only cancels the debates around political mobilization but introduces another sinister perspective in analyzing American constitutional history (and somehow regarding any constitutional history): if there was a constitutional moment *precisely because there was blood.*

According to my idea, the "dramatic circumstances" and not the mobilization of the citizenry (or its participation through deliberative procedures), are the decisive factor in order to recognize the emergence of a constitutional transformation. In other words, the popular involvement, the mobilization of the masses, is rather expressed through wars and all sort of massacres later exploited by the elites for their own sake. Violence and the personal sacrifices derived from a brutal confrontation are the perfect narrative to consolidate the national sense of belonging and thus, the legitimacy of the rule that organizes said national community. The higher the sacrifice is in terms of deaths, the stronger the legitimacy of the resulting constitutional endeavour is.

American constitutional history is a vast field of knowledge composed of countless contributions. In contrast to what occurred in Germany regarding the foundation of the 1949 German Basic Law, in the American tradition the narratives on constitutional legitimacy rooted in historical episodes have been fully developed. As an outsider of American constitutional thought, the aim of the following writings does not consist in offering a theory on American constitutional law. Rather, I would limit my contribution in alluding to the different episodes defined by Ackerman and others as "constitutional moments" but only as long as they serve my theory on constitutionalism and violence. I would not get into the sophisticated theories on American constitutional interpretations that have been extracted from history. My analysis shall be encompassed by exploring such episodes only to confirm the importance of coercion both in the foundation and in the evolution of a constitutional system.

Precedents: the Mayflower Compact and the colonization

Since American history provides a myth regarding the foundation of a political community within a no man's land, philosophers and historians have identified some episodes of colonization as one of the rare real experiences of free consent among individuals on the creation of a political community and the adoption of society's basic rules. As is well known, one of the main figures responsible for tracing the line of legitimacy that reaches the U.S. Constitution from the time of the colonization and, specifically, from the episode of the Mayflower Compact was, in fact, the main theorist that gave account of the legitimacy of the American constitutional foundation given a supposed relatively non-violent character of the American Revolution: Hannah Arendt (1963, pp. 166–178).

Arendt, grounding herself on the narratives of the origins of American constitutionalism provided by some previous authors (see, for instance, Craven, 1956; McLaughlin, 1932), saw in the Mayflower Compact a social contract arising from a group almost thrown into a state of nature, a situation which somehow was reproduced during the colonization in some charters[1] and, after the independence, while framing the American States' constitutions.

Regardless of the historical evidence that the episode of the Mayflower Compact scarcely had any influence in the theoretical framework of the generation that carried out the revolution and triggered the constitution-making processes both in the States and in the Federation (Topf, 2019, p. 59 n.36), the point here is that the Mayflower Compact episode as described retrospectively by Arendt and the authors that inspired her from the interwar time is, considering the historical context that surrounded the arrival of the ship near Cape Cod (Johnson, 1997, pp. 28–31), far from encapsulating an example of forming a political order through the action of free people.

To begin, we must not lose sight of the fact that the ideas concerning the foundation of the political community by a compact to which all the individuals give their consent flourished from *a religious* background (Lutz, 1988, pp. 24–27; Robertson, 2015, p. 19); the same religious vision that had forced the Mayflower passengers to flee from England in order to establish themselves in North America. So, the Mayflower travel itself was marked by the shadow of oppression, indeed being the outcome of previous violence: that which King James of England and Scotland and his officials exercised pursuing members of the Protestant dissidence to the English Church (Solt, 1990, 145–146). Despite this circumstance, the so-called Pilgrim Fathers concluded their agreement declaring themselves "loyal subjects of our dread Sovereign Lord King James," that is, without breaking whatsoever with the political regime under which their adventure was being developed. It was not an entire "new beginning" out of the pre-existent political sphere. Considering that the Pilgrims and those Europeans that landed in North America by the first half of the seventeenth century saw themselves as fabricants of new governments, as Arendt pretends, is inaccurate. Both the Mayflower Compact and the subsequent colonial charters that provided for structures of government emphatically asserted royal authority for doing so (Topf, 2019, pp. 62–63).

Yet, from the perspective of the epistemological analysis, it is no wonder that Arendt relied on a religious conception provided by the Pilgrims and the Puritans, in which collective oaths played a central role, to justify the main tenets of her theory on the sources of power. As had been underscored by some of Arendt's commentators (Miller, 1979; Sternberger, 1977, p. 145; Topf, 2019, p. 60), her insistence on focusing on the agreements among men as the pillar of political authority by denying the historical contingencies of the creation of a political order is only understandable under religious assumptions. To explain that men came together to found an enduring, stable, and legitimate political order, and that the progress shown by the American republic in contrast with other experiences, such as the French or the Russian ones, is precisely due to the terms of its creation through such free consented covenants is not scientifically sustainable under any historical methodology. To use James Miller's terms, Arendt's descriptions applied to the American developments from the Mayflower Compact are "magical" (1979, p. 181 and p. 183).

Digging up some more historical details on the Mayflower's vicissitudes, it is not difficult to realize that anything agreed there was not a product of the inclusive participation of all the members concerned. Not all the people placed in the ship had been involved in the conclusion of the compact. The agreement only involved the males that belonged to the religious group of the Congregationalists, the only ones that were allowed to participate in the establishment of the political body. The compact was concluded with the exclusion of the women and the other passengers of the ship, such as adventurers, tradesmen, and servants, referred to by the Pilgrims as "the Strangers." The foundation of the new order began, thus, *with the segregation* on both gender and religious grounds. Majority decision-making was a rule not extended to the whole of the human group that took part in the expedition, but only to the group defined by a part. The creative act was, from the outset, an act defined by its ability to exclude.

Colonization was not an occupation of a *terra nullius* either. The agreements among the settlers, the Mayflower Compact and those adopted some years after providing the regulations of the settlements, as the Fundamental Orders of Connecticut, had not taken place within a territory free from any other human presence. The political articulation during the colonization was seeded in a ground already politically organized by other human groups against whom the newcomers were preparing themselves to fight, to assimilate, and to destroy.[2] The settlers had to pave the way by killing and looting the indigenous peoples that they found when they arrived at the North American eastern coasts, before agreeing on the basic rules that would rule them. Still, the fundamental decisions on the colonies' governance were taken given the confrontation between the settlers and the indigenous local population in a way that the latter neither participated in the rules that would organize the colonies of the Europeans, nor would be members of the political community once the legal framework was established. The shaping of a legal framework for a colony was, indeed, the signal of its consolidation in spite of the indigenous pressure, if not the mark of the indigenous defeat. The North American germinal fundamental orders were, accordingly, also the consequence of existential conflicts for the control of land and resources and it was not rare to find in the beginnings of the odyssey of colonization, particularly when they were still unsafe in confrontation with the Indian polities, that the rules of organizing the colony *were directly dictated and imposed by the directors of the private companies* that have invested in the North America colonialist endeavour, as happened, for instance, with the colony of Jamestown established under the auspices of the Virginia Company by the beginning of the seventeenth century (see Acemoglu and Robinson, 2012, p. 25), a model which is the antonym of the consent among free men that Arendt had depicted.

Generally, thus, coercion accompanied all of the fundamental regulations that were adopted in North America from colonization to the entry into force of the Federal Constitution, including the decisive caesura represented in the American Revolution which was no more than a war of secession.

The "dramatic circumstances" and the origins of the U.S. constitutional order

The foundation of the American system relied decisively on a war of secession which displaced the rule of the loyalists by the local elites, who then gained a full scope of political decision. As we have suggested, however, violence had already been exercised before the 1770s by some groups which would accede to sovereignty with independence. In fact, the constitutional structure of the new republic, in the same way as described in our general theory on the constitution, would be used to entrench the dominance of the elites consolidated by the secession upon the groups that they had already subdued under British rule, essentially, upon the indigenous peoples, the slaves, and the popular strata of American society. The latter group, even though they had been fighting side by side with the elites in the war, were contained and marginalized by the big landowners and merchants with the creation of the Federation.

Slaves

The exclusion from the American demos of both the slaves and the Indian tribes was decisive in the construction of the U.S. constitutional framework (Zurn, 2010, p. 192). In the case of slavery, its maintenance during the foundation of the Republic was compelling to obtain the support of the Southern States whose rapid economic development relied on the labour force provided by the population recruited in Africa and transferred to America by coercive means.[3] After all, the successes of the Revolution and the establishment of the federal government were achieved due to the impressive economic development provided by the production of slave-grown crops of tobacco, rice, sugar, and cotton that slave owners sold on the international market (Berlin, 2004, p. 1257). Slave trade to the American colonies had thrived with the liberalization adopted by the British Crown in 1712 which may be estimated as one of the consequences of the liberal revolution that had taken place in England a couple of decades before

(Pettigrew, 2007, p. 4). It is somehow paradoxical that the beginning of liberalism in England was associated with the intensification of the traffic of human beings to the colonies. A similar pattern between a liberal revolution and increase of the slave trade would be observed with the American emancipation. By 1775 there were around 400,000 black people scattered in mainland colonies, approximately 17 per cent of the population (Middlekauff, 2007 p. 32). After independence, the number of slaves increased and their distribution spread (Johnson, 1997, p. 158). The number of slaves in Virginia, for instance, doubled between 1755 and the end of the conflict in 1782 (Morgan, 1975, p. 298).

Under such circumstances, the 1787 constitutional agreement was basically an agreement to tolerate slavery: the most important compromise in the original Federal Constitution, the fundamental decision on the allocation of power that encompasses the idea of constitution according to my approach, was that between the States committed to maintaining slavery and the States that had either abolished human bondage or were in the process of doing so (Graber, 2006, p. 93). Such a compromise had, essentially, its institutional translation in the veto power that was conferred to the Southern States through political representation in order to block any national measure deemed injurious to a Southern economy grounded on forced labour.

The 20-year exemption of the slave trade from federal control, as entailed in Article I, Section 2, Clause I of the original draft, for instance, may be read as an expression of the compromise reached between the Southern delegates and the Northern delegates at the Philadelphia Convention (Fehrenbacher, 2001, p. 37). That the mentioned temporary preservation of the slave trade was a determinant issue of the constitutional product is underscored by the fact that the clause stands as the first independent restraint on congressional powers, prior even to the restriction on the power to suspend the writ of habeas corpus (Spalding, 2014). The North–South agreement on preserving slavery embedded other clauses of the constitutional text: Northern States were placed under an obligation to return slaves who escaped to freedom back to their owners, and the apportionment of seats in the House of Representatives took slavery into account by giving slave States a bonus: each slave would be counted as three-fifths of a freeman in order to determine the number of representatives that each State, according to its population, would send to the Federal House (Ohline, 1971). The mechanism to elect the presidency had also been considered as part of the great compromise between Northern and Southern States with some ramification concerning the issue of slavery (Tushnet, 2009, p. 12): the president would be chosen through an "electoral college" whose members would be elected in the States (with each State getting a number of electors equal to the number of Representatives it had plus two) in a way that gave Southerners the confidence that they would retain a considerable influence on the presidency, enabling them to protect their interests in the preservation of the slave trade, against any congressional regulation. Until the middle of the nineteenth century, and with the exception of John Adams and his son John Quincy Adams, all the United States presidents had Southerner origins.

The revolution for national liberation and the constitutional Convention, in short, led to the creation of a slaveholding republic. Worries, such as that expressed by John Adams or Thomas Jefferson on pursuing the virtue and the equality that were supposed to cement the new republican government (see Wood, 1998, p. 123) did not encompass any concern towards those groups of the American population subordinated by the most hideous coercions. Even though Jefferson wrote that "all men are created equal" and tried to blame American slavery in the Declaration of Independence's original draft, such movements had not deprived him from being a slaveholder himself, as were the majority of the figures of the Founding, and some political leaders of the next generations [from George Washington, James Madison, James Monroe, and Andrew Jackson through to John Tyler, James Knox Polk, and Zachary Taylor (on the contradictions between the liberal ideals of the American founders and the institutionalization of slavery see Bailyn, 1992, pp. 232–246 and Berlin, 2004, p. 1257)]. Already a visionary, Madison understood that the compromises adopted in the constituent moment in relation to slavery were an evil that was necessary to prevent the "dismemberment of the Union" (Fehrenbacher, 2001, p. 37), dismemberment that would overshadow the United States 74 years later.

It was, certainly, when the founding equilibrium was broken by the different economic developments between the industrious and urbanized North and the rural South that the 1787 original compromise was at stake. This equilibrium was particularly threatened when, given the overwhelming economic development of the North, a demographic expansion was experienced both within the North itself and within the Northwest areas colonized by population from slavery free States (in a way that the majority of representatives and the presidency could be elected without the consent of the Southern citizenry). Northern States integrated by masses of waged free-labour workers (who were employed by capital owners paying salaries) would not tolerate the unfair competition through slavery developed by their Southern counterparts. As James McPherson pointed out (1988, p. 8) tensions between the North and the South escalated when the Federation expanded westwards and, specifically, when an enormous amount of surface was annexed from Mexico after the war against that country in 1846–1848. The question of slavery would become explosive given the territorial gains, since establishing if the new dominions would be free or subjected to human bondage would in effect mark the respective spheres of influence of both Northern States and Southern ones.

Slavery and the evolution of American constitutionalism provide, furthermore, an example that would explain the distinction that I have described in my theoretical elaborations between constitutional transformations vis-à-vis constitutional amendments. If the 1787 Federal Constitution, as I mentioned above, was built upon the consent of the participants in the Convention on exploiting other humans for the sake of the (Southern) elites, the Civil War would make the original agreement burst into pieces, preparing the ground for a new allocation of powers that in fact would not be consolidated until a century later through the Civil Rights Revolution (see Ackerman, 2014).

The 13th, 14th, and 15th Amendments would certify the Union victory over the Confederative States and would demolish the infrastructure of slavery in the original Constitution entailed in clauses such as the Three-Fifths Clause, the Fugitive Slave Clause, the Importation Clause, and the Proportionate Tax Clause (Albert, 2018, p. 4) but if the decision on the new allocation of power was not implemented shortly after the Civil War, that happened because the military triumph of the Northern elites did not crush completely the dominion of the Southern elites. The Southern planters had lost the war but would win the peace. Slavery would have been abolished and African Americans would have been entitled with the right to vote after 1865, but the economic system of the South based on plantation-type agriculture with cheap labour and the ownership of the land in few hands would persist (Acemoglu and Robinson, 2012, pp. 353–357).

Indigenous peoples

The westward expansion of the United States, that had poisoned the U.S. national politics by the middle of the nineteenth century with the disputes on human bondage, would show another history of violence, killings, and plundering in the contraction and defeat of the original American Peoples, a history that, as we have seen, had already begun during the colonial period and had had, by the founding of the American Republic, its peculiar constitutional translation.

Slavery and aggressions against the indigenous population were two sides of the same coin of oppression. Slaves worked on lands previously looted from the Native Americans. In the first phase the extermination of indigenous nations and the displacement of entire populations were executed under the auspice of British colonization. But the narrative of the independence of the American States added a supplementary degree of cynicism, since the supposed fight against the colonialism of the British Empire established a regime that embraced the settler colonialism on a bigger scale.

In fact, in the case of North America, one of the factors that led to the separatist movement was a pro-Indian policy displayed by the British authorities shortly after the expulsion of the French (Johnson, 1997, pp. 131–133) in the aftermath of the Seven Years War (1756–1763). In a royal proclamation of October 7, 1763 (known as the Great Proclamation) it was established that Americans would be forbidden to settle in the territories reserved to Indians "beyond the heads or sources of any of the rivers which fall into the Atlantic Ocean from the West to Northwest." Such a regulation created an Atlantic-fringe America, inwardly blocked by an Indian interior, and motivated a strong opposition among the colonies since it was seen as an obstacle to the expansion of the American settlers to the boundless lands of the interior. Some of the future leaders of the Revolution, including George Washington (to whom access to land on the frontier was a matter of the utmost importance) saw the Great Proclamation as the main challenge against their development perspectives and, thus, caused a turn in their loyalties. The Great Proclamation had been indeed a British initiative to finish with a war of extermination against the Indians caused by the American westward movement. The expansion of the colonists had been responded to by the Indians with the so-called Pontiac's Rebellion adopting the name of the leader of the Ottawa, Chief Pontiac, who tried unfruitfully to stop the white settlers' advance over their lands (Middlekauff, 2007, pp. 59–60).

With independence, and definitely released from the British constraints, the form of colonialism that the new authorities practised might be plainly qualified as a genocide (Dunbar-Ortiz, 2014, pp. 6–9): it included "killing members of the group," the inflicting of "serious bodily or mental harm to members of the group," the "deliberately inflicting on the group conditions of life calculated to bring about its physical destruction in whole or in part," the imposition "of measures intended to prevent births within the group," and the transfer "forcibly of the children of the group to another group." All these measures were accompanied by the unrestrained taking of land and resources backed by armies in an atmosphere of tremendous violence.

Throughout the decades that encompass the fight for independence, the Confederation, and the framing of the U.S. Constitution, it must be observed that the conflicts between the separatists and the indigenous groups were deployed on multiple fronts. The settler's war against the British overlapped a series of Indian wars against the Shawnee and the Delaware Nations in Ohio (Anderson and Cayton, 2005, pp. 104–159; Grenier, 2005, pp. 170–172) against the Cherokee through the attacks launched from Virginia, Georgia, and North and South Carolina (Grenier, 2005, pp. 51–53) and against the Six Nations Iroquois at the western edge of New York (Dunbar-Ortiz, 2014, pp. 166–168). In all of them separatist settler-rangers used extreme violence against indigenous non-combatants with the goals of total subjugation or expulsion. During the War of Independence some indigenous nations still had indeed the opportunity to negotiate an alliance with the British against the separatists, thus reinforcing their resistance against settler-squatters. But afterwards, with Britain's withdrawal in 1783, the new authorities' atrocities against indigenous nations were unrestrained. The fight between the American Republic and the Indian tribes was a crucial factor in the creation of the U.S. Federation, since it propelled the consolidation of the federal army and, thus, a basic means of coercion. It also provided a huge area with resources to be exploited, including the revenues obtained by the federal government (the primary revenue source for the federal authorities) when it sold the confiscated land to the settlers.

Indians had been explicitly treated by the constitutional system as outsiders of the Republic. That basically happened through both (1) the provisions of the Federal Constitution that conferred to the Federal authorities the powers on commerce and treaty-making with the Indian tribes and (2) the regulation that excluded Indians from taxation [which was likely to allude to the Indian's exclusion as citizens (Pommersheim, 2012, p. 3)]. The 1787 Constitutional design, summarily, handled the American native population as aliens. Such an approach (that may be defined under the same logic that ruled the relations between the United States and other sovereign entities) did not give account, nevertheless, of the status of the tribes *already absorbed* within the 13 original colonies. The making process of the U.S. Federal Constitution certified the subjugation of the Indians, the violence exercised upon them, and the land usurpation that they had to suffer before the establishment of the Federation. Such invisibility of the Indians as members of the original American States and such denial of the illegitimate means by which they were dispossessed of wealth and political status in the time of the colonization would be, in fact, transferred to the other Indian tribes settled westwards as long as the Federal authorities conquered their territories and the American white citizens occupied their lands.[4] Federal authorities, beginning with the Supreme Court, didn't hesitate in refusing to admit consequences for the breach of the treaties that the U.S. maintained with the tribes once the army and the settlers occupied Indian territories. Indian tribes began to be considered dependent nations in a state of pupillage as they had no rights upon the land which they inhabited [*Johnson v M'Intosh* 21 U.S. (8 Wheat.) 543 (1823); *Cherokee Nation v Georgia* 30 U.S. 1 (1831)] and Congress was considered to have plenary authority over such Peoples [*Lone Wolf v. Hitchcock* 187 U.S. 553 (1903)]. The Supreme Court, as long as those tribes were falling into de dominions of the U.S. jurisdiction, displayed its doctrine on the blindness towards any Indian identity-grounded claim arguing that any special recognition towards the indigenous peoples would curtail the principle of formal equality [*Williams v Lee* 358 US 217 (1959)]. But, certainly, the strict application of formal equality in handling with Indian claims only supposed the refusal by the U.S. authorities to consider the Indian's sovereign situation and its control of land and resources *before the usurpation*.

Integration of the indigenous peoples through constitutional transformations was even still less visible than the path taken through the abolition of slavery (to the extent that one may doubt that the question of the Original Peoples has whatsoever impinged in the allocation of power that the American constitutional system represents). At any rate, by the time in which the struggle between the elites around the cause of slavery exploded in the Civil War, the European settlers' descendants carried on with the carnage against the Indians, confirming the original decision already envisaged in the founding, that is, the exclusion of the Indians from the political community. At the end of January 1863, less than a month after Abraham Lincoln issued the Emancipation Proclamation to free slaves during the Civil War, his Union Army committed the worst massacre of Native Americans in U.S. history when they murdered 400 Shoshone at the Bear River. Previously, in December 1862, 38 Dakota men from the hundreds that had been interned in a sort of concentration camp in Minnesota after the Dakota War had been hanged.

Popular classes

As I have suggested, furthermore, the original Constitution as an expression of the allocation of power conceived by the elites to subject other collectives *was also focused on the domination of the popular classes within the American citizenry.*[5] Inequality and social stratification had been developed during the eighteenth century and marked the generation of the Revolution. Besides the sumptuous landlords of the Hudson Valley, for instance, whose status resembled that of the European feudal lords, there coexisted a wide range of small freeholders and a still larger mass of poor tenants with scarce possibilities to become freeholders (Middlekauff, 2005, pp. 41–42). The growth of the cities also led to the growth of the urban poor population. Gary Nash, in his study on America's pre-revolutionary urban inequality (1976) asserts that in Boston and Philadelphia the lower half of society only held 5 per cent of the taxable wealth and that by 1772 one in four adult men in Philadelphia was poor by the standards of the day.

As we shall see, after independence, the centralization of power that the federal constituent operation represented was considered a reaction against the popular turmoil which spread across some of the States in the 1780s. It had been widely believed, at least since the publication in 1913 of Charles A. Beard's *Economic Interpretation of the Constitution*, that the 1787 Federal Constitution was a device by which men of property, particularly those holding securities of the State or continental governments, sought to protect themselves and their financial holdings against the dangers of popular rule. As has been widely studied by the American doctrine, the Federal constitutional system is marked by a gamut of instruments devoted to the restraint of popular governance.

Inequality among white Americans meant inequality in the recognition of rights. The regulation of the right to suffrage during the creation of the American Republic gives a good account of that [not to mention women, who in most parts of the United States were going to be excluded from voting for more than a century (Keyssar, 2000)]. The consent of the members of the community in establishing the basic rules of society was, thus, far from being attained, whether during the approval of the States' Constitutions or during the framing of the Federal Constitution (Beard, 1964, pp. 24–26). By 1776 all of the recently independent States retained some sort of tax-paying or property qualification for suffrage (Keyssar, 2000, pp. 8–20; Wood, 1998, pp. 167–170). Even the Pennsylvania Constitution, passed within the context of a radical revolution, required the paying of public taxes in order to have the right to vote. In spite of the fact that some States temporarily set aside these property qualifications and allowed all free adult male citizens to vote in the election for the Federal Constitution ratifying Convention (Amar, 2006, p. 7), by the 1790s only about ten to sixteen per cent of America's population could vote. Pecuniary qualifications were still higher for eligibility. According to the 1780 Massachusetts Constitution, for instance, the governor was required to have a freehold worth at least one thousand pounds, senators a freehold of three hundred or six hundred pounds total estate, and representatives a freehold of one hundred pounds or two hundred pounds total estate (Palmer, 1968, p. 352).

Universal white male suffrage was not going to be expanded until the so-called Jacksonian democracy and the requirements to own property or to pay taxes would not be dropped for this sector of population until the fifties of the nineteenth century (North Carolina was the last State to abolish property qualifications for white men by 1856). Once former slaves gained the right to vote after the Civil

War, and the passing of the 15th Amendment, some Southern States, however, adopted poll taxes that had the effect of disenfranchising many blacks, as well as poor whites. Poll taxes, which were an indirect way to deprive some parts of the citizenship of the right to vote, would not be completely abolished until the 1960s through the approval of the 24th Amendment to the Federal Constitution and the passing of the *Voting Rights Act* (Ackerman, 2014, p. 10).

Wars of State-building and constitution-making

The American Revolution was a breach in the existing order; it was a bloody revolutionary triumph achieved not through an inclusive and rational debate, but through the effective use of force.

However much Hanna Arendt (1963, p. 169) insists on "the generation of political power through the mutual contract by which people bind themselves together in order to form a community," in delving into the specific facts that marked the emancipation of the 13 North American colonies even she had to observe that:

> The force of this power, engendered by action and kept by promises, came to fore when, to the great surprise of all the great powers, the colonies … *won the war* against England.
>
> (Arendt, 1963, p. 175, italics mine)

The war against England was, certainly, won, and it was won through military organization and not through the free and sincere promises kept by the separatists. It must be not forgotten, in addition, that the other European "great powers" did not watch passively the action of the American patriots enforcing their promises. American independence was possible because ***absolute monarchies*** such as both France and Spain, representing the contrary of the American republican ideals, provided the rebels with crucial military and financial support. The aspiration of founding a new political space in which democracy finds its seeds is undermined when the genealogical analysis reveals the wide range of coercions that accompanied the secession. Such coercions have simply nothing to do with "mutual consent," "covenants," and the "free and sincere promises of men together" but with the *expulsion* of some elements as a result of shaping a new political community. The American revolutionary war was won *against someone*. There was a replacement of a cadre of organized men, able to enforce a legal order, through arms by another one. The triumphant soldiers of the battles of Saratoga or Yorktown forced the migration of the losers, namely, the columns of around 80,000 loyalists that left the American States and went to England, to the other colonies of the Crown in the West Indies, or north to Canada where the vast majority of the British subjects finished their journey. Their properties in the American States had been confiscated without qualms (Palmer, 1968, p. 359) even though "possessing property" was considered an "inherent right" according to some of the States' Constitutions.

If some modern political analysts have distorted the determinacy of the means of warfare in explaining the revolutionary success, it may be due to the narratives displayed by the American founding generation itself. As we have seen, the colonists had already donned blinkers in relation to the exclusions and the violence that, during the times of the Crown's sovereignty, had carved their privileged position over other groups. Barely a few years before the clash, the revolutionaries themselves were not considered oppressed (Middlekauff, 2007, pp. 5–6). As Gordon Wood remarks in the opening of his magnificent study on the creation of the American Republic, the Americans of that time knew that they were probably freer and less burdened with cumbersome feudal and hierarchical restraints than any part of mankind in the eighteenth century (Wood, 1998, p. 3). After all, the Americans of the eighteenth century had been born under the rule of the English constitution emerging from the 1688 Glorious Revolution which was considered even in the New Continent "the best model of Government that can be framed by Mortals" (so Adams quoted by Wood, 1998, p. 11). A perception that would suddenly change when the inhabitants of the colonies (Green, 1968, p. 20) began to realize that the British parliamentarian supremacy established in the aftermath of the expulsion of James the II also represented British parliamentarian arbitrariness (Amar, 1987, p. 1430). The transformation of Britain into a world power and its involvement in several military adventures required huge amounts of money and, in their purpose of increasing the sources of revenues, the landowners that dominated the British Parliament turned their view, as the eighteenth century advanced, to their wealthy American counterparts. The Seven Years War finished in 1763 with an overwhelming victory for the British but the national debt the war had represented was overwhelming too, and most of the costs were due to the permanent stationing of British military forces in mainland America. The expenditure in order to maintain such an army would carry on since the conflicts with the indigenous peoples in the West would not be mitigated, and Britain had the intention to consolidate the new territorial gains obtained with the war. Then was when Grenville's government decided to tighten the screws on the colonies by imposing certain taxes on trade. The Revenue Act of 1764, or Sugar Act as it was popularly called, was a relevant step in that direction and was easily passed in the British Parliament because (an issue that later would appear as one of the Americans' most fundamental claims) the colonies were unrepresented in the British Houses (Middlekauff, 2007, pp. 61–73). But the Sugar Act was just the beginning. Taxing the colonies without the consent of the American representatives would still lead to more serious and pressing crises such as the rioting and mobbing that ensued with the approval of the Stamp Act in 1765.

It might be reasoned that, given such antecedents (the relatively liberal frame in which the American rebellion took place and a vindication in the first stages centred in economic demands) it is not incoherent that the contemporaries of independence preferred to explain themselves by associating their political struggle with the gathering of people in all sorts of meetings and congresses than with the killing of British soldiers.

But the simple historical truth is that a harsh conflict was needed to make the American constitutional developments flourish. What is in fact particular to the American Revolution is that the American States' constitutions were being drafted *in the midst* of a war of secession, the American case thus being a scenario in which the violence displayed both during State-building and during the constitution-making process is intertwined at the very same time. Most of the States' Constitutions were passed in a moment of uncertainty on the outcome of the fight: ten States out of 13 gave themselves new constitutions in 1776 and 1777 (Palmer, 1968, p. 342). The possibility of the total military defeat of the rebels, such as when George Washington had to remain in retreat at Valley Forge in the winter of 1777 after losing Boston, New York, and Philadelphia (Ackerman, 2019, p. 364) was even overshadowing most of the constitution-making process, a circumstance that in the case of being consummated would probably have deprived the American constitutional proposals of any force.

The immediate call of the Continental Congress for the adoption of written constitutions for the States (Topf, 2019, p. 59) was conceived as a move to confer legitimacy to the revolutionary struggle while the challenge against the previous order was taking place. The constitutive initiative launched by the American elites (as soon as they definitely had joined the cause of the independence) sought, in the first instance, to reduce the vacuum of authority for the shortest time possible and, in the second instance, and probably more important, to galvanize the masses around the defence of their rights in order to mobilize them for the military goals.

The constitutional creation of the American States might be in that fashion considered as a means of recruiting manpower to fight in the war. If all men were declared "equally free and independent" and entitled with rights, as for instance the Virginia Declaration of Rights drafted by George Mason in June 1776 established, that was because the highest number of mobilized men was needed to face up to the British and their local followers. The generosity in recognizing liberties and in designing participative institutional structures instigated by the urgency of gaining the widest popular support to combat the royalists would have thorny consequences, once the war concluded, for the stability of the constitutional system.

The American Revolution sharply illustrates to what extent the design of a participative government and the recognition of fundamental rights emerge as incidental outcomes of the struggle for power and why they could be perceived as concessions bestowed by the elites to the lower strata of the society in order to consolidate the assault of the former to the rule of the new political body. As some historians explained many decades ago, the shifting point in the relatively harmonious relations between Britain and its North American colonies, up to 1763, may be situated in the conflict around the ambitions of rival factions *among* the American elites (see, for instance, Green, 1968, p. 28). The debate on the political status that the colonies deserved in their relationship with Britain represented the occasion for one faction to gain political predominance at the expense of its rivals as happened with the opposition to the Stamp Act in

Connecticut or in Rhode Island in 1765 (Middlekauff, 2007, pp. 106–107). Thus, it was when some of such factions within the American elite began to realize that they would never enjoy the privileges and the opportunities recognized for their counterparts in Britain and, furthermore, that they began to understand that their property rights were being threatened by British rule, that their support of the Crown began to stagger. But to get rid of British dominion and to fight and defeat the loyalists, such circles needed the support of the popular classes. It was in that time, only shortly before the Revolution, around 1774, that the idea of involving the people in the rule of society began to circulate (Bouton, 2007, p. 31; Turner Main, 1968, p. 322). Prior to the moment in which the rupture with Britain was looming, the democratic approaches developed by some theories, such as by the Whigs, understood that a modicum of democracy had to be balanced by equal parts of aristocracy and monarchy, obviously excluding ordinary people from holding any office. Still, as late as the outbreak of open hostilities between Great Britain and the 13 colonies in the spring of 1775, there were many Americans who felt that no political change was needed except the expulsion of the British (Palmer, 1968, p. 342). Colonial institutions such as the States' Houses elected before the war were overwhelmingly controlled by representatives coming from the highest economic and social ranks, and they had no desire to relinquish their predominance in the management of public affairs. On their concept of property, for instance, the American oligarchy did not provide any innovation in comparison with the ideas developed by the English Whigs (Adams, 1980, p. 190). Their only ambition was related to ensuring the protection of their wealth in a way that British Parliament had been incapable of doing in North America, and it was only in order to achieve said goal that the inclusion of the right to property in a written constitution was accepted. Consequently, since the safeguard of property rights through a Constitution was a concern of the ones that had something to protect, the first American Constitutions did not place restrictions on the individual's rights to dispose of his property, nor did constitutional framers doubt the utility of imposing property qualifications for suffrage or office holding (Rankove, 1981, p. 299). In following the path of the origins of the right to property in the constitutional language, it is not difficult to find that, both in the State's Constitution and later in the Federal one, the well-to-do were behind such developments precisely to contain the rising democratization that resulted from the war and the break up with the British system.

The regime change, however, was accompanied by an extension of political participation to wider parts of American society. The military command had no other alternative but to include people of humbler origins in the decision-making processes if it had the intention of winning the fight. After all, modest farmers were falling before one of the best equipped armies in the world (Bouton, 2007, p. 49) and the leaders of the pro-independence movement could not overlook them in the creation of the new constitutional framework, at least while the war was ongoing. Whether in the case of assemblies inherited from the previous regime or in the case of new representative chambers (indistinctly of the fact if they had been transformed through legal or extra-legal means), ordinary yeoman and artisans gained more presence with the change. Being because of the greater number of representatives established for the legislatures, or being because, with reduction of the property qualifications for voting, people chose more men of their social condition, the point is that politics were open to new agents. The extent of this phenomenon varied from moderate in Virginia and Maryland to radical in New Hampshire and New Jersey, but everywhere the same process occurred (Turner Main, 1968, p. 335).

The American elite, notwithstanding, did its best to conduct the reconstitution of power according to its interests, which meant giving the populace as little institutional weight as possible. One common strategy adopted relied on avoiding the election of constituent Conventions to discuss and pass the drafting of fundamental rules. In a revolutionary atmosphere, the calling of elections to a conventional body might have instigated the hasty entry in the institutions of new elements. While it is true that the presence of small farmers, mechanics, and moderate properties had increased in the provincial congresses from 1774 (Turner Main, 1968, pp. 328–329), wealthy merchants, lawyers, and large property owners still had a strong influence in the representative instances in which the elaboration of constitutions might be placed. In Maryland and North Carolina, the constitution-making process would be provided with a measure of popular ratification (Palmer, 1968, p. 343) but the constitutional design had been already coined by an upper-class-dominated assembly. The central role of the elites in exercising the constituent power within ordinary assemblies would also be the rule, apart from the mentioned experiences in Maryland and North Carolina, in New Hampshire, New York, Delaware, and Georgia. While in Rhode Island and Connecticut there would be no constitution-making process at all, and the colonial charters would remain in force for decades (in Massachusetts the colonial charter was maintained until 1780), the only place in which a constitutional Convention was envisaged was also the scenario in which things got out of hand for the conservatives: Pennsylvania. Pennsylvania was a breeding ground for the radicalization of the revolution (Bouton, 2007, p. 33; Palmer, 1968, pp. 344–345) and it would be on occasion of Pennsylvania's constitutional change that social turbulences among Americans, particularly intense in the following decade, would be inaugurated.

Internal revolution

Even though the American Revolution was accompanied by democratic demands that had some impact during the framing of States' Constitutions, those who enjoyed wealth and political power did their best in using the constituent power to undermine the democratic and economic claims of the masses. As the historian Merrill Jensen wrote in the 1948 preface to the second printing of his book *The Articles of Confederation* (p. xvii)

> The fact is that during and after the Revolution the patriot members of the old aristocracy and its rich new members fought hand in hand to hold their position, or to regain it in states where it had been lost.

There had been a conflict between the American revolutionaries and the British loyalists but there were also going to be conflicts *among the citizens of the new American States.* As mentioned above, Pennsylvania, already shortly before the Declaration of Independence, represented the first serious clash between the privileged classes and a revolutionary mass of farmers and artisans organized in committees, associations, and militia (see Douglass, 1955, pp. 120–122; Hawk, 1961; Thayer, 1953; Wood, 1998, pp. 83–90). It has been observed (Palmer, 1968, pp. 344–345) that the harsher turn experienced in Pennsylvania with the fight among Americans had been precisely due to the persistence of loyalism among Pennsylvania's elites expressed in a desire of conciliation with the metropolitan power. But in 1776, after a year of open war with Britain, and when the conservatives opted, not without reluctance, for leaving behind their Anglophile sensibilities, their position became so weak that they found their desire of containing the democratic impetus of the masses impracticable.

In the summer of 1776, radicals captured the control of the Pennsylvania constitutional Convention and wrote a draft that reflected the egalitarian ideas developed by the Whigs and, particularly, by the British radical and in that time an enormously popular figure in America: Thomas Paine (see Gargarella, 2010, pp. 13–14; Selsam, 1971; Wood, 1998, pp. 85, 137–139). The Pennsylvania Constitution reserved a central role for the legislature and created a weak executive: the governor was totally eliminated and replaced by an Executive Council of 12, who were elected directly by the people. Pennsylvanian constitution-makers also suppressed the institution of the Senate and opened up to the public the decision-making process. The draft did not contemplate any of the counter-majoritarian knots that would afterwards be scattered in the U.S. Federal Constitution and that were still defining the institutional design in most States through which the elites kept their hands on the reins of power (the persistence of a second legislative chamber with property thresholds of large estates to access office is an example of this).

The example of Pennsylvania had some influence in the drafting of other States' constitutions (see Lutz, 1988, pp. 104–105; Nevins, 1927, pp. 117–170) but the institutional democratization expressed in some particular constitutional regulations was more marked by the local needs given the military situation or by the colonial background on organizing the government[6] than by the spreading of radical revolutionary trends that had Pennsylvania as an epicentre. In any case, the well born and the socially qualified chiefly conducted the constituent processes developed between 1776 and 1777 in the rest of the States, and even regained the power in Pennsylvania a few years later.

The 1776 Pennsylvania Constitution was one of the most democratic constitutions produced in the eighteenth century, at least according to its formal provisions, but in a similar way as happened with the 1793 French Constitution, the American text did not work in practice under its democratic principles, and became an example of the authoritarian turn that populism may cause (Palmer, 1968, p. 345) a circumstance that was conveniently invoked by the Pennsylvania upper classes in order to derogate the regime in 1790 once they recovered from their weakness under the protection of the constitutional structure that had been assembled at the federal level (Bouton, 2007, p. 171).

But social tensions became even more acute by the conclusion of the peace with Britain and the entering into force of the Articles of the Confederation in the decade of the 1780s. Some of the recently independent American States had to tackle an important and controversial demand among the bulk of the American population: the issuance of paper money. Most people were highly indebted after the war, and the printing of paper money appeared to offer the only escape from this situation (Beard, 1964, p. 28; Gargarella, 2010, p. 14). But money creation provoked serious concerns among creditors, landowners, and the American political elite because it reduced the value of their assets. Debt relief laws passed by some State legislatures forced creditors to accept repayment in devalued paper currency (Fritz, 2008, p. 123). It is not casual that some of the drafters of the U.S. Constitution that belonged to the group of owners and creditors opposed fiercely the printing of paper money, and that issue was often remembered by them as an example of the infamous consequences that the conquer of the power by the masses and the prevalence of the decisions of the majority would entail (Jensen, 1967, p. 313).

Rhode Island offers a good example to illustrate these political and economic dynamics. The same State that did not send delegates to the 1787 Philadelphia Convention and the State which was most reluctant to ratify the Federal Constitution, was also the place where the question of printing paper money in order to satisfy debtors' claims reached its peak (Nevins, 1927, p. 518). Jonathan Hazard, the leader of the debtors' group, was in 1786 directly elected as the governor of Rhode Island. He controlled the State legislative branch through his supporters as well. Such a position allowed Hazard to pass diverse laws favourable to debtors' interests and promoted the issue of paper money, as well as the establishment of fines for the creditors that did not accept the bills and the possibility of bringing them before the State's courts if they persisted in refusing paper money. The situation in Rhode Island was harshly criticized by James Madison, who in a letter sent to his brother, Ambrose, remarked on the economic and social chaos into which the State had fallen.[7]

Also in a stable State, in Maryland, the House of Delegates in the winter of 1786–1787 attempted to bring pressure on the Senate by urging the people at large to instruct the members of the upper house to pass paper money bills (Wood, 1998, p. 369). The opponents of this measure avoided its enaction by remarking that the Senate, which they controlled, was equally representative of the people as the House of Delegates and, thus, representatives were not bound to the instructions given by the electors. The case of Maryland on the issue of paper money expressed the tension between the House of Delegates in which the radicals were more influential and the Senate, which, as in many States, remained a stronghold of the elite.

But other dramatic events would break out across the American State under the Confederation that would instigate the future U.S. President John Quincy Adams in July 1787 to speak of the "critical period." The elite was especially alarmed by the protests that spread in Massachusetts from the summer of 1786 under the leadership of Daniel Shays, a bankrupt farmer and former army captain, whose name was given to the rebellion.[8] Rebels, made up of farmers and small debtors, sought to force the Massachusetts legislature to drop direct taxation, lower court fees, and make other fiscal concessions to the mob. Protests degenerated into riots, assaults on State institutions, and clashes with the State militia, which at the very beginning was proved to be unreliable. The tumult only could be suppressed by the funding of a private army assembled with donations coming from more than one hundred merchants. Some historians have interpreted Shays' Rebellion as containing elements of class warfare (Collier and Collier, 1986, p. 12). It represented a peak of the confrontation between the local population and some parts of the oligarchy that already began to operate at a supra-State level.

From another strand, some scholars have interpreted the Shays' Rebellion as a postcolonial conflict (see, for instance, Rana, 2020, p. 77; Szatmary, 1980, pp. 19–36; on the consequences of postcolonial conflicts regarding the constitutional evolution of the liberated States, see Ackerman, 2020, p. 387). According to them, the convulsions experienced in Massachusetts by the mid-eighties of the eighteenth century crystallized the potential threats of dissolution and European subjection that confronted the new independent States. The rebellion itself was initially precipitated by the decision of the British merchants to close their doors to American business. The attitude of the British actors might be inferred as a sort of economic retaliation against those that had challenged the situation of colonial domination. Either way, disregarding the role of the former metropoli in instigating the crisis, the American elites that later would gather in the Philadelphia Convention were convinced that a stronger central government was needed in order to face also the external threats and, particularly, those coming from the appetite of the British to keep control of their former colonies.

In the 1787 Massachusetts elections the supporters of the popular claims gained the majority in the House (although the Senate remained under the control of the establishment) and elected a new governor inclined to enforce the various devices that the legislature would pass in order to suspend the ordinary means for the recovery of debts. Such a shift in the institutions of Massachusetts in the aftermath of the rebellions increased the criticisms of the people's government. Personalities such as Henry Knox began to speak of "mad democracy" not only in Massachusetts but from "almost every legislature" (quoted in Fritz, 2008, p. 113) and the voices warning of the danger of the "majoritarian tyranny" and urging to find institutional remedies to contain it were common among the parts of American society that represented the creditors (Wood, 1998, p. 411). "Every state has its Shays" would be later written by a supporter of the Federal Constitution at the beginning of the ratification campaign (Richards, 2002, p. 139). In fact, when Madison argued for constitutional restrictions to the overbearing power of a majority in order to protect rights, he was mainly concerned about the protection of property rights, given the crises unleashed by the debtors. He asserted in *The Federalist No. 10* that "the first object of government" was "the protection of different and unequal faculties of acquiring property" (1989, p. 58). Furthermore, Madison, as most of the American elite, thought that the revolutionary principles of government left the rights of property vulnerable to the excesses of popular government (Nedelsky, 1990, p. 21). The American wealthy class that complained about the crippling of property rights by the British Parliament before the war realized that the same insecurities towards the protection of their assets may be found in their dispossessed fellow citizens when they acted through the representative institutions. Yet, as Ackerman remarked (1993, pp. 170–171), given the convulsions experienced during the Revolution and its aftermath, the American elites already faced up to a problem that would become a classic in the following age of the revolutions of the nineteenth and the twentieth centuries, namely, how to avoid that someone else might challenge the established authority gained through the revolution with *another revolution*. Just as the revolutionaries challenged the British authority, so can others challenge the regime of the Confederation and the independent American States. If the legal order has been broken once, it could be broken more times.

As is well known, Madison was compelled by such issues when he wrote the *Federalist No.10* and analyzed the question of the factions (1989, pp. 56–65). The point was that once the constitutional order was established, no faction could claim that it spoke in the name of the People in the same way that the revolutionaries did when they broke with the British order and displaced the British ruling apparatus applied in the colonies and by the social class that had benefited from British authority.[9] If the revolutionaries gained their legitimacy by the supposed concrete assent of the People, despite the illegality, some faction would be able to invoke *its* popular support, "the superior force of an interested and overbearing majority" (1989, p. 57) in order to infringe the new constitutional order. The solution, according to Madison, was to conceive a constitutional device capable of neutralizing the faction and its power to undermine the regime. One might read Madison's proposals as the search for a constitutional design engaged with the aim of preserving the principles of the Revolution, channelling the influence of factions by playing each interest group off against others (see Ackerman, 1993, p. 181). Madison didn't deny the possibility of appealing to the will of the People under the constitutional framework but pleaded to subject such appeal to extraordinary occasions expressed through the constitutional amendment process.

The Federalist constitutional science described by Madison, however, might be shown under another, and darker, narrative: the revolutionary elite, eager to perpetuate its power *used constitutionalism to constrain other candidates from speaking in the name of the People*. In other terms, the Founders were nothing but a faction; the faction integrated by white male merchants and landowners who had led and won a war and who were trying to exclude other factions from the control of legal authority.

Even though lots of criticism has been expressed in recent decades of the historiographical thesis on the conservative turn among the American elites after the Revolution, more recent approaches remark that the link between the anarchic unravelling of the Confederation and the endorsement of a less egalitarian set of constitutional principles by the Federalists "undoubtedly" existed (Nelson, 2014, p. 184). As McIlwain had already pointed out (1923, p. 59) the reaction of the majority of the members of the Philadelphia Convention contained fundamentally an anti-Whig perspective. The Federal Constitution would be the solution that Washington, Madison & Co. would find to the democratic malaise that according to them was devastating the young American experiment.

The road to the illegal founding

During the years of the Confederation, thus, the need to build a strong central government was extended among the leading class of the American States. The anxiety of creating the Federation was not so much inspired by the aim of strengthening the Union in its relationships with foreign powers. The issue that predominated in the minds of the Federalists was to found a new constitutional framework in order to confront the disarray of American society and the upside-down changes in the political and social hierarchy that the Revolution had released (Wood, 1998, p. 475).

If we read the expressions of the Federalists, we find disdain everywhere towards the infusion of new classes that acceded to power during the breakup with the English empire and the formation of the Confederation (Main, 1966, pp. 391–407). The revolution allowed government to fall "into the Hands of those whose ability or situation in Life does not entitle them to it,"[10] "men, respectable neither for their property, their virtue, nor their abilities,"[11] "men whom Wisdom would have left in obscurity,"[12] "men without reading, experience, or principle."[13] According to the Federalists, it was time to return the control of the government to the owners, the talented, and the respectable people.

The Founders would invest themselves with the authority of the "We the People" in order to block the People's effective rule. Basically, the main aim of the national political elite was the neutralization of the States' legislatures, bodies in which, after such experiences as those mentioned in Pennsylvania, Rhode Island, or Massachusetts (McDonald, 1968, p. 4) some of the Federalists saw the confirmation of all their fears regarding populism, the direct intervention of the people in political affairs, and the threat of individual rights. "In our Governments the real power lies in the majority of the Community" wrote Madison to Jefferson in a letter "and the invasion of private rights is chiefly to be apprehended, not from acts of Government contrary to the sense of its constituents, but from acts in which the Government is the mere instrument of the major number of constituents."[14]

Besides the opposition of James Madison, it is not difficult to find hundreds of writings of other prominent figures in the creation of the American Republic criticizing the power of States' elected representatives. Alexander Hamilton, for instance, denounced the usurpation of power by the legislature and warned his peers at the prospect of seeing the people's representatives transformed into "perpetual dictators" (Hamilton, 1962, p. 605). George Washington himself, in a letter to Madison, considered that the State legislatures were invaded by "prejudices" and by "irrational jealousies and local interests" (Madison, 1979, pp. 161–162). Such a state of things allowed some historians of the period such as Gordon Wood (2002, 142–143) to state that:

> By the mid-1780s many American leaders had come to believe that the State legislatures, not the governors, were the political authority to be most feared. Not only were some of the legislatures violating the individual rights of property-owners through their excessive printing of paper money and their various acts on behalf of debtors, but in all the States the assemblies also pushed beyond the generous grants of legislative authority of the 1776 Revolutionary constitutions and were absorbing numerous executive and judicial duties directing military operations, for example, and setting aside court judgments.

Undermining the State legislatures' powers, particularly the States' Houses of Representatives' powers had been in the mind of the future U.S. Constitution drafters during the years of the Confederation, to the extent that the first move in order to reach this purpose once the Federal constitutional draft was passed, relied on placing the ratification of the document not in the legislatures but in special Conventions. It is not casual that the notion of constitution conceived as a set of fundamental rules able to bind the elected representatives (thus, the rules able to limit democratic decisions) was from 1776 developed by groups where confidence in the existing legislative assemblies was weakest (Wood, 1998, pp. 267–268). Mistrust in the States' legislatures also explains the formation of the judicial review of legislation at the State level under the Confederation, as it would later explain the development of such an institution at the federal level.

The operation deployed during the making of the U.S. Federal Constitution consequently sought, first of all, to circumvent as much as possible the influence of legislatures in the establishing of the constitutional framework. To this end, the idea of calling a constitutional Convention composed of delegates chosen with the special intention to frame a Constitution would be invoked. Such a body, that had already been present during the Revolution inspired by some episodes of English constitutional history, was conceived as a special representation of the People, expressing the consent among society on creating a set of rules superior to those enacted by the legislatures. But the calling of the Philadelphia Convention was a movement oriented to jeopardize the more radical representation in order to promote the selection of candidates closer to the interests of the privileged few. The theory of the Convention allowed the Founders to simulate the emergence of a special representation of the People while at the same time cutting the influence of the people at large both by (1) depriving the citizenry of the vote for the delegates and by (2) manipulating the legislatures, particularly through the Senates existing in most of the States, to ensure that the delegates appointed were supporters of the centralization of power. Curiously, as we have seen, when in 1776 most of the legislatures were integrated by conservatives, the calling for a constituent Convention was refused in all of them except Pennsylvania (and later in Massachusetts). But when in 1787 the democrats entrenched their majorities in the Houses of representatives, the Federalists understood that only the calling of a Convention with opaque methods of selecting the delegates would allow them to frame a constitution for the Union according to their interests.

In a long and detailed article devoted to showing all the range of illegalities that the Federalists perpetrated during the Founding, Bruce Ackerman and Neal Katyal (1995) argue that the violation of the Confederation legal framework was planned by the leaders of the Federalist movement from the outset. It was not only a matter of the violation, as we shall see, of Article XIII of the Confederation by which any alteration to such articles required the unanimous consent of the 13 States [while the Federal Constitution only required in its Article VII the consent of nine States to enter into force][15]; *it was a recurrent infringement of most of the procedural requirements in order to amend the existing framework.* As Ackerman and Katyal remarked, the composition of the Convention was irregular since "the convention was itself a secessionist body" (1995, p. 480). Also, Kay (1987, p. 57) did not hesitate in stating that:

> This foundation of American legality was itself the product of a blatant and conscious illegality.

Maintaining some analogies with the European integration process in the twentieth century, the immediate precedent of the American Federation was the struggle for a commercial union that had to be outlined by a general trade Convention which met in Annapolis, one year before the calling for the Convention on the Constitution (Farrand, 1960, pp. 7–11; Jensen, 1964, p. 33). The Confederation had been shown incapable of developing a successful economic policy because of the Congressional lack of authority to tax, to regulate commerce, or to control credit (Kay, 1984, p. 125; Ackerman, 2019, p. 368). The central government was incompetent either to establish national tariffs or trade policies and this, under the perspective of the Federalists, resulted in a serious disadvantage in competing or negotiating with other countries. Large agriculture producers and merchants were therefore interested in adopting a common trade policy, but the commissioners sent to Annapolis and the organizers of the Convention (Hamilton among them) quickly realized that their flourishing commerce and economy needed a new political and legal framework to ensure respect for the rights of property and to provide order and stability. The fragmentation of political authority was, in the view of such circles, a major obstacle to progress (Kay, 1987, p. 63). The Annapolis Convention did not accomplish the purpose of establishing a general trade agreement because only five States were represented. It might not have gone very far, but the Shays' Rebellion highlighted among merchants, politicians, and generals the need for a strong national government (Elster, 2012a, p. 18). Accordingly, the commissioners recommended to the legislatures of the States and to the only body authorized by the Articles of Confederation to propose amendments, the United States in Congress Assembled, to set up another Convention of wider scope.

The Congress adopted a resolution on February 21, 1787, in favour of a Convention. The Congressional resolution calling the Convention restricted the Convention's mission to "revising the Articles of Confederation and reporting ... alterations and provisions therein" (Kay, 1984, p. 126) but the delegates assembled in Philadelphia worked on a complete replacement of the Articles of the Confederation from the start (Bowen, 1986, p. 117). The Congress resolution, on the other hand, had provided that delegates should be "appointed by the States" without establishing any specific procedure for that purpose. The leaders of the Federalist movement were confronted with the pretension of convincing the legislatures, and particularly the members of the legislatures related to the large groups of economic interests, to send delegates to Philadelphia (Beard, 1964, p. 64). Naturally, those most concerned with the necessity of constitutional change were more receptive to becoming candidates. The supporters of the Federal Constitution were able to use a substantial part of the institutional framework of each State to ensure that delegates would satisfy their expectations in defending the creation of the central government and introducing the proper checks to restrain democratic excesses. This aim was helped by popular indifference and ignorance prevailing during the formation of the Convention and the discussions regarding the structure of the central power.

At the stage of sending the delegates, the only place where the purpose of the Federalists failed in part because the tensions around the debt issue were still vivid, was in Rhode Island, which did not respond to the call and renounced to send any commissioners to Philadelphia. Other States sent delegates but barred the delegation from agreeing to any proposal that affected equality in voting power as was regulated under the Confederation Articles (as in the case of Delaware, whose delegation recognized that it had acted in contempt of its commission). In the case of New York, three delegates were sent to the Convention but two (John Lansing and Robert Yates) withdrew from the sessions upon observing the pronounced centralized bias of the Federalist majority. Only Alexander Hamilton remained at the secret sessions and, consequently, the Convention did not even pretend that Hamilton's signature would suffice to bind the State, explaining why among the State delegations enumerated on the final roll call as approving the Constitution, both that of Rhode Island and New York were omitted from the list (Ackerman and Katyal, 1995, pp. 481–482; Ackerman, 2019, p. 369).

The change of the constitutional framework also undermined some limits established by the State constitutions. After all, the legal status of each ratifying Convention depended on its particular State constitution (Kay, 2011, p. 728). There were some State constitutions that contemplated the use of Conventions and there were others that did not. Among the States' constitutions that provided for the use of Conventions several mechanisms existed which allowed for the summoning of a Convention that were not satisfied in the 1787 process (in Massachusetts, for instance, it required two-thirds of the towns to agree; Pennsylvania required two-thirds of a specially elected body of Censors). There were other State constitutions that provided for the intervention of the States' legislatures in some stage of the revisionary mechanism (precisely the body that some Federalists sought to elude). And, furthermore, some States' constitutional provisions forbade any Constitutional amendment until a certain date beyond the time in which the Federal Constitution was planned to be ratified. Either way, the Federalists lacked the legal authority to change the method of constitutional revision designed by the existing State constitutions.

The legal infringements to draft the U.S. Constitution were, in conclusion, constant.

Framing the U.S. Constitution

The Philadelphia Convention represented a great opportunity for the American ruling class across the continent to re-encounter itself. Among the 55 delegates that first gathered on May 25, 1787, all of them were white males, more than half were lawyers, another quarter were owners of large commercial farms or plantations, and only two of them were small farmers from the class that made up 85 per cent of the population (Collier and Collier, 1986, p. 76). As Charles Beard highlighted (1964, p. 30), there was more identity interest among Langdon of Portsmouth, Gerry of Boston, Dayton of New Jersey, Robert Morris of Philadelphia, McHenry of Baltimore, Washington on the Potomac, Williamson of North Carolina, the Pinckneys of Charleston, and Pierce of Savannah than between these several men and their debt-burdened neighbours at the back door. Beard suggested that the decisions adopted by the framers at Philadelphia were motivated by the satisfaction of their direct personal interest. This thesis, however, has been contested by some historians (Brown, 1956; McDonald, 1958) arguing that it has not been convincingly demonstrated that only economic benefit determined the vote of delegates. The question of the scarce protection that bondholders (among whom one could count some of the delegates in the Convention) would enjoy under the constitutional provisions is an example that shows that not everything was defined by the zeal for personal enrichment. Notwithstanding this objection, one cannot affirm that the behaviour of the representatives who met at Philadelphia was not primarily conducted *by the defence of their class interest as a whole.*[16] The military organization provided in order to prevent future revolts, for instance, gives a good account on the influence of the elite's interest in outlining the constitutional institutions. The Southern planter or the creditor in Massachusetts, would feel more secure against, respectively, slave rebellions or debtors' riots since they would know that under the new constitution the governor of his State might call in the strong arm of the federal administration in case of a domestic disturbance. In this vein, it might be stated that the main issue that instigated the strength of central institutions reflected in the Federal Constitution was the threat to the "domestic tranquility" (as was included in the constitutional preamble), and this tranquillity had been put in danger by events such as the Shays' Rebellion.

As I have explained, the Shays' Rebellion had been stifled due to the initiative of the Massachusetts governor to recruit, with private funding, an army against the mob, but the circles that supported the call for the Federal Convention (and most of the delegates gathered at Philadelphia) understood that such a situation could not take place again, and that it was peremptory for the authorities to provide themselves with a stable military framework to crush any other attempt that might demolish the existing order. In short, the Philadelphia constituent process was essentially determined by the need to consolidate monopolistic exercise of physical violence in the hands of the government. The American case confirms that constitutionalism is basically related to the organization of force to defend the new order created and, particularly, to the shaping of an instrument of State violence able to repress popular violence (Elster, 2012, p. 37). Several provisions of the 1787 constitutional draft are motivated by the aforementioned strand: the goal of cracking down future Shays-like upheaval may be perceived in the authorization in Article I.8 placed in the Congress "to provide for calling forth the militia to execute the laws of the union, suppress insurrections, and repel invasions," in Article IV.4 according to which "the United States shall ... protect [every State] against invasion, and on application of the legislature, or the executive (when the legislature cannot be convened) against domestic violence," or in the affirmation in Article I.9 that "The privilege of the writ of habeas corpus shall not be suspended, unless when in cases of rebellion or invasion the public safety may require it" (Elster, 2012, p. 20). In a draft in which a bill of rights was still not incorporated even the rights there recognized, such as habeas corpus, were regulated under the possibility of suspending them in case of tumult. Although Article I.8 Clause 16 is reserved to the States, the "appointment of the officers, and the authority of training the militia" powers are developed "according to the discipline prescribed by Congress."

Generally, the whole institutional design of the Federal Constitution was conceived to put up barriers against popular participation, whether that was exercised through institutional means or through direct action. Virginia's governor and a member of the State's delegation at the Convention, Edmund Randolph, admitted that:

> Our chief danger arises from the democratic parts of our constitutions. It is a maxim which I hold incontrovertible, that the powers of government exercised by the people swallows up the other branches.
>
> (quoted by Bouton, 2007, p. 171)

In order to prevent such supposed popular abuses Randolph, as most of the other delegates, proposed a gamut of checks that would shape the famous counter-majoritarian institutions within the American constitutional system: the Founders canvassed an almost monarchical presidency with legislative veto power [which by 1787 was only acceptable through the immense prestige of the figure of George Washington who also contributed to the legitimacy of the Philadelphia Convention by chairing it (Ackerman, 2019, p. 365; Elster, 2012, p. 19)] and vested the Senate [which in the first stance was removed from direct popular control (Middlekauff, 2007, p. 673)] with decisive attributes including the appointment of the federal judiciary that later would develop the constitutional review of legislation at federal level.

From the conception of the constitution as a decision on the allocation of power that I have described, the main expression of the move experienced in Philadelphia in 1787 was the configuration of a strong central power at the service of the American upper classes. There were, however, some other controversial issues related to the decision on the framework of domination that found a solution in the constitutional draft, basically (1) the fear of the small States of a Union dominated by the larger ones and (2) the already mentioned Northern and Southern disputes concerning the question of slavery (Brant, 1950, pp. 55–70; Tushnet, 2009, p. 12).

On the first question, the solution was chiefly found through the equal representation of the States in the Senate (Collier and Collier, 1986, p. 114; Middlekauff, 2007, p. 659). That the equal representation of the States in the Senate was central in designing the U.S. constitutional architecture was revealed by the particular amendment procedure conceived to change such a point. Leaving out the particular path to amend the constitution by calling a Constitutional Convention on the application to the Congress of the legislatures of two-thirds of the States (on this procedure, see Dellinger, 1979), the equal representation of the States in the Senate created an exception to the general formal amendment rule in the constitution as established in Article V of the U.S. Constitution.

Whereas a formal amendment ordinarily requires Congress and the States, respectively, to propose a formal amendment by two-thirds vote and to ratify it by three-quarters supermajority vote, a formal amendment diminishing a State's representation in the Senate requires in addition, as provided by Article V of the U.S. Constitution, that "no State, without its Consent, shall be deprived of its equal Suffrage in the Senate." Since it is hardly conceivable that any State would consent to a change that resulted in the direct or relative diminution of its power in American federalism it has been argued that the so-called Equal Suffrage Clause concerning the States' representation in the Senate may be considered an unamendable rule (see Albert, 2019, p. 160). Furthermore, it has been assumed that a change concerning any State's deprivation of the equal suffrage in the Senate in fact requires the unanimous consent of all States (and not only the ratification by a three-quarters supermajority plus the consent of the affected State). The reason becomes clear if we consider that if any State sees its representation in the Senate reduced, all other States would see their own Senate representation altered in relation to the State that has consented in its deprivation of equal suffrage (see Albert, 2019, p. 160; Levinson, 1996, p. 122; Levinson, 2001, p. 271 and p. 284). In sum, the Equal Suffrage Clause in the Senate and its virtual unamendability might be perceived as the legal translation of one of the main pillars concerning the decision on the allocation of power that the American framers adopted in the Convention.

Small States were also satisfied by the design of the House of Representatives' composition which initially envisaged a formula of one representative for every 40,000 inhabitants (Middlekauff, 2007, p. 659) but the resulting reduced number of the lower house representatives deserved both the criticisms of the most populated States' delegates at the Convention and, afterwards, of the Anti-Federalists by accusing the federal legislature of being an instrument conceived to entrench "an aristocracy" of rulers. Before the closing of the Convention even Washington himself, as President of the body, accepted *in extremis* an amendment to strike out the proportion of 40,000 to elect a representative in the House and insert instead a 30,000 clause (Amar, 1998, pp. 12–13). But when the draft reached the Conventions for ratification, Federalists had to counteract the Anti-Federalists' accusations regarding the "aristocratic character" of the Congress by offering an amendment to the Constitution. Said amendment, the first amendment to the Constitution among the 12 proposed in the First Congress, was never approved given precisely the opposition of small States (Amar, 1998, p. 17).

Besides the special amendment procedure above mentioned concerning the Equal Suffrage Clause in the Senate, it might be observed as well that the ordinary amendment process to the Constitution, requiring at least the consent of three-quarters of the States to be approved, favoured likewise the small States, given that any structural change needed the support of some of them.

Small States' interests were also covered with the federation blueprint towards western lands. Some small north-eastern States would become bigger if a strong central government would safeguard their expansion to the west at the expense of the Indian territories. Connecticut, Pennsylvania, and Maryland contained many land speculators holding titles to territories in the West based on Indian deeds which might only be enforced through the performance of federal forces (Brant, 1950, pp. 62–65). After all, common interests among both large and small States were stronger than their differences, and that may explain why it was possible to reach an agreement, although not without strains. Large and small States supported the regulation of commerce; both feared upheavals which a national government might forestall or speedily suppress; both had a stake in solid public finance and the protection of creditors; both saw that a national government might stimulate the economy; and both saw the need for protection of the republic against external enemies (Middlekauff, 2007, pp. 647–648).

As we have seen, the constituent decision on the issue of slavery meant that the federal government would be barred from prohibiting the inter-State trade of slaves for two decades; that northern States would have the obligation to return slaves and that the apportionment of seats in the House would take slavery into account. The delegates at Philadelphia reached the so-called three-fifths compromise which was revealed as determinant for the success of the constituent Convention (Fehrenbacher, 2001, p. 44; Lynd, 1966) since it contained the differences between the Southern States claiming for the preservation of slavery and the reluctance of the Northern States to maintain it. Its effect was to give the Southern States a third more seats in Congress and a third more electoral votes than if slaves had been ignored, but fewer than if slaves and free people had been counted equally.

From the point of view of the procedural perspective, it should be pointed out that the Convention was conducted in secrecy by a small group, and the public was completely excluded, even as observers, from the discussion and deliberation of the constitutional decisions and regulations (Ginsburg, Blount, and Elkins, 2008, pp. 361–362; Rakove, 1997, p. 13). One reason for adopting the secrecy rule was related to the delegates' consciousness of the fact that if it began to come out that the Convention was considering this or that course of action, there would be a public uproar, which might set the country against the whole proceedings (Collier and Collier, 1986, p. 83). Most of the delegates (if not all of them, since the secrecy rule was not contested) suspected that they were on the verge of doing something against the opinion of the majority.

As Robert Dahl remarked, several crucial votes in June and July 1787 were taken with only 11 State delegations. In addition, votes were counted by States although members of State delegations were occasionally divided, being unable, because of their division, to cast the vote (Dahl, 2002, p. 2). The ratification process within the elected Conventions of each State would not minimize the fact that the whole constitutional architecture had been already established by a minority and that the public represented by the States' Conventions, despite some attempts, had no right to amend the constitutional product.

The ratification of the Federal Constitution

The framing of the U.S. Federal Constitution was, thus, carried out with a violation of the Articles of the Confederation. Thirty-nine of the 55 delegates dispatched to the Philadelphia Convention decided to go ahead with the new constitutional draft even though its approval procedure was not compatible with the unanimous consent of the States required by the provisions of the Confederation agreement. The unanimous consent rule of the Confederation's articles had been changed to the two-thirds consent rule, leaving out the issue of the manner in which the nine States were to signify their approval.[17] Article XIII of the Confederation foresaw that the enacting of any alteration required the confirmation of the legislatures of every State while Article VII of the Federal Constitution draft provided that the ratification shall be decided by special constitutional Conventions of the States. As Elster (1994, p. 81) rightly observed, the decision included in the constitutional draft involved *a double break* with the Articles of the Confederation, which demanded unanimous ratification by the State legislatures for all alterations. States' legislatures had been thus bypassed again by the Federalists, who succeeded in restricting the legislatures' performance only to the call for elections of the ratifying Conventions (Middlekauff, 2007, p. 680).

Supporters of the drafters' initiative have been, of course, prone to justify the conventional ratification solution under a democratic perspective. If the delegates of the Philadelphia Convention considered that they were able to act without legal warrant under the pre-existing articles, it was because they argued that they were acting in a revolutionary manner according to the will of the People (Ackerman, 1993, pp. 41–42). The ratification procedures through the States'

Conventions were regarded as an expression of democratic deliberation able both to sustain constitutional supremacy (Richards, 1992–1993, p. 587) and to justify the breach of previous existing legal rules.

Such was the theory outlined by James Wilson in Pennsylvania ratifying the Convention when he refuted the idea held by the Anti-Federalists according to which the approval of the Federal Constitution and the violation of the Articles of the Confederation undermined the States' sovereignty. Wilson (quoted by Wood, 1998, pp. 530–531) said:

> In all governments, whatever their form, however they may be constituted, there must be a power established from which there is no appeal, and which is therefore called absolute, supreme, and uncontrollable. The only question is where that power is lodged? … for in truth, it remains and flourishes with the people … . The supreme power *resides* in the People, as the fountain of government.

The invocation of "the People" covered the legal breach. In the early years of the American Revolution, the people's constituent power was considered to be external to and above the constitutional order (see Jacobsohn and Roznai, 2020, p. 228; Partlett, 2017). That has been a usual move within the history of constitutionalism to confer authority to elude the existing institutions (Kay, 1987, p. 72). Alexander Hamilton stressed as well the need for recourse to the sovereign people in circumventing the State legislatures and proposing the ratification by special State Conventions ("Federalist 22," Hamilton, Madison and Jay 1989, pp. 145–146) and, decades later, Chief Justice Marshall in *M'Culloch versus Maryland* also insisted on the Constitution's direct origin from the People while denying the authorship of the States' sovereignties [*M'Culloch v. Maryland*, 17 U.S. 316, 363, 377–378, 403–405 (1819) see Gilhooley, 2019, pp. 100–104]. The idea was that whereas for ordinary decisions of law and government, the ordinary lawmaking institutions might be adequate surrogates for "the People," in a constituent process "the People" would have to speak with an alternative voice able to transcend the agencies of government (Palmer, 1966, pp. 354–357). Also, Madison focused on the special popular participation as a measure to repair the breach of the previous legal framework. In "Federalist 40," Madison wrote (Hamilton, Madison and Jay, 1989, pp. 265–266):

> The delegates must have reflected that in all great changes of established governments, forms ought to give way to substance … . They must have borne in mind, that as the plan to be framed and proposed, was to be submitted *to the people themselves*, the disapprobation of this supreme authority would destroy it forever; its approbation blot out all antecedent errors and irregularities.

Thus "the unanimous consent" of the States was sacrificed by giving prevalence to the will of "the People:" in 1787 not only "the People" within the States but the "We the People of the United States" as mentioned in the preface of the Federal Constitution. However, it is difficult to sustain that the will of "the People" was expressed during the ratification of the new constitutional framework. Rather, the genealogical analysis shows to what extent the approval of the federal government depended on the mobilization of a minority rather than on the consent of the majority.

To begin, the involvement of the People, according to the Federalists, did not represent a call to direct democratic channels of participation. Thus, as in Madison's view, thousands of people could not have immediately and equally participated in the countless specific decisions implicated in drafting a Constitution clause by clause (Amar, 2006, p. 14). In a different sense, and according to the Founders thought, large-scale direct referenda would have prevented the ultimate ratification votes from benefiting from detailed presentation of competing arguments. Would it be fair to ask every voter in America to drop everything for so long a period? But such arguments provided by Madison and his fellow Federalists in support of representation against popular referenda do not conceal that the representative argument for the Conventions did not affect the role of the legislatures as a representative body, the annulment of which, as we have seen, constituted the real agenda of the Philadelphia drafters.

The Convention method supposedly provided a reinforcement of the political participation of citizenry in the approval of the Constitution since the draft would be ratified not by the people's ordinary representatives but by special delegates chosen for the occasion. This *ad hoc* character of selection of candidates fostered, first, that only the personalities most favourable to the federal project would be inclined to present their candidatures to the Conventions' elections; and second, as some critics noticed (Beard, 1964, p. 219) that being the delegates chosen by "the People" for the particular purpose of ratifying the Constitution, the subject would be more candidly discussed and the supporters of the Constitution would better be able to concentrate their campaign of persuasion than if the debate had taken place in the legislatures. The idea of Conventions provided to the drafters a perfect masquerade to pretend that "the People" had concurred in the approval of the new federal government while, in fact, all the process would have been developed with the marginalization of a great part of the population.

As suggested above, if there had been any real intention of the framers to submit the approval of the Federal Constitution to "the People," there would have always been the possibility to call for a popular referendum on the approval or the rejection of the draft in each State. Nevertheless, the idea was precisely to take away the Constitutional debate from populism, and this solution would have left, as Edmund Randolph observed, the discussion on the new constitutional framework at the mercy of the local demagogues (quoted by Beard, 1964, p. 219). Besides that, it should be noticed that there had already been some negative experiences within the States on popular votes regarding the approval of a Constitution, such as the Massachusetts Constitutional draft passed by the legislative body but rejected by the voters in 1778 (Richards, 1989, p. 19; Palmer, 1968, p. 349). The framers of the Federal Constitution were not willing to risk again the construction of the central government leaving the final decision on the new legal framework to the people at large.[18]

Though stated that the Federal Constitution was an expression of the will of the whole "People," without the submission of the popular vote it is difficult to determine to what extent how many of "the People" favoured the adoption of the new instrument. "The People" were only allowed to participate in choosing the delegates to the State Conventions and a considerable proportion of the adult white male population was debarred from participating in the elections of delegates to the ratifying State Conventions by the prevailing property qualifications on suffrage. Despite the lack of materials regarding the vote on delegates to the States Convention in each town and county, there are some signs and data coming from dispersed places that demonstrate the tiny percentage of the population involved in the vote on the delegates. From such percentages related to the population entitled to vote [which run between 5 per cent and 10 per cent in the counties where some data are available (Beard, 1964, p. 244)] might be inferred a low turnout. The latter would indicate that the Federalists would have been successful in ensuring that the debate on the Federal Constitution would not generally have inspired the attention of the masses and, thus, that the supporters of the new regime were the ones more inclined to be mobilized.

In a different way, the Federalists were able to control the whole ratification process in the States, conducting the calling from the States' Conventions, the elections of delegates, and the deliberation and voting in the Conventions with unseemly haste, in order to impede the organization of the opposition. Such tactics were especially intense in Pennsylvania,[19] Connecticut, New Jersey, Georgia, and Delaware. In places where the new instrument was more contested, some irregularities were perceived both in the processes to elect delegates and in the developments of the Convention, so happening in Virginia (Ackerman and Katyal, 1995, pp. 530–533) in New York, in New Hampshire, and in Massachusetts, where the popular vote had been adverse for the Federalists, probably because in such States property qualifications for the vote had been set aside in the 1788 election for the Conventions (Amar, 2006, p. 7). At any rate, the conversion of some a priori Anti-Federalist delegates secured the ratification of the Constitution (Ackerman and Katyal, 1995, pp. 526–530; Beard, 1964, pp. 237–238; McDonald, 1958, p. 183). Such a combination of Federalists' manoeuvres at the different phases of the ratification procedure in order to disarticulate the popular opposition to the Constitution and foster the action of the supporters to the central government might be condensed in the following remarks recited by 21 members of the Pennsylvania Convention who opposed the ratification (quoted by Beard, 1964, pp. 233–234):

> The convention was called by a legislature made up in part of members who had been dragged to their seats and kept there against their wills, and so early a day was set for the election of delegates that many a voter did not know of until it was passed. Others kept away from the polls because they were

> ignorant of the new plan; some because they disliked it and some because they did not think the convention legally called.

The irregularities that tarnished the calling and gathering of some Conventions within the States did not hinder, however, that when New Hampshire became the ninth State to ratify the Constitution (doing so in June 1788), the general view that the constitutional draft had been made law was entrenched (Barczentewicz, 2019, p. 85; Maier, 2010, p. ix).

The Federalists, in spite of such success, did not obtain the ratification of Rhode Island and North Carolina in the first instance. Both were not brought into the Union until the new federal government was established, and both were convinced with an intense economic pressure that made the isolation of such States unviable (Ackerman and Katyal, 1995, p. 480). The prospect of coercion exercised by the government of the United States was especially intense in the case of Rhode Island, which was combined with the threat of domestic insurrection since the city of Providence planned to join other Federalist towns and to seek the protection of the federal government (Beard, 1964, pp. 235–237).

To sum up, the Federalists manipulated the invocation of "the People" during the ratification process by alienating substantial parts of society that had been politically active during the independence of the American States and the years of the Confederation. Looking at such developments allowed, for instance, Governor Clinton of New York to charge that the Federal Constitution had been "founded in usurpation" (quoted by Kay, 1984, p. 159) and that a significant part of the Anti-Federalists struggles were oriented in claiming that the Constitution had been the result of a conspiracy of the wealthy to betray the Revolution by imposing a kind of aristocratic government (Banning, 1978, p. 115). The Founders would not let radical democratic initiatives go further in the government or in defining the framework that would rule the community in the future.

The bill of rights

Several delegates at Philadelphia considered that it was not necessary to incorporate a bill of rights into the text of the Constitution since the Federation would not be conferred with powers able to abridge citizen's liberties. James Wilson, for instance, argued that the Congress would not be able to regulate issues in which free press or other traditional rights were concerned (quoted by Middlekauff, 2007, p. 677):

> it would have been superfluous and absurd to have stipulated with a federal body of our own creation, that we should enjoy those privileges, of which we are not divested either by the intention or the act, that has brought that body into existence.

In a similar vein, Madison emphasized that federalism, that is, the precise enumeration of the powers given to the national government, and the separation of powers would both emerge as guarantees to protect fundamental rights (Tushnet, 2009, pp. 15–16). But during the ratification campaign, Madison himself and other Federalists realized that the absence of a bill of rights in the constitutional draft was the Anti-Federalists' most politically effective argument (see Kenyon, 1955, pp. 18–21) and that the success of the establishment of a central government hinged on the promise that the Constitution would soon be amended in order to add the rights able to be invoked at the federal level. It is likely that the Federalist commitment to fundamental rights was crucial for the ratification of the Constitution in New York where the fight with the opposition was close. The debate around the bill of rights was also relevant at both the Massachusetts and Virginia Conventions (Middlekauff, 2007, pp. 682–683). Afterwards, when the Constitution entered into force and the elections to the first Congress were organized, Madison went to the campaign for the seat in the House of Representatives (the Virginia legislature had already refused to elect him to the Senate) upholding as well the promise to introduce a bill of rights (Tushnet, 2009, p. 17). Consequently, in the same fashion as had happened in the Revolution during the drafting of the States' constitutions, the elites were obliged to proclaim fundamental rights if they wished to gain popular support for their cause. In other words, rights were recognized in constitutional provisions not because the leaders of the process believed in liberty but because *they had no other alternative if they wanted to consolidate their power.*

Once assumed by people such as Madison or Hamilton that there would not be federation without rights, they did their best to redirect the sense of the bill of rights to the general intention that they had in building the national government, that is, *to make a strong central government able to trump the States* in case of dissidences. The federal bill of rights was not conceived as a device to limit the power but *to create* power. On the first stance this move did not accomplish its goals but, nevertheless, it laid the foundations for the constitutional change that would take place more than half a century later with the Reconstruction.

If we look closer at the elaboration of the current First Amendment (I leave aside now the circumstance that the first and the second original amendment proposals were not ratified in 1791), we shall find that Madison had in mind to protect "freedom of speech," "freedom of the press," or "free exercise of religion" *from State interference*, the action of which through the majorities gathered in the State legislatures, was deemed more dangerous than any eventual regulation provided by the federal Congress (Amar, 1998, p. 22). Madison's proposal, however, was not passed in the Senate and the possibility to include, for instance, the speech and press clauses against the States would have to wait until the approval of the Equal Protection Clause of the 14th Amendment occurred after the Civil War.

It may be argued that Federalists had more success in using the bill of rights to strength the Federation vis-à-vis the States through other clauses such as the Second Amendment, guaranteeing the right to raise "a well-regulated Militia, being necessary to security of a free State" and "the right of the people to keep and bear Arms." The argument might be outlined by underscoring the authority that Article I of the Constitution gives to the Congress to federalize the "well-regulated Militia" of the Second Amendment and eventually launching against States in case of insurrection (Amar, 1998, p. 54). But it seems that the bill of rights' drafters, being still afresh from the fight against Great Britain, were rather thinking of the Second Amendment as a right of the People to raise arms in the case of a tyrannical regression of a general government or in the case of an abusive behaviour of the federal army (though the wording of the Amendment speaks of "a free *State*"). Again, it would be the experience of the Civil War that would incorporate the Second Amendment as a limit on the encroaching liberties exercised by individual States.

The considerations of the ten first amendments to the U.S. Constitution here presented allow me to stress the already mentioned (in the previous chapter) difference between a "constitutional amendment" and a "constitutional transformation." As suggested, the 1791 inclusion of the bill of rights was achieved without great convulsions and the promise of its drafting made by the Federalists represented a relevant argument to persuade the representatives in the Conventions where the ratification had to be discussed. The bill of rights, thus, as some scholars argued (Berkin, 2002, p. 179; Collier and Collier, 1986, pp. 249–250), rather than being perceived as a constitutional change, it might even be doubted if it was a constitutional amendment at all (though formally it was) or a mere *epigone* of the constitutional foundation. The point here is that the violence and open wars that accompanied some of the further U.S. constitutional developments accurately illustrate to what extent a real constitutional change, a structural one, is rather linked to extreme conflicts and political catastrophes than to public involvement and deliberations. Precisely the different role of the bill of rights bestowed by the 14th Amendment and its capacity to be invoked, from the Civil War onwards, against the States, demonstrates that idea.

Constituent power and beyond: constitutional transformations

Violence embedded any subsequent rearrangement of the U.S. constitutional system beginning with the territorial enlargement of the federation. The absorption of new territories and their conversion into new States of the Union were only possible through a reinforcement of the Federal authorities' military resources that the constitutional draft had foreseen. The expansion of the Union, from the conflicts with the indigenous peoples shortly after the constitutional establishment (Dunbar-Ortiz, 2014, pp. 81–94) to the clashes with the armies of European monarchies or, later, with authorities of other recently independent countries (such as México) was the outcome of many acts of violence. Constitutional changes enshrined in the early American national period such as the ones related to the right of suffrage, to the formation of political parties, or to the conception of the presidency which appeared during Andrew Jackson's era (Tushnet, 2009, pp. 20–21) were also the product of wars, population removals, or secessionist crises.

The involvement of violence in American constitutional transformations is self-evident in describing the consequences of the Civil War for the legal system: the nationalization of the protection of individual rights against States' abridgments, the abolition of slavery, the configuration of "equal protection" and "due process of law," the emergence of safeguards on voting rights against racial discrimination, and the changes in the interaction between Federal Law and States Law (Ackerman, 1993, pp. 82–83; on the interpretative consequences of the Civil War see Monaghan, 1981, p. 356). In short, the strength of the central authority boosted by the Republican nationalism that accompanied the Reconstruction was not a product of the people gathered and deliberating but the corollary of military conflict (Levinson, 2004, pp. 461, 471). Reconstruction depended on maintaining the Union by the force of arms between 1861 to 1865 (Levinson, 2014, p. 2656).

The relationship between the North and the defeated South after the Civil War, as Noah Feldman pointed out (2004–2005, p. 859) resembled those historical scenarios in which a constitutional settlement is imposed by a foreign power, such as the examples that in the twentieth century will be developed in postwar Japan or Germany. Occupied Southern States in the aftermath of the Civil War were refused to be represented in Congress and to be readmitted to the Union until they ratified the 13th and the 14th Amendments to the Federal Constitution (Levinson, 2014, p. 2657). The political will of the Union was, thus, expressed independently of the true will of the "renegade States that had illegitimately made war upon the Union" (Tribe, 1995, pp. 1294). The constitutional transformations experienced in such a context were, thus, clearly a consequence of an act of force and a military occupation. Even the United States Supreme Court in reviewing the validity of some measures passed by the States that seceded from the Union in 1861 admitted that the legitimacy of its decision declaring void such acts of rebellion *was a matter of something conquered by force*. While in judgements such as *Texas v. White* [74 U.S. 700 (1869)] such a conclusion remained more or less concealed, in *Daniels v. Tearney*, for instance, the Court openly declared:

> That the ordinance of secession was void is a proposition we need not discuss. The affirmative has been settled by the arbitrament of arms.
>
> [*Daniels v. Tearney*, 102 U.S. 415 (1880)]

Bruce Ackerman (1998, pp. 21–22) also openly admits that violence was in the grounding of U.S. constitutional amendments during the Reconstruction:

> Granted, there is something fishy about the Fourteenth Amendment. But surely Reconstruction was an exceptional time, full of the passions of the Civil War. It was the blood and sacrifice at battles like Gettysburg not the nationalistic model of constitutional change, that legitimated the Civil War amendments.

But Ackerman not only highlights the importance of battlefield victories in exploring what lies behind a successful constitutional transformation. He also emphasizes the involvement of a different conception in changing the Constitution. In Ackerman's approach, unconventional political reform is likely to be coached by political initiatives that succeed in presenting themselves as speaking in the name of the People. The point that rather arises in such analysis is that the unconventional innovation of the constitutional order *is a necessary* condition to achieve constitutional transformation and that such illegal struggle is but the consequence of the violence previously unleashed. The American Reconstruction after the Civil War (and also the American Founding) represented a constitutional transformation since it was sustained by both the battles and the legal breakup. Thus – it is from the legal breakup, backed by violence, that higher lawmaking emerges.

The American Civil War and the Reconstruction Amendments also reveal both (1) the nature of constitutional rules as legal translation of dominant powers and (2) the notion of constitutional transformation regarding the decision on a new allocation of powers. Even though the issue of slavery finally dominated the vision that persisted around the Civil War and the constitutional developments that accompanied it [an idea proclaimed by Lincoln when he recognized that only the constitutional abolition of slavery would give the war an enduring and constitutional meaning (quoted by Richards, 1992–1993, p. 590)] the American conflict had its background in a fight for power among different groups of American citizenry that had been socially, economically, and legally differentiated since the beginning of the Federation. The American Civil War was primarily a consequence of challenging the Union by those in the South who sought to gain more power within another political structure (Buchanan, 1991, p. 1). There was a clash among groups and the triumph of one group upon another that only incidentally left the benefit of emancipating the slaves and advancing in terms of human rights among a more general reconfiguration of the American constitutional structure. As we have seen, nevertheless, since the elites of the South persisted after the Civil War, the constitutional transformation was not complete, and the effectiveness of the Reconstruction Amendments had to wait almost a century to be appreciated through the so-called Civil Rights Revolution.

In a different sense, the very notion of the American People (Weiler, 2003, p. 56; Ackerman, 1997, p. 792) was not obvious in the self-conscience of the American citizens since, precisely, the aftermath of the Civil War and the Reconstruction. In other words, a Civil War was needed to create the idea of a unitary people, sustaining the legitimacy of the Federal Constitution. Before then, the "We the People of the United States" was a more ambiguous notion given the association with the State's citizenship and the discussion on sovereign attributes of the State. The view according to which the Union was an agreement among the States grounded the interposition and nullification theories concerning the role of the states in determining as a final authority the limits of federal government's power and their capacity to reject, or nullify, the federal law passed *ultra vires* (Corwin, 1950, p. 10). Such debates would last until the challenge posed by Southern States' secession and the victory of the North. As Ackerman (2014,

p. 30) wrote also regarding the transformations of the American constitutional system that followed the Civil War:

> Only the bloodbath of the Civil War gave birth to a stronger national identity. In contrast to the Founders, Reconstruction Republicans won the authority to declare, in the Fourteenth Amendment, that national citizenship was primary and state citizenship was secondary. With these words, the Republicans aimed to transform the Federalists' state-centered federation into a nation-centered federation.

It may be argued that in the case of Ackerman's third constitutional moment, the struggle between Franklin D. Roosevelt's Presidency and the Supreme Court during the Great Depression, was the only genuine democratic transformation. But the global background of such developments was anything except calm. The First World War, from which the United States had emerged as a great new industrial power, was not so distant. The America economic and social counter model, the Soviet Union, had precisely stemmed from the ashes of the Great War, and the shadow of the First World War would expand over American society especially once the stock market crashed in 1929, and the illusion of prosperity that had dominated the twenties, vanished. Assuming that, as Eric Hobsbawm classically affirmed (1996, pp. 36–37) the First World War and the Second World War were indeed the same conflict that began in 1914, the American constitutional changes in the 1930s would have been established in the very middle of such an age of extremes. The Great Depression, furthermore, that was the immediate antecedent of Roosevelt's challenge, was itself tarnished by some violent episodes as well. On March 7, 1932, there took place, for instance, the so-called "Ford Hunger March" in which more than 3,000 unemployed workers demonstrated going from Detroit to Dearborn in an attempt to present some demands to the Ford Motor Company. The march resulted in four workers being shot to death by the Dearborn Police Department and security guards employed by the Ford Company (a fifth worker died some months later) and over 60 workers injured. In late spring and summer of 1932 an assemblage of First World War veterans and their families (known as the Bonus army) gathered in Washington in order to demand cash-payment redemption of their service certificates. The World War Adjusted Compensation Act of 1924 had awarded them bonuses in the form of certificates they could not redeem until 1945. Each service certificate, issued to a qualified veteran soldier, bore a face value equal to the soldier's promised payment plus compound interest. Since the Great Depression had expelled the veterans from the labour market and they were sunk into poverty, they demanded the immediate cash payment of their certificates. Two veterans were shot by Washington Police, and one died. Afterwards, President Hoover ordered the army to clear the veterans' campsite and General MacArthur launched a brutal cavalry charge against the veterans, their families, and the camp followers which was followed by the intervention of the infantry using fixed bayonets and tear gas.

Strikes and violent conflicts carried on also during President Roosevelt's first mandate in spite of his reformist agenda and the new frame of relations between workers and employers. Workers' protests were answered also by employer campaigns in defence of entrepreneurial freedom. Moreover, the lack of jobs triggered an explosion of racism since the desperate white workers struggled to snatch the low paid jobs previously assigned to the blacks.

And the convulsive consequences of the Great Depression led to another open global conflict. In this sense, it might be suggested that the constitutional changes developed in the New Deal needed the experience of the Second World War to be consolidated. It was not only the democratic expression of "the People" in 1940 supporting Roosevelt for a third presidential term that solidified the Democrats' new constitutional conception. It was rather what followed from the Pearl Harbour attack in December 1941 that decided the fate of the New Deal measures introduced in the thirties. According to such an interpretation, if in the two previous constitutional moments (the Founding and the Civil War) violence occurred at the beginning of the political events that crystallized in the constitutional regulation (or throughout their evolution) in the third one, the New Deal, the most acute expression of violence appeared at the end of the process in the form of a total war. The Second World War was, thus, a challenge that the New Deal's constitutional transformations helped to overcome and, at the same time, the context that conferred permanence to changes from which the modern constitutional configuration of America was born.

The next stage of the American constitutional transformations, the Civil Rights Revolution, was also defined by upheavals and horrendous crimes. The opening of the civil rights debate, symbolized by the Supreme Court decision *Brown v. Board of Education* [347 U.S. 483 (1954)], happened within an atmosphere of violent racism that was corroding American society during that time.

From the issuing of *Brown* to the passing of the 1968 Fair Housing Act there was a gap of almost 15 years plagued by all sort of attacks, murders, vandalism, and riots, including the assassination of the United States President, John Fitzgerald Kennedy, on November 22, 1963, and the assassination of the leader of the Civil Rights Movement, Martin Luther King, Jr., on April 4, 1968. In such a context of social unrest and fierce confrontations with the background of persistent racial discrimination, it is quite doubtful to state that the constituent moment represented by *Brown*, and the statutes that followed the Supreme Court's decision (the 1964 Civil Rights Act, the 1965 Voting Rights Act, and the mentioned 1968 Fair Housing Act) was a transformation grounded in a calmed debate.

Finally, in order to view some recent debates on American possible constitutional changes, I refer to the issue of mass murders and the right of the People to keep and bear arms according to the Second Amendment to the Federal Constitution. The fact that such controversy was not explicitly displayed through the formal channels of constitutional change[20] did not exclude its constitutional character. After all, the American constitutional changes in the twentieth century relied more on judicial adjudication (or even on judicial appointments) rather than on formal amendments (Jackson, 2015, p. 576).

The right to bear arms was inherited from a period in which the monopolization of the use of the force by the State was not complete, and citizens themselves were called to protect order by their own means. It could be argued even that an inherent social contract in modern societies by which citizens deliver their means of warfare to the State in order to receive the protection of the public authorities was not concluded in all its terms in American constitutional history. It might be thought that the right to bear arms reveals to what extent freedom within a political community requires the means of self-protection that were exercised before said political community was constituted [or, as some authors affirm (Scarry, 1991, p. 1257) that the social contract is precisely ensured by the fact that the population carries guns, the "We the People" would, thus, be inextricably associated with "We, the Armed People"]. Either way, the permanence of the right of the People to keep and bear arms in the core of the U.S. Constitutional system also confirms, in spite of the time that has elapsed from the Foundation, the links between current constitutional developments and the origins of the Constitution. Any constitutional change regarding such an issue, through formal constitutional amendment or through constitutional reinterpretation, and given the problem of social violence surrounding the constitutional debate, would never be free of a background of destruction. A constitutional transformation on the right to bear arms would have required a great deal of victims (*homines* and *mulieres sacri* in Agamben's terminology). The latter would have been not only those fallen as a consequence of the colonizers' self-protection in the first steps of American history [Hartmann (2019, pp. 6–9) calls this the unholy alliance between genocide and guns] but would also be the children murdered in American schools during the last decades by disturbed people who had been constitutionally authorized to bear weapons designed for mass murder.

The Supreme Court sought to reinterpret the right to bear arms dismissing a Second Amendment challenge regarding a California regulation which provided a ten-day waiting period for new gun purchases. But during Donald Trump's Presidency, a more profound constitutional debate on that issue was blocked due to President Trump's firm support of a wide conception of the right in dispute. The Presidential position did not change despite the crimes that occurred during his term of office. Instead of reconsidering the scope of the Second Amendment, the solution proposed by the chief magistrate concerned the militarization of classroom teachers making, consequently, more evident the original link between the right to bear arms and the right of self-defence. Under such a conception, thus, the exercise of legal violence would be shared by the State and the individuals just as happened in the stages that preceded the consolidation of the modern State.

Notes

1 On the 1639 Fundamental Orders of Connecticut see, for instance, Kay, 1984, p. 134 n.112.
2 Such historical remarks represent one of the main objections to the constitutional theory in the West as was developed by James Tully in his survey of 400 years of

constitutional practice with special attention to the American Aboriginal question, see Tully, 1995.

3 On the issue of American Slavery in the origins of the United States see, among many others, Berlin, 2004; Feagin, 2014; Fehrenbacher, 2001; Horton and Horton, 2005; Mason, 2006; Pettigrew, 2007; Richards, 2000.

4 A good summary on the position of the Indian Tribes within the U.S. Constitutional system and its evolution may be found in Breda, 2018, pp. 142–148.

5 On the social conflicts during the creation of the American Republic see, among many others, the works of Charles Beard (1964) and Merrill Jensen (among them see Jensen, 1964, 1967, and 1976). See, more recently, the contribution of Terry Bouton (2007).

6 The only State that adopted in its new constitution a one-chamber legislature besides Pennsylvania was Georgia but it is likely that such a decision was more related to the circumstance that Georgia already had one chamber as a representative body under the British rule than to Pennsylvania's revolutionary influence (Palmer, 1968, p. 358). In fact, Pennsylvania itself had only a one-chamber legislature during the colonist regime in a way that one can doubt if also some of the Pennsylvania revolutionary constitutional arrangements were not somehow rooted in the previous political tradition.

7 Madison wrote on Rhode Island: "a large sum has been struck down and made a tender, and coin. The consequence is that provisions are withheld from the Market, the Shops shut up ... a general distress and tumultuous meetings." See Madison, 1979, p. 89. Later Madison wrote in *The Federalist 51* that "it can be little doubted that if the State of Rhode Island was separated from the Confederacy and left to itself, the insecurity of rights under the popular form of government within such narrow limits would be displayed by such reiterated oppressions of factious majorities that some power altogether independent of the people would soon be called for by the voice of the very factions whose misrule had proved the necessity of it" (see Madison et al., 1989, p. 352).

8 Among the oceanic literature on the Shays' Rebellion see Fritz, 2008, pp. 80–116; McDonald, 1968, pp. 103–107; Richards, 2002, and Szatmary, 1980. On the consequences of the Shays' Rebellion for the creation of the Federation and the calling of the constitutional Convention at Philadelphia see Elster, 2012, p. 9. Ackerman (1998, p. 44) in a different position, minimizes the role of the Rebellion as a catalyzer of the constitutional Convention.

9 On James Madison's theory of the faction and its influence in American constitutional creation see Richards (1992–1993).

10 Johnson to Iredell, December 9, 1776, quoted in Wood, 1998, p. 477.

11 Charleston *Columbian Herald*, September 23, 1785 quoted in Wood, 1998, p. 477.

12 Jay to Hamilton, May 8, 1778, quoted in Wood, 1998, p. 477.

13 Johnson to Iredell, December 9, 1776, quoted in Wood, 1998, p. 477.

14 Madison to Jefferson, October 17, 1788 quoted in Wood, 1998, p. 410.

15 On this point see also Jacobson (2014, p. 9) and Levinson (2004, p. 468). Levinson considered that the "1787 Constitution could itself be viewed as a secessionist act."

16 It should be mentioned that Beard's thesis in the hard sense of finding a direct correlation between the Philadelphia delegates' economic interest and the decisions adopted while drafting the constitution had been rehabilitated in the last decades of the twentieth century and the beginning of the twenty first with the works of McGuire and Ohsfeldt (McGuire and Ohsfeldt, 1984 and McGuire, 2003). See on this debate also Heckelman and Dougherty, 2007.

17 According to Article XIII of the Confederation and Perpetual Union "the Articles of this confederation shall be inviolably observed by every state, and the union shall be perpetual; nor shall any alteration at any time hereafter be made in any of them; unless such alteration be agreed to in a congress of the united states, and be afterwards confirmed by the legislatures of every state." Article VII of the original Constitution provides: "The Ratification of the Conventions of nine States shall be sufficient for the Establishment of this Constitution between the States so ratifying the same." On the break of Article XIII of the Confederation by Article VII of the 1787 U.S. Constitution draft see Ackerman, 1993, pp. 41–42 and 168; Ackerman and Katyal, 1995, pp. 470–480; Kay, 1987, p. 68. Van Middelaar, in comparing the creation of the American Federation with the European integration process, offers a candid reading on the passing of Article VII of the Federal Constitution according to which "it is curious that the revolutionary Article VII was so little disputed" (Van Middelaar, 2013, p. 85). However, the apparent lack of controversy concerning such an article that might have been appreciated during its approval at the Convention does not minimize the criticism of the departure from the Confederation's rules of amendment during the ratification process and after, to the extent that the question regarding the position of the States vis-à-vis the Union would be central throughout the American history of the nineteenth century until the Civil War and the Reconstruction. For an argument on the adjustment to the law of treaties of the Philadelphia Constitutional Convention's departure from the rules of amendment under the Articles of the Confederation see Amar, 1994, p. 465. Amar's approach, following Madison's arguments, holds that according to the law of the treaties, the breach of the Articles by some States allowed others to declare them void. On this point see also Ackerman and Katyal, 1995, pp. 509 and 547 and Tribe, 1995, p. 1289. In "Federalist 43" Madison wrote: "[I]t is an established doctrine on the subject of treaties, that all the articles are mutually conditions of each other; that a breach of any one article is a breach of the whole treaty; and that a breach committed by either of the parties absolves the others; and authorizes them, if they please, to pronounce the treaty violated and void;" see Hamilton, Madison and Jay, 1989, p. 297. Madison had raised the breached-treaty argument at the Philadelphia Convention as well. For example, on June 5, 1787, he noted, "[A]s far as the articles of Union were to be considered as a Treaty only of a particular sort, among the Governments of Independent States, the doctrine might be set up that a breach of any one article, by any of the parties, absolved the other parties from <the whole> obligation. For these <reasons as well as others> he thought it indispensable that the new Constitution should be ratified in the most unexceptionable form." See Farrand, 1966, pp. 122–123.

18 There was a State, however, in which a referendum on the Federal Constitution was held and the draft was rejected: Rhode Island. See Ackerman and Katyal, 1995, p. 527.

19 Pennsylvania's Constitution required a six-month pause between the time amendments were proposed and the time a Convention would be elected. The Federalists pushed forward with a plan to hold an election within nine days in order to catch their opponents by surprise. See Ackerman and Katyal, 1995, pp. 517–519 and 525.

20 A constitutional debate developed in the last decades more centred in triggering the Article V U.S. Constitution might be found in the reaction to the U.S. Supreme Court decision *Citizens United v. Federal Election Comm'n* 558 U.S. 310 (2010) seeking to override the Court's decision, a case holding that cor-

porations may spend unlimited amounts of money in federal elections as long as they do not coordinate their spending with candidates (Albert, 2019, pp. 177–178). However, no constitutional change according to the opposition to Citizens United has taken place neither under a formal constitutional amendment nor under a different constitutional adjudication (see Jackson, 2015, pp. 584–590).

4 Constituent power without "We the People"

The foundation of the Federal Republic of Germany

Introduction

To date, the constitutional system of the Federal Republic of Germany may be considered one of the most successful political experiences among the liberal democracies. Even though there is widespread awareness of the violent origins of that system (linked to the total collapse of the Nazi regime in a way that is difficult to conceive a constitutional rule more dependent on the crimes and coercions that surrounded its birth), less shared is the perception of the scarce involvement of the citizenry in the adoption of the fundamental decisions in Germany's constitutional history from 1949.

While in the twenty-first century people's participation, as we have seen, has been a recurrent topic concerning the constituent processes that have taken place in some parts of the world, few observers have remarked to what extent the German system is far from fulfilling *any* of the democratic requirements that now are so passionately discussed and claimed regarding other constituent scenarios. It may be argued, with a certain wicked intention, that, given the previous experiences of the twentieth century, depriving the German people from participating in the constituent debate is an important factor on which the success of the model has relied.

The silence about Germany in regard to the democratic constitution-making process is still more shocking considering that the Germans had another opportunity to trigger a participative revision of their constitutional framework in a more peaceful and placid context, as was the one that followed the fall of the Berlin Wall in 1989. Instead, they relinquished any coaching of Germany's national reunification with a broad popular involvement on the new constitutional foundations. I may doubt, accordingly, that in spite of the profound political significance of the absorption of the former German Democratic Republic, this move might be considered a "constitutional transformation" at all. The strict continuity with the system of the 1949 Basic Law, from Bonn, and the fact that the final outcome represented little more than a mere expansion in terms of territory and population makes one rather associate the events of 1989–1990 with a "constitutional amendment" in the sense that I have used in this book: a change that does not affect the core decision on the allocation of power.

German constitutional developments have been also, as reflected in my theory, processes conducted by the elites. Although the German political cadres in the constitutional-making phase represented a break with the immediate, Nazi, past the *economic* elites in Western Germany that were behind the political decisions adopted in 1949 had been involved to a great extent with the previous regime (Arendt, 1976, pp. 326–339) and, as we shall see, would assume progressively a relevant role in the governance of the new republic with the consent of the Western Allied Powers. Unsurprisingly, Bruce Ackerman (2015, p. 710) also views the Basic Law as the product of "elite construction" which in his account means that it is "not a revolutionary creation." The German path to constitutionalism would thus be an example of a constitutional order emerging from the embers of an old regime boosted by cadres (including some of those involved in the Third Reich) who, despite their claims to have acted in the name of the people, generate a new constitutional order in the absence of any genuine popular participation (see on this point also Jacobsohn and Roznai, 2020, p. 134).

Obviously, the presence of the Soviet Union and the beginning of the Cold War by the winter of 1948 would instigate the leadership of the United States and Great Britain (France was another matter) to tolerate the redemption of the German industrialists and bankers that had behaved themselves in compliance with Hitler's regime. If the German Federal Republic had to be in the first line of the fight against Communism and if that struggle decisively depended on the economic success of the Western part of Germany vis-à-vis its Eastern counterpart, liberal democracies needed to co-opt the German economic powers by forgetting their previous political allegiances (see, among many other historians, Mazower, 2008, p. 575).

The reunification process in 1990 was also a process monopolized by both the political and the economic elites of Western Germany with the consent of the victors of the Second World War. As I will point out, the constitutional system resulting from the incorporation of the five new *Länder* was not developed through any constitutional Convention nor through a vote of the German citizenry in a referendum. Chancellor Helmut Kohl, the figure that led the process, from the Christian Democratic Union, would not allow the leftists from the former Eastern Germany (or even the socialists from Western Germany itself) to become a majority in an eventual constituent Convention nor to exercise a relevant role in transforming the German constitution with a more social and egalitarian blueprint (see Ackerman, 2015, p. 711 and 2019, p. 20).

But let us now examine the time in which the present Germany has its origins from the constitutional point of view, and that means to place us in the scenario that stemmed from the immediate aftermath of a war that Germany lost.

Die Stunde Null

The strongest constitutional culture in Europe departs from a constituent power deprived from the People.[1] The German Basic Law was the direct consequence of one of the most outrageous periods of violence that humankind has seen, the Second World War and the defeat of the Nazi regime, and the path that led to its drafting was accompanied by all sorts of coercion caused by the Allied occupation, in terms of physical destruction, imprisonments, displacements, and vengeances.[2] Laying aside some three million dead German soldiers, by May 7, 1945, at least 1.8 million German civilians had perished and 3.6 million homes had been destroyed (20 per cent of the total) leaving 7.5 million homeless. As many as 16.5 million Germans were to be driven from their homes. Of these some two and a quarter million would die during the expulsions from the south and east (McDonogh, 2009, p. 1). Approximately 12 million Germans were expelled from areas in Eastern Europe considered German for hundreds of years such as Pomerania, East Brandenburg, Lower and Upper Silesia, East Prussia, and the port of Danzig (De Zayas, 2006, p. 156; Lowe, 2013, p. 231). Such was one of the biggest removals of people in modern history (if not in all of humankind's history). The scenario of Germany by the end of the war, and to some extent, of great areas of Europe, is a place where:

> Law and order are virtually non-existent, because there is no police force and no judiciary. In some areas there no longer seems to be any clear sense of what is right and what is wrong. People help themselves to whatever they want without regard to ownership – indeed, the sense of ownership itself has largely disappeared. Goods belong only to those who are strong enough to hold on to them, and those who are willing to guard them with their lives. Men with weapons roam the streets, taking what they want and threatening anyone who gets in their way. Women of all classes and ages prostitute themselves for food and protection. There is no shame. There is no morality. There is only survival.
>
> (Lowe, 2013, p. xiii)

Germany and the German people were, thus, absolutely devastated and the Basic Law that four years later would emerge from the ashes would be chiefly conceived by the Powers that were occupying the Western regions of the country. The constitutional law scholar C.J. Friedrich made it clear at the time:

> Any consideration of this Basic Law should start from the fact that the charter *is not the creation of a free people*, and that it will have to function within limits, both territorial and functional, which severely handicap its chance of becoming a genuine constitution, securely anchored in the basic convictions of the people.
>
> (Friederich, 1949b, p. 704)

Even the name of the document, the Basic Law, makes somehow explicit both to the Allies and to the Germans that the new State's framework was not provided by a Constitution in the sense of a rule passed with the consent of the governed (Patberg, 2017, p. 56). The Zero Hour, *die Stunde Null* (Röhrich, 1997, pp. 30–32) after the Nazi surrender, was anything but a scenario of people deliberating on their future. Instead, when popular mobilization *took place*, it was in the final stages of the Weimar Republic and allowed the Nazis to seize power and to be sustained in it during the war (being the latter one of the most disquieting phenomena concerning modern democracy). Somehow, Nazism had been a rogue product of modern democracy coupled by the idea of nation as the most important category for organizing human affairs (see, among many others, Arendt, 1976, pp. 305–326; Slobodian, 2018, p. 29).

Such aversion to the populism that had led to catastrophe would be reflected in the Basic Law's lack of provisions concerning mechanisms of direct participation by the citizenry in decision-making processes. While in the America of the eighteenth century the "People-out-doors," as we have seen, was associated with revolution and emancipation, in post 1945 Germany "the People" unrestrained had other darker reminiscences. Among them, for instance, might be highlighted some expressions of direct acclamation by the People, such as the referendum held on August 19, 1934 by which Adolf Hitler's assumption of supreme power was passed, the referendum concerning the annexation of Austria and the approval of a single list of Nazi candidates for the Reichstag (held on April 10, 1938) or Nazi meetings such as the one that took place on February 18, 1943, on the occasion of a speech delivered by the German Propaganda Minister Joseph Goebbels calling for a total war shortly after the collapse of the German forces in Stalingrad: "*Wollt ihr den totalen Krieg?*" "Do you want total war?" was the question launched by Goebbels to an enthusiastic audience which feverously and unanimously replied: "*Ja!*" ("Yes"). A total war that certainly brought total defeat (Röhrich, 1997, p. 30). Taking such a background into account, the total mobilization of the People fostered by the Nazi regime caused Möllers (2007) to illustratively characterize the German constituent power behind the 1949 Basic Law as "We (are afraid of) the People."

Aside from the spurious use of mechanisms of direct popular participation by the Nazis, the system of the Weimar constitution, even before Hitler was appointed Chancellor in 1933, had been much richer in providing channels of public involvement than the 1949 Basic Law would ever be. The Weimar constitution-making process itself (Klein and Sajó, 2012, p. 249) developed after the military defeat in the First World War and a sequence of revolutions and coups d'état, at least relied on special elections arranged to choose the representatives that would gather themselves in a constituent assembly, the *Nationalversammlung*.[3] Weimar's constitutional design, in addition, included some other devices of political participation of the citizenry, such as the direct election of the *Reichspräsident* or the mentioned referenda that would not be maintained in the Basic Law, because then prevailed the opinion that, partially, the failure of the Weimar system was caused by excessive openness of the constitutional system to the will of the masses. The Weimar precedent explained why distrust towards any popular constituent agency was in 1948–1949 not only a matter of the occupant forces but also a concern shared by the German representatives. For example, both the decision to eliminate plebiscites and the restriction of popular input to changes of *Länder* borders (Markovits, 2008, p. 1312), were products of local initiative.

Even though the idea of a completely new beginning for Germany from May 1945 is contested by some historians and some relevant lines of continuity with the past may be appreciated (see Spevack, 2001, pp. 58–59), it was in the described paramount of total physical and moral devastation and a profound caution towards democracy where the path that led to the *Grundgesetz* approval was inaugurated.[4]

The disintegration of the German nation

The German constitutional developments between 1945 and 1948 were oriented by the will of the Allied Powers to undermine the German nation. Somehow the idea of the constituent power observed in the German process may be qualified as the contrary of what Sieyès exposed in his theory: if according to Sieyès the constituent power relied on the nation, the Allied Powers undertook, instead, the mission to build a political structure *without* a nation, or to be more precise, they designed a constitutional framework while they were demolishing the German national structures existing until the end of the war. Only reluctantly the Western Allied Powers accepted the recentralization of power in a Western German Federation, and that happened because in 1948 they had no other alternative given the consolidation of the Communist bloc and the beginning of the Cold War.

The strategy of disbanding the German nation activated from *die Stunde Null*, however, persisted in the constitutional proposals that would crystallize in the 1949 Basic Law. The new constitutional system represented a refusal of the ethnic and cultural perception of the nation that had flourished from the Romantic movement between the end of the eighteenth and the nineteenth century, and to which the Nazis added supremacist attributes. That concept of nation had, furthermore, its territorial consequences since it encompassed not only the ethnic German inhabitants within the borders of the Reich existing before 1945 (which included Eastern Prussia or Silesia) but also the Austrians and the ethnic and cultural Germans (*die Volksdeutsche*) that had lived for generations in vast territories of Eastern Europe (from the Sudetes in what is now the Czech Republic to the Baltic States or Ukraine) and it was precisely such a territorially expanded idea of Germany that the Allies sought to take down in the first stance through the political decisions that they adopted.

Plans for dismembering Germany had already been formulated in the midst of the war (see Backer, 1981, pp. 23–32; Graml, 1983, pp. 23–31; Stolleis, 2003, p. 275; and Vogel, 1967). As early as in the Moscow Conference of October 1943, which brought together the Allied Ministers of Foreign Affairs, and in the summit of the Allied leaders in Teheran (November 28–December 1, 1943) was outlined the Soviet annexation of a part of Eastern Prussia, Polish administration in some of the Eastern German territories, the internationalization of the Ruhr and Saarland or the control of Hamburg and the Kiel Canal in Western Allied hands. "Decentralization" of Germany was already a keyword used in the Tehran Conference while referring to the political organization of the future Germany (Stolleis, 2003, p. 275). Later on, the London Protocol of September 12, 1944, went forward in the partition of the Reich, confirming the Soviet administration of Eastern Prussia, the Polish administration of a part of Pomerania and the Upper Silesia, the control of Bremen and Bremerhaven by the Americans, Austria's independence, or the establishment of three zones within the German borders of 1937.

But even more relevant than the Allies' attitude towards the German nation was that the spirit of overcoming the ethno-cultural approach was internalized by the Germans themselves and would decisively mark German political culture until our times in terms of intellectual creation, such as the idea of Constitutional Patriotism (*Verfassungspatriotismus*) that are only understandable considering the context of the total defeat of Germany in 1945, and the enormous moral burden that the actions of a German nationalistic regime transmitted to the following generations of Germans.[5]

The constitutional rules established after the Second World War, in summary, reflected the intention to hamper forever the resurrection of a unified and strong German nation. Scholars such as Kirchhof (2004, p. 265) or Isensee (1992, p. 288) underlined that beyond the democratic deficits that surrounded the creation of the 1949 Basic Law, said constitutional framework was born within a context of a "national" deficit that required the amputation of the constituent agent.[6]

A nation of refugees

The Allies carved up, territorially, the annexations carried out by the Reich and the Nazis but, ironically, due to the waves of German refugees coming from Eastern Europe, postwar Western Germany achieved in the long run the goal of cultural and ethnic homogeneity that Hitler had envisaged, though on a smaller scale. Some historians such as Mark Mazower (2008, p. 63) or Toni Judt (2000, p. 298) suggested that the ethnically purified model of the nation-State that stems from the massive deportations of the 1940s contributed to postwar political stability in some countries of Central and Eastern Europe including Western Germany. According to such authors, internal cohesion would also later lay the groundwork for integration into supranational organizations, as was the case of the European Union.

But the final outcome would not be achieved without a preliminary phase of profound German internal divisions and an immense amount of outrages, including the perishing of at least half a million Germans in the three different phases in which the removals occurred (the evacuation organized by the Nazi government in the face of the Red Army advance, the chaotic fleeing immediately following the unravelling of the Third Reich, and the expulsions decided by the Allies from the former German territories transferred to Poland, Russia, or Czechoslovakia).

The landscape that the newcomers found was daunting: since most of the German cities had been reduced to rubble by Allied bombing, the country's infrastructure was unable to offer shelter, medical aid, or food after their journey (Lowe, 2013, p. 244). Some, the most vulnerable, were interned in refugee camps for several years (De Zayas, 2006, p. 136). The sheer dimension of the migration caused a demographic shock, particularly in those zones in which the refugees concentrated. German inhabitants of the Sudetes and Silesia, for instance, were forced to move from their homelands mainly to Bavaria where as late as 1960 some 28 per cent of the federal government employees were expellees (Judt, 2000, p. 297). In the North of Germany, to which 6,000 "eastern" Germans were transported per day for a full year and a half (Lowe, 2013, p. 243) there were *Länder*, such as the agrarian State of Schleswig-Holstein, where the population doubled (Hahn, 1995, p. 32).

Given the misery in which everybody had to live, conflicts between the native population and the deported spread in several places. On the one hand, the refugees were bitter over the fact that the natives enjoyed better housing, jobs, and living conditions. The native population, on the other hand, often regarded the refugees as unwanted additional burdens to be housed, fed, and clothed at a time when existing supplies did not meet the elementary demands of the resident population (Fischer, 1974, p. 95) The *Volksdeutsche*, in spite of the former Nazi propaganda and the fact that the 1949 Basic Law would recognize them as German citizens (Article 116 of the Basic Law) were sometimes regarded as foreigners by other Germans. They themselves did not recognize Western Germany as their home and their alienation from the political community went to the extent of founding a party, the Union of Expellees and Dispossessed (*Block der Heimatvertriebenen und Entrechteten*: *BHE*), more commonly known as the Refugee Party, that in the 1953 Federal election entered the Bundestag Parliament with 27 seats and became coalition partner in Adenauer's second cabinet.

The path of the German refugees from Eastern Europe ended with assimilation but it might not have been so if Adenauer had not acted with shrewdness when the Refugee Party reached its high point in 1953. Had the Chancellor not brought about the decline of that force by breaking it up and bringing one faction to his Christian Democratic party, those millions of German refugees might have jeopardized the very foundations of the new Republic (Mazower, 2000, p. 288).

The refugees' final integration into Western Germany had another postponed consequence by the time of the German reunification that up to now is still maintained: the German government's complete relinquishing of the territories east of the Oder–Neisse line that before 1945 were inhabited by a large German population. The conclusion of the German–Polish Treaty in 1990 covered by the treaty between Western and Eastern Germany and the Allied Powers that allowed reunification (the Treaty on the Final Settlement with Respect to Germany or the "Two Plus Four" Agreement) signified the legal certification, with its constitutional reverberations in terms of institutional settlement, of one face of the national dismemberment that the Allies had planned by 1944–1945.

The two Germanies

The decision to go ahead in building the German Federal Republic was somehow the answer of the Western Allies at the end of the London Six-Power Conference, by February 1948, once the relations with the Soviet Union were irreversibly broken by the Communist takeover in Czechoslovakia, the withdrawal of the Soviet delegation from Berlin's Allied command, and the beginning of the Berlin-Blockade (Mußgnung, 2003, pp. 321–322). But the Western movement towards a divided Germany had not only been inspired by the Soviet shadow. The willingness of the Americans, the British, and, especially, the French to keep Germany divided had also been a motivation to act beyond Soviet initiatives. In fact, as we shall see, the Soviet challenge triggered the American and British efforts to build a more centralized Western Germany than they originally planned and that the French rejected at first (Hahn, 1995, pp. 14–17).

Already during the war in 1944, and while the Allies seemed to be approaching victory, the Americans conceived a plan for a future defeated Germany which included not only the total destruction of Germany's industrial power and its reduction to a rural economy, but also the division of the country in two sides. The "Morgenthau plan" named after the United States Secretary of Treasure, Henry Morgenthau Jr., reveals clearly that the idea of dividing Germany was in some Western Allies' minds whatever the relations with the Soviet Union were going to be. In fact, the Morgenthau plan was accepted by both Roosevelt and Churchill, but it was later abandoned due to the strong opposition that German deindustrialization faced among their advisers. The idea was finally excluded from the 1945 July–August Potsdam Agreements (Churchill, 1954, pp. 138–139; Graml, 1983, pp. 283–299; Spevack, 2001, pp. 58–59) because some of the strategists in London and Washington already envisaged that they could take some profit from the industrial remnants that, particularly in West Germany, had eluded obliteration. The Cold War started under the shadow of this strategy.

I have noticed that among the Allies the will to territorially divide Germany was coupled, looking back at the Weimar experience, with their plans to avoid such mechanisms in the constitutional design that might eventually enable the Germans to participate by direct democratic means. But the circumstance of the German division between the Western and the Eastern zone also explained the unwillingness to include devices of popular direct participation in the constituent process *on the part of the German representatives*. Since the Western German negotiators during the Basic Law drafting did not want to identify the Western constituent initiative with the acceptance of the definitive partition of Germany, they were also suspicious towards any expression of popular participation prone to confirm that the popular basis of the German Federal Republic were only the Western Germans (Preuss, 2006–2007, p. 476). The latter may justify, for instance, that even the Occupation Powers in the West were likely to conceive a popular referendum as a final stage in the approval of the German Basic Law. Those who set out the strongest objections against such a referendum on the ratification of the Basic Law were precisely the German politicians [to the extent that such a disagreement on the constitution-making procedure and the involvement of the Western German People almost led to the collapse of the Allied-German negotiations (Markovits, 2008, p. 1309)]. The locals, thus, were mainly motivated by the aim of national division, and as such were those who avoided any full democratic legitimation of the new charter which, as we shall see, was only passed by the ratifying vote of the *Länder*'s assemblies.

Fragmenting the nation through federalism

But probably the main strike to the notion of the German nation was represented by the Western Allied imposition of federalism. After the war, some of the new *Länder* had been artificially outlined since they did not reflect the territorial entities existing under the Weimar Constitution or even during the empire. The most powerful of them (Prussia) was eliminated[7] and besides the recognition of their role of constituent agents they were chiefly conceived to counterweight the future federation. One evidence of the *Länder*'s relevance vis-à-vis the federation was that the Basic Law would prohibit any constitutional amendment related both to the abolition of the division between the *Bund* and the *Länder* and to jeopardize the *Länder*'s participation in the federal legislative process [Article 79.3 of the Basic Law (see Blank, 1995)]. While in the United States federalism was motivated by the urge to create a strong national government, in postwar Germany the Allies saw in federalism a way to contain the empowerment of the centre.

As I have remarked, a decentralized Germany had been the option proposed by the Allies already in the conferences celebrated during the war and it was reiterated in Potsdam (Friedrich, 1949a, p. 465). Among Western Allies circulated the idea of splitting Germany into small States and establishing weak ties among them limited to economic and foreign policy. Though the French did not participate in said conferences, they were the main supporters of such a German confederation (Mußgnung, 2003, p. 321; Spevack, 2001, p. 116). After all, a centralist and militarized Germany had invaded their country[8] and they were obsessed with preventing such a situation from happening again. By contrast, Stalin, before his rupture with the Western Allies, was not completely opposed to a more centralized German postwar government since he deemed that a neutral but united Germany in a first phase would be easier to turn into a socialist State. But, as I have said, it was precisely the entrenchment of the Soviet Union's position in Eastern Europe, including its German occupied zone, that was the reason that compelled the Americans and the British to depart from the confederative plans for Germany that the French so warmly supported. It was necessary to reshape their respective occupied zones into a stronger entity, with a central Parliament elected by universal suffrage and a federal executive, able to raise itself as a stronghold of free market liberal democracy in Central Europe (Hahn, 1995, p. 16).

The *Länder*, thus, would become the main channel of German local involvement in the 1949 Basic Law drafting process, but such participation would be developed through levels of representation distant from the citizenry. While it is true that popular participation was more intense in the drafting of the previous *Länder* constitutions [to the extent that even there were examples of referenda in ratifying the texts passed by the *Länder* parliaments, as happened in Bavaria, Hessen (both referenda took place on December 1, 1946) and Rhineland-Palatinate (referendum of May 18, 1947)] it cannot be omitted that the settlement of German's postwar *Länder* had been all along supervised by the occupying forces in their respective assigned zones. As Ulrich Preuss admitted (2006–2007, pp. 475–476), the peoples in the *Länder* did not strictly speaking exercise their constituent power when they enacted constitutions because the supreme authority was vested, with full effect in international law, either jointly with the Allied Powers or with any one of them in respect of the part of the German territory placed under its administration. The Western Allied Powers, indeed, decided, as I have mentioned before, on some *Länder*'s borders, contributed decisively in the determination of the *Länder*'s constitutional framework (Fait, 1985; Lewis, 1948), and even vetoed some excessively centrifugal trends, as was shown by the American attitude towards Bavarian separatism (Hahn, 1995, p. 10; Spevack, 2001, p. 102).

Once it was decided by the occupants to organize a central government in Western Germany, the *Länder*'s *assemblies were the bodies that appointed the representatives* that would gather themselves in the kind of constitutional Convention that would discuss the German Basic Law: the Parliamentarian Council (*der Parlamentarische Rat*). The German citizenry, thus, *did not participate at any level* in the 1949 German federal constitution-making process. Although the members of the *Länder*'s assemblies had been elected by the people of each State, the drafting of a Federal Constitution was not an issue when elections took place between 1946 and 1947 (Neuberg, 2001), at which the citizenry could not choose between eventual constituent ideas proposed by the different parties that participated in the electoral contest. As Donald Kommers explained (quoted by Ackerman, 2015, p. 711), opinion polls of that time showed that a majority of the respondents were not even aware of the Parliamentary Council's existence. In May 1949, a survey found that two-thirds of the respondents were not sure what the Basic Law was.

It may be argued that, as I have explained in the previous chapter, the lack of popular involvement in 1949 Germany was not so distant in comparison with what happened in the American States by 1787 when the delegates appointed by the States' legislatures met at Philadelphia after the Continental Congress called for a constitutional Convention. However, at least in the America of the eighteenth century, the citizenry of the States had the opportunity, disregarding the manoeuvres of the Federalists, to choose representatives for the State Conventions whereby the ratification of the constitutional proposal was discussed. In the Western Germany of 1949, there were no specially elected Conventions in the *Länder* to deliberate on the draft passed by the members of the Parliamentarian Council. The proposal went to the same bodies (the *Länder*'s legislatures) that had appointed the delegates and proceeded to the debate on ratification (Mußgnung, 2003, p. 255; Schneider, 1992, p. 22). Also different from the American experience (aside from the resistance shown by Rhode Island which in the end ratified the Federal Constitution) in Germany there was one major *Land* that *never* ratified the Basic Law: Bavaria.[9] Since the Bonner draft established that the consent of two-thirds of the *Länder* would be sufficient to enter into force (Article 144 of the Basic Law) it was considered that a Bavarian legislative supporting vote would not be needed in order to give birth to the German Federal Republic. It was scarcely argued if the German federation might anyhow run *leaving Bavaria aside* as it was likely to have been in America if Rhode Island had not ratified the Federal Constitution. It was taken for granted that Bavaria was a part of the new German federation without considering the fact that the integration was not supported by *any* democratic argument. Only afterwards, when the Bavarian people participated in the first elections to the *Bundestag*, as they have been doing since then, can the democratic legitimacy of Bavarian belonging to the German federation be appreciated. Certainly, the participation of the Germans in *ordinary* elections to the *Bundestag* would be repeatedly invoked to silence the objections to the weakness of the German constitution-making process. But I shall later isolate some of the problems entailing such a strategy of appealing to the day-to-day democratic procedures in order to conceal the democratic lack of the founding moment.

The position of the *Länder* concerning the federal constituent process might be summarized by observing that:

1. on the one hand, the system recognized the *Länder* as constituent agents. The Parliamentarian Council was composed by delegates chosen by the *Länder* legislatures, the constituent draft had to be ratified by at least two-thirds of those entities, and the division between the federation and the *Länder* was intangible to future constitutional amendments.
2. on the other hand, federalism, as was going to be constant in German postwar constitutionalism, represented a mechanism to tame democracy to the extent that the constitutional system might be applied to a space in which its inhabitants did not support the Basic Law by democratic means (neither directly nor indirectly). Federalism was also seen as a safeguard against the resurrection of the German nation expressed by the democratic will of a single people (Dietze, 1960, p. 130). Due to the problem regarding the division between Western and Eastern Germany, the German drafters themselves refused to attribute the constitutional decision to a performance exercised by the German citizenry considered in its entirety. But from the preamble of the Basic Law in 1949 may be inferred a reluctance as well to recognize the involvement of the People in grounding the Federal Republic independently from the *Länder*. The latter may be noticed from the mention of the People as a subject that lies "*in* the *Länder*" [the expression "in the *Länder*" was not even changed when the preamble was amended in 1990 with reunification].[10] In a different sense to the American case, it is not the "We the People" who introduces an idea of unity beyond the fragmentation of the States (and, as

we have seen, a source of popular legitimacy upon the States) but in Germany the States were outlined as barriers of the people's scope of action.
3. even considering the *Land* a pillar of the Western German constitutional order, its will did not mean much, as the Bavarian case made clear, because what mattered was the will of the powers that occupied Bavaria at that time and the Americans wanted a territory that bordered the Communist bloc to be *inside* Western Germany whether the Bavarian representatives voted in favour or not.

That last point leads me to tackle the structure of power that materially founded the German constituent process in 1949: the Western Allied Powers.

Western Allied tutelage in the constitutional framing

The Allied influence in framing the German Basic Law is still a controversial issue among historians. There are several and radically confronted interpretations which have consequences in the present German constitutional narrative. Basically, the extreme points of such discussion are marked by, on the one hand, the view arguing that the Basic Law was a German free and unbound creation in which the Allies played a marginal role[11] and, on the other hand, the view that saw the Basic Law as an Allied dictate.[12] Even though the present constitutional approaches (including some statements arising from the German Constitutional Federal Court) tend to support the idea of a freely drafted constitutional framework triggered by powerful German agency, the historiography mainstream is closer to the view that there was dominant and decisive Allied intervention (Spevack, 2001, pp. 21–22). After all, even supporters of some German room of manoeuvre during the making of the Basic Law concede that the Western Allies (1) did initiate the constitution-making process, (2) intervened decisively during the process, and (3) that the final product could not begin to function without their approval.[13] This was, for instance, the position expressed by Hahn (1995, p. 8) when making the following statement on analyzing the foundations of Western Germany:

> the United States, Great Britain, and France had a decisive role in the constitutional reconstruction of Western Germany after 1945, when they began the democratization of local and State government in their zones. The Basic Law, which capped the process, was initiated by the Western powers, vetted by them as it was being drafted, and ratified only after their approval.[14]

The decision to build a Western German Republic corresponding to the three zones occupied by the Western Allies was adopted by their authorities in the London Six-Power Conference developed between February and June 1948 [called "Six-Power" because it gathered not only the three Western Second World War military victors, the United States, the United Kingdom, and France, but also the three neighbours of Western Germany to its west, Belgium, Netherlands, and Luxembourg (Görtemaker, 1999, pp. 45–50; Wehmer, 1994)]. As evidence that the core decisions regarding the constitutional future of Western Germany were in the hands of the Allies, it might be mentioned that from the conclusion of the London Conference to the passing of the *Grundgesetz* in spring 1949, Allied policy on the Bonn drafting was always officially referred to as "implementation of the London decisions" (Spevack, 2001, p. 113). Besides that, the London agreement included a confidential "Letter of Advice ... Regarding German Constitution" to help the military governors assess the Basic Law (Hahn, 1995, p. 24).

The London Conference conclusions would be reflected in the recommendations that later would be issued by the three Western military Governors in Germany to the minister presidents of the Western Germany *Länder* in the so-called Frankfurt Documents, which established the main premises of the future Western Germany constitutional settlement (Benz, 1984, pp. 156–161; Eschenburg and Benz, 1983, pp. 459–462). The first Frankfurt Document authorized the *Länder* minister presidents to convene a constituent assembly; the second authorized them also to review the *Länder* boundaries [a consequence of that would be the foundation of Baden-Würtemberg in 1952 (Mußgnung, 2003, p. 323)]; and the third one included provisions regarding the occupation statute (Hahn, 1995, p. 22). The central issues concerning Germany's future constitutional framework, thus, were entitled in Frankfurt Document I, where it was established that a constitutional Convention had to draft a new Constitution which had to provide German division into *Länder*, as well as guarantees on human rights. That draft, according to the Frankfurt Document I, would require the consent of the military governors to be passed, and the ratification by two-thirds of the 11 German Western States (Mußgnung, 2003, pp. 323–324). Foreseeing that the constitutional architecture designed by the Allied Powers would confirm the division of Germany into two zones, the only substantial concession that the minister presidents of Western Germany succeeded in obtaining from the Allied Military powers (as a consequence of the minister presidents meeting at Koblenz from July 8–10, 1948) was that the foundation of the Western German Federation would only have a provisory character. The latter explains why the constitutional product finally adopted was labelled under the name of *Grundgesetz* ("Basic Law") and not a "Constitution," hoping that the "German constitution" would be passed in the future when reunification would take place (Kommers, 1997, p. 30; Preuss, 2006–2007, p. 478).

The Western Allied Powers controlled every step on the path which shaped the 1949 German Basic Law: the assembling of the constitutional Convention (the *Parlamentarischer Rat*) and its deliberations (Benz, 1984, pp. 191–200; Eschenburg and Benz, 1983, pp. 483–490; Görtemaker, 1999, pp. 59–65; Spevack, 2001, pp. 357–393) as well as the works of the first Basic Law drafting by a commission of constitutional experts who met at Herrenchiemsee Abbey in Bavaria (Eschenburg and Benz, 1983, pp. 479–483). All these stages needed the consent of the Western Allies representation. The final draft had also to be approved by the occupying Powers (Schneider, 1954, p. 937), a consent that was given on May 12, 1949, after the Basic Law had been passed by the *Parlamentarischer Rat*. For the reasons exposed, basically the fear of the German politicians to make Germany's division perpetual, the result of the deliberations of the Parliamentary Council was not submitted to plebiscitary approval (Merkl, 1963, pp. 128–129; Preuss, 2006–2007, p. 479).

Although there is relevant evidence that the German agents in the *Parlamentarischer Rat* provided the Basic Law draft with ideas coming from the German legal tradition [Steinberg, 1990, pp. 41–70][15] and that the stubborn stand of some German politicians transformed the Basic Law into something different from what the Allies ideally wished (Grabbe, 1978, pp. 393–418; Benz, 1984, pp. 212–226), it is historically hardly undeniable that the Allies remained the main actors in setting the entire framework of the Western German State.

The Allies and the majority of the German domestic actors, nevertheless, shared similar conceptions on the rule of law and constitutional supremacy as constraints on democracy. The Weimar experience, as I have outlined, had shown to what extremes an omnipotent democracy may lead and, accordingly, the basic aim of the drafters was to achieve an order grounded in law, but shielded from the potential disruptions that the democratically empowered masses may cause (Preuss, 2006–2007, p. 480). Gottfried Dietze (1960, p. 123) captured such a point when he wrote that one of the main motivations in the German constituent process was:

> to prevent the creation of a type of democracy under which the individual would be in danger of being absorbed by the *volonté générale* and subdued by the majority. Therefore, a system was established under which the democratic principle, while recognized as an ideal, was, as a mere means, subordinated to the liberal principle of the protection of individual freedom, as an end.

One watchful eye was kept towards the Nazis' immediate totalitarian past. But the other, more concerning issue, was the socialist world that was being organized in the backyard. The fear that an unrestrained democracy would derive into socialism was acute for actors as diverse as the Americans or Adenauer [who was a vehement anticommunist (Stadelmann, 1995, p. 2)]. But in order to place some principles beyond democratic accountability (as happened with the clause that prohibited the core of the constitutional system from being amended, the so-called "eternity clause," *die Ewigkeitsklausel*, in Article 79.3 of the Basic Law) another source of legitimacy, different from that provided by the will of the people, was needed. That source was the system of fundamental rights safeguarded by constitutional supremacy and able to trump democratic majorities. Entrenching rights for citizens and requiring the State to defend those rights against violation would represent the foundation of postwar German constitutional architecture (Bark and Gress, 1989, p. 225).

Fundamental rights were another topic on which both the locals and the occupants coincided, particularly because they were mostly restrained to a liberal conception though, given both the Nazi experience and the Soviet threat, emphasizing the centrality of the humanist ideal of dignity (Article 1 of the Basic Law). The drafters of the Basic Law intended to make human dignity its primary constitutional value and, consequently, it would permeate the entire legal order (Albert, 2019, pp. 52–53).

A potent welfare State would be later developed in Western Germany as a consequence of economic growth without precedent. But in the 1949 Basic Law there were scarce traces of mechanisms for establishing redistributive politics and there were still fewer expressed in the language of fundamental rights. The most relevant commitment to social justice was the definition of the Federal Republic enshrined in Article 20 of the Basic Law which proclaimed with solemnity that the German Federal Republic was a federal, democratic, and *social* State (a definition also excluded from the amendment processes as were both federalism and fundamental rights) but whereas the liberal rights were intended to be strongly enforced by the courts against the legislator, the precision of the social clause was left to the democratic majorities of the day-to-day political debate and always insofar as the legislative decision on redistributive politics did not affect individual liberties. In contrast with the strong mark of social concerns that embedded both the 1946 French Fourth Republic Constitution and the 1948 Italian Constitution, the 1949 German Basic Law was quite meagre in constitutional provisions envisaging a more egalitarian horizon. It was not unrelated to this circumstance that Communists influenced the constituent processes both in France and in Italy and even they had been integrated into the respective provisional governments (they had gained considerable prestige in the resistance against the Germans) while the German Basic Law was precisely being drafted *against* the Communist model that was being built in Eastern Germany and, generally, in Eastern Europe.

At any rate, the cornerstone of Western Germany's constitutional design composed of federalism, free market economy, and democracy limited by the rule of law and fundamental freedoms conceived as an irradiating instrument of political legitimacy was sculptured through the decisions adopted by the Western Allies to which the German representatives accommodated with more or less enthusiasm providing their autochthonous vision of the different institutions according to their legal tradition. Not surprisingly, as I suggested, such decisions defined the eternity clause and were the fields excluded from the constitutional amendment altogether (that is, completely unavailable to democratic deliberation). As Ackerman remarked (2015, p. 711), it is doubtful to know what it means to proclaim "democracy" as an eternal value when the proponents of the Basic Law refuse to submit it to a vote.

Another piece of evidence that shows that the Basic Law was to a high degree imposed was that in the final article of the Basic Law, Article 146, in which there is provision for a procedure to call for the constituent power and, thus, according to part of the German doctrine, even able to amend the principles included in the eternity clause[16] it was established that in applying such a provision the German people would give itself "freely" a constitution as insinuating that the adoption of the Basic Law in 1949 was not genuinely free. We shall see to what extent the abandonment of Article 146 of the Basic Law by the political cadres as a procedure to carry out reunification would explain that question.[17]

Involvement of elites in the shaping of the German constitutional framework

The German People did not give its consent to the German Basic Law passed in 1949. But, as Noah Feldman argues in his study of imposed constitutions, any constitutional framework, even those designed from the outside by foreigner powers, need at least the consent of a substantial part of the local elites to be established (Feldman, 2004–2005, p. 880). In fact, as was outlined in the case of the United States, a constitutional foundation is always a matter of the elites, regardless of whether the constitutional boost comes from outside (as in Germany) or from inside (as happened with the events that followed the independence of the American States). As has already been noticed, passing a constitution is the legal translation of the existing network of forces and the consolidation and enforcement of a constitutional regime depends on the support of the social and economic powers to the institutional design provided by the constitutional drafters.

But which elites were present in Germany after the destruction of the war?[18] The political cadres involved in the formation of the Bonn Republic were mainly composed by former opponents of the Nazi regime or from institutions, such as the churches, that although they did not directly fight Nazism they had at least expressed their discrepancies with Third Reich policies and had not collaborated with its atrocities.[19] Such actors, people like Konrad Adenauer (CDU), Carlo Schmid (SPD), or Theodor Heuss (FDP) still preserved some moral authority before the eyes of the occupants. Almost three-quarters of the delegates in the *Parlamentarischer Rat* had been professionally disadvantaged in the Hitler years, but prison sentences under the Nazis among the mentioned group, except for some of the Socialists and the two Communists, had been relatively rare (Markovits, 2008, p. 1310).

In a country in which Nazism was so widespread and deep-rooted, retribution did not concern all the individuals that had been engaged with the regime. The retaliations and the punishments dictated by the Allies had a limited impact on the Nazi leadership,[20] but other strata of German society went through denazification with relative indemnity. After all, Germany's reconstruction needed some elements of the previous power structure to be grounded (Preuss, 2006–2007, p. 475). As General Lucius Clay, the American Military Commander, pointed out regarding the organization of a German administration:

> our major administrative problem was to find reasonably competent Germans *who had not been affiliated or associated in some way with the Nazi regime … . All too often, it seems that the only men with the qualifications … are the career civil servants … a great proportion of whom were more than nominal participants (by our definition) in the activities of the Nazi party.
>
> (quoted by Judt, 2005, p. 56)

Already having in mind the aim to create a new political entity, the future West German Chancellor Konrad Adenauer, on May 5, 1946 spoke out against the denazification measures demanding that the "Nazi fellow travelers" be left in peace. The political leaders that were being envisaged for the new German beginning, thus, considered it more prudent to encourage silence on the social support that Hitler's regime had had.

Among such "Nazi fellow travelers," in the territories controlled by the Western Allies, an important part of the German economic oligarchies could be included. In spite of the general devastation of the country, some productive structures survived the catastrophe. During the last months of the war the Third Reich Minister of Arms and War Production, Albert Speer, worked to circumvent Hitler's instructions regarding the destruction of German industry in the territories that were going to fall into the hands of the Allies (the so-called Nero Decree). Speer's struggles enabled him to keep relatively safe some German industrial facilities that would be needed after the war (Herbst, 1982, pp. 345–347). Physical destruction of industrial assets was quite limited, for Allied bombing had focused on the transportation infrastructure and civilian housing, and gross industrial capital in fact grew by a fifth between 1936 and 1945 (Scheidel, 2017, p. 152).

However, most business owners of the surviving industrial premises had played an active role under Hitler's dictatorship. It was not only that the punishment against capitalist Nazi supporters was light at the end of the war, but also that their engagement with the future Federal Republic would be crucial in order to have some perspective of stability and economic recovery (and certainly to compete with the Soviet-occupied Germany, where the action of Soviet authorities was focused on expropriating and finishing economic elites in order to erect a communist regime).

Indeed, the relevant part of the German capitalists that supported Hitler were going to play a prominent role in the development of West Germany and would also emerge as an important social agent in the reconstruction of the whole continent through a European integration process grounded on the principles of the market economy. In the European arena, some of those German industrialists that regained their position after 1945 would meet with businessmen from France, Belgium, Luxembourg, or the Netherlands who had been involved a few years earlier in negotiations when the Nazi Economics Ministry of Germany had talked about organizing European cartels and output planning (Mazower, 2008, p. 571).

In spite of the abundance of material on the German oligarchies provided by sociology and political science [mostly concerned with the character of the German elites and their contribution until 1945 to the historical failure of democracy (see, among many others, Beyme, 1971; Dahrendorf, 1967; Hoffmann-Lange, 1991; Zapf, 1965)], approaches that stress the *continuity* in Western Germany of the economic elites involved in the Nazi regime have been scarcer. Some examples on this issue, nonetheless, might be mentioned: Friedrich Flick, convicted as a war criminal in 1947, was released three years later by the Bonn authorities and restored to his former eminence as the leading shareholder in Daimler-Benz. Flick became the richest person in West Germany during the Cold War and was one of the richest people in the world at the time of his death in 1972. Senior figures in the incriminated industrial combines of I.G. Farben and Krupp (like Otto Ambros and Alfred Krupp) were all released early and re-entered public life little the worse for wear. By 1952, Fordwerke, the German branch of Ford Motor Company, had reassembled all its senior management from the Nazi years (Judt, 2005, p. 58). Harald Quandt, the son of Günther Quandt and Magda Behrend, who later would marry Joseph Goebbels, also ran with his half-brother Herbert Quandt, the industrial empire inherited from his father after the Second World War. Günther Quandt, Harald's father, was arrested and interned in 1946 but was soon released, in 1948, considering that while he accepted Nazi ideology, he supposedly did not take an active part in crimes. Harald Quandt served as a lieutenant in the Luftwaffe and was captured by Allied troops in Italy but was also soon released, in 1947. The Quandts, among other businesses, are owners of about 46 per cent of the *Bayerische Motoren Werke* (BMW) vehicle manufacturing company until the time of writing. The owner of the clothing company that designed and supplied the Nazi uniforms from the twenties, Hugo Boss, was only condemned to a fine of 100,000 German marks for being a supporter and beneficiary of National Socialism. Also from the textile industry, the support to the Nazis given by the Dassler brothers did not stop them, in the postwar period, from making burgeoning businesses through their firms: Adidas and Puma. Companies such as BASF, Hoechst, Siemens, Henschel, Volkswagen, Adam Opel AG, Bayer, and Deutsche Bank, which profited from slave labour during the Nazi era, also carried on with their activity and even expanded from 1945 (Lübbe, 2005). The Nazi intellectual cadres would not be alien either to the smooth transition towards the Federal Republic, beyond the most-known cases of philosophers such as Martin Heidegger, there were more concealed examples of accommodation into the new regime, and more effective in the building of the new economic and social order: such was the history of Reinhard Höhn, a young sociologist and law professor under the Nazi regime who was considered the father of the intellectual arm of the *SS*: the *Sicherheitsdienst* (*SD*). Nevertheless, when times changed, Höhn founded the Harzburg Academy for Economic Leadership and became the management studies guru of 1950s West Germany (Mazower, 2008, p. 234).

In summary, most of the pre-war economic powers and academic staff integrated decisively in the constitutional movement that led to the approval of the 1949 Basic Law and underpinned its consolidation. The legal framework there provided, especially on the point concerning the guarantees on liberal economic individual rights and the constraints on radical democracy, was designed to protect the interests of such elites. Accordingly, the Basic Law constitutional devices that were foreseen to limit democratic excesses that had emerged during the Weimar Republic might also be interpreted in another fashion: the restrictions on popular participation would be seen as particularly suitable for the elites in order to exclude political mobilization against the pillars of the liberal economic order. After all, as was observed in analyzing the composition of the Parliamentary Council, the German Basic Law drafters were mostly "formed by bourgeois-liberal conceptions of a constitution" (Werner, 1996, p. XV). Making again an analogy with the events that motivated the creation of the United States Federal Constitution and the willingness to protect the interests of the oligarchies against the revolutionary masses, the drafting of the German Basic Law after the Second World War also contemplated counter-majoritarian institutions to safeguard the capitalist and free market economic order. With the paradox, in the German case, that many of those who were benefited by such restrictions on political participation were also relevant industrialists, businessmen, or landowners that had constituted the economic elite under the former regime.

We have defined our theory of the constitution as a legal document that translates a decision on power previously gained by violence. However, the mention of the German Basic Law constituent process is likely to be to some degree contradictory with such an idea since it might be considered a rare example of a constitutional framework conceived to design the allocation of power among *the defeated*. To which constellation of powers would German postwar constitutionalism serve in its attempt to perpetuate the structures previously gained by violence? This question has a historically clear answer, albeit concealed by the circumstances: the German Basic Law sought to consolidate the power of the Western Allies and the forces of liberal capitalism against the danger represented by the Soviet Union. If the Allied political and military leadership sought to pass a Basic Law initiated with the protection of human rights and the statement: "Human dignity shall be inviolable," it was not because they felt sympathetic towards a people who had been involved in horrible crimes (and who had been their enemies not long ago); it was, instead, because they needed to obtain their loyalty in order to contain the Soviet threat.

The role of the 1949 German Basic Law in strengthening the existing powers in the territories controlled by the Allies represented, in conclusion, the alliance between the foreigner occupants and the German capitalist forces, most of these related to the former Nazi regime, and easily redeemed after a short conviction (or after not being convicted at all). For the constituent forces, human rights were important, but they were important to be recognized besides provisions emphasizing capitalist economic safeguards (such as, for instance, Article 14 of the German Basic Law ensuring private property and right to inheritance). The aim was to ensure capitalism in Western Germany as a first step to designing a capitalist free market area at the level of Western Europe able to compete against its socialist alternative.

Conferring democratic legitimacy to the Basic Law

The lack of a real active democratic subject in Western Germany's historical constitution-making process has forced the focus on the reconstruction of the people's consent within the *constituted* power (Möllers, 2007, p. 98). German doctrine, as we have seen that also political theorists such as Habermas held, focuses on the vision according to which a Constitution is more a matter of future than a matter of memory, somehow recognizing thus that a degree of memory-distortion is needed in order to enforce the constitutional order. In this way, Kirchhof (2004, p. 273) for instance, stated that:

> It is not the past, but the future of constitutional law the issue of a constitution.

The basic ideas of such "reconstruction" theory within the German version are, on the one hand, that democratic legitimacy is seen within the ordinary democratic constitutional procedures (Böckenförde, 1992a, p. 105) and, on the other hand, that the German fundamental constitutional discourse has been de-politicized, and put into the form of constitutional interpretation beyond democratic theory (Möllers, 2007, p. 97). Regarding the latter strategy, German doctrine has centred its analysis in the constitutional conflicts before the Constitutional Court: the constitutional judicial review of legislation (and particularly, the individual complaints lodged to the Federal Constitutional Court) emerges as the occasion to transform a constitutional significance through an act of political participation (Dietze, 1960, p. 138; Markovits, 2008, p. 1337). Granting the judiciary the power to interpret the meaning of some constitutional concepts (such as those stemming from human dignity or sprinkled within the articles in which fundamental rights are recognized) was predictable taking into account that they had been codified against amendment (see Albert, 2019, p. 53). In this fashion may be understood some theoretical proposals, such as the one represented by Peter Häberle (1996) whose theory of the open society of constitutional interpreters is partially an attempt to organize the reconfiguration of constitutional concepts through the dialogue that several agents within the society hold with the *Bundesverfassungsgericht* in the present. But, at the end of the day, interpretation through the conflicts that are developed before the judiciary cannot subvert the constitutional meanings and, thus, the objection according to which there is a limit composed by core decisions that had not been adopted by the citizenry, still subsists.

Already at the beginning of the regime of the Bonn Basic Law, a scholar such as Schneider (1954) suggested that the postwar German constitutional framework gained democratic legitimacy through the high voter turnout in the regular elections to the *Bundestag* that took place shortly after the passing of the Basic Law. According to Schneider, 78 per cent of those Western Germans entitled to vote cast their votes in the 1949 first *Bundestag* elections and thus indicated their willingness to accept the new system.[21] Furthermore, wrote Schneider, only 13.2 per cent of the eligible voters voted for parties which, like the Communists, the Centre Party, the Bavarian Party, and the German Party, rejected the Basic Law for one reason or another (on that point see also Kloepfer, 1983, p. 59). The argument according to which the German Basic Law already enjoyed a popular endorsement through every national election since 1949 was repeated during the reunification of Germany in 1990 by those that sought to avoid a comprehensive constitutional debate appealing to the people (Chambers, 2004, p. 166).

But, as has been remarked, ordinary participation for the legislative does not say many things about a majority supporting the constitution. And, on the other hand, regarding the postwar German particular circumstances: ***had the Western Germans any other alternative*** than to participate in the elections of the bodies designed by the Basic Law? Was that really a *free* participation under a system imposed by the war victors, with all the constraints of the Cold War at its peak and with the possibility of prohibiting any political party challenging the Western Allied decisions as finally happened in the fifties?[22] The high voter turnout in the first general elections to the *Bundestag* and the electoral preference for the parties that supported the *Grundgesetz*, as Schneider argued, was not equivalent to popular consent for the new regime, and it might be stated that voters were forced by the facts. The participation in such electoral processes only expressed the lesser evil. Rather than showing the acceptance of the constitutional framework, a high voter turnout and wide support for the "pro constitutional" parties in legislative elections might reveal the fear of coming back to the clashes that had marked German life until the Nazi defeat.

Something similar might be said of the argument regarding the frequent constitutional amendments to which the German Basic Law has been submitted (Kloepfer, 1983, p. 59, Murswiek, 1978, p. 176; Steiner, 1966, p. 225). Constitutional amendments achieved by two-thirds of the representatives of both federal legislative chambers might hardly be considered an expression of the German citizenry and an example of general political mobilization. Basic Law amendments are closer to an act of ordinary politics than to a "constitutional transformation." What is rather the problem is precisely that that citizenry has ***always been excluded*** from constitutional amendments, counting also those amendments passed in the reunification process. Such amendments that have scrupulously followed the constitutional procedure without any popular involvement and grounded just in ordinary elections may strictly be considered *pouvoir constitué* (or, more precisely, *pouvoir constituant dérivé*), but not constituent power.

What really conferred legitimacy to the Western German constitutional system from 1949, as happened in other European countries in the postwar period, were the extraordinary economic growth and the social advantages that derived from it. Prosperity in the early phase was sharply boosted by the liberalization of trade that accompanied the adoption of Marshall Aid and by the recovery of international markets. The Basic Law, with the primacy of the rule of law above democracy in defence of property rights and the market economy that had been consecrated, became the perfect legal receptacle to foment such a golden age. Western Germany led most of the economic indicators of growth. Its foreign trade, for instance, increased by an astonishing average of 16 per cent *per year* between 1948 and 1962 (Kershaw, 2018, p. 135). Such sustained high rates of growth permitted the increase of wages and salaries in real terms, improving living standards. At the same time, the governments, even liberal conservative ones at the federal level and in some *Länder*, benefited from the gain of additional tax revenue to fund social welfare programmes. The harshness of the crises in the seventies did not hamper, once the path of prosperity was reassumed in the eighties, Western Germany's definitive triumph over the communist Eastern part of the country.

The People and the constituent power in Germany's reunification

From the constitutional point of view, the events in Germany in 1990[23] did not differ substantially in comparison to those experienced in 1948–1949 at least regarding two basic characteristics: (1) the 1990 German Reunification was supervised by the powers that had won the Second World War (this time including Gorbachev's agonizing Soviet Union) and (2) the German citizenry, except in the first phase of demonstrations in Eastern Germany in the fall of 1989 and with some constitutional initiatives coming also from the East, *was displaced from adopting political decisions directly*. The constitutional amendment process was, in the end, monopolized by the representatives.

The German "national deficit" that some scholars such as Kirchhof or Isensee mentioned, envisaging the direct involvement of the German People in giving itself a constitutional framework, was not remedied in 1990.

Reconstruction theories such as the ones commented on in the previous section, such as giving significance and democratic legitimacy to the constitutional provisions through the procedures developed in the day-to-day functioning of the German Republic, were nonetheless still invoked by the doctrine after 1990 as the opportunity to strengthen the democratic foundations of the system. Yet, the preservation in 1990 of the basic decisions on the allocation of power assumed in 1949 (the constitutional principles of the eternity clause, the liberal market economy, the dependence on foreign powers, and the restrictions on public involvement in deciding on constitutional issues) makes it difficult to state that constitutional changes displayed in 1990 represented a "constitutional transformation" in the terminology that I used here.

Take the reading of Article 146 of the Basic Law, for instance – that provision which foresaw precisely the scenario of reunification and that, nevertheless, did not apply to the very case for which the article was intended (Möllers, 2007, p. 99). If we look at Article 146 of the Basic Law as amended in 1990 (Wiederin, 1992, pp. 427–429 and pp. 433–436), we shall easily realize that the constitutional amender considered that the "unity and freedom for the whole German People" had been fulfilled (such statement, however, might be arguable since the German minorities in other territories that were Germany before 1945 such as in Eastern Prussia or Upper Silesia had been left aside). But, in another way, from the wording of the new Article 146 it might also be admitted that the decision of the German People regarding its constitutional framework *was still pending*. Such a conclusion can be reached from the fact of maintaining in the Article 146 of the Basic Law the possibility of replacing the Basic Law by a brand new *Verfassung* through the "free" consent of the German People *as such consent had not been "freely" given in 1990, either* (Heckel, 1995, p. 491).

The consent that was required for uniting both German States, instead, was that of the Allies through an international treaty: the Treaty on the Final Settlement with Respect to Germany of September 12, 1990 between the German Federal Republic, the German Democratic Republic, the Soviet Union, the United States, the United Kingdom, and the Republic of France, also known as the "Two plus Four" Treaty (Kilian, 2003, pp. 632–635; Quaritsch, 1995, pp. 383–400; and Schweitzer, 1995). It was not until the conclusion of the Two plus Four Treaty that the Allied Powers considered the rights and the responsibilities towards Germany to be finished and that, consequently, the full sovereignty of Germany to be restored.[24] In fact, what the Americans, the British, the French, and the Soviets thought to avoid in concluding the Treaty was precisely the involvement of the German People considered in its unity in accepting the new political status. It is likely that the lack of application of Article 146 of the Basic Law in the reunification process was a direct consequence of the negotiations with the participants of the Two plus Four Treaty (Kilian, 2003, p. 656; Quaritsch, 1995, p. 390). The memory of the war made some Western European leaders at that time such as the French President, Françoise Mitterrand, or the British Prime Minister, Margaret Thatcher, admit that they were swallowing a bitter pill in agreeing that the Germans unite in a single republic. The French or the British would probably not have tolerated that the Germans achieved their political goal if they had done it through a constitutional revolution, as may have been expected given the popular mobilizations that took place in Eastern Germany around the end of the Communist regime.

In a similar vein as experienced in 1949, Western Allies worries were shared by Western German political elites. Both deemed that the farther the process be kept from direct public involvement, the better. Indeed, for many members of the German political and academic establishment in 1990, the idea of a full-scale constitutional debate on the Basic Law seeking democratic endorsement for a new constitution was horrifying (Chambers, 2004, p. 165; Schäuble, 1991, pp. 287–307). The Western German government, furthermore, did not want to miss the chance of proceeding with a fast reunification within an internationally favourable atmosphere and pondered that a long deliberation on the constitutional status may put the whole political operation at risk. In the end, the constituent power of the now united German people was invoked only by politically marginal groups in the two German States (Preuss, 2006–2007, pp. 479–480).

The most intense public discussion on constitutional matters occurred shortly after the fall of the Berlin Wall, when the possibility of maintaining the German Democratic Republic as a separate State with its own constitutional framework was discussed. In the first weeks after the events of November 9, 1989, spontaneous roundtable discussions sprang up throughout East Germany: meetings of civic-minded citizens, dissenters, local officials, and ordinary citizens who got together to debate how the political energy exploding all around them could be funnelled into the creation of a democratic German Democratic Republic (GDR) (Markovits, 2008, p. 1324).

A central Roundtable of the German Democratic Republic was established on December 7, 1989, adopting the decision on drafting a new constitution for East Germany. But all such channels of deliberation began to decline, in the first instance, when it began to be perceived that the roundtable was used as a device by the Eastern Germany authorities to retain some legitimacy and, in a second instance, when it became clear, by the spring of 1990, that Germany would be reunified by a simple accession of the GDR to the Federal Republic. A freely elected Parliament in Eastern Germany, the *Volkskammer*, might have played the role of a constituent assembly, but in the elections held in Eastern Germany on March 18, 1990, the conservative alliance obtained an outstanding result and they pressed, following the intention of the Western German Chancellor, Helmut Kohl, for swift unification.

In spite of the original efforts in the German Democratic Republic to produce a new constitution in a process of communication free of domination by the elites the final product of the unification under the system of the German Basic Law was decided by a reduced group of politicians. The roundtable drafting committee handed over its work to the newly constituted *Volkskammer* three weeks after the elections in the GDR (Markovits, 2008, p. 1331) but the Christian Democratic majority in the chamber considered that the constitutional draft would jeopardize reunification and decided not to transfer it to the competent committee.

In the end, thus, the way chosen to complete reunification was that of the former Article 23 of the Basic Law, which foresaw the extension of the German Federal Republic constitutional regime to newly incorporated *Länder* [the same way that had been used with the integration of the Saarland in 1957 (Chambers, 2004, p. 166; Lerche, 1995, pp. 421–424; Kilian, 2003, pp. 637–639; and Quint, 1992–1993)]. No new constitutional order would be created, but German reunification would merely be an extension of the 1949 Basic Law to other territories. The application of the former Article 23 of the Basic Law required just a limited amendment concerning the preamble, the legislative composition, some transitional regulation, the derogation of Article 23, and the already mentioned amendment of Article 146 of the Basic Law (Klein, 1995, pp. 577–588). These amendments to the Basic Law were formally adopted through another international treaty: the Unification Treaty between the German Federal Republic and the German Democratic Republic,[25] whose approval was carried out with notorious participative and deliberative shortcomings.

In spite of the fact that a subcommittee of the two houses was established to discuss the constitutional arrangements derived from reunification (the Joint Constitutional Commission) the substance of the debate was quite narrow and its ultimate recommendations were minimal (Benz, 1994). Around 800,000 submissions from the citizenry were received by the Joint Constitutional Commission but it was never clear what happened to them (Chambers, 2004, p. 167). The Unification Treaty was finally passed by a two-thirds vote of the German Democratic Parliament (which would cease to exist with the Treaty's entering into force) and, in West Germany, by two-thirds of the votes of the *Bundestag* and the *Bundesrat* (according to Article 79.2 of the Basic Law that entails the general procedure to amend that rule) but this vote had been delivered in a procedure in which no amendments had been allowed (Quint, 1992–1993, p. 694). The constitutional amendment procedure was challenged and upheld by the Federal Constitutional Court. The Court, nevertheless, rejected the complaint, that had been lodged by a small number of conservative *Bundestag* members, and justified the use of an extraordinary procedure.[26] The decision of the *Bundestag*, thus, was a decision to approve or ratify a decision already made by treaty negotiators without transparency (Quint, 1992–1993, pp. 694–695).

Following the same logic that was alleged after the settlement of the Western German Federal Republic, the democratic justification of the constitutional arrangements carried out by reunification was extracted from the first *ordinary* elections of the unified Germany to the *Bundestag* held in December 1990 (Heckel, 1995, p. 510; Kilian, 2003, p. 658). Since the vote of German citizenry was for those parties that gave their support to the reunification under the terms that were finally consummated (and, particularly, they voted for the Christian Democrats that had led the process) that was interpreted as the people consenting to the constitutional change as a whole. Again, thus, the democratic legitimacy of the constitutional structure under the system of the Basic Law was confined to the regular procedures of political participation.

The outcome of the modest amendments to the Basic Law made in 1990 revealed, thus, that at the end of the twentieth century the German political and social background was still anchored in the framework of powers and fears that surrounded the original approval of the Basic Law (Preuss, 2006–2007, p. 480). The winners of the Second World War imposed their will again in several ways: by prohibiting, for instance, any territorial stretch by Germany beyond the Oder–Neisse line, by forcing German politicians to commit themselves to the European integration process once reunification was achieved (Kumm, 2016a, p. 923), or by limiting the direct participation, by German citizenry, in decision-making processes, confirming that the current German constitutional system was still the product of a military defeat or, to say it in another way, that the German constitutional settlement was the consequence of a violent context.

The political mobilization in 1989 was not translated into a constitutional transformation able to leave behind the inheritance of the postwar period. Had the German reunification boosted a "constitutional transformation" through a free and massive political participation, capable of challenging the order established after the 1945 capitulation, such a movement would probably not have lacked convulsion, or, at least, would not have been easily accepted by the Allies.

Although some German authors such as Jaggi (2016a, 2016b) hold a complacent view on the events that brought about the German reunification and argue that they were marked by a popular mobilization in the East from which somehow the resultant constitutional system of the Basic Law was benefited, I would remain closer to the interpretation provided by Bruce Ackerman on the issue. Ackerman did not see, in 1990, any trace of the popular involvement with which he characterizes a revolutionary constitutional movement and, consequently, offered an ambivalent assessment of the German Basic Law model from the democratic point of view (1992, pp. 101–112). While appreciating the success of the German Federal Republic from the point of view of the rule of law (partially expressed in the enormous prestige of the German Federal Constitutional Court and its commitment to the defence of the fundamental political principles and fundamental rights), Ackerman admits that the German constitutional development is a "second-best" or "half as good" as a model triggered by political mobilization or by, as Ackerman calls it, a "constitutional moment" in the midst of a liberal revolution. According to this interpretation, that I share, the German constitutional experience after the fall of the Berlin Wall was too dependent on the benign decisions of a political and judicial elite to define and guarantee basic rights, and as such it could not be associated with a true revolutionary liberal movement. In short, Germany has managed to forget the fact that, in both 1949 and 1989, its political elite refused to place the constitution before the voters for their considered judgement (see Ackerman, 2015, p. 711).

Violence founded the 1949 German Basic Law, and the remembrance of such violence avoids any constitutional transformation of the system even today. One of the main devices which guarantees the impossibility of reproducing violence again is the set of limitations on popular involvement, designed to put insurmountable obstacles in the way of the German people freely deciding, because somehow, though generations pass, the responsibility of the collective descent towards totalitarianism is still attributed to the democratic decision adopted by the Germans. Such an "anti-populist" strand devoted to introducing bounds on the decision of the people, which dominated the founding of the 1949 Basic Law and its subsequent developments, has had a prominent influence on the contemporary constitutional discourses on the question of drafting a Constitution. Populist fears and the remembrance of violence have marked not only the constitutional paradigm for Germany and Central Europe but also the European integration process itself, to which the German constitutional developments had been a source of inspiration.

The interactions between the German Federal Republic and the European Union constitutional models: liberalism, rule of law, cosmopolitanism

Postwar German constitutionalism, a model designed to establish a thriving free market economy with particular concern for the defence of property rights, delighted the liberals, who by the time in which the Basic Law was drafted exercised a powerful influence on political and economic thought. Most of them, such as Hayek, von Mises, Haberler, or Röpke, came from the German-speaking world, and had already fled from Germany or Austria to Switzerland, or to the United States, before the Second World War. While the particular ascendance of these authors in the German constituent process is uncertain, the truth is that their ideas modelled the understanding of the Basic Law and marked the action of the first German federal governments, especially through the figure of Ludwig

Erhard who was, besides his affiliation to the mentioned neoliberal strand, Minister of Economic Affairs in the Adenauer governments and later Chancellor of the Federal Republic.[27]

The Western German model alluded to most of the characteristics that the liberals had outlined in designing political institutions, beginning with a deep distrust towards nationalism and democracy as threats to the functioning of the market order. Hayek, for instance, understood that the democratic expression of nationalism would lead inexorably to socialism. Through democracy, nationalism and socialism were "inseparable forces" (Hayek, 1976, p. 134). Liberalism was essentially cosmopolitan and conceived a world of political entities focused only on enforcing the law to guarantee economic freedoms such as the freedom of trade, the free movement of capitals, the freedom to invest,[28] and the freedom to consume. Hence it is not surprising that some of the authors mentioned were sympathetic towards a political system grounded on federalism and on the minimization of national impulses, a trend that would be later reproduced in the formation of the European Communities (Weiler, 1999, pp. 324–357).

In fact, Western Germany would become a laboratory of the liberal conceptions that would be later displayed through the European institutions: the centrality of the rule of law expressed in constitutional supremacy (the supremacy of the European Constituent Treaties at the European level), the preference of adjudication by judges and scholars above the decisions adopted by the representatives of the people (and from this claim may be explained both the decisive role assigned to the German Federal Constitutional Court within the German constitutional structure, and the importance that the European Court of Justice would gain as European integration went forward), and the ability of the interpreters of the law to ensure fundamental rights (emphasizing economic freedoms) to override anything decided through popular involvement. Needless to say, in the liberal set of coordinates it is irrelevant whether the people had participated, or not, in the foundational decisions of the system. According to the liberal criteria, it was better that the populace be excluded from the institutional design since their demands for redistribution were seen as the root of all economic problems.

The tenets of liberal constitutionalism were also maintained with the constitutional changes that reunification brought about: its internationalism was, for instance, revealed by the circumstance that the constitutional amendments were linked to international treaties such as the Four plus Two Treaty, the Unification Treaty, or even the treaty between the German Federal Republic and Poland on the Eastern German border (Kumm, 2016a, p. 923). As we have seen, in addition, the reunification of Germany was accepted by the Allies as long as the new Germany was committed to European integration, as would be explicitly inserted in the new wording of Article 23 of the Basic Law, also known as the "European Article." Legalism, the contention of the citizenry in the constitution-making process, or the fact that the united Germany represented the abduction of a former socialist economy into a free market economy (which, at the very same time, was deeply integrated in a larger liberal structure which was the European

Common Market) reaffirm the persistence of the neoliberal pattern in defining the German constitutional culture.

On the other hand, this strand of cosmopolitanism in defining a constitutional framework in a global arena, detached from a demos and essentially built on the idea of the rule of law is still reflected in the work of present German scholars. As we have seen in the second chapter of this book, the struggle to surmount the association between the constituent power and a national sovereign through supranational structures has been mainly developed by German authors such as Nico Krisch, Mattias Kumm, and Bardo Fassbender. German liberal constitutionalism played a significant role in defining German policies as well, both in the years that preceded the European Sovereign debt crises, and in the years that followed these crises. The beginning of the twenty-first century was a time of relative economic stagnation for Germany, against which a Social Democratic Chancellor, Gerhard Schröder, applied a neoliberal recipe, that allowed his successor, Angela Merkel, to tackle the world's Great Depression from 2008 in better conditions than most Western economies (Tooze, 2018, pp. 94–95).

Germany, given its economic success derived from the liberal reforms adopted by the beginning of the century and the accumulation of fiscal surpluses, would later lead the crises of the Euro and would determine the economic policies of some Southern European States that were strongly indebted to German lenders. Some of them, such as Greece or Spain, were forced to ask for bailouts from the different European and global funds that were at that time constituted to rescue fragile economies, with an important level of German design of these funds.

Constitutional identity or the return of the German nation

In spite of the background described, even before reunification, there may be observed within the German constitutional context, a resurgence of a nationalistic vision of the Basic Law that, paradoxically, was justified by a strong concern for the defence of democracy and the rights connected to political participation. Still more perplexing was that such a discourse on German national democratic sovereignty was, from the seventies, cultivated by the apex of German legalism, the German Federal Constitutional Court, in its debate vis-à-vis the European institutions (preeminently the European Court of Justice) on European integration.[29] In that regard, it was somehow peculiar that the German Federal Constitutional Court undertook the task of tracing the limits to the European Union integration process, by invoking the democratic source of the German constitutional framework which, as we have seen, had been very feeble both in 1949 and in 1990. In spite of the struggle developed by a relevant part of the doctrine in order to describe the German constitutional identity as mainly focused on the traces of the Basic Law itself performing (through the defence of fundamental rights, democracy, federalism, and the *Rechtsstaat*) a critical redemptive role against an identitarian understanding of the German State that was prevalent in the past (Häberle, 2000, p. 87; Kokott, 1998, p. 90; Kotzur, 2012, p. 128; Rosenfeld, 2005, p. 321), the truth is that judicial engagement with the constitutional identity has been surrounded by an old-fashioned sovereigntist atmosphere. Such was also the opinion of some legal scholars in rejecting the German Federal Constitutional Court decision in the *Lisbon Treaty Case* which encapsulated the doctrine on German Constitutional identity as a boundary to European integration. Thus, Jo Eric Khushal Murkens (2010, p. 540) for instance, stated that

> The tenor of the Court's judgment … is that "identity trumps integration"

while Roland Bieber (2009, p. 397) observed that

> The Union is presented as a foreign entity, not as part of German's identity. Hence, the main task of the Court seems to be the defense of Germany against intrusions by this entity.

The basic idea concerning the constitutional identity in the German Constitutional Court's approach, might be, thus, that every State action, even those exercised through representatives in transnational organizations, must find through a non-interrupted chain their last resort of legitimacy in the will of the People (Böckenförde, 1992b, p. 302) defined in a hard sense. In the German postwar scene such democracy, as I have explained, had to be understood only in reference to the *constituted* German democracy, and always limited to a representative democracy.

Using the words of the German Constitutional Court in the *Lisbon Judgement*, for instance,[30] it might be asserted that, according to such interpretations, the German constitutional State is the primary democratic space ("*demokratische Primärraum*") in which the self-determination of the German people is achieved.[31] The people, with some degree of unity or (national) consciousness, give themselves a constitutional framework that, in its essence, cannot be conferred to supranational institutions such as the European Union. So, as the German Federal Constitutional Court states:

> The Basic Law does not grant powers to bodies acting on behalf of Germany to abandon the right to self-determination of the German people in the form of Germany's sovereignty under international law by joining a federal State.[32]

Such an interpretation would hold that the only hope for legitimate governance lies in the domestic constitutional framework and the governance structures should be conceived, and constructed, as ultimately flowing from and controlled by national political and constitutional processes. Sovereignty, thus, would be characterized as the right of the people to decide the basic questions of their own identity constitutively. Such an assertion, according to the German Federal Constitutional Court[33] would be derived from the recognition of the democratic principle (Articles 20.1 and 20.2 of the German Basic Law) and specified in the individual right of German citizens to vote to the legislatures (Article 38.1 of the

German Basic Law), which confers the possibility of challenging, by individual complaints, European Union legal provisions able to undermine German Constitutional identity (on German's constitutional identity see Ingold, 2015; Polzin, 2016). Thus, through such types of "popular action" articulated around the constitutional individual complaint against European Union regulations (or their implementation) the German Constitutional Court assumes the role of controlling any European Union measure considered to put at risk, through excess of competence (*ultra vires*) German constitutional identity as expressed by the German people's self-determination.[34] The idea is that any substantial appropriation, via transference of competences to the European Union without the consent of the German citizenry, of core decision-making on constitutional issues, would be rejected.

Constitutional identity would, thus, operate as a limit of a constitutional amendment provided by a European Union act (Ingold, 2015, pp. 6–9 and pp. 10–12; Schneider, 2014). Even though it is not completely clear in the German Constitutional Court jurisprudence if the constitutional identity relates to a concept beyond the material limits of the Basic Law amendments entailed in Article 79.3 of the Basic Law (Polzin, 2016, p. 431), from the first judgements in which the German Constitutional Court outlined the limits to European integration, the eternity clause in Article 79.3 GG appeared as the core of decisions that could not be affected by supranational provisions. The eternity clause entailed in Article 79.3 of the Basic Law is, consequently, a way to identify the "German constitutional identity" (Ingold, 2015, p. 10; Polzin, 2016, pp. 424–426). But ironically, as we underlined before, the limits to the Basic Law constitutional amendment to which Article 79.3 of the Basic Law refers (such as the Basic Law principles, fundamental rights, or federalism) *were not decided by any popular instance*. The limits to European integration expressed through the eternity clause conceived as the German constitutional identity, by which the ultimate public authority must lie in the German people … have *never* been decided by the German people.

The Court aimed, thus, to give the ultimate authority to the German people through the eternity clause (interpreted as the German constitutional identity) *which basically was conceived to keep the issues therein mentioned out of the scope of people's decision*. On the one hand, the Court stressed the importance of linking every step to a European "closer union" to the will of the Germans but, on the other hand, the definition of what the constitutional identity is has been from the outset excluded from the consent of the Germans.

The jurisprudence of the German Federal Constitutional Court regarding the limits of European integration, in a different way, also implied the resurrection of the idea of a German nation that had been proscribed since the end of the war, the nation as a culturally and socially homogeneous group. The idea of associating the preconditions of democratic process within the constitutional State with some homogeneous factors assigned to the People was deeply elaborated by Carl Schmitt in the interwar time [which included a famous critique of the federation's national pluralism (Schmitt, 1993, pp. 375–376)]. Schmitt's idea was that the constitutional provisions that represented the fundamental decisions given by the people in exercising their constituent power were outside the scope of constitutional amendments (see Polzin, 2016, pp. 419–420). The latter happened even in the case, as the Weimar Constitution showed, in which there were no material limits to constitutional change. The aforementioned fundamental decisions signalling constitutional identity had to come from a politically united body in which, following the path of Sieyès' idea of nation, national homogeneity was to be considered essential.

Schmitt's approaches were revisited by the German Constitutional Court shortly after reunification, in examining the compatibility between the 1992 European Union Treaty and the German Basic Law (see Hestermeyer, 2013). The Court's reasoning on the nature of the demos that constitutes a limit to integration may be encapsulated in the following statement:

> States need sufficiently important spheres of activity of their own in which the People of each can develop and articulate itself in a process of political will-formation which it legitimates and controls, in order thus to give legal expression to what binds People together (to a greater or lesser degree of homogeneity) spiritually, *socially*, and *politically*.[35]

The German Constitutional Court perspective, that has been reiterated, for instance, on the judgements concerning the European institutions managing the sovereign debt crises, envisages a democratic theory grounded on an idealized interpretation of the historical facts. The Court, often accompanied by some sectors of the doctrine, has devoted itself to extract a past on the German people's involvement in constitutional decisions *that has never been*, a past that, in fact, has fluctuated in an almost completely opposite direction to the image presented, with the intention of restraining the supremacy of European governance.

Such indicated trends in the German Constitutional Court's jurisprudence were, for instance, confirmed in its decision issued on May 5, 2020 in which the Court arrogated itself the power to control the European Union law under the parameters of the German Basic Law.[36] The Court declared that the programme of sovereign debt purchasing launched by the European Central Bank had been developed beyond the powers transferred to the European Union and encroached on the democratic principle, fundamental rights of political participation, and, consequently, the German constitutional identity. The idea, in sum, was grounded on establishing an exception to the primacy of the European Law when the German Constitutional Court considered that it violated the core of the German national interests. Through the defence of the German companies' competitiveness and the German savers the Court envisaged, thus, a German *national* project, namely, to entrench the German economic hegemony even against the formal rhetoric of the Federal Government and the *Bundeskanzlerin* Angela Merkel, which given the Covid-19 problem, were at that time (in a different vein as to what had happened in the 2012 sovereign debt crises) supporting the gathering of European common funds to assist the most vulnerable countries.

Being aware of the legitimacy problems of invoking the emergence of the people within the German constitutional system, consequently, it is not casual that such idealization of the centrality of the German citizenry has been close to an approach on the constituent power as a reconstruction. More than in other constitutional systems, the German one is focused on the *ex post facto* resurrection of the foundation through the democratic channels provided by ordinary politics in the way conceived by Lindhal, Loughlin, or, among the German doctrine, Böckenförde. In sum, the democratic foundations of German constitutionalism represent an attempt to cling to the well-functioning present democracy in order to forget the deficits of the past. The constituent agency invoked to democratically cement the system, however, is precisely that from which arose all the demons of the past, namely, the German people conscious of its *national* unity, an agent able to undermine the whole constitutional architecture forged by the Allies when they attended the laying of the first stone of the Basic Law.

The constitutional resurrection of the German nation stems from the German Constitutional Court doctrine towards the European Union, but also in relation to the *Länder*, which the Allies had perceived as one of the main safeguards to prevent the return of a German unitary power. In a relatively unnoticed resolution, some judges of the German court identified the German Federation with the idea of *nation-State* (*Nationalstaat*), an association for many years surrounded by the taboo that accompanied the word "nation," given the memories of the Nazi past.

While analyzing an individual constitutional complaint concerning the celebration of an independence referendum in Bavaria, judges Huber, Kessal-Wulf, and König rejected the claim by stating that:

> In the Federal Republic of Germany, which is a nation-state based on the constituent power of the German people, *Länder* are not "masters of the constitution."[37]

In a few words, the Court contradicted the historical context in which the Federal Republic emerged (a constituent process that between 1946 and 1949 was initiated by the *Länder*) and prepared the grounds to allow the reappearance of a unitary conception of the German people *within* the German nation.

The voice of the German People

In an era in which democratic-based nationalism is engulfing great parts of the Western liberal democracies, the German constitutional system has remained relatively untouched by such a movement. Postwar German constitutional history (in which there was conceived a legal structure designed precisely to prevent the reappearance of a strong German national conscience by democratic means) is partly responsible for this contention. But beyond the constitutional developments, German postwar stability has found its legitimacy in economic prosperity: a trend that has been maintained and even enhanced in the midst of the monetary turbulences that convulsed the Eurozone and that reached their peak in 2012.

The German Federal Republic has not departed from its international commitments, beginning with its leading role in the European integration process, which also represented barriers against populism and policies exclusively centred on the satisfaction of national interests. Liberalism, rule of law, the defence of fundamental rights, and openness to international systems, were the principles that shaped the main characteristics of the German constitutional order, and still do. The fidelity of the German political and intellectual cadres to these fundamental mandates had been compensated by the enthronement of the German Republic as a global economic hegemon. Germany's success in terms of growth and welfare has also implied, however, *the renouncement* of the German elites of access to global political power, which their antecessors in the first half of the twentieth century had tried to obtain (Kundnani, 2015, pp. 13–15).

Several questions from the present context may arise: until when will German economic growth be sustainable? Until which point can the condition of economic hegemon be compatible with an irrelevant level of political power at the global scale? What relationship may be established between the German Republic and the European Union and to what extent should the German Republic use the European Union as its instrument to strengthen its political position within the global arena? But, given the present approach centred on the question of the constituent power, the question would be *until when will the German elites and the German citizenry put up with the circumstance of being ruled by a constitutional system determined by the winners of the Second World War?*

The seeds of the return to a German national-centred constitutional approach have already been planted in the developments of the jurisprudence of the German Constitutional Court. The guardian of legalism has become the main voice of the narrative as well regarding the democratic foundations of the German Republic, and also the main promoter, through the doctrine of the constitutional identity, of attaching the idea of a constituent agency to that of the German nation.

Even though, in the debates between the German Constitutional Court and the European Court of Justice concerning the Euro crisis, the German Court's claim based on the German constitutional identity arose in defence of liberal economic policies, the German opposition, let's say, to the monetary policies of the European Central Bank, was built in defence of German *national* interests and, particularly, in defence of the German financial establishment which retained the bulk of the sovereign debt of the countries of the south of Europe. The German actors lost the dispute and, for the sake of a European process profoundly affected by the withdrawal of the United Kingdom, did not insist on contradicting the European instances. Again, a political sacrifice was experienced by the German political and legal bodies in order to safeguard a stable constitutional framework that, after all, had allowed them to enjoy great economic benefits.

However, multiple factors, from an economic depression to a change in the German political leadership, might make this type of sacrifice less viable in the future. In such a situation, if the German side is at some point convinced that German national interests have to prevail over international commitments, and that need is democratically appreciated, a turn of this nature would probably have constitutional consequences, including a real "constitutional transformation" in which, as states Article 146 of the Basic Law, the German People would have the final word.

Notes

1 See the description of the German Basic Law drafting process provided by Ackerman and his interpretation on the role of the German Basic Law in his theory on constitutional dualism (Ackerman, 1992, p. 103) According to Ackerman, "the Basic Law was originally promulgated without a full-fledged mandate from the German People." See also Klein and Sajó, 2012, p. 432: "[The German Basic Law] was thus not approved by the people."'
2 For some basic contributions to the history of the last days of the Nazi regime and the immediate aftermath of the Second World War in Germany see Beevor, 2007; Jäckel, 1983; Lowe, 2013; Mac Donogh, 2009.
3 The circumstance that such elections took place only four days after the crush of the far-left Spartacus League and the murder of their leaders Rosa Luxemburg and Karl Liebknecht, might indeed raise again the question on the relationship between violence and constituent power.
4 Among the large bibliography concerning the 1949 German *Grundgesetz* creation we have consulted the following works: Benz, 1984; Eschenburg and Benz, 1983; Feldkamp, 1998; Friederich, 1949a and 1949b; Gimbel, 1968; Görtemaker, 1999; Hahn, 1995; Merkl, 1963; Murswiek, 1978; Mußgnung, 2003; Pfetsch, 1990; Preuss, 2006–2007, pp. 474–481; Spevack, 2001; Stolleis, 2003.
5 The notion of *Verfassungspatriotismus* was conceived by Sternberg, 1982, but it was the author Habermas (1987) that popularized it.
6 On the democratic deficits during the creation of the 1949 German Basic Law see generally Schneider, 1992, p. 22.
7 See Control Council Law No.46 of February 25, 1947 (*Abolition of Prussia*). The preamble of the Control Council Law states that "The Prussian State which from early days has been a bearer of militarism and reaction in Germany has de facto ceased to exist." See Huber, 1951, p. 648.
8 Hitler had reduced the *Länder* to mere administrative units, *die Gaue*, which were extended to the other areas annexed to the Reich from 1938 such as Austria (Dietze, 1960, p. 128; Mazower, 2008, p. 48).
9 The Bavarian legislative rejected the Federal Basic Law draft in a session developed during the night between the 19th and the 20th of May, 1949, with 101 votes against the draft, 63 in favor, and nine abstentions (seven parliamentarians were absent).
10 Preamble of the German Basic Law in 1949: "Conscious of its responsibility before God and mankind, filled with the resolve to preserve its national and political unity and to serve world peace as an equal partner in a united Europe, the German people *in* the *Länder* Baden, Bavaria, Bremen, Hamburg, Hesse, Lower Saxony, North Rhine-Westphalia, Rhineland-Palatinate, Schleswig-Holstein, Wuerttemberg-Baden and Wuerttemberg-Hohenzollern has, by virtue of its constituent power, enacted this Basic Law of the Federal Republic of Germany to give a new order to political life for a transitional period" (emphasis added).
11 This view agrees with the statement made by Konrad Adenauer in his speech opening the work of the *Parlamentarische Rat* in September 1, 1948, claiming that the Parliamentary was "completely free and unbound" in its decision-making

powers (quoted by, Lange, 1993, p. 23). See also on this point Merkl, 1963, pp. 114–115 and Spevack, 2001, p. 13.

12 Such a view is chiefly represented by Schulz (1984). The idea of the Allied Dictate is also supported by the former liaison officer to the *Parlamentarische Rat*, Hans Simons, who in a lecture entitled "The Bonn Constitution and its Government" delivered at the University of Chicago in 1951 stated that: "[t]he West German constitution was developed primarily as a consequence of the conflict between the United States and the other western powers, on the one side, and the Soviet Union, on the other, and not primarily in order to please the Germans or do something good for the Germans." See Simons, 1952, p. 114. See also Hahn, 1995, p. 7 and Spevack, 2001, p. 27.

13 There is some consensus, however, in appreciating that the local involvement in the 1949 German Constituent process was more intense in comparison to the Japanese constitutional drafting which may be more assimilated to the idea of an Allied dictate. On the differences between the German and the Japanese case see Jackson, 2008, pp. 1263–1265; Otake, 2001.

14 In a similar vein, Gimbel, 1968, p. 30; Golay, 1958, pp. 108–110; and Merkl, 1963, pp. 114–115.

15 This was for instance the case of Hans Nawiasky (Zacher, 1993, pp. 677–692) who was behind both the drafting of the Bayern's Constitution and, later, the configuration of institutions such as the Constitutional Court at the federal level.

16 On the relationship between Article 146 of the Basic Law and Article 79.3 of that text see, among many others, Heckel, 1995, pp. 531–553; Polzin, 2016, pp. 429–430. Polzin argues that the German Federal Constitutional Court's approach is likely to hold that Article 79.3 of the Basic Law does not apply within the context of Article 146 since the latter refers to the constituent power which is not bound by the material limits contained in the eternity clause.

17 In a famous article written before the reunification, in 1983, Professor Michael Kloepfer while admitting the lack of democratic legitimacy of the Basic Law in its origins (given the context of occupation, the lack of citizenry involvement, or the tensions derived from the partition and the Cold War) suggested that such gaps might be covered considering the provisory character of the *Grundgesetz* and the pending decision of the German People decision as foreseen by Article 146 of the Basic Law. But, since the word was not given to the German People either in the terms prescribed by Article 146 of the Basic Law at the time of the reunification it may be considered, as we shall see, that the democratic shortcomings of 1949 were not repaired.

18 Regarding the social frame of postwar Germany see Judt 2005, pp. 53–63.

19 "At the time when every other German institution appeared discredited by Nazi collaboration, the spiritual authority and administrative continuity of the Protestant and especially the Catholic Church accorded religious leaders enormous prestige," see Mitchell, p. 27.

20 In the Western zones more than 5,000 people were convicted of war crimes or crimes against humanity, of whom just under 800 were condemned to death and 486 were eventually executed (Judt, 2005, p. 53)

21 On the 1949 first *Bundestag* elections and its plebiscitarian character see Benz, 1984, pp. 251–270; Görtemaker, 1999, pp. 78–83; and Mußgnung, 2003, pp. 352–353.

22 The German Federal Constitutional Court banned the Socialist Reich Party in 1952 (considered successor of the National Socialist German Workers' Party – NSDAP) and the Communist Party of Germany in 1956.

23 On the constitutional development concerning the 1990 German Unification see, among countless literature examples, Frowein, 1992; Heckel, 1995; Jaggi,

2016a and 2016b; Kilian, 2003; Klein, 1995; Lerche, 1995; Quaritsh, 1995; and Wiederin, 1992.

24 See Article 7 of the Treaty on the Final Settlement with Respect to Germany of September 12, 1990 between the German Federal Republic, the German Democratic Republic, the Soviet Union, the United States, the United Kingdom, and the Republic of France.

25 Treaty on the Unification of Germany between the Federal Republic of Germany and the German Democratic Republic of September 12, 1990 (on this treaty see Quint, 1992–1993, p. 692).

26 *Unification Treaty* Judgment *BVerfG*, 2 *BvE* 2/90 of September 18, 1990.

27 In the description of the neoliberal thought tenets I follow the work of Slobodian, 2018, particularly pp. 271–272. On the influence of the neoliberal ideas in the formation of the West Germany economic order under Adenauer's government see Bank, 2013.

28 It may be noticed that thebelieved to be first Bilateral Investment Treaty, an instrument that confers protection to the foreign investor against the expropriations carried out by the State that hosts the investment, was signed between West German and Pakistani governments in November1959 under the auspices of the neoliberal approaches (Slobodian, 2018, pp. 142–143).

29 Among the different resolutions of the German Federal Constitutional Court that may be mentioned on the limits of the European Law regarding the German Constitutional Law see *Solange I* Judgment *BVerfG*, 2 *BvL* 52/71 of May 29, 1974; *Solange II* Judgment BVerfG 2 BvR 197/83 of October 22, 1986; *Maastricht* Judgment *BVerfG*, 2 *BvE* 2134, 2159/92 of October 12, 1993; *Lisbon* Judgment *BVerfG*, 2 *BvE* 2/08 of June 30, 2009, or *European Central Bank OMT-Programs* Judgment *BVerfG* 2 *BvR* 2728, 2729, 2730, 2731/13, 2 *BvE* 13/13 of June 21, 2016. Among the scholars that have shared the vision of the German Constitutional Court see Böckenförde, 1992a, 1992b, and 1999 (whose interpretation embedded the Court's vision when he served in it as a judge) and Kirchhof, 1992 and 2004.

30 Among the comments of this judgment in the German doctrine see Von Bogdandy, 2010; Classen, 2009; Halberstam and Möllers, 2009; and Tomuschat, 2009.

31 *Lisbon* Judgment *BVerfG*, 2 *BvE* 2/08 of June 30, 2009 (para 399).

32 *Lisbon* Judgment *BVerfG*, 2 *BvE* 2/08 of June 30, 2009 (para. 228).

33 See, for instance, *European Central Bank OMT-Programs* Judgment *BVerfG* 2 *BvR* 2728, 2729, 2730, 2731/13, 2 *BvE* 13/13 of 21 June, 2016.

34 *European Central Bank OMT-Programs* Judgment *BVerfG* 2 *BvR* 2728, 2729, 2730, 2731/13, 2 *BvE* 13/13 of 21 June, 2016 (para 129–135).

35 *Maastricht* Judgment *BVerfG*, 2 *BvE* 2134, 2159/92 of October 12, 1993 (para 88). On support of the German Constitutional Court thesis see Kirchhof, 1994.

36 Judgment *BVerfG* 2 *BvR* 859, 1651, 2006/15, 2 *BvR* 980/16 of May 5, 2020.

37 Judgment *BVerfG*, 2 *BvR* 349/16 of December 16, 2016.

5 "New constitutionalism" and the emergence of constituent power in some recent experiences

Constitution-making in modernity

Although the involvement of "the People" in the constituent foundations of existing liberal democracies is, as we have seen in the previous chapters, very contested from the historical point of view, this circumstance has not refrained actors and observers of constituent processes that have taken place during the last decades to sustain a discourse grounded on people's participation, inclusiveness, mobilization, and deliberation as a principal source of legitimacy and effectiveness of higher lawmaking (see, among many others, Eisenstadt et al., 2017; Elstub and Pomatto, 2018; Ginsburg et al., 2008; Hart, 2003; Klein and Sajó, 2012, pp. 435–436; Suiter and Reuchamps, 2016). In a widely shared normative view in constitution-making, the involvement of citizens before, during, and after constitution-writing is supposed to enhance the sense of collective ownership of the new text, promote a democratic institutional design, and facilitate its enforcement (see Negretto, 2020, p. 206).

Different contexts have arisen; thus, the discussion on the democratic conditions that must surround the constituent moment: to what extent does the popular constituent agency have to be vested with special channels of participation, different to those displayed in normal politics? Generally, it has been recognized that forms of popular participation had to be expanded well beyond ratification through a referendum on a product written by elites (Landemore, 2020, p. 180) and indeed various experiences have been recorded around the world in which members of the public (directly elected or through their leadership in civil society) or even citizens' assemblies composed of people chosen at random from the population, may participate in processes to set the agenda for constitutional negotiations, including the adoption of basic principles within which constitutional choice must occur (Choudhry and Tushnet, 2020, pp. 173–174). Compared to older constitutional processes, the novelty of the participatory constituent processes would mean that the citizenry would have a direct influence on the content and the shape of the constitutional text itself (Elster, 2012b, p. 148; Landemore, 2020, p. 180).

Such premises embed a movement that in some of those constituent workshops have been known as "new constitutionalism," according to which, while admitting that in the past constituent power was expressed mainly by violence, revolutions, or impositions, in the twenty-first century and in the age of the consolidation of democracy, constitutional transformations should be oriented by the effective role of "the People" in the creation and mastery of the constitutional framework.[1]

The association between constitutional drafting and a moment of special democratic sensibility characterized with the label of "new constitutionalism" was proposed within a Latin American context (Carbonell, 2003; Martínez Dalmau, 2009; Salazar Ugarte, 2013) and, particularly, within a Mexican context both while discussing the convenience of a new constituent moment during the celebration of the 1917 Mexican Constitution centenary, and during the drafting of the State Constitution of Mexico City (2016–2017). Such concerns, however, could be appreciated in other parts of the globe in spite of the fact that they may be expressed in other terms.[2]

Under the aforementioned perspectives, transformations in constitutional creations are likely to be triggered and coached by technological developments which allow a deeper involvement of a greater part of the population within specific and democratic contexts. Constitution-making in terms of participation in a fair process should not, thus, be the same as it was in the eighteenth century in the twenty-first century digital era (Rowe and Frewer, 2015; Suteu, 2015, p. 258). Such assumptions, on the other hand, would be handled both from a normative perspective (defending an ideal of people's special participation and deliberation while discussing the basic rules by which the society will be organized in the future) and from a descriptive perspective (arguing that such popular participation has been given in particular constituent processes that are fully analyzed). Complementary to citizen participation, normative assessments emphasize other values that modern constituent processes somehow related to the mentioned notion of new constitutionalism that should be taken into account. Arato, for instance, in what he calls the "post-sovereign" approach, insists that constituent decisions ought to be oriented by values such as pluralism, inclusion, publicity, fairness, compromise, generosity, and legality (2016, p. 11). He appreciates the fairness in the initiative of creating a new constitutional framework by extending in time the deliberative forums of constitution-drafting through conventions, constituent assemblies, and roundtables (2017, p. 376) without excluding the approval of interim constitutions able to ensure the stability of the transition between regimes (2016, p. 13; 2017, p. 377). Visions on more intense processes of popular mobilization through more refined forums in comparison with the old revolutionary tradition have been perceived in some of the constituent processes developed during the first two decades of the twenty-first century, such as the ones that took place in Iceland, Ireland, Chile, Catalonia (in its attempt to secede from Spain), or even in the European Union.

However, the point that I wish to highlight from the outset is that most of such constituent processes theoretically dominated by the willingness to give the voice to the people through uncountable channels of participation *have failed or are likely to fail.* At least, they might be considered failed as patterns of constitution-making developed under full democratic conditions and high standards of specific political mobilization by the citizenry. As we shall see, the negative evaluation of those constitution-making experiences from the normative perspective is rooted in the course that the mentioned processes have taken. There are two main scenarios that may derive from the modern constituent initiatives:

1. on the one hand, from the complexity of a participative and deliberative popular involvement while creating a new constitution in deepening democracies has resulted, after all, in the *abandonment of the constitutional blueprint* (the Icelandic case would be illustrative of that trend).
2. on the other hand, a specific and highly participative invocation of the constituent power has instigated a violent reaction on the part of the incumbent authorities in a manner that the proposed mechanisms of constitutional enactment *reproduce the old patterns* described in this book on coercion and abuses determining the constituent moment (the examples of Catalonia's secessionist struggle and that of the movement for a new Chilean Constitution are clear examples of this point).

My idea is that, given the historical background on constitutional creation that I have previously portrayed, the failures of modern processes somehow committed to providing a sophisticated web of channels of citizenship participation are foreseeable: an intense popular participation seeking a constitutional transformation is hardly compatible with an open, calm, inclusive, and specific deliberation. A constitutional transformation, as we have seen, is devoted to *the expulsion of the previous elite* which had designed the constitutional structure to serve its needs of perpetuation. Consequently, the consolidation of the structure of a new power through other agents is not likely to be produced without harsh convulsions.

In a different vein, even in supposedly advanced constitutional democracies, the need for comprehensive constitutional change is usually triggered by some sort of cataclysm. In both Ireland and Iceland, the initiative to enact brand-new constitutions circulated in the midst of the financial collapse caused by the 2008 global crises. Such States did not have the resources, the institutions, or the political capacities to deal with the gigantic shock to their overgrown financial sectors (Tooze, 2018, p. 167). In more divided and authoritarian regimes, the 2008 crash also had constitutional consequences, as in some Arab countries, but the constituent impulses, disregarding their success or not, were accompanied by instances of violence and sacrifice of human life.

In Northern Africa and the Middle East, the initial abuses perpetrated by the established regimes nourished a bigger contestation that, except in the case of Tunisia, evolved in an ineffective constitutional change given an authoritarian regression (as in Egypt) or straightforwardly into civil war, chaos, and the failure of the State (as in Libya, Syria, or Yemen). At any rate, historical events with their constitutional repercussions in the Northern Africa and Middle East landscape probably represent the opposite fashion of the normative proposals that the new constitutionalism has in mind when pondering the premises of legitimacy of a constituent process. Even the case of Tunisia, which may be qualified as the most successful experience in that area regarding the transition towards a constitutional democracy, did not escape from the plague of serious upheavals and mortal victims at the beginning of the process (Eisenstadt, Carl LeVan, and Maboudi, 2017, pp. 57–58; Gardbaum, 2020, p. 144).

In the middle term between the inclusive and specific constituent experiences in Iceland or Ireland (though buried in Iceland and incomplete in Ireland) and the brutal scenarios for constitutional developments recorded in the Arabic world, would be situated some of the Latin American constituent episodes which, as I mentioned before, coined the expression "new constitutionalism" and paved the way to rethink the constituent process as a participative and deliberative instance.

In spite of the more or less honest theoretical efforts to see in constituent processes such as the ones displayed in Venezuela, Bolivia, or Ecuador opportunities to set out a constitutional framework grounded in an intense and popular mobilization (Martínez Dalmau, 2009, pp. 265–269), the truth is that the constitutional elaborations achieved in these States coincide with the formerly described vision of a constitution as the legal certification of the victory of one group over the others by coercive means (Brewer-Carías, 2007, p. 71). The replacement of a decision on the allocation of power by another (the definition of the material constitution according to my approach) entails, predictably, the eruption of violence in some of the phases that encompass the life of those constitutional systems: while tumults and deaths were given by the creation of the new constitutional orders in Venezuela and Bolivia, unrest and victims were counted in Ecuador in 2019 once President Moreno sought to consolidate his position in opposition to his antecessor and founder of the new constitutional order, President Rafael Correa.

The stalemate of the constituent process promoted by President Maduro in Venezuela with the creation of the Constituent Assembly in 2017 (with the less concealed intention to retain political power that the regime had lost through the supermajority gained by the opposition in the 2015 National Assembly elections) revealed that the fierce fight between the political groups was not over and, thus, that the new decision on the allocation of power had not yet been adopted.

Bolivia's constitutional evolution maintains some analogies with those described in Venezuela, in the sense that the assembling of a majority by a group until that moment excluded from power, combined with social turmoil, propels a new brand of constitutional configuration (the 2009 Political Constitution of the Multinational State) which is used by the newcomers to consolidate themselves in the State's institutional architecture. However, when the opposition finds the opportunity to seize power (as it did in November 2019 by sending President Evo Morales into exile), the effectiveness of the constitutional order designed by the previous hegemonic group is questioned and the shaping of a new constitutional structure, adapted to the new partisan interests, is envisaged.

The constitutional dynamic in both Venezuela and Bolivia shows another characteristic typically associated with the emergence of constituent power in modernity: the use of constitutional politics by a strong (but temporary) majority which seeks to maintain its political predominance through the constitutional rules created under its auspices (Chambers, 2019, p. 1118). The cases mentioned reflect with remarkable precision the constitutional cycle described in the theory exposed in Chapter 2 of this book: the constitution as the legal correspondence to the assault on power performed by a given elite, by a faction, in a way according to which when some political cadres are replaced by others; such movement is also followed by a constitutional somersault. The formal constitution may be transformed, through regular or irregular means, because the underlying allocation of power, what I call the material constitution, has also been affected in its core.

Recent constitutional history in Chile is likely to evoke a different paradigm from those observed in Venezuela and Bolivia but, nevertheless, leading to a similar conclusion. While the need for constitutional change had been appreciated in Chile from the time of the transition to democracy at the end of Pinochet's dictatorship, the Chilean case is one of the rare examples in which a new constitutional blueprint was not activated by a social or economic commotion. In addition, the constituent process was encouraged from above, from President Bachelet's government, in a procedural plan able to capture all the concerns pointed out by the new constitutionalism approach: citizenry participation, pluralism, openness, inclusiveness, and deliberation. The result was that the Chilean constitutional-making process fell into a cul-de-sac, just as had happened in the experiences recorded among advanced European democracies. Citizenry responded to the government's constitutional struggle with apathy, to the degree that in the following presidential elections, Sebastián Piñera won, having run on an electoral platform which rejected major constitutional changes. However, scarcely one year passed since Piñera took office before virulent riots exploded across the country, placing the demand for a new Chilean constitution at the centre of the agenda. Given the threat of an open revolution, Piñera had no alternative but to commit himself to foster another constituent process by calling for a plebiscite in 2020 in which the citizenry would decide if they would vote for the drafting of a new constitution.

The point that I wish to stress here, however, is that the uproar which broke out in the fall of 2019 caused a death toll of at least 34 people. Before, there had been any mortal victims and the constituent process was conducted in a civilized manner, popular mobilization for a new Chilean constitution was discrete. When protests turned into violent upheavals, however, the aspiration for a total constitutional change grew among the citizenry. It should be underscored, in a different vein, that none of the constituent processes developed in Latin America, including the Chilean one in the case that someday a new constitution is approved, would satisfy the normative test proposed in these pages: the "no victims rule." In all these cases, constitutional transformations in some of their stages implied a cost in terms of human lives.

The constituent-making culture appreciated in Venezuela and Bolivia grounded in the subversion of constitutionalism by shaping new constitutions to suit selfish political agendas had been generalized in Africa as well (see

Albert, 2019, p. 113). The use of constitutional politics to entrench the violent occupation of power by new elites has not only been regular during Africa's first three decades of independence, but it has also traced some of the more recent African constituent experiences. Thus is seen, for instance, in the constituent process in Kenya reflected in the 2010 Constitution which had its origins in the humanitarian crises unchained in 2007 when the former President Mwai Kibaki was declared the winner of the presidential election held in December of that year. According to Duncan Okubasu (2017, p. 331) in some African countries, constitutional politics are

> appropriated by the ruling elites such that a constitution is important as formally legitimizing a regime and also for thwarting threats toward the regime.

In this chapter I am going to comment in more detail on some of the aforementioned constitution-making processes developed in the last decades to confirm the described oscillation of constitutional experiences between the specific (and tedious) participative frameworks that some liberal democracies have unfolded to establish new (and usually frustrated) constitutional arrangements, and the revolutionary instances that involve a disruption in the allocation of power and, consequently, an entire transformation of the constitutional system.

I shall begin in Europe and I shall finish in Europe. In the first and in the last cases I shall allude to a background which may be not considered "constitutional" since it clings on to international treaties: those organizing the European Union. In the next section I shall revisit a process already forgotten but, in its time, quietly discussed (though, and that was the problem, both within academic circles and within European political, economic, and administrative elites) regarding the replacement of the European treaties by the Treaty Establishing a Constitution for Europe. I conclude the narrative on recent appearances of the constituent power with another controversial invocation of European Union law: that related to the withdrawal of the United Kingdom from the European organization. Brexit, while debatable whether it is a constitutional transformation or not, deserves some considerations in the context of my descriptive and normative vision on constitution-making processes and, though it may sound a bit enigmatic concerning the United Kingdom, their relationship with violence.

European Union: Treaty Establishing a Constitution for Europe (2001–2005)

As is the case of much of the existing international legal order, the European Union (in its origins the European Communities) was a direct consequence of tremendous violent disturbances. The latter not only included the Second World War, but also the loss of Empire by the Western European Powers that founded the European Common Market. The creation of a free trade space was vital for the economic growth within a continent whose States had suffered a long haemorrhage of resources, financing colonial adventures, and had lost their privileged access to markets and raw materials in their former dominions (Garavini, 2012).

All in all, by the beginning of the twenty-first century, the European elites embarked themselves on a comprehensive reform of the architecture of the European Union without any immediate political or economic turmoil. It is true that the fragile sensation overshadowing the Western world as a result of the attacks on New York and Washington on September 11, 2001 might have motivated the need to accelerate the political integration of the continent (in fact, the European Council that called for the European Convention took place in Laeken in December 2001, barely a few months after the attack) but institutional reform had already been conceived in the Intergovernmental Conference held in Nice in December 2000, when few turbulences were visible on the horizon. Rather than terrorism or the fears of an economic default, the main concern of the European leadership, causing them to promote the change in the legal framework of the European Union (EU), was marked by the enlargement of the Union towards the former Communist States in Eastern Europe. In a sequence relatively rare in comparative perspective, the European constituent initiative was not a consequence of a humanitarian disaster (though challenges of such a kind would arise shortly after with profoundly divisive repercussions among the Europeans once the United States launched their crusade against Afghanistan and Iraq in retaliation for the September 11 attacks) but an attempt to digest a success: the victory of the European liberal democracies upon their socialist counter-model in Eastern Europe, a victory which, with the exception of the disintegration of Yugoslavia, had been developed in quite peaceful terms.

The process towards what had to be called the Treaty Establishing a Constitution for Europe was not, in summary, inspired by any collective tragedy. Together with the fact that the drafting proposed did not represent a radical mutation in the allocation of power between the States and the Union (the States still were characterized as "the masters of the Treaties") the reasons for the failure of the reform were unsurprising. The European Union would continue to be a Union of States, in which said States would still retain their basic attributes of sovereignty, including the right to secede unilaterally from the organization. Though the Convention in which the European constitutional Treaty was drafted mirrored itself on the 1787 Philadelphia Convention, few people, apart from those participating in the refined debates at the academic level, saw in the new constitutional proposal a transformation which might be compared with the transformation experienced in America in the transit from the Articles of the Confederation to the Federal Constitution.

The shrining of the word "Constitution" in the title of the treaty equally did not mean that the European process could be identified with the scene of a demos giving itself a constitutional framework, as had happened with the constitutional movements in revolutionary France. To begin, there was no demos (nor was there a common European political space) and that was, precisely, the main deficiency. The different *demoi* within the European nation-States were not likely to be very interested in the operation promoted by their respective elites, in spite of the fact that such elites, eager to consolidate a fully liberalized market within the new legal framework of the Union, habilitated different channels to ensure the participation of European citizenry in the process.

Beyond the formal and informal mechanisms of submitting proposals by a wide range of actors, some governments decided to call for referenda on the ratification of the text. Giving the voice to "the People" within the Member States revealed itself to be a deathblow for the reform. In some cases, as in Spain, the test was passed. Apathy generally characterized the following of the constitutional debate by the citizenry (neither transparency nor modernized access to the discussions in a growing digital society was provided) and once some sort of public mobilization was boosted, as in the examples of the referenda held in France and the Netherlands, it happened that both the French and the Dutch people repudiated the change.

The lesson was well learned by the European elites and the following reforms entailed in the Lisbon Treaty, straightly presented as an international treaty change dispossessed of any constitutional resonance, were passed without being ratified through referendum by the citizenship of the Member States (with the exception of Ireland, whose Constitution required a referendum to be held on such matters. The Irish People refused in the first term the Lisbon Treaty in 2008, a decision that was reversed in a second referendum in 2009).

The European experiment developed between 2001 and 2005 was ambiguous in its constitutional character. No immediate tragic precedent had instigated the drafting, and there had not been any disruption affecting the continuity of European elites which were the main actors pushing towards the achievement of the reform. If approved, given the scarce affection on the balance of powers, less could be really said regarding the constitutional theory that I have exposed. The thesis would be able to be maintained: after all, there would have not been a real constitutional transformation since the process had emanated from a violent background. But in its failure, we may find further evidence to support the idea that sober discussions, no pressing conflictive circumstances, and public indifference (probably explained because those dramatic circumstances are not given) do not lead to any significant event in constitutional terms.

States' Constitutions within Federations and constitutional transformations

I have mentioned in the introduction of this chapter that the ideas on popular participation while drafting a constitution (which I have gathered under the label of 'new constitutionalism') had one of their high points in the amendments to some States' constitutions within federations. Precedents on exploring new avenues of participatory and partially citizen-led decision-making processes on constitutional issues were seen in the citizen assemblies created on occasion of the electoral reform in British Columbia and Ontario (Suteu, 2015, p. 252). After those experiences, the integral drafting of a brand-new State constitution under the principles of popular engagement might be found in the elaboration and approval of the Constitution for Mexico City (2017).

With some of those examples in mind, I would ask if such successes regarding constitutional change in States belonging to wider federations may contradict my thesis, suggested above, according to which constitutional transformations are likely not to happen in specific, inclusive, and deliberative contexts.

Some North-American authors such as Sanford Levinson (2014) John Dinan (2006), and Alan Tarr (2006) have argued that instead of focusing at the United States national level to search for the involvement of the people in creating constitutions, scholars should pay more attention to the State level, in which some satisfactory stories from the point of view of fulfilling democratic premises while drafting fundamental rules might be told. American State constitutions have been amended over 7,500 times, amounting on average to 150 amendments per State (Albert, 2019, p. 113) and, as John Dinan's historical analysis revealed (2006, p. 63), most of these amendments were achieved through the action of an informed, participatory, and peaceful citizenship.

However, some precisions might modulate such optimistic observations on the exercise of power to both create and amend constitutions at the State level. On the one hand, it may be remarked that beside successful stories on constitutional change within the States, the shaping of State constitutions might be doomed to failure as well. Voters rejected, for instance, many times and in many American States the call for a State constitutional Convention to draft a new constitution (for instance, in New York in 1957 or in Missouri in 1962 and 1982).

On the other hand, it is quite arguable that the State-level experiences in constitutional creation may be compared to the federal ones (or the "national ones" with all the significance that the use of the latter adjective reveals). The revision of a State constitution is always given in a *limited* way. With the sole exception of secessionist challenges or annexations (also reflected, for instance, in the wave of constitutional replacements that the Southern American States experienced as a result of the Civil War and its aftermath) *existential decisions are only stated by the federal (national) level.* In other words, issues related to sovereignty, to the profound constellation of powers that dominate a given political community, are not concerned by State constitution-drafting (and maybe it is not therefore casual that people's participation is more tolerated in that constrained locus, since the real fundamental decisions are not affected). Changing a State constitution in a frame of very limited public powers is somehow inoffensive for the given structure of domination ruling in a society and is not likely to lead to violence, but it is not likely to lead to a real constitutional transformation, either.

Iceland: a never-ending constituent-making process

As a consequence of the financial crash that involved the default of all three of the country's major privately-owned commercial banks in late 2008, the demand for a radical constitutional change grew among Icelandic society, and the leftist government of Jóhanna Sigurdardóttir assumed the challenge by triggering in

2009 a process to replace the 1944 Constitution.[3,4] The independent Icelandic republic had certainly never autonomously written a brand-new document matching the nature of an independent republic since the 1944 constitution focused on ending the Danish monarchy and was otherwise largely a copy of the 1874 Danish constitution (Bossacoma, 2020, pp. 319–320; Meuwese, 2013, p. 473). Also in the Icelandic case, thus, and even in a stable democracy, constitutional change was at the outset associated with social unrest.

The crisis opened the door to reviewing the pillars of the Icelandic constitutional framework under profound innovations concerning the amendment procedure. The reform was inspired by the view that the people, as constituent agent, should have a direct impact on the constitution's contents and values without major involvement by the political parties (at least during the initial stages of the drafting). Deliberation and inclusiveness were intended to be the vectors to organize the new constitutional arrangements.

Shortly after the collapse of the Icelandic economy, a grassroots association calling itself "the Anthill" organized a large public event called a "National Forum" to discuss the future of Iceland. This National Forum gathered 1,500 individuals most of them randomly selected from the National Population Register, in a one-day exercise that consisted of articulating the values and priorities that should guide the renewal of government and public administration (Landemore, 2020, p. 186; Suteu, 2015, p. 261). The success of this first National Forum, and the media attention that it received, pushed the Icelandic Parliament to organize a second one already inserted in the formal constituent process.

Indeed, on June 16, 2010, Parliament had passed the constitutional act initiating the constitutional revision process and providing the shaping of a Constituent Assembly in charge of writing the constitutional draft. On November 6, 2010, a Constitutional Committee appointed by Parliament organized the aforementioned second National Forum, which encompassed 950 randomly selected citizens tasked with establishing "the principle viewpoints and points of emphasis of the public concerning the organization of the country's government and its constitution" (Landemore, 2015, p. 170, and 2020, p. 183; Suteu, 2015, p. 261). The National Forum's report constituted the starting point for the deliberation of the Constitutional Assembly, with 25 members from 522 candidates elected on November 27, 2010. The elections to the Constitutional Assembly showed, however, the first cause of disappointment in the constituent process: only 37 per cent of the electorate turned up at the polls (Thorarensen, 2017, p. 107). Such low turnout, much lower than for the elections of candidates to the legislature (which generally exceeds 80 per cent) was not certainly the best credential for a constituent process supposedly characterized by "the exceptional mobilization" of the people, to say it in Ackermanian terms.

Among the reasons suggested for the low turnout in the Constitutional Assembly elections was that the large numbers of candidates in the election made it difficult for voters to pick candidates from the great number of mostly unknown people (Thorarensen, 2017, p. 107). As the candidates had no connections with political parties and acted solely in their own personal capacity, it was likely to be difficult for voters to assess what policies they advocated. Such detachment of the candidates to the Constitutional Assembly from the political establishment, considered as a cause that might explain the low turnout, maybe suggests that even in constituent moments popular mobilization requires some sort of relation between the constituent agent and the immediate political debates developed by the representatives. The Icelandic experiment shows to what extent the interaction between constitutional politics and ordinary politics is twofold in nature: on the one hand, an excessive involvement of the ordinary representatives in the constituent process may lead to the use (and to the manipulation) of constitutional instruments for short-term politics. But, on the other hand, from the parallel running of the two tracks there may result a lack of interest on constitutional proposals among both the citizenry and the political staff.

Beyond the problem of the low turnout, the elections to the Constitutional Assembly had to surmount an invalidating ruling of Iceland's Supreme Court since a request concerning the candidates' legitimacy was held (Saunders, 2012, p. 6). The election of the Constitutional Assembly was disputed on the grounds of various alleged electoral defects in its execution, among them the violation of the right to vote by secret ballot (Thorarensen, 2017, p. 108). The 25 delegates originally elected were, on March 24, 2011, nevertheless, appointed by the Parliament to a body, whose name had been changed, called from then on the "Constitutional Council," which was given the same consultative role as the Constitutional Assembly had been intended to perform (Contiades and Fotiadou, 2017, p. 20). This decision by the Parliament was severely criticized by the opposition parties in the Parliament arguing that it constituted a circumvention of the decision of the Supreme Court (Thorarensen, 2017, p. 108). The change of the name would not cancel the problems of legality and legitimacy in which the creation of that institution incurred.

The Constitutional Council, however, convened and began to work. The Council basically sought (1) to inform the public of its progress, (2) to encourage public participation, and (3) to make suggestions as discussions went forward (Suteu, 2015, p. 262). For these purposes all sorts of social media were used including Facebook, Twitter, YouTube, and Flickr (Meuwese, 2013, p. 470). This phase of direct participation by the citizenry in the drafting included a series of 12 crowdsourcing moments (Landemore, 2020, pp. 189–190). Meeting schedules and minutes were posted online, and the Council's website was updated with news and a weekly newsletter. By the end of the Council's work, the public had made some 360 proposals and more than 3,600 comments on the platforms (Suteu, 2015, p. 262). The crowdsourced phase was not exempt from criticism among some local observers. Professor Helgadóttir (2014) for instance, pointed out that the internet consultations during the discussion on the 2011 constitutional draft did not foster the inclusion of traditional politically marginalized groups. It rather confirmed the empowerment of the native-born and middle-aged males who were by far the most active in using the social media to submit their proposals.

The Council's proposals were unanimously approved by all delegates on the council and submitted to the Althingi as a bill for a new constitution of Iceland at the end of July 2011. In the Parliament parties did not move much in terms of the next steps to be taken on the bill. Instead of preparing and processing the constituent task further, the bill was referred to one of the parliamentary standing committees which blocked the process for more than a year (Thorarensen, 2017, p. 109). Since the Parliament was strongly divided by the constitutional revision issue (a bill proposed by the Council with no intervention by Members of Parliament – MPs) it was likely that the political establishment opted for the typical option taken when the representatives do not want to go forward with something: sending it to a committee. In the end, however, the majority of MPs in the governing coalition parties decided to hold an advisory referendum on the original proposals on October 20, 2012 (Landemore, 2015, p. 170). Six questions were posed in this referendum, including "do you wish the Constitutional Council's proposals to form the basis of a new draft Constitution?" (Suteu, 2015, p. 263). In a low turnout of 49 per cent (higher than in electing the Constitutional Assembly but lower than in ordinary elections to the legislature) 64 per cent of those who voted on the question indicated that they wanted the Constitutional Council's proposals to form the basis of a new draft constitution (Thorarensen, 2017, p. 110). It should be underlined that the Council's proposals were submitted to the Venice Commission which issued a report expressing serious doubts about such constitutional proposals.[5] The Venice Commission saw a risk of political obstruction and instability that could undermine the country's good governance (Landemore, 2020, pp. 190–197).

Despite the results of the advisory referendum, political parties were unable to fully consider the draft before the general election in April 2013 (Bergsson and Blokker, 2014, p. 165). The bill with the constitutional proposals had been discussed twice in Parliament before another bill was passed in March 2013 which effectively postponed the third and final discussion for the new legislature which was going to be voted on that spring. Total constitutional revision needed a final and favourable vote of the Althingi to be passed. However, such a vote never occurred since in the mentioned elections on April 27, 2013, the conservative parties opposed to the new constitutional arrangements won a majority of seats and paralyzed the process (Landemore, 2020, p. 184).

The resignation of the conservative Prime Minister, Sigmundur Davíð Gunnlaugsson, in April 2016, the problematic dissolution of the Parliament, and the elections that finally were held in October 2016 did not invigorate the debate on the constitutional revision mainly because in spite of the fact that the forces which took power in January 2017 accepted some kind of constitutional changes, they disagreed about the character and the intensity of such changes (Helgadóttir and Ingólfsdóttir, 2017, p. 3). Again, the supposed "extraordinary politics" attached to a constitutional transformation were subordinated to the fate of the day-to-day democracy developed by the representatives of the Parliament. While two of the three members of the coalition (*Bright Future* and *Viðreisn*) believed in finishing the total revision of the Constitution by using the previous draft and enhancing direct democratic devices to allow popular participation, the *Independence Party*, which had been part of the previous anti-revisionist coalition between 2013 and 2016, admitted the need for constitutional changes but limited to certain points instead of drafting a completely new instrument.

In spite of such disagreements, among the three parties the 2017 coalition agreement stated the commitment to carrying on the work of revising the Constitution on the basis of the previous contributions but remarking the central role of the Parliament in the process: the work on the draft had to be mainly developed in a parliamentary committee. However, the Icelandic Government formed in January 2017 was disbanded after only eight months in power, due to several scandals affecting the Prime Minister Bjarni Benediktsson, and new elections were held in October 2017.

A new coalition government was concluded under the leadership of Katrín Jakobsdóttir between the *Leftist-Green Movement* (a left-leaning socialist party), the *Progressive Party* (centre), and the liberal conservative *Independence Party.* The mentions of constitutional change in their agreement were still scarcer than in the previous political phase. Nevertheless, in January 2018, Prime Minister Katrín Jakobsdóttir announced a new effort towards constitutional reform in Iceland, but on this occasion, it was planned from the outset that the constitution-making process would take a long period of time (seven years, two parliamentarian terms) in order to ensure a broad social and political consensus around the reform. Jakobsdóttir's initiative envisaged the reemergence of innovative public consultation means but the cornerstone of the proposal relied on recognizing the centrality of the Parliament in the whole process. The failure of the 2011 drafting process revealed that constitutional change would not have any prospect of success if it does not couple the public engagement expressed in innovative channels of participation, with the will of the political representatives in the existing institutions.

Aside from the evolution of the process and its possible conclusion with a "holistic reform" of the Icelandic Constitution, the constitutional product is not likely, however, to come from "a revolutionary moment" nor to represent a constitutional transformation, either, as shortly after, the economic crisis appeared to be the case. In the new horizon of the revision process, the key decision body has been placed on a committee composed of the leaders of the parties with representation in the Parliament in a way that although it makes the parties the central players of the process, thereby increasing the likelihood of ratification of the draft, it also increases the likelihood that the changes will be minor and that the input from the public will not have a significant impact (Hudson, 2018).

In the Icelandic case, some paradoxes might be observed: despite the support for the new constitutional settlement, the general election in 2013 was won by anti-revisionist parties. To some extent a part of the electorate which once supported the constitutional change from 2009 had, in the 2013 parliamentary elections, voted for the parties opposed to that change. Thus, the Icelandic experience shows that even the highest level of concern of public participation, mobilization, and deliberation on constitutional issues may lead to a stalemate, particularly if those opposed to the revision get the constitutional changes proposed watered-down or dissolved by the passing of time. The world's so-called first "crowdsourced" constitution-making (see Colón-Ríos, 2012, p. 182; Landemore, 2020, p. 189; Saunders, 2012, p. 6; Suteu, 2015, p. 261) was a process in which the citizenry not only behaved with relative indifference (it participated less in the election to the Constituent Assembly than it did in parliamentarian elections) but, furthermore, voted for the representatives that proposed the abandonment of the initiative. If political mobilization regarding the claim of passing a new constitution had been strong enough, this demand would also have been translated into legislative representation. The lower turnout to both the November 2010 elections to the Constitutional Assembly and the October 2012 advisory referendum on the questions relating to the constitutional revision also confirm that Icelandic society was more concerned by other issues than constitutional reform or, more precisely, that it saw the opportunity to overcome the crises without the necessity to change the legal framework altogether.

Another contradiction of the Icelandic events arises from the subordination of the Constituent Assembly to the legislature. Instead of being led by "extraordinary politics," it was "ordinary politics" which marked the tempo of the constitutional discussions. In spite of the initial financial shock, the constituent process never set out a complete replacement of the incumbent elites, the citizenry initiative to create a new constitutional order had to coexist with the representatives who finally managed to abort the attempt. Putting it differently: leaving aside the first expectations arisen while the Icelandic financial system was collapsing, the constituent process was never intended to be revolutionary – it was finally assumed that somehow the amendment of the rules in the existing constitution had to be respected including the fact that the Parliament had to hold the final word on the approval of a new constitution. The resignation with which the citizenry accepted that its proposals would need the final consent of the politicians may explain the apathy which progressively dominated events. Either way, the "crowdsourced" Icelandic constitutional process did not succeed in allowing "the People" to speak in creating a set of constitutional rules effectively passed.

The economic and social turmoil caused by the 2008 crash had not affected the grounds of Icelandic liberal democracy. Constitutional transformations and the appearance of the constituent power as we understand them are not likely to occur within stable contexts, meaning that the decisions on the allocation of power are not questioned at the most fundamental level.

Republic of Ireland: from comprehensive constitutional revision to punctual change

As happened in Iceland, the outburst of the 2008 financial crises strengthened the claim for a deep constitutional review among Irish society.[6] The failure of Ireland's governmental institutions to anticipate and then adequately address the economic difficulties contributed to a substantial decrease in recorded levels of trust in the Irish government (O'Sullivan et al., 2014, p. 554). Even the first public reaction adopted an anti-establishment character, demanding more efficient control and accountability of public bodies (De Londras and Morgan, 2013, p. 179). Protests, notwithstanding, did not become a breakup. Changes would be developed within the existing constitutional amendment procedure and the replacement of the political cadres would take place through ordinary electoral processes, such as those in the 2011 general election, which swept from power the party (Fianna Fáil) that had formed the Irish government for 61 of the 79 years since it first came to office in 1932. However, the fact that even in 2011 the voters also chose other establishment parties (though they had been out of power for 14 years) also reduced the momentum for a more radical constitutional reform.

Already in the previous mandate the Parliament Joint Committee on the Constitution had debated the need for a constitutional amendment focused on electoral reform (Čolić, 2014, p. 10; Suteu, 2015, p. 264). The Committee report, issued in July 2010, proposed the establishment of a Citizens' Assembly to consider this question, a concern that was shared by the major Irish political parties which concurred to the 2011 election supporting the call for a Constitutional Convention "to consider comprehensive reform" and, thus, extended to other issues beyond electoral design. In July 2012, the Irish Parliament passed a resolution establishing the terms for Convention integrated by (1) a majority of citizens randomly selected among those entitled to vote at a referendum (66 members), (2) 33 elected legislators of the political cadres (29 of these from the Irish Parliament and four from the Northern Ireland Assembly), and (3) the Chairperson, Tom Arnold, appointed by the Government (Carolan, 2015, p. 739; Farrell, 2014, pp. 103–104; Farrell et al., 2017, pp. 122–123; Suteu, 2015, pp. 265–266). This composition of the Convention led to different sorts of criticisms. Previous experiences on assemblies created for debating constitutional changes proved that a process completely independent of party politics fostered the risk of political detachment.[7] But, in an opposite direction, it was argued that the involvement of political establishment members would lead to the blocking of a radical reform (Carolan, 2015, p. 740; Farrell, Harris, and Suiter, 2017, pp. 125–126). There was generally the fear that the politician members might seek to dominate the discussions and the decision-making proceedings. This fear was, however, likely to be mitigated by training facilitators to ensure that all members had an equal chance to contribute to discussions and by secret ballot (Farrell, Harris, and Suiter, 2017, p. 126). In another sense, the representativeness and the inclusiveness of randomly selected citizens by a survey company brought about lots of doubts: was, thus, statistical representativeness by itself adequate to ensure the legitimacy of the body? (Carolan, 2015, p. 742). Was a statistically representative sample of citizens enough to represent the attitudes that exist within the community at large on different controversial issues? What contribution was made by the random selection of citizens to the Convention beyond what was provided by ordinary representatives in the legislature? Which were, in short, the merits of the randomly selected citizens in order to debate on the grounds of the political system? (see Ólafsson, 2021).

Such questions, however, did not thwart the Convention's work which began on December 1, 2012, and sought to produce reports on several constitutional issues [the Convention terms of reference listed eight issues but the Convention proposed other relevant amendments (Farrell, Harris, and Suiter, 2017, pp. 122–124)]. The government, in addition, committed both to respond to each Convention's report within four months and to indicate a time frame for submitting accepted recommendations for a referendum (Suteu, 2015, p. 266). However, this point was also controversial since it was considered that the government had the final word in deciding which questions would be addressed to the people in the referendum and that the Convention only played an advisory role (Farrell, Harris, and Suiter, 2017, pp. 122–129). The established constitutional amendment process did not render other options. Since the Constitution provided that an amendment has to be approved by both Houses of Parliament before holding a referendum, it was considered that the government, which typically controls a majority in the Parliament, had the power to choose the issues put to the people in a referendum. The gathering of the Convention did not preclude, accordingly, the following of the constitutional amendment rules.

The Convention received thousands of submissions, especially on the more controversial issues discussed such as same-sex marriage and the relationship between church and State. In the same way as in the Icelandic Constitutional Council, the Irish Constitutional Convention works were uploaded onto its website and social media such as Facebook, YouTube, and Twitter, which were used in order to interact with the citizenry (Suteu, 2015, p. 267).

Yet what seemed an initiative leading to a substantial amendment of the Irish Constitution as an outcome of a complex and inclusive participatory process (28 discrete recommendations had been made by the Constitutional Convention) was finally reduced to only three issues: the recognition of the right to marriage for same-sex couples, the reduction of the minimum age of 35 years to 21 to access the Presidency of the Republic, and the removal of blasphemy as an exception to the right to express convictions and opinions freely. In 2015, two referenda were held on both the question of same-sex marriage and the minimum age to accede to the Presidency of the Republic, but only the recognition of the right to marriage of same-sex couples enjoyed majority support among the voters (the reduction of the threshold age to be President of the Republic was rejected).

Regarding the removal of blasphemy as an exception to free speech, the Constitutional Convention proposed in 2013 the replacement of blasphemy in the Constitution with a prohibition on incitement of religious hatred, but the reform was suspended until 2017 when it was announced that the English comedian Stephen Fry was under criminal investigation for blasphemy about comments made in a 2015 interview with Gay Byrne. The public indignation caused by the criminal charges against Fry led the government to accept the holding of a referendum on simply removing the word "blasphemous" from Article 40.6.1 of the Constitution (different from what the Constitutional Convention had proposed). The referendum took place on October 26, 2018 and the "Yes" won by 64.85 per cent of the vote, allowing the Thirty-Seventh Amendment of the Constitution to be passed.

But there was no further progress concerning the remaining issues handled by the Convention. The government infringed the terms on giving response to them, and that happened even considering that the executive had committed itself to call for a referendum in some additional questions, such as in the case concerning the reduction of the voting age to16 (Farrell, Harris, and Suiter, 2017, p. 131).

In parallel to the work developed by the Constitutional Convention, there was launched the proposal to abolish the upper house of Parliament, the *Seanad*. Such an amendment would have represented by itself a relevant change for the Irish constitutional system, since it intended not only to abolish the Senate but also to reconstitute the legislature as a unicameral Parliament (Albert, 2019, p. 66). Such change would have concerned the nature of legislative representation, the lawmaking process in its entirety, the separation of executive-legislative powers, and the functioning of democracy (Doyle, 2013a, pp. 199–200). The Thirty-Second Amendment of the Constitution Bill concerning the Senate issue contained therefore over 40 discrete amendments to the Constitution (Albert, 2019, p. 66; Doyle, 2013b). However, none of these questions were discussed through the Constitutional Convention nor were attached to the comprehensive participatory process to amend the Constitution. The Irish government precluded the Convention from being involved in the design of the legislature (Doyle, 2013b), a decision that confirmed that popular participation on the debate around structural issues had its boundaries. Citizenry only had the opportunity to debate on the abolition of the Senate, and all the linked amendments regarding the legislative functions on occasion of the campaign preceding the holding of the referendum on the bill. In the fall of 2013, notwithstanding, Irish voters narrowly refused the constitutional amendment proposal by 51.8 per cent to 48.2 per cent (Albert, 2019, p. 66).

Both the 2016 and the 2020 Irish general elections showed a fragmented legislature that even made it difficult to form government, not to mention to go ahead with an ambitious constitutional reform. However, between both elections was discussed and approved another amendment to the Irish Constitution. That change was of the utmost transcendence given the background of Irish constitutional history: the Thirty-Sixth Amendment which permitted the Irish legislature to regulate for abortion (De Londras and Enright, 2018). The Thirty-Sixth Amendment repealed the Eighth amendment, introduced in 1983, that had safeguarded the right to life of the unborn, and had made abortion illegal unless there was a serious risk to the life of the mother. By the beginning of the 2010s, the social atmosphere regarding the question of the termination of pregnancy had completely changed (partially motivated by the death in 2012 from septic miscarriage of Savita Halappanavar, whose request for an abortion was denied) and in the run up to the 2016 general election, five parties concurred with the commitment to hold a referendum to repeal the Eighth Amendment. When the Fine Gael-led government was formed and Enda Kenny took office as Taoiseach, he promised a randomly selected Citizens' Assembly to report on possible changes to the Eighth Amendment. The Citizens' Assembly (inspired in the citizenry branch of the previous Constitutional Convention) discussed the issue from November 2016 to April 2017, with invited experts and stakeholders, and voted to recommend repealing the existing text and replacing it with an explicit mandate for the Oireachtas to legislate on abortion. The bill was discussed and passed by the Irish legislature and ratified in a referendum held on May 25, 2018, in which the Yes won, gathering 66.4 per cent of the votes with a remarkably high turnout (64.13 per cent). The Thirty-Sixth Amendment to the Irish Constitution concerned a very sensitive issue, caused an unprecedented popular mobilization, and the citizenry was involved in the deliberation through innovative mechanisms such as the Citizens' Assembly.

Popular mobilization and discussion on abortion and same-sex marriage (after all, together with the removal of the offence of blasphemy from the Constitution, same-sex marriage was the only relevant issue that came out from the Constitutional Convention) shows to what extent a constitutional change depends on the presence of a conflict hovering in society (and on the passion that it awakes) to go forward. As had been pointed out (Sinnott, 2002, p. 815), Irish politics have been for decades dominated by a powerful religious-conservative versus secular-liberal cleavage regarding to which both groups, conservative and liberals, had developed strategies grounded on constitutional change to advance in their own position (Doyle, 2017, p. 11). Whereas in other contexts such controversies on moral issues would only be displayed through ordinary legislation in Ireland, given the influence of the Catholic Church since the foundation of the State, debates around sex, marriage, abortion, and blasphemy had been constitutionalized and, indeed, as we have seen, were the ones to be considered and approved by formal constitutional amendment in the last decade. Regarding same-sex marriage, for instance, it has been admitted that no constitutional change was required to allow it (O'Mahony, 2012; Tobin, 2016) however, taking into account the position of other significant constitutional actors on the question [such as the courts, arguing for the constitutional ban of same-sex marriage (O'Mahony, 2012, pp. 200–214)] and the aforementioned context of conservative-liberal disputes, the question was finally raised both by the legislature and the Constitutional Convention to the constitutional track.

Allowing the regulation of abortion or same-sex marriage instigated citizenry participation and reflected the ascendency of the liberal part of the cleavage and the dilution of the Catholic characteristics that had marked the 1937 Irish Constitution (Doyle, 2017, p. 10) but it is arguable that such changes represented a *real* constitutional transformation in the sense here described as a reassignment of powers. If we consider that such a series of constitutional changes represent a marginalization of the conservative trend and a minimization of the Catholic Church's power upon Irish institutions, and we observe that no violence was displayed in the process, the Irish reforms of 2015 and 2018 might be deemed as one of the scarce examples of a constitutional transformation that respects the no victims rule (though maybe a feminist account would consider, not misguidedly, that Savita Halappanavar's death as a consequence of the septic miscarriage encroached that rule).

At any rate, in my opinion, it is difficult to find even within the Irish context and regarding the Catholic Church (which, in another sense, has seen its influence reduced at the global scale) a regime change by constitutionally regulating abortion, same-sex marriage, or by removing blasphemy as an exception to free speech. At the end of the day, the conservatives still play a relevant role in Irish politics, even integrate the majoritarian parties (though possibly not as they did some decades ago) and, as we have seen, the more radical constitutional change envisaged by the beginning of the 2010s (which might have provided the complete reallocation of power) fizzled out.

Why, thus, was comprehensive constitutional reform abandoned in the Irish case? Several hypotheses might be suggested: as happened in Iceland, the complexity of citizenry involvement in discussing structural questions of the amendment of the Constitution paralyzed the process and the dynamic of normal politics devoured the higher lawmaking pretensions. As we have seen, the Irish government maintenance of the final word regarding any recommendation on constitutional reform was deemed also as a shortcoming that undermined the ambition of the change. The concern for opening channels of direct political participation did not avoid placing the final decision in the hands of the representatives. Interests regarding the short-run political questions prevailed upon the urge to create a brand-new constitutional framework.

Some observers, however, considered the Irish Constitutional Convention a success since at least the question concerning same-sex marriage had been passed resulting from a process of deliberation (see Suteu, 2015, p. 267). But adopting same-sex marriage is not a total revision of the constitutional pillars, and certainly does not represent the emergence of the constituent power, and one might consider that it may even be doubtful if regulating such questions concerning family law belongs to the realm of constitutional politics. In another sense, if the economic crises instigated the call for a total constitutional revision, it was not clear if, already from the proposals of the Convention, the recommendations had anything to do with the issues highlighted by the economic crisis (what connection may we find, for instance, between the social and economic collapse, and same-sex marriage?). Anyhow, as the intensity of the economic malaise diminished, also so did the ambition for constitutional reform which basically spun around issues that had already been discussed at different levels (constitutional, legislative, or judicial) in the previous decades.

This latter consideration leads us to a general observation in regard to constituent processes developed in stable democracies and, as both in the Irish and in the Icelandic cases, grounded on the principle of public engagement: the point is that once the people themselves are called to discuss constitutional reforms, even to the degree of setting up the constitutional agenda (as did the random citizens selected for the Irish Constitutional Convention), *they do not really know what they are expected to deliberate on.* Arguing for a radical measure against the structure of power (to which the constitution represents the legal translation as, let's say, against the free market economy) is excluded from the outset. That is probably why the deliberation is reduced to secondary things (such as the age of voting or same-sex marriage) that do not really put at stake the foundations of the system.

Violence and constitutional change in the hands of temporary majorities: Venezuela, Bolivia, and Ecuador

The new constitutionalism as understood regarding some Latin American scenarios had a twofold dimension: on the one hand, it alluded to a pledge for a wider recognition of social and environmental rights in order to entrench more egalitarian societies and, on the other hand, was linked to normative proposals of procedure concerning constitutional enactment by promoting equal participation of the citizens in the discussion and decision on the new constitutional framework. If people had to be equal within the society, they were supposed to participate equally as well in creating the rules that would govern such a society (Colón-Ríos, 2012, p. 36; Martínez Dalmau, 2009, p. 267).

The ideal, nevertheless, contrasted with what happened in places such as Venezuela, Bolivia, and Ecuador in which the socially and politically egalitarian discourse on the exercise of the constituent power covered an operation that confirmed the imposition of the power of one faction upon another. A temporary majority used its newly acquired power to hammer out a constitution: it shielded itself through the constitutional structure to safeguard its hegemony.

Indeed, President Hugo Chavez in Venezuela was not likely to respect the values of pluralism and inclusiveness when in 1999, shortly after he entered office, he called for elections to a Constituent Assembly grounded on the popular will expressed in a previous referendum which, although organized in violation of the amendment rule of the 1961 Venezuelan Constitution then in place, was authorized by the Venezuelan Supreme Court (Judgement No. 17 on the referendum for Convening Constituent Assembly of January 19, 1999, see Colón-Ríos, 2020, p. 281). Hence, via reform of the electoral system, it was ensured that 95 per cent of the members elected in the Constituent Assembly were aligned with the President (Brewer-Carías, 2007, p. 72). The wide recognition of fundamental rights, the concern for indigenous communities, or the design of participative mechanisms for the citizenry entailed in the 1999 Venezuelan Constitution did not impede that the so-called "Bolivarians" used the constitution-making process to solidify their control of the State. They invoked plebiscitarian mass support in order to transform the constitutional structure, dismantled checks and balances, concentrated power in the figure of the President, and promoted the immediate reelection of the representatives loyal to the regime (Weyland, 2013, p. 22).

As mentioned before, the successor of Chavez, President Maduro, sought to display an analogous operation by convening another Constituent Assembly in 2017 dominated by his acolytes. But Maduro's attempt (though it allowed him and his followers to retain rule while the opposition had obtained the majority of seats in the Parliament) did not repair the deep political division spreading across

Venezuelan society in a conflict that had no prospect of being solved and that became particularly acute when the President of the National Assembly, Juan Guaidó, proclaimed himself Venezuelan President in January 2019, gaining some international recognition.

As had happened in Venezuela by the end of the nineties, with social disturbances preceding the constituent manoeuvre, also the immediate background of the constituent process in Bolivia, developed in the 2000s, was defined by the fight for natural resources between the elites and the indigenous people and labour groups, causing terrifying bloodbaths and leading to the resignation of two presidents, Sánchez de Lozada, and Mesa, before the election of Evo Morales (Massüger Sánchez Sandoval and Welp, 2016, p. 112). The accession of Morales to office was accompanied by the penetration into the State apparatus of Bolivian social segments traditionally excluded from the political decision-making processes. The new majority, however, did not miss the opportunity to redesign completely the Bolivian institutions through the approval of a new constitutional framework in order to ensure that the people that had just been included into the system were not going to be expelled again. Such an operation required the transformation of what was called to be a temporary rule, into a permanent regime. If the Constitution was the product of a faction, other factions would not see any possibility to reach power again if they followed the rules of the Constitution. Accordingly, they would have more incentives to demolish the constitutional system by the force of facts than by trying to become a majority under the constitutional provisions conceived by their adversaries. That was exactly what happened when after a series of protests claiming some supposed irregularities in the general elections of October 2019 (which encompassed the doubts around the reelection of Morales as President), some elements of the army and the police changed sides and forced Morales to resign. Although the 2009 Bolivian Constitution remained nominally in force, and even though the Constitutional Court accepted the self-proclamation as President of Jeanine Áñez, this political change did not occur through legal means. In October 2020, nevertheless, Morales' ally Luis Arce won by a landslide in the Bolivian presidential elections making predictable the return of the social cadres that had supported Morales in power and, thus, the maintenance, at least for a while, of the constitutional regime.

One cannot say for sure that the drafting of the 2008 Ecuadorian Constitution was not dominated by the social disturbances that surrounded both the drafting of the Venezuelan Constitution in 1999, and that of the Bolivian Constitution, in 2009. But political convulsions had been taking place in Ecuador for more than ten years before the new Constitution was ratified by referendum on October 20, 2008. The constitutional regime that was in force when President Rafael Correa called for the gathering of the Constituent Assembly was that of 1998 which had been enacted as a consequence of the coup d'état that had removed President Bucaram in 1997. Constitutional rupture, thus, had already been perpetrated by the 1998 Constitution, opening a lapse of time that witnessed profound economic, social, and institutional breakdowns, including the ruling and fall of five presidents between 1998 and 2006, and the Supreme Court cessation of activity for almost a year. The temporary popular support expressed through the election of President Correa was used to promote, in the words of the President himself, a "radical, deep and fast change of the political, economic and social system" for which it was necessary to circumvent the constitutional provisions in force. In a similar way as in Venezuela and Bolivia, the constitutional barrier was surmounted by calling to "the People," firstly, in a popular consultation on the convenience of setting up a Constituent Assembly (April 2007) that the 1998 Constitution did not contemplate and, secondly, in the elections to that Assembly (September 2007) in which Rafael Correa's political party, *PAIS Alliance*, won the majority of the 130 available seats.

If the events that led to the 2008 approval of the Constitution, though on occasions turbulent, did not reach the same degree of violence that was present in the prelude of the constituent processes both in Venezuela and Bolivia, the enforcement of the Ecuadorian constitutional provisions had not been entirely specific: in the autumn of 2019, serious upheavals erupted as a response to President Moreno's economic initiatives which brought at least eight deaths (some organizations, such as the Confederation of Indigenous Nations, claimed that there were more than one hundred missing people) and around 1,500 injured. At any rate, violence has been present with more or less intensity in some stage of the three Latin American constituent experiments here described.

David Landau (2013a) in analyzing the constituent-making processes in Venezuela and Bolivia (he added the Egyptian constitutional drafting that followed the fall of Hosni Mubarak in February 2011) did not hesitate in qualifying such experiences as failures. Indeed, political developments would confirm Landau's predictions, and of the three regimes two, Bolivia and Egypt, collapsed through a coup d'état and the third, Venezuela, as we have seen, is besieged by constant political, economic, and social crises. But at least the constituent processes in Venezuela, Bolivia, and Egypt may be qualified as a success under the main perspective that might be taken into account when assessing the emergence of a new constitutional framework, namely, *that a constitution was effectively passed.* Landau warned about the danger of regime transitions where there was an absence of clearly defined and credible institutions and rules. He also pointed out the manipulation of temporary majorities to reshape the political system in an illiberal manner and denounced the use of constitutionalism to conceal undemocratic practices (see also Albert, 2019, p. 50). In such scenarios, the introduction of formal safeguards, such as a wider recognition of human rights, may be read as a "collateral effect" of the main goal pursued by the constituent agents: to entrench their recently obtained political hegemony. But the question is if *any* constitutional experience seeking to be completed (and differently as to what had happened with the abandonment of comprehensive constitutional changes in Iceland or in Ireland) did not require a quantum of harm. If a constitution is a decision on the allocation of power conveying the replacement of an elite by another through violent means, it is not surprising that, even under the coverage of the effusive language on democracy and fundamental rights, constitutional achievement understood as the approval of an entirely new political system only emerges in a context of conflict and polarization, in which there are winners and losers.

After all, and aside from the disgraceful paths that had been taken in Venezuela, Bolivia, and Ecuador from 2019, their respective constituent processes had culminated, the rupture with the old regime had been consummated, and the new regimes, even with authoritarian features, had been consolidated. That was much more than experiences in some European democracies might say in spite of their overwhelming concern for the political participation of the people. Maybe Carl Friedrich would agree in stating that processes such as the Icelandic or the Irish ones were not real manifestations of constituent power. According to Friedrich (1968, p. 130), constituent power must be "always employed to establish a constitution" and, thus, if a constitution is not established, that means that the exercise of the constituent power has been an illusion.

In the previously mentioned comment by Landau on Venezuela and Bolivia he concludes that:

> An important paradox of modern regime transition is that it might sometimes be necessary to preserve undemocratic enclaves in a regime in order to create a viable democracy.
>
> (2013a, p. 980)

But such an observation might be applied to a more encompassing view of constitutional transitions: the failure of constitutional transformations in stable democracies without coercion maybe shows that the "preservation of undemocratic enclaves" can be distinguished regarding *all* the constitution-making processes that effectively pass a constitution. If we associate the aforementioned allusion to the "undemocratic enclaves" with factual reality, power, and imposition, it is unavoidable not to come back to the idea according to which it is difficult to find the establishment of a new constitutional regime without the infringement of the no victims rule in some stage of its evolution, even in the case that such constitutional framework (whether in reality or as a façade) is devoted to preserving the rule of law, human rights, and democracy.

Republic of Chile: from sober deliberation to attempted revolution

In October 2015, the President of Chile, Michelle Bachelet, announced the opening of a process of adopting a new Constitution for Chile with the intention to repeal the current Constitution, which was passed in 1980, during the era of the dictatorship of Augusto Pinochet.[8] In 1988, a plebiscite was held in which the "no" campaign opposing Pinochet's continuity in the presidency won nearly 56 per cent of the vote. The social and political rejection of the dictatorship was at that time strong enough to remove Pinochet from office, but it lacked the wide majority support to instigate a constitutional revolution that might dismantle the dictator's constitutional legacy. Even though several packages of amendments had been passed from 1989 that aimed to set aside the authoritarian sections of the Constitution, and go forward with the democratization of the system, discontentment around the constitutional framework had subsisted in large sectors of Chilean society for decades. After all, the 1980 Constitution in force was still that which had been approved under an authoritarian regime and the high quorums required to amend the nuclear sections of the Constitution conferred the heirs of Pinochet's regime a kind of veto power over the political process (Bellolio, 2016; Carrillo, 2002).

Echoing such claims and hoping that over the years a wider majority for constitutional transformation had been consolidated, President Bachelet triggered a constituent process with the aim of passing a newly branded Constitution able to replace any vestige of the authoritarian past (Heiss, 2017, pp. 472–473). At the same time, given the context in which the constitutional movement was going to be developed, a stable democracy in the digital era, the constitutional process was committed from the outset to a crowdsourced paradigm grounded in deep public involvement, transparency, and inclusiveness. The Chilean struggle for the new Constitution, thus, would take place on "a long and winding road" (Coddou McManus, 2016) composed by seven successive stages which had been conceived as avenues of direct democratic engagements: (1) a phase of "civic and constitutional education," (2) local and regional "dialogues" to gather citizens' opinions at the local, provincial, and national levels called *cabildos* o *encuentros* besides a parallel process of consultation with indigenous peoples, (3) the creation of a "National Council of Observers" to overview the organization of such *encuentros*, (4) the drafting of a new constitutional baseline grounded on the outcomes of the dialogues, (5) constitutional reform to allow for the wholesale replacement and not just the mere amendment of the current Constitution, (6) Congressional debate of the constituent mechanism. The latter debate might be developed by the Congress, by a mixed Convention with congressmen and women plus citizens, by a proper Constituent Assembly, or even through a referendum to delegate this decision to the people, and (7) finally, there would take place a referendum to approve or reject the new text.

The Chilean constitutional initiative, however, had to face up to some important challenges that diluted the whole process. First, as I had already suggested in commenting on the European Union struggle to pass the Treaty Establishing a Constitution, constitutional transformations were not likely to be achieved in time of ordinary politics and lacking a political, economic, or social crisis. Bachelet's mandate between 2014 and 2018 was a relatively calm and prosperous one. Though the enormous social differences and inequality that were, under the surface, nourishing the restlessness that would arise in 2019, by the mid-2010s the Chilean recovery from the previous global crises had been quite successful.

Although the constituent process had been celebrated by several regional and international organizations, such as the OECD, it did not generate a massive mobilization of opinion, nor a passionate debate among citizens. Furthermore, the constitutional agenda, during Bachelet's initiative, had not been detached from that developed by the ordinary institutional debate. In fact, as the constitution-making process had been designed and scheduled, ordinary debates on politics had been intertwined with constitutional discussions: the discussion on the Constituent mechanism, for instance, was foreseen to take place after the 2017 Presidential and Parliamentarian elections leaving therefore the future of the constitutional reform clinging on to the regular elections of the representatives. Bachelet herself sought for another term in office presenting herself as the candidate of constitutional reform but, set against the case of Roosevelt and the New Deal (in which the constitutional discussion was linked to the presidential candidate solutions for the great economic disorder) the case of Bachelet, without any structural crisis to surmount, reduced the constitutional debate to the assessment of the ordinary presidential administration. In lacking turmoil, the risk of confusing the constitutional agenda with the ordinary agenda (something as prosaic as winning ordinary elections) was higher. What was worse: some accusations of corruption that tarnished Bachelet's last months in office also promoted scepticism around the constitutional blueprint that was associated with her figure.

Another paradox shown by the Chilean case during Bachelet's mandate lay in the fact, as happened in Iceland, that even though some part of the society might have been mobilized, decisive groups remained unconcerned (such as the conservative and liberal establishment). Ordinary politics had not been abandoned and, consequently, nothing substantial happened to persuade them to participate in debate with those that supported a constitutional change.

In the 2017 presidential elections, the constitutional transformative project proposed by the left and led by President Bachelet was confronted with that of the right-wing candidate Sebastián Piñera, who rejected the creation of a new constitutional arrangement. According to the right-wing/liberal vision represented by Piñera, the majority of Chileans did not appreciate the need for any structural reform to the economic and political arrangements that embedded Pinochet's Constitution. After all, the existing constitutional framework had provided impressive economic growth sustained for almost 40 years. Hence, the changes proposed from the conservative side were restricted to some institutions [such as the presidential period and the convenience of extending it to six years (Verdugo and Contesse, 2018)] but a major constitutional transformation was outright rejected. Piñera's victory in the December 2017 presidential elections consequently blocked a comprehensive amendment of the Chilean constitution, at least provisionally.

Yet, in autumn 2019, the context changed completely. The frustration among wide sectors of Chilean society with the political system's incapability to distribute the benefits of economic growth in an egalitarian way was expressed from October 18, in an explosion of riots and violence known as *el estallido social* (Atria, 2020, p. 53). The demands on the streets seemed to be miscellaneous, but most of them targeted the privileged political class which was perceived as the main cause of inequality (Verdugo, 2019a). Popular claims interpreted constitutional arrangements inherited from the Pinochet era as the institutional resorts that had permitted the entrenchment of such privileged cadres at the expense of an impoverished and precarious majority and, accordingly, most citizens insisted that the total constitutional replacement was a *conditio sine qua non* for any social transformation.

The events in Chile in 2019 adopting a revolutionary character encapsulated some features of the constitutional theory here described:

1. the 1980 Constitution, in spite of its partial amendments, embodied the particular decision on the allocation of power assumed during the dictatorship and grounded on a neo-liberal socio-economic model that enabled the consolidation of a political and economic elite.
2. the social opposition to the system (not only against Piñera's government but adopting a general distrust towards the whole arch of the political establishment) urged to embrace another decision on the allocation of power pivoting around a more just and democratic order.
3. the constitutional system is deemed as the cornerstone of the operation: there shall not be profound social change if a new constitution does not replace entirely the old one (disregarding whether the formal codified constitutional amendment procedures are respected or not).
4. the constitutional change is expected to bring about inclusion in the political, economic, and social life of parts of the society previously marginalized.
5. violence is a determining factor in the impulse for change. The demand for constitutional replacement did not gather supra-majorities both within the society and the representatives until the scene began to be coloured by blood and violations of human rights.

After the initial resistance of Piñera's government expressed in the declaration of a state of emergency, and harsh repression against the protesters, precisely the victims that such reaction caused meant that the consensus for constitutional revamping was generated. The intensity of the confrontation brought Piñera to capitulate and to commit himself to reforms. As we have seen regarding other experiences, only when those holding the power see their position stagger, do they assume the demands of the outsiders and relinquish to their prerogatives. The waters of the revolutionary impetus calmed when representatives, heeding the popular clamour, reached an agreement called "for Social Peace and a New Constitution" in which the authorities accepted the call for a binding, national plebiscite to decide whether and how to write a new Constitution (Atria, 2020, pp. 55–56). The plebiscite, after a postponement caused by the Covid-19 crisis, was finally held on October25, 2020. According to the agreement that had been concluded in November 2019, the people had to vote for two questions on the ballot: the first question was if they wanted a new constitution (which had to be answered by "Approve" or "Reject") and the second question was related to the organization of the Constituent Convention. The ones that approved the drafting of a new constitution (which were the majority by obtaining the 78 per cent of the votes in the referendum) had to choose between the two forms that the constituent body might take: a mixed Convention, half of whose members would come from the sitting Congress and half who would be elected uniquely for the Convention, or a fully separate constituent Convention, whose members could not be sitting members of Congress and whose mandate would be limited to writing the new Constitution (Hilbink, 2019). The majority opted for a fully separate constituent Convention (79 per cent of the "Approve" votes) to draft a new constitution. The constituent Convention had to be formed by 155 members guaranteeing equal gender representation. The people elected to the Convention would have 12 months to draft the constitutional text which must be adopted by a vote of two-thirds of the members of the constituent body. The draft has finally to be confirmed by the Chilean citizenry in a ratifying referendum.

Whether the Chilean Agreement "for Social Peace" and the subsequent episodes in the path for a new Chilean constitution were signs of the Chilean constitutional system truly transforming, or represented a stitch-up by the political elite to contain popular rage, will be appreciated in the following years. A constitutional movement able to turn the existing structures of power in Chilean society upside down might, in another sense, even reverse the democratic achievements of the post-authoritarian era (see Verdugo, 2019b, pp. 204–205) and become thus an additional example in Latin America of the use of the constitutional framework for the sake of a punctual democratic majority built aside the traditional political class. At any rate, it might be already presumed that the Chilean demand for a new constitution translating a new distribution of power was, given the convulsive nature of the 2019 events, more likely to succeed than its previous attempts.

Constitutional transformation and authoritarian constitutionalism in Hungary

It is somehow ironic that one of the rare cases in which both a constitutional transformation was involved and the no victims rule was respected reflected the passage from a liberal democracy to a regime with authoritarian tenets in the heart of Europe. Another characteristic of the Hungarian path to constitutional creation has been that the dismantlement of the previous basic constitutional structure had been undertaken through constitutional amendments enacted in accordance with procedures stipulated within the constitutional norms in force (see Jacobsohn and Roznai, 2020, pp. 61–62). It might be argued that somehow such a kind of substantial replacement of a constitutional order by another through formal and procedural adjusted amendments has been taking place in Hungary not only in the constitutional transformation that culminated in 2011 but also in the 1980s as a transition from communism to liberal democracy (even though, as the supporters of the 2011 constitutional change stated, the problem was that in 1989 no real constitutional transformation took place).

The transformation of the Hungarian constitutional system into something different from a liberal democracy has not only been recognized by many scholars[9] but also by the main architect of the process, the Hungarian prime minister from 2010, Viktor Orbán, who had not hesitated in declaring that the political and legal changes that he had promoted represent the building of "an illiberal State, a non-liberal State" that respects community rather than the individual.[10]

As I have mentioned in Chapter 2, we have witnessed several comprehensive constitutional revisions concerning some different European States during the last decades. Those were the cases of both the Swiss (1999–2000) and the Finnish (2000) new constitutions which, aside from a mere codification of existing constitutional rules in a more accessible format, did not entail a change in the decision on the allocation of power. As we saw in the Swiss case, the different allocation on the powers between the cantonal governments and the federation, and the creation of new bodies linking both levels of government had not to be confused with an *existential* reconfiguration on the material structure of powers that lie behind the formal constitution as is expressed according to my definitions. While some authors might disagree with the following observations (see Albert, 2019, p. 7), something similar as the statements on the Swiss Constitution might be extended to the 2000 Finnish Constitution which essentially represented a formal updating and editing of rules that before were disaggregated. The truth is that the new Finnish Constitution also included an entrenchment of the powers of Parliament, and the reduction of those previously attributed to the President (Ojanen, 2013) but, in the same fashion as happened with the Swiss experience, such different distributions of the roles of different bodies in the decision-making process do not constitute an existential change to the material powers upon which Finnish society and politics are sustained.

The contrast between both the Swiss and the Finnish constitutions with the 2011 Hungarian constitution is, in the perspective pinpointed, clamorous. The Hungarian 2011 constitutional case effectively reflects a change on the allocation of power which might be more precisely described as the movement from a temporary majority that still left space to other political options, to the monopolization of power by a hyper-majority.

The operation undertaken by the Fidesz party, despite radical ideological opposition, had some analogies with what happened in Venezuela and Bolivia, in which a temporary majority adopted constitutional language to perpetuate itself in power (Uitz, 2015, p. 292). Until the present, however, Fidesz has been more successful than its Latin American counterparts. The Hungarian party maintained its hegemonic position through reiterated support in parliamentary elections, and both the creation and the enforcement of the new constitutional regime were developed without mortal victims. Furthermore, Orbán's regime is not likely to be threatened by an extra-constitutional putsch by the Opposition, such as the one that besieged Maduro in Venezuela, or the one that demolished Morales' government.

Several observations might be suggested in order to explain the singular evolution taken by the Hungarian constitutional path.

From 2010, Orbán's Fidesz and its allies managed to concentrate a huge democratic majority around them. In the Hungarian parliamentary elections of

2010, the alliance of Fidesz and the Christian Democratic People's Party won the majority of votes (53 per cent) and obtained more than two-thirds of the seats in Parliament (263 of 386 MPs), a circumstance which allowed Orbán to foster radical changes to the Hungarian political system (Bogaards, 2018, p. 1487). The overwhelming electoral support was crucial to understand why Orbán's political acolytes found the perfect conditions to reconfigure the allocation of power without violent contestation. The replacement of the previous 1949 constitutional framework (as amended after 1989) only required the votes of two-thirds of members of Parliament.[11] There were no unamendable provisions (the German Basic Law ordinary amending procedure also requires a two-thirds majority of both legislative chambers but as, we saw in Chapter 4, there are in the German constitutional system clauses excluded from the amendment) and no referendum or any other form of ratification was foreseen. In Hungary, the qualified consent of one legislative body was sufficient to adopt a brand-new constitution (Kovács and Gabor, 2011, p. 186).

That the passing of the 2011 Fundamental Law represented a change in the allocation of powers might also be derived from some statements of the politicians that led the reform. Orbán himself argued that the new constitutional framework completed the transition to democracy[12] and the Fidesz parliamentary group chairman, János Lázár, declared that the constitutional change marked a definitive break with Hungary's Communist past.[13] The idea that such politicians sought to convey was that if there had not been a formal complete revision of the Hungarian constitution until 2011, it was because the powers that had been present during the Communist era *still persisted* despite the amendments post-1989. The Hungarian constitutional system had been the only one in the former Eastern bloc that did not experience a total revision shortly after 1989. According to the vision of the ideologues of Fidesz, the convulsion caused by the financial shock of 2008 (paradoxically a capitalist crisis) had been necessary to carry away the remnants of the political culture previous to the fall of Communism, which was associated with scandals, corruption, and the chaotic situation that besieged the Social Democratic governments of Prime Ministers Gyurcsány and Bajnai.

Indeed, Orbán and his parliamentarian majority took advantage of the same context that had instigated the constitutional revision processes in Iceland or in Ireland: the economic crisis which lacerated Eastern Europe in its earlier phases (Tooze, 2018, p. 139). Differently to Iceland or Ireland, however, the Fidesz hyper-majority concluded its constitutional plans by passing a Fundamental Law whose drafting process might be defined as the antithesis of the popular participative structures that defined both Icelandic and Irish constitutional *fora*.

With the exception of an initial stage in which a National Consultation Body was set up with the aim of sending a questionnaire composed around 12 constitutional issues to every citizen in Hungary (Kovács and Gabor, 2011, p. 197), public involvement was scarce. There were not citizenry assemblies nor was a constitutional Convention called. There was not a cross-party consensus among the citizenry representatives either. Also, in contrast with what we have seen in Venezuela or Ecuador, Orbán, given both his super-qualified parliamentary majority and the relatively flexible constitutional amendment procedure, had no need to address the people through referenda to assert his constitutional initiative or to ratify the draft. The Hungarian citizenry had already delivered to him full powers, through ordinary elections, to change the constitutional system as he pleased.

Orbán's hyper-majority had been maintained for more than a decade [both in the 2014 and in the 2018 Parliament elections (Gabor, 2019, p. 300), in the latter the Fidesz and its allies obtaining 133 seats of 199] which facilitated the consolidation of the constitutional reforms. It is true that such constitutional manoeuvres and the progressive control by Orbán loyalists of the State apparatus had undermined basic tenets of a liberal democracy, such as free speech or judicial independence, but the bullying of particular elements of the opposition through the limitation of these rights and principles did not exclude the regime from enjoying remarkable popular support [strengthened, it has to be said, by electoral reforms that benefited the ruling party (Bogaards, 2018, pp. 1485–1486)].

The European Union institutions, furthermore, in turning a blind eye for many years to Orbán's policies [at least until September 2018, when the European Parliament launched the opening of an Article 7 Treaty on European Union (TEU) procedure against Hungary (Gabor, 2019, p. 300)] somehow confirmed that, though human rights count among the Union's founding values, other dimensions of legitimacy concerning the Hungarian constitutional system could not be underestimated. The reluctance shown by the European Union institutions and its Member States to sanction the Hungarian authoritarian turn has, in fact, worked as both supporting and legitimizing factors for the Hungarian regime (Bozóki and Hegedűs, 2018, p. 1178).

The appearance of a constitutional transformation without violence may be, as suggested, mainly explained through the impressive and sustained democratic support that the regime has obtained in successive parliamentarian elections. Orbán described it as "revolution through the ballot box" (Bogaards, 2018, p. 1481) and in my opinion he was not completely wrong. In the end, a fundamental law was passed entailing a complete rearrangement of values and powers without having to count any row of dead bodies, as usually happens with revolutions. But it is precisely this transformative character derived from the Hungarian constitutional operation (even expressed in democratic terms and culminated following the formal amendment rules) from which any prediction of its evolution or possible crises may be inferred.

On the one hand, the path to an authoritarian government opens the door to strengthening the coercive means of power to enforce the regime and, consequently, the growth of resistance among the opposition and the appeal to break with the system through a revolution. The Fidesz may lose elections and be removed from the Hungarian government, but the newcomers to power are not likely to obtain the sufficient electoral support (translated into two-thirds of the seats in Parliament) to reverse Fidesz's constitutional work. Since it is not likely, either, that any alternative majority would allow Fidesz to rule from the grave through constitutional limitations and its control over other constitutional bodies (Arato, 2016, p. 222) the temptation will exist to promote a constitutional change without following amendment provisions.

On the other hand, Orbán's success in consolidating his constitutional regime is highly dependent on his leadership and his charisma, neither of which will endure forever. Indeed, both authoritarian regimes and constitutional democracies grounded in the revolutionary struggle of a charismatic leader share the same problem (Ackerman, 2019, pp. 3–4; Snyder, 2018, p. 38): how to handle the succession of the leader (or the succession of the founding generation). The harsh disturbances that we have not found at the beginning of the Hungarian constitutional system might appear during the process of Orbán's succession, contradicting thus the preservation of the no victims rule in any stage of constitutional evolution.

Secessionism in Catalonia

Secessionism may be considered a sort of constituent action.[14] In fact, it reflects with precision the foundational moment to which I alluded when I defined the idea of constitution as a decision on the allocation of power. Secession clearly represents the replacement of the elite controlling a territory and a population by another: the elite inhabiting the seceding territory claims to expel that of the parent State in order to monopolize the power upon a smaller portion. The independence of the American States, as we have seen, gives a good account on such a notion of the constituent moment. The formal translation of America's unilateral secession was, first, the Constitutions of the States and the Articles of the Confederation and, second, the U.S. Federal Constitution, but none of these episodes would be materialized without the decision that represented the Declaration of Independence in 1776 and the ability to defend it by military means.

The constituent agent awakens through secession, not through the constitutional drafting which merely represents the certification of the situation entrenched by the rupture with the previous sovereign. As Pau Bossacoma (2020, p. 355) wrote interpreting the sense of a declaration of independence in Kelsenian positivist terms, such unilateral declarations may be understood as norms that, though not derived from any previous internal constitutional norm, identify and seek to give validity to the birth of a new legal-logical constitution.

In Catalonia, in which one sees one of the most vigorous secessionist movements in Western Europe, there had been several discussions on the character that the future constitution of the new State should adopt. There had been some constitutional drafts proposed to the Catalan authorities during the 2010s and, after 2018, a group of experts was appointed by the Catalan President, Joaquim Torra, in order to think about the constitutional design of the future republic. But all such controversies on the Catalan constitutional framework had been evaporated by not assuming the "principle of reality," namely, that first of all secession from Spain *had to be consummated* and that only the success of this separation and the way to achieve it could determine the specific content of an eventual formal constitution. Secession from Spain, if perpetrated, and the different allocation of power that such a move might bring shall be Catalonia's constitution.

Secessions are rare in liberal democracies since minority nations within a larger State may find some kind of accommodation through the participative channels that democratic mechanisms provide. Pluralist democracies tend to respect the will of the peoples coexisting within their borders by allowing them to determine their political status in whatever form they choose: mere administrative decentralization, political autonomy, federal statehood, or even co-sovereign partnership. Even in those democratic areas in which the secessionist experiences have been closer to the claim for creating a new independent State, as happened in Quebec or in Scotland, central authorities of the parent State agreed, or at least tolerated, the holding of a referendum on sovereignty. Somehow, to say it in terms of international law, the respect of the right to the internal self-determination of the minority nation by the central authorities through democratic structures of decision-making have prevented (within the contexts mentioned in Canada or Great Britain) the exercise of the right to external self-determination by the peoples of Quebec or Scotland, respectively (López Bofill, 2019b, pp. 988–989). Both citizenries voted to remain in the existing States. Both in Quebec (in 1980 and in 1995) and in Scotland (2014) there were debates on the question in specific terms, there was no violence, and the pro-secessionist sides lost the referenda. There was not secession and, accordingly, there was not a different allocation of powers.

What makes the Catalan case so peculiar is that it had been developed within a supposed liberal democracy (Spain) which, regarding the defence of its national unity behaves rather as an illiberal State (López Bofill, 2019a, pp. 967–969). Spanish central authorities have not attended to the demands of the Catalan citizenry for further self-government for decades (even when expressed entirely by specific means) and had responded to the secessionist challenge by repressing the holding of a referendum on independence through the application of criminal law and the imprisonment of the Catalan leaders. Such a harsh reaction blocking any Catalan decision-making on the national political status has done nothing but foster the consolidation of a sustained pro-independence majority in Catalan institutions.

The crisis between the Catalan government and the Spanish institutions began to be envisaged when, after a long process of amending the Catalan Statute (*Estatut d'Autonomia*) passed both by the Catalan Parliament and the Spanish legislature and ratified by the Catalan citizenry in referendum, this text was declared unconstitutional and void in its basic tenets by the Spanish Constitutional Court.[15] The Spanish Constitutional Court decision on the amendment of the Catalan Statute may be deemed as the first stage in the escalation of the conflict in which the Catalan people's right to (internal) self-determination had been frustrated: the Statute had been passed by three democratic instances (the Catalan Parliament, the Spanish *Cortes*, and the Catalan citizenry) following the formal paths of amendment of the Statute according to the Spanish Constitution, but the

Spanish Constitutional Court dismantled the main principles which had inspired the change. The Catalan government sought to redress the loss of powers that the Constitutional Court ruling had represented by at least enhancing the Catalan financing with an agreement with the Spanish Government. But the latter, at that moment led by Mariano Rajoy of the conservative Popular Party, refused *a limine* even to open negotiations on the financial issue with the Catalan president then in office, Artur Mas.

The response in Catalonia was a march of hundreds of thousands of people on Catalonia's national day (September 11) in 2012 claiming for independence and the calling of snap elections by Artur Mas with a commitment to organize a consultation on Catalonia's political status. The expected consultation was held on November 9, 2014 in the form of a "participatory process" (Bossacoma and López Bofill, 2016, pp. 122–128) but President Mas and other members of the Catalan government that had been involved in the organization of this consultation exercise had to face criminal trial on the grounds of disobedience, prevarication, embezzlement of public funds, and usurpation of functions. They were finally convicted on the grounds of disobedience, which implied disqualification for office. Prison punishments would be dictated later, on occasion of the second round of events concerning Catalonia's struggle for independence that would be developed from the elections that were held in autumn 2015, which were won by the pro-independence forces, obtaining the overall majority of seats in the Catalan Parliament (Martí and Cetrà, 2016).

The first step given by the majority in the path to the creation of a new State was the passing of a parliamentary resolution[16] which, even though it was not considered legally binding, was immediately referred by the Spanish Government to the Spanish Constitutional Court and declared unconstitutional and void.[17] In the aforementioned resolution, it was stated that "[t]he Parliament of Catalonia solemnly declares the beginning of the process of creation of an independent Catalan State in the form of a republic."[18]

The response of the Spanish central institutions was that since the Spanish Constitutional Court considered the parliamentary resolution incompatible with the Constitution, any subsequent step taken by the Catalan MPs or any other Catalan authorities connected to the aim of "creating an independent Catalan State" could be prosecuted and punished through criminal law.

The electoral programme backed by the pro-independence parties in the Catalan parliamentary elections of September 27, 2015, was likely to opt to proceed with a declaration of independence and to seek international recognition for the new State. But secessionists, who were led by a new president, Carles Puigdemont, starting in January 2016, changed the aim of declaring the independence to that of holding a referendum on the independence of Catalonia scheduled for October 1, 2017 (López Bofill, 2019a, p. 963).

In contrast to the "participatory process" held on November the 9, 2014, the 2017 process was directly laid out as a referendum understood as a consultation addressed to the Catalan electorate in which a single and clear question was posed ("Do you want Catalonia to become an independent State with the form of a republic?") able to be answered with a "yes" or a "no." The Catalan referendum on independence was planned to be covered by an ad-hoc piece of legislation regulating only one referendum process: the referendum on the secession of Catalonia from Spain. In September 2017, the Catalan Parliament passed the referendum bill to provide the legal framework for organizing the October 1 referendum to which the Catalan president had committed.[19] Even though the mere drafting of the bill was covered by the prohibition of the Spanish Constitutional Court and reinforced by the threat of indicting the president of the Parliament of Catalonia and four other members of the Parliament's bureau, the plenary debated and passed the bill in one day and, thus, the Spanish central authorities had no time to interrupt the parliamentary session and to impede the bill's adoption.

However, the Spanish central institutions did not feel concerned by the Catalan sovereign proclamation entitled in the self-determination referendum bill and, as expected, the Spanish President of Government Mariano Rajoy lodged several appeals of unconstitutionality before the Spanish Constitutional Court.[20] The Court admitted the appeals, suspended the provisions of the referendum bill, and issued a warning towards 77 Catalan officials that any act related to the holding of the referendum could imply criminal liability.

More measures were taken by the Spanish government, the prosecutor, and the Spanish judiciary in order to impede the referendum: campaign material and ballot papers were seized, orders to seal off the entrance to polling stations were issued, newspaper editors were accused of aiding the preparations for the referendum, more than one hundred websites which provided information on the referendum were closed, public meetings called to discuss the issue were banned, and thousands of paramilitary officers depending on the Spanish administration (la *Guardia Civil*, the Civil Guard) were sent to occupy Catalan government buildings, and arrested some Catalan officials charging them with the crime of sedition (punishable by up to 15 years of prison).

Finally, the referendum on October 1, 2017, awoke to a fierce storm by the Spanish police at polling stations causing almost 900 hundred people to be injured and produced terrifying images that scandalized the international public in the West. In spite of such enormous pressure, including the closing of 14 per cent of the polling stations, the confiscation of thousands of votes and repeated cyber-attacks caused by the Spanish forces, Catalan people voted in a turnout that reached 43.03 per cent of citizens with franchise (the final outcome was of 2,020,144 "yes" votes for independence against 176,566 "no" votes, with 65,715 being void or blank).

The Catalan Parliament declared independence on October 27, 2017 but the Spanish government immediately seized the Catalan self-government, dissolved the Catalan Parliament, and removed the Catalan government. Charges for rebellion, sedition, embezzlement, and disobedience were lodged against the members of the Catalan government, the Catalan Parliament chairwoman, and two pro-independence grassroots leaders. Some of them fled into exile, and others were detained, trialled, and finally convicted in October 2019, to punishments that added up to more than one hundred years of prison.[21]

In the elections called by the Spanish government and held on December 21, 2017, pro-independence parties, in spite of such pressing circumstances, again won the elections and formed a government under the presidency of the pro-independence leader Joaquim Torra. Secessionists also won in Catalonia all the following elections to the Spanish Parliament (April 2019 and November 2019), to the European Parliament (May 2019), as well as the elections to the Catalan municipalities (May 2019). Pro-independence Catalan parties also won the elections to the Catalan Parliament held on February 14, 2021. The situation regarding the Catalan politicians in prison also led to some decisions of European instances estimating that imprisonment had violated parliamentary immunity and political rights.[22] However, Spanish authorities did not liberate the politicians concerned.

Despite the severe repression displayed by the Spanish central authorities in penalizing any attempt to organize a secessionist referendum, the Catalan process would, in case of being completed in the near future, still pass the test on the no victims rule. Indeed, the violence exercised by the Spanish authorities has been acute (in that regard I may mention the aggressions against voters during the referendum of October 1, 2017, by the Spanish police and the serious physical harm suffered by some of them), but *still nobody has died* for political reasons related to the constitutional transformation that the emergence of a new State might represent.

It is nevertheless true that Catalan independence is still a chimera, although it may be reasoned that the Declaration of Independence was already issued on October 27, 2017 and that the new republic at least exists in the realm of rules, only pending, as any declaration of independence, on the recognition by other sovereign States.

However, the recognition of that State is attached to the practice observed in international law according to which the newly proclaimed independent State has to enjoy effective control of the territory and the population upon which it claims its sovereignty (Bossacoma, 2020, pp. 189–207), and in this sense it is not unthinkable to predict that the degree of violence, encompassing mortal victims, might increase if the Catalan authorities struggled to achieve an effective control of the territory and population, if the Spanish authorities tried to prevent it.

At the moment of writing, the no victims rule has not been infringed in the Catalan-Spanish conflict but it might be stated as well that no Catalan independence has yet been made real and that, consequently, no constitutional transformation has taken place either.

Brexit or the *Mulier Sacer*

Is the withdrawal of the United Kingdom from the European Union an example of a constitutional transformation? What Brexit has indeed confirmed is that if there is a real constitutional change at the European level, that can only be provided through a domestic constitutional development. The capacity to trigger the constitutional mechanisms in order to secede from the Union, as the United Kingdom did, reveals that the adoption of the most relevant political decisions is still placed in the hands of the Member States' authorities. It might be observed, thus, that in recognizing a unilateral right of secession to the States [through Article 50 of the Treaty on European Union which foresees the possibility of State secession once the term of two years is reached from the notification when there is no agreement][23] the Union renounces the assumption of any sovereignty attributes understood as original and inner supreme power.

Under a different perspective, it is arguable whether Brexit has activated a constitutional transformation within the United Kingdom. Generally, it is difficult to appreciate the character of a radical constitutional change within a system of flexible constitution such as the British one. The statutes concerning the integration of the United Kingdom in the European Communities (the 1972 *European Communities Act*) or its separation from the European Union (the 2018 *European Union Withdrawal Act* and the 2020 *European Union Withdrawal Agreement Act*) may be considered a component of the British constitution such as the 1689 *Bill of Rights* or the 1701 *Act of Settlement* are, but it is harder to affirm if European membership or its ending changed somehow the nature of the British "regime."

According to the series of constitutional discussions that arose in the British Parliament, in the Courts,[24] and within the citizenship during the process of withdrawal from the Union, it could be suggested that Brexit represented a relevant transformation for the United Kingdom constitutional system. I argue in the following lines that the adhesion of the United Kingdom to the European Communities was somehow a result of a different allocation of power that represented the end of the empire and that the subsequent Brexit process was as well inspired by the pretension to redraw a different position of the United Kingdom in the world that, at the end of the day, was devoted to reconfiguring the internal relations of domination. What is relevant to my analysis concerning the concept of constitution is that none of the episodes, the integration and the separation, took place in a completely specific, inclusive, and deliberative atmosphere.

From the second half of the sixties, the United Kingdom was tackling a difficult situation in terms of political stability and economic stagnation that would become worse during the decade of the seventies. By that time, the bulk of the colonies and dominions had already been lost in more or less convulsive procedures (Buettner, 2016, pp. 23–73). The Middle East mandates (including Palestine and the fierce conflict that the British withdrawal supposed), India, Pakistan, Burma, the possessions in the Malacca Peninsula, Egypt, Sudan, enormous extensions of territories in both West and East Africa … everything was gone, and while enormous pieces of territories were being divided from the motherland, the British institutions still thought that they could cope with the juncture by their sole national means. But it was soon evident that the loss of markets and wealth caused by the disintegration of the Empire had to be found somewhere else. The Macmillan government already launched Britain's first application to join the European Economic Community in 1961 propelled by shifts in British trade towards advanced industrial European markets. This first membership application would meet, however, the same fate as the second: the reluctance of General De

Gaulle to allow Britain's integration in the European project and the consequent French veto to Britain's adhesion [so, it is not surprising that when De Gaulle left office in April 1969, the prospects of widening the European Community to include the United Kingdom improved sharply (Judt, 2005, p. 212)]. But finally, the British internal crisis, and particularly, the territorial crises and the sense of weakness that overshadowed British politics (combined with the unexpected victory in the June 1970 elections of the Europhile conservative Edward Heath) were the factors that counted in explaining the interest of the British society in the club that had been formed on the other side of the Channel.

By the beginning of the seventies, nevertheless, the big political and humanitarian shock was not in any distant British colony but in the very backyard of the metropolis: Northern Ireland. In summer 1969, following the Apprentice Boys' March, a battle had spread through the streets of Derry between the unionist police forces and the Republican residents of Bogside that led to the deployment of the British Army. But the British military presence, in the beginning conceived to act as a neutral force to come between both fighting communities, only made things worse. The Irish Republican Army reorganized with the split into the "Provisional" and the "Official" factions in a way that the Provisional one embarked itself in an armed struggle to defend the Catholic community against British rule.

Following the killing of a British soldier in February 1971, the British government introduced internment without trial; a decision that radicalized still further the Catholic community, since they perceived that they had been flagrantly discriminated against in the struggle of the British authorities to restore order (Walker, 2006, p. 27). Finally, violence reached one of its peaks on January 30, of 1972 when the British First Battalion Parachute Regiment killed 13 unarmed civilians and injured more than 14 people who were marching peacefully, in the events that were to be known as "Bloody Sunday." The point that I would like to observe here is that such an orgy of violence happened only seven days after Edward Heath signed the accession Treaty to the then European Communities (on January22, of 1972) and just at the beginning of a dark year of armed conflict that left 146 members of the security forces and 321 civilians killed (Judt, 2005, p. 466) in what might be qualified as a latent civil war. The United Kingdom needed, in short, integration into a supranational organization as a proxy to contain a confrontation that was savagely evolving against British interests and against Britain's territorial integrity. In such a context, the United Kingdom's accession to the European Communities, disregarding if it represented a real constitutional transformation or not (that I would not dare to qualify as such), did not occur in a calm and sober discussion.

Almost 50 years after, the United Kingdom's process of leaving the EU did *not* occur in an absence of violence, either. Not only was the debate on abandoning the EU strongly affected by the crisis of refugees arriving to Europe from the countries of the Middle East or the threat of terrorism from ISIS and Al-Qaida; not only was the referendum campaign surrounded by both passions and a context of aggression (the opposite of what had to be expected in a reasonable deliberation) but also, on June 16 2016, Jo Cox, a Labour MP defending the idea that the UK should remain in the EU, was killed by a man allegedly with several connections to ultra-right movements in favour of Brexit.

The assassination of Jo Cox was clearly a political killing in spite of the fact that the killer, Thomas Alexander Mair, had a long history of mental-health problems (one may argue that some Nazi hierarchs, including Hitler, suffered mental diseases and the latter had not cancelled out, as it didn't in the case of Mair, the political nature of their deeds).

Brexit, even organized by means of unambiguous democratic rules and following the required constitutional procedure, *was attached to direct or subjective violence*, in Zizek'z terms. In the context of constitutional convulsion during Brexit, Jo Cox may be considered *the death* which would be prohibited according to our normative requirement regarding the legitimacy of the constitution-making. Jo Cox would be, thus, put it in Agamben's words, our *mulier sacer*. The latter would appear as additional disturbing evidence of the connections that we have abundantly noted throughout this work between violence and the configuration of a new constitutional order.

In addition to that, the definitive constitutional status on the United Kingdom territorial integrity as a consequence of Brexit is still pending. As 50 years ago, though now without victims, Northern Ireland and the horizon of the unification of the island of Ireland became one of the main focuses of political stress. Although the text of the 1998 Good Friday Agreement (by which the bloody conflict between unionists and Irish nationalists began to be superseded) did not include many references to the European Union, it has been admitted by different actors that European Union membership facilitated the design of the agreement (Meehan, 2000; Skoutaris, 2020, p. 4). George Mitchell, for instance, a United States senator who performed as a mediator in the forging of the Good Friday Agreement, stated that the European Union played a part in thawing relations between the Republic of Ireland and the United Kingdom which enabled the Northern Ireland peace process.[25]

The Agreement, although highlighting that Northern Ireland is an integral part of the United Kingdom, also recognized the right of the region to secede.[26] Such a particular status of Northern Ireland within the British constitutional framework might accordingly experience some variations in the context of Brexit. As Nikos Skoutaris pointed out (2020, p. 4), if the European Union coverage no longer provides a paradigm of power-sharing between the Irish nationalists and the unionists, a part of the segmented post-conflict society of Northern Ireland might reject the strengthening of more UK-centric notions of sovereignty derived from the withdrawal from Europe.

But constitutional change grounded on the Northern Irish question might be pushed due to more mundane reasons concerning the economy and, particularly, the status of the island of Ireland as a single economic unity that Brexit threatens. The decision of the United Kingdom government to leave both the European Union single market and the Customs Union meant that a Customs border might be re-established between the Republic of Ireland, as an EU Member State, and the United Kingdom as a third country. The alternative to maintaining the EU single market and the Customs Union in Northern Island, the proposal for a "backstop" arrangement to avoid a hard border dividing the island of Ireland, became the sticking point of the Brexit negotiations and, in addition, was a determining factor in the evolution of British domestic politics.

British Prime Minister Theresa May was unable to find parliamentary support for her Brexit deal proposal, mainly due to the objections to the backstop. One of the main actors responsible for May's parliamentary defeats was the vote coming from the Northern Ireland unionists MPs of the Democratic Unionist Party (DUP), who rejected the Prime Minister's plan for the withdrawal from the EU precisely because such a plan foresaw a backstop arrangement that would effectively place Northern Ireland under the European Union regulations. The backstop solution was qualified by the Northern Irish unionist leader, Arlene Foster, as a European Union "annexation" of Northern Ireland.[27]

The immediate reaction of the Prime Minister was to reopen the negotiations on the status of Northern Ireland in order to gain the support of the DUP MPs and the hard-line pro-Brexit Tories who feared that some part of the United Kingdom might remain within the European Customs Union. And May's struggle in breaking Brexit deadlock included the possibility of replacing the backstop in Northern Ireland *by rewriting the 1998 Good Friday Agreement.*[28] The British nationalist hubris on the complete separation from the European Union was going to lead May's government to put at risk the main device that had ensured the peace in Northern Ireland for two decades. But instead of causing the collapse of the Good Friday Agreement, what collapsed was May's government itself. May's parliamentary weakness and the disagreements within the government on the way in which the Prime Minister was conducting the process of withdrawal from the Union (criticisms that included the resignation of several ministers) paved the way for May's nemesis and her succession by Boris Johnson.

Johnson, however, would also find in the Irish backstop a hard nut to crack. Johnson's arrangement for Northern Ireland was indeed not so distant from that proposed by May. The main change was provided by recognizing that *de jure* Northern Ireland remained within the United Kingdom Customs Union. But instead of threatening the Good Friday Agreement, Johnson sought political understanding with other actors involved in the peace process, mentioned in the Agreement, such as the Irish Taoiseach. Resulting from conversations with Leo Varadkar, it was emphasized that the differentiated treatment on the region concerning the application of EU law to keep the Irish border open could only be abandoned if the regional parliament decided so (or if a future arrangement supersedes it). Such a proposal, consequently, took into account the right of the self-determination of the Northern Irish people as provided in the Good Friday Agreement which includes that the governance of the region is based on the consent of both ethno-religious communities (Skoutaris, 2020, pp. 10 and 18). The Irish border remaining open to traffic and trade, and the new economic border between Britain and the European Union placed squarely in the Irish Sea, as foreseen under Johnson's proposal also deserved the criticism of the Irish unionist MPs of the DUP since they feared that leaving Northern Ireland open to cross-border traffic and trade with the Irish Republic (and with the European Union) would represent the first step to the political unification of the island and the permanent validity of EU law on Northern Irish soil.

In the first stance, Johnson succeeded in passing the bill on the new agreement between Great Britain and the EU with the modifications on the Irish backstop, but failed to fast-track a bill on the Agreements' approval before October 31, 2019, which had been announced by the Prime Minister as the deadline for achieving Brexit. However, Johnson called for a general election in December 2019, in which he obtained a great success, and the Brexit bill was finally approved by the Commons in January 2020. The withdrawal of the United Kingdom from the European Union was finally consummated on January 31, 2020. But the EU-United Kingdom deal on Brexit still establishes a provisory regulation that might suffer some variations after the definitive relationship is arranged. In this vein, the final agreement might determine if the Northern Irish citizenry activates the mechanisms entailed in the Good Friday Agreement to express their consent to the political status of the region, with all sorts of political consequences that such a movement might represent.

It could be argued that, in fact, the invocation of the mechanisms included in the Good Friday Agreement, even if they would eventually lead to Irish reunification, would not represent a constitutional transformation since they are already part of the British constitutional framework. Such an observation might be acceptable but then it should be admitted that what signified the British constitutional transformation was *the Good Friday Agreement itself, which was grounded on thousands of victims.*[29] An eventual unification of the island of Ireland, even developed specifically in the years to come, would not cancel consequently my theses on the link between violence and constitutional transformations.

Apart from the question of Northern Ireland, Brexit opened the Scottish front as well. The withdrawal of the United Kingdom from the European Union instigated the claim for a second independence referendum in Scotland which, differently to what happened regarding the referendum held in 2014, is not likely to count with the consent of the British central authorities. The general election of December 2019 signified a victory for Boris Johnson and Brexit finally went ahead. But also, in December 2019, the Scottish National Party obtained a remarkable result by gaining eight seats and entrenching with 48 seats its third position in the House. For the Scottish Prime Minister, Nicola Sturgeon, her party's success led to renewed calls for a secessionist referendum. For Boris Johnson, Scottish independence was a matter concluded by the defeat of the pro-independence side in 2014, at least for a generation.

In conclusion, watching political developments both in Northern Ireland and Scotland, it is doubtful that further British constitutional changes grounded on territorial amputation are going to be achieved fulfilling the no victims rule. Considering the circumstances of a political entity that once ruled over more than one-quarter of the Earth's land surface, it is rather likely that the nationalistic *tour de force* between England and the peripheral sub-State nations within the United

Kingdom shall follow the usual coercive pattern that I have described in this book, when existential matters are at stake.

Paradoxes of the new constitutionalism in higher lawmaking

The experiences described above on the emergence of recent constituent processes and their attempt to frame a constitution in a pure deliberative manner, asking for maximum popular participation, and preventing violence, convey some paradoxes.

One contradiction emerges in the relationship between popular mobilization and political stability. On the one hand, it is claimed that the benefits of increased participation in constitution-making require a minimum of order, democratic consolidation, and social homogeneity (Landau, 2013a, p. 934; Widner, 2008, pp. 1529–1533), while on the other hand, what we usually find in stable democracies involved in a constitutional change is apathy among the citizenry, lack of participation, and, at most, a popular mobilization *against* the constitutional proposal.

It is thus hardly conceivable to encourage a massive participation within a context of normal politics in which no pressing constitutional debate might be appreciated, not to mention the difficulties in triggering participation in power and institutions, when constitutional questions are far from the day-to-day worries of most citizens. Experiences such as the European Treaty on the Constitution or President Bachelet's proposal to reform the Constitution of Chile showed that there is no popular mobilization able to promote a constitutional transformation *without a conflict* (a conflict which, as we have seen, usually derives in violence). The will to change the basic premises of a political organization is not suddenly born from nothing.

In this vein, the case of the European Treaty Establishing a Constitution was eloquent. Member States' governments and the European Union institutional representatives embarked themselves on a supposed constituent proposal that did not really involve a reallocation of power because it did not allude to any immediate conflictive background. However, the constituent *mise-en-scène* transmitted by the Convention alerted some parts of the electorate within the Member States that a reform could pave the way to build structures at the European level able to lead to deeper social and economic inequality across the continent. In other words, the European elites *created* the problem and, as a consequence of their initiative, grassroots activism within the Member States mobilized, but *to repudiate* the new rules erected by the political cadres (as was shown by the 2005 referenda held in France and in the Netherlands, which buried the constitutional draft).

Differently, in more divided and irritated societies, a deeper and more intense popular mobilization may be recorded but such assertion by the citizens may also appear tarnished by the destructive impulses that obliterate any deliberative structure or by the will of a faction and its charismatic leader that push for the monopolization of power. Venezuela, Bolivia, or Hungary would be examples of "abusive constitutionalism" as David Landau (2013b) qualified the phenomenon which uses mechanisms of constitutional reform to erode the democratic order. Where there is a calm deliberation without popular passion, constitutions are not finally passed. Instead, where there is impetus and conflict, constitutions may be finally approved because the winning group imposes its will without great concern for pluralism and inclusiveness.

The juxtaposition of what has been called "populist constitutionalism" [that is, the struggle of some populist movements to attain political self-perpetuation through constitutionalization (Dixon, 2017; Chambers, 2019, p. 1117)] vis-à-vis a supposed "deliberative constitutionalism" [in which the largest possible amount of individuals within a given society participate, discuss, and agree on the constitutional rules (Chambers, 2019, pp. 1125–1128)] also reflects another disturbing phenomenon, namely, that within the contexts of populist constitutionalism constitutions are approved and enforced while deliberative constitutionalism cannot exhibit *any single example* of a comprehensive constitutional reform associated with a real transformation regarding the allocation of power.

Before the wave of authoritarian regression that is eclipsing some constitutional democracies, it has been argued that constitutions are being transformed from rules of the game of democratic competition into instruments designed to shield the majority party from competition and criticism (see Grimm, 2020, p. 15). But, in my opinion, the role of constitutions at the service of the faction that has temporarily taken the control of the State and uses the constituent track to entrench itself in power *lies behind the very concept of constitution*. Further still, adopting a constitution contributes to legitimate what in other circumstances would be a raw contention of dissidence through coercive means.

In another respect, in such places in which the transformative forces do not count with the application of physical violence, as happened for instance in Catalonia, the change in the political framework is not achieved, because the supporters of the status quo have only to abstain themselves from participating in the constitutional initiative and trusting in the repression displayed by the establishment. In other words, specific and democratic movements for constitutional revolution are likely to fail in circumstances where the boycott of the adversaries may interpose a kind of veto. Such context also depicts the fragile dialectic between democracy and political apathy in the face of a constitutional change but from another perspective. It could be said that the persistence of the lack of involvement of one side precisely reveals that the constitutional change is not backed up by an extensive, intense, and sustained popular mobilization that may legitimize the transformative movement in a pure, violence-free context (see Bossacoma, 2020, p. 348). But it is not clear at all if the boycott of the adversaries succeeds in refraining the change precisely because they are backed by the violence (or the threat of violence) exhibited by the State apparatus on which they rely or, conversely, if the big majority pushing forward the transformation, disregarding how wide it is, fizzles out because it does not count with the decisive coercive means to impose its will. It would be thus, in conclusion, not a matter of democracy but a matter of force.

At any rate, what a constitutional transformation denotes is that *there is a fundamental cleft in the society that excludes a unitary solution.* In fact, the constitutional process itself may contribute to enforcing the divisions within the society. Invoking a complete constitutional rearrangement in which the conflict, while existing, is latent, may boost its eruption and hence make impossible any constitutional agreement since the resulting disputes have gone too far. Whether the conflict within the society is not pressing enough to incite the majority of the people to jettison political stability (as seemed to happen in Iceland or Ireland), or because the division is already too profound that no constitutional agreement may be reached (as might happen in Catalonia and its secessionist attempt from Spain), the outcome would be the same: the failure of political and institutional reform. In order to ensure the achievement of the constitutional transformation the part of the society backing up the new regime has not only to be willing to risk losing the stability provided by the old regime, but also has to be able to enforce the constitutional change towards the adversaries, disregarding the attitude of the latter which may be radicalized with the constitutional dispute. Constitutional politics are, in sum, polarized politics (Elster, 2000b, p. 348).

The myth of constitutionalism is grounded on the idea according to which "We the People" gives itself a constitutional framework. Both old and new experiences of constitution-making processes (from the drafting of the United States' Federal Constitution to the developments seen in the new constitutionalism) rather demonstrate, however, that real political change emerges where the People *is divided* and, accordingly, constitutions are finally passed in those places in which a part of the society dominates the other parts.

Constituent processes are not developed in an arena where political mobilization and deliberation is general as the emergence of the We the People is likely to allude. Instead, as long as a part of the citizenry expresses its eagerness to challenge the basic rules, such struggle is paid at the cost of deepening the divisions in society and dissolving the very notion of the People. The document that is supposed to be founded on a common political unity has its origins in the fiercely internal fight within such a group, while its outcome represents the interests of one faction. The People cannot be in such a narrative the agent of the constituent impulse because a constitution is rather the product that expresses its dismemberment.

Notes

1 A variant on the discourse of enhancing citizenship participation on constitutional decision-making is traced in the United States by supporting the popular involvement against "the purported evils of judicial supremacy" (Kramer, 2004).

2 That using of the term "new constitutionalism" is appreciably different than Ran Hirschl's (2007) idea regarding the fortification of judicial review mainly caused by the supranational legal integration processes. It should be also distinguished from the use of the expression "new constitutionalism" here offered from the approaches by Stephen Gill (2008, pp. 137–138) and David Schneiderman (2008, p. 38) when they associate the new constitutionalism with the institutional manifestation of disciplinary neoliberalism. So understood, the new constitutionalism would

insulate key aspects of the economy from the influence of politicians and the mass of citizens by imposing, internally and externally, binding constraints on the conduct of fiscal, monetary, and trade and investment policies. Such description would perfectly suit with the *opposite* concept until now refereed in which the popular participation in creating fundamental rules (including the economic ones) plays a fundamental role. Nevertheless, the considerations developed by the analyzers of the neoliberal constitutional set of rules would, in a different way, have some relation with our ideas on constitutions as devices by which the existing distributions of wealth and elite privileges are consolidated since they disempower the people from deciding about some fundamental economic relations.

3 The pattern of new constitutions emerging from violent revolutions and coups d'état in which is outlined the seizing of power by new elites has been generalized in Africa. Among many cases observed in the last decades may be mentioned the Constitutions of Guinea (2010), Madagascar (2010), and Niger (2010).

4 On the Icelandic constitutional process see, among many others, Bergmann, 2016; Bergsson and Blokker, 2014; Landemore, 2015 and 2020; Meuwese, 2013; Sanders, 2012, p. 6; Suteu, 2015, pp. 260–264; Thorarensen, 2017.

5 Venice Commission Opinion 702/2013, available at http://www.venice.coe.int/webforms/documents/default.aspx?pdffile=CDL-AD(2013)010-e

6 On the Irish constitution-making process see Carolan, 2015; Čolić, 2014; De Londras and Morgan, 2013; Farrell, 2014; Farrell et al., 2016 and 2017; O'Sullivan, Healy, and Breen, 2014; Suteu, 2015, pp. 264–268.

7 It is likely that the Irish Convention was inspired by the assemblies on electoral reform in the Canadian province of British Columbia established in 2004 (see Farrell et al., 2017, p. 124).

8 On the first phase of the Chilean constitutional change attempt see Quiero and Gajardo, 2016.

9 Among many others see Arato, 2016, p. 161; Bogaards, 2018; Gabor, 2019; Halmai, 2018, p. 219; Jacobsohn and Roznai, 2020, pp. 89–101; Pichl, 2019; Sólyom, 2015.

10 Prime Minister Víktor Orbán's Speech at the 25th Bálványos Summer Free University and Student Camp, available at www.kormany.hu/en/the-prime-minister/the-prime-minister-s-speeches/prime-minister-viktor-orban-s-speech-at-the-25th-balvanyos-summer-free-university-and-student-camp

11 On the causes of the 2011 authoritarian turn rooted in the deficiencies of the 1989 constitutional process see Arato, 2016, pp. 161–222.

12 "Hungarian lawmakers approve socially and fiscally conservative new constitution," *The Wahington Post*, April 18, 2011.

13 "Hungarian Parliament Approves New Constitution," *The New York Times*, April 18, 2011.

14 On secessionism as the emergence of the constituent power see, among many others, Albert, 2019, pp. 64–66 and Bossacoma, 2020, pp. 354–357.

15 Spanish Constitutional Court Decision 31/2010 of June 28, 2010. On this ruling see my work López Bofill, 2014, pp. 70–85.

16 Resolution 1/XI, November 9, 2015, of the Parliament of Catalonia, on the beginning of the political process in Catalonia as a consequence of the outcome of the elections held on September 27, 2015.

17 Spanish Constitutional Court Decision 259/2015 of December 2, 2015.

18 Point 2 of the Resolution 1/XI, November 9, 2015, of the Catalan Parliament.

19 Catalan Parliament Statute 19/2017, of September 6, 2017, on the self-determination referendum.

20 Among them the Appeal of Unconstitutionality number 4334-2017 against the Catalan Parliament Statute 19/2017, of September 6, 2017, on the self-

determination referendum. There were other appeals concerning, for instance, the Catalan Government Decree 139/2017 of September 6, 2017 calling for the self-determination referendum on October 1, 2017 and the appointment of the members of the supervising referendum body provided by the Statute.

21 Catalonia's former vice-president Oriol Junqueras was convicted of sedition and misuse of public funds and sentenced to 13 years in prison. He was also banned from holding public office for 13 years. The former Catalan foreign minister Raül Romeva, labour minister Dolors Bassa, and regional government spokesman Jordi Turull were each convicted of the same offences and sentenced to 12 years' imprisonment and handed 12-year bans on holding office. Carme Forcadell, a former speaker of the Catalan Parliament, was sentenced to 11 and a half years, while the former interior minister Joaquim Forn and territorial minister Josep Rull got ten and a half years each. Two pro-independence grassroots activists, Jordi Cuixart and Jordi Sànchez, were found guilty of sedition and given nine-year sentences.

22 European Court of Justice C-502/19, December 19, 2019, *Junqueras Vies.*

23 On Brexit and, generally, the withdrawal of a Member State from the Union according to Article 50 of the Treaty on European Union as a modality of secession see Bossacoma, 2017, p. 15; Ferreres, 2018, p. 141.

24 See, for instance, on the parliamentarian authorization to leave the Union, the United Kingdom Supreme Court judgement *R. (Miller) v. Secretary of State for Exiting the European Union* [2017] UKSC5 (appeal taken from Eng.).

25 See December 2017 George Mitchell's interview by the BBC available at www.bbc.com/news/uk-northern-ireland-42412972

26 See points 1 (i) and 1(ii) regarding the Constitutional Issues of the 1998 Good Friday Agreement between the Government of the United Kingdom and the Government of Ireland: "The participants endorse the commitment made by the British and Irish Governments that, in a new British-Irish Agreement replacing the Anglo Irish Agreement, they will: (i) recognize the legitimacy of whatever choice is freely exercised by a majority of the people of Northern Ireland with regard to its status, whether they prefer to continue to support the Union with Great Britain or a sovereign united Ireland; (ii) recognize that it is for the people of the island of Ireland alone, by agreement between the two parts respectively and without external impediment, to exercise their right of self-determination on the basis of consent, freely and concurrently given, North and South, to bring about a united Ireland, if that is their wish, accepting that this right must be achieved and exercised with and subject to the agreement and consent of a majority of the people of Northern Ireland."

27 "DUP leader prefers no Brexit deal to EU 'annexation' of Northern Ireland," CNBC October 13, 2018 available at www.cnbc.com/2018/10/13/dup-leader-prefers-no-brexit-deal-to-eu-annexation-of-northern-ireland.html

28 "PM's Plan B: Good Friday deal could be rewritten," *The Daily Telegraph*, January 21, 2019.

29 Total number of mortal victims derived from the Northern Irish conflict available at www.theguardian.com/news/datablog/2010/jun/10/deaths-in-northern-ireland-conflict-data.

Conclusions

The main thesis of this book is that political orders are founded on violence and that constitutions, including those establishing liberal democracies, are the legal translation of this seminal coercion. In spite of the huge literature that has in recent times exploded around the constitution-making processes, the factor of violence has been scarcely considered in the assessment on the appearance of a brand-new constitutional framework. Instead, as had been developed by constitutionalism since the American and French eighteenth-century transitions, scholars have been more centred in observing the public involvement in the drafting of fundamental rules and, thus, associating popular mobilization and deliberation with constitutional legitimacy. Struggles were focused in building a narrative able to justify why a constitution enjoys supremacy over other popular representative institutions. To put it in a very reductive way: "if a constitution prevails over other norms adopted by the People's representatives, that happened because the constitution was not passed by the representatives but by the People itself." Here is, in a nutshell, the popular narrative on which constitutional legitimacy is grounded. But, as a historical analysis reveals, it has been violence, and not a collective action of "the People," which usually (or always) has surrounded the formation of a constitution and ensured its effectiveness.

Taking this premise, and though my approach is mainly descriptive, I have suggested a normative background to evaluate the interaction between the claims on popular participation and the influence of violence in constitution-making processes. My idea is that, if instead of focusing on the devices of popular participation (elections to a constituent assembly, constitutional conventions, round-tables, or referenda) we pay attention to the coercions involved in such processes, we should conclude that wars, genocides, killings, or massive infringements of basic human rights *cancel* any narrative on the democratic grounds of fundamental laws.

The normative statement that I propose might be summarized in the principle that I have called the "no victims rule." It may be formulated as follows: "democratic participation is relevant in assessing the democratic foundation of a constitution as long as there has not been any mortal victim in the whole process." The "no victims rule" would in that sense work as a minimal moral constraint. It would not be incompatible with assessing a constitution-making process through judgements grounded on political participation, mobilization, democracy, equality, or inclusiveness but it would be enshrined *as a necessary condition* that would have to be fulfilled before examining the other parameters of evaluation.

In the description of "the victim" that lies behind the constituent foundation I have taken the figure identified in Giorgio Agamben's works and known as the *homo sacer*. In my analysis, furthermore, I have considered "the whole process" of constitutional creation in a wide sense: not only the constitution-making phase *stricto sensu* but also the creation of the political entity. The latter has been motivated by the idea that a constitution is the legal extension of the events displayed during the creation of the State.

Constitutionalism has been shown as an ideology concerned with the limitation of power, but in these pages, we have rather seen its role as a device used to confirm the power previously gained by violence. That has induced me to outline a concept of constitution related to the fundamental decisions given in a society about the allocation of power. In spite of the fact that the narrative of constitutionalism offers the idealized picture of a mobilized people united around the creation of a political body regulated through constitutional rules, historical experience points out that a constitution is an outcome spreading from profoundly divided societies. And it is precisely the annihilatory violence between groups and the triumph of one constellation of powers over others that are the factors that made possible the erection of a political order grounded on the fiction of political unity which legalized the outcome of the conflict. In this vein, a constitution-making moment is only given when the existing decisions on the holding of power are reviewed in their entirety. I have described the latter movement as "constitutional transformations" in opposition to a mere "constitutional amendment" which is developed not at the level of the existential decisions on power but through the channel of the so-called "constitutional laws" (formal constitutional changes that do not touch the core of a regime described as the established network of forces).

Other consequences of the reasoning displayed here stress the difficulty of handling the discussions on the fundamental decisions about power with the language of democracy and the rule of law. On the rule of law, it might be stated that implementing a constitutional system that breaks with the previous establishment requires also a break of the chain of legality and, particularly, on the formal ways that the previous system provides for amendment (remembering that violence is predictable when the bounds of the pre-constitutional legal order are at stake). Such is the space in which the theory of the constituent power moved from the French eighteenth-century transitions and their theorization by Sieyès, according to whom the constituent power had no previous legal bounds.

But conflicts about the creation of a political body and the constitutional rules that are going to regulate it are also hardly compatible with democratic procedures of negotiation and deliberation. Debate or conflict about the most fundamental characteristics of a given society makes it difficult to have such discussions in a calm and sober way. As recent experiences on constitution-making processes have suggested, if the constitutional change is only constrained to the level of "constitutional laws" without concerning the essence of the structure of power, the public involvement is weak and the constituent struggle will tend to fade. But if the reform challenges the pillars and the existential decisions about the nature of the society as a whole, popular mobilization (usually boosted by that part of the society that had been excluded from the previous reconfiguration of power) is likely to act through revolution and arbitrariness and, in sum, through the force of the facts.

We have seen with some detail to what extent violence has dominated the process of constitutional creation of two of the major constitutional traditions of our times, the American and the German one, although their foundational experiences took place in different ages and circumstances. Both were the outcome of great bloody confrontations, and despite their day-to-day functioning under the parameters of rule of law, free elections, or human rights, their foundations were developed in a context in which some of these principles (or all of them) were infringed.

A constitution represents the remnants of the coercions given in the beginning and is obeyed as long as such remnants persist in the ordinary times of the constituted power. As we have seen in the American experience, constitutional transformations, even though they have not been reflected in the replacement of one constitution by another, lead to a significant change of the regime accompanied by onslaught and destruction. In fact, as notoriously happens with the American Civil War or the so-called Civil Rights Revolution, it is violence that allows us to identify the moments in which we are witnessing a constitutional transformation.

Another thing might be said regarding the case of the Federal Republic of Germany which, although having the experience of reunification in 1990, since no violence concurred and the system was still marked by the violence given during the World War, no constitutional transformations had really taken place.

Finally, my exploration has been focused on recent constitution-making experiences from the beginning of the twenty-first century. We have seen that in the Western space, renovated devices (such as random citizen constituent assemblies, partial referenda …) have been introduced while debating and drafting a constitution. However, in such countries where the "no victims rule" has been respected and democratic procedures have been scrupulously followed a constitutional transformation (a reconfiguration of the power allocation among groups) and, thus, a total constitutional revision, has not been achieved.

On the contrary, as some experiences in Latin America or in the Middle East express, within the context of divided societies and harsh conflicts with a lot of victims, at least new constitutions dismantling the old order have been adopted (disregarding the question about whether such new constitutional systems have persisted or they have themselves sunk in a subsequent whirlwind of confrontations, carnage, counterrevolutions, or authoritarianism).

My analysis would need a great deal of empirical data to accompany it, regarding the violence committed in different historical developments and its particular influence in the determination of constitutional arrangements. A detailed approach of this kind would make the research closer to the statements of science (after all, a murder is a fact empirically verifiable) than to the building of intersubjective narratives. However, my proposal still belongs to the realm of such intersubjective reality created by the stories that people tell each other. In a world of competing interpretations that surround history, sociology, political philosophy, or law, the narrative on the original violence embedding constitutional provisions and ensuring their force through the memories of devastation is likely to be more convincing than the mobilization and deliberation of free and equal individuals who decide to give themselves a set of fundamental rules.

Although being a narrative dependent on the empirical data, research centring on the violent backgrounds witnessed during the forging of constitutional regimes at least simplifies normative discourses and aspirations to tame constituent power: under my perspective one political death is enough to invalidate the whole constituent struggle.

Will we see constitutional experiences, constitutional transformations as I defined them, *without deaths* in the future? To do so, a radical change in the idea about the State is probably required: indeed a radical change in the ways that human beings organize society is probably required, if not a radical change about human nature itself.

Bibliography

Abat Ninet, A. (2013) *Constitutional Violence: Legitimacy, Democracy and Human Rights*. Edinburgh: Edinburgh University Press.

Abat Ninet, A. and Tushnet, M. (2015) *The Arab Spring. An Essay on Revolution and Constitutionalism*. Cheltenham: Edward Elgar Publishing.

Acemoglu, D. and Robinson, J.A. (2012) *Why Nations Fail. The Origins of Power, Prosperity, and Poverty*. New York: Penguin Random House.

Ackerman, B. (1992) *The Future of Liberal Revolution*. New Haven, CT: Yale University Press.

Ackerman, B. (1993) *We the People I: Foundations*. Cambridge, MA: The Belknap Press of Harvard University Press (1st edition 1991).

Ackerman, B. (1995) Higher Lawmaking. In: Levinson, S. (ed.) *Responding to Imperfection: The Theory and Practice of Constitutional Amendment*. Princeton, NJ: Princeton University Press.

Ackerman, B. (1997) The Rise of World Constitutionalism. *Virginia Law Review* 83(4): 771–797.

Ackerman, B. (1998) *We the People II: Transformations*. Cambridge, MA: The Belknap Press of Harvard University Press.

Ackerman, B. (2007) *The Failure of the Founding Fathers*. Cambridge, MA: Harvard University Press.

Ackerman, B. (2014) *The Civil Rights Revolution (We the People III)*. Cambridge, MA: The Belknap Press of Harvard University Press.

Ackerman, B. (2015) Three Paths to Constitutionalism and the Crisis of the European Union. *British Journal of Political Science* 45: 705–714.

Ackerman, B. (2019) *Revolutionary Constitutions. Charismatic Leadership and The Rule of Law*. Cambridge, MA: The Belknap Press of Harvard University Press.

Ackerman, B. (2020) The Race Against Time. In: Albert, R. (ed.) *Revolutionary Constitutionalism. Law, Legitimacy, Power*. Oxford: Hart Publishing.

Ackerman, B. and Katyal, N. (1995) Our Unconventional Founding. *The University of Chicago Law Review* 62(2): 475–573.

Adams, W.P. (1980) *The First American Constitutions: Republican Ideology and the Making of the State Constitutions in the Revolutionary Era*. Chapel Hill, NC: The University of North Carolina Press.

Agamben, G. (2000) *Means Without End: Notes on Politics*. Minneapolis, MN: University of Minnesota Press.

Agamben, G. (2003) *Lo stato di eccezione. Homo sacer: II*. Torino: Bollati Boringhieri.

Agamben, G. (2005) *Homo sacer: Il potere sovrano e la nuda vita*. Torino: Einaudi (1st edition 1998).
Agamben, G. (2019) A Jurist Confronting Himself: Carl Schmitt's Jurisprudential Thought. In: Meierhenrich, J. and Simons, O. (eds.) *The Oxford Handbook of Carl Schmitt*. Oxford: Oxford University Press (1st edition 2016).
Agne, H. (2012) Democratic Founding: We the People and the Others. *International Journal of Constitutional Law* 10(3): 836–861.
Albert, R. (2018) Constitutional Amendment and Dismemberment. *The Yale Journal of International Law* 43: 1–84.
Albert, R. (2019) *Constitutional Amendments. Making, Breaking, and Changing Constitutions*. New York: Oxford University Press.
Albert, R. and Guruswamy, M. (2019) Introduction. Mapping the Founding. In: Albert, R., Guruswamy, M. and Basnyat, N. (eds.) *Founding Moments in Constitutionalism*. Oxford: Hart Publishing.
Albertus, M. and Menaldo, V. (2018) *Authoritarianism and the Elite Origins of Democracy*. Cambridge: Cambridge University Press.
Althusius, J. (1995) *Politica An Abridged Translation of Politics Methodically Set Forth and Illustrated with Sacred and Profane Examples*. Indianapolis, IN: Liberty Fund (1st edition 1603, 2nd edition revised 1610).
Amar, A.R. (1987) Of Sovereignty and Federalism. *The Yale Law Journal* 96(7): 1425–1520.
Amar, A.R. (1994) The Consent of the Governed: Constitutional Amendment Outside Article V. *Columbia Law Review* 94(2): 457–508.
Amar, A.R. (1998) *The Bill of Rights. Creation and Reconstruction*. New Haven, CT: Yale University Press.
Amar, A.R. (2006) *America's Constitution. A Biography*. New York: Random House.
Anderson, F. and Cayton, A. (2005) *The Dominion of War: Empire and Liberty in North America*. New York: The Viking Press.
Arato, A. (1992–1993) Dilemmas Arising from the Power to Create Constitutions in Eastern Europe. *Cardozo Law Review* 14: 661–690.
Arato, A. (1995–1996) Forms of Constitution Making and Theories of Democracy. *Cardozo Law Review* 17: 191–225.
Arato, A. (2000) *Civil Society, Constitution, and Legitimacy*. Lanham, MD: Rowman & Littlefield.
Arato, A. (2016) *Post Sovereign Constitution Making. Learning and Legitimacy*. Oxford: Oxford University Press.
Arato, A. (2017) *The Adventures of the Constituent Power: Beyond Revolutions?* New York: Cambridge University Press.
Arato, A. (2020) Revolution on a Human Scale. Liberal Values, Populist Theory? In: Albert, R. (ed.) *Revolutionary Constitutionalism. Law, Legitimacy, Power*. Oxford: Hart Publishing.
Arendt, H. (1961) *Between Past and Future*. New York: The Viking Press.
Arendt, H. (1963) *On Revolution*. New York: The Viking Press.
Arendt, H. (1976) *The Origins of Totalitarianism*. San Diego, CA: Harvest and HBJ Book.
Aristotle (2005) *Politics*. Oxford: Oxford University Press.
Atria, F. (2020) Constituent Moment, Constituted Powers in Chile. *Law and Critique* 31(1): 51–58.
Babst, D. (1972) A Force for Peace. *Industrial Research* 14: 55–58.

Backer, J.H. (1981) *Die Entscheidung zur Teilung, Deutschlands. Die amerikanische Deutschlandpolitik 1943–1948.* München: C.H. Beck.
Bailyn, B. (1992) *The Ideological Origins of the American Revolution.* Cambridge, MA: The Belknap Press of Harvard University Press.
Balkin, J.M. (2011) *Constitutional Redemption: Political Faith in an Unjust World.* Cambridge, MA: Harvard University Press.
Balkin, J.M. and Levinson, S. (2001) Understanding the Constitutional Revolution. *Virginia Law Review* 87(6): 1045–1104.
Bank, M. (2013) *Stunde der Neoliberalen? Politikberatung und Wirtschaftspolitik in der Ära Adenauer.* PhD Thesis. Köln University.
Banks, A. (2008) Expanding Participation in Constitution Making. *William and Mary Law Review* 49: 1043–1069.
Banning, L. (1978) *The Jeffersonian Persuasion: Evolution of a Party Ideology.* Ithaca, NY: Cornell University Press.
Barabas, J. (2004) How Deliberation Affects Policy Opinions. *American Political Science Review* 98(4): 687–701.
Barczentewicz, M. (2019) I Am Not Your (Founding) Father. In: Albert, R., Guruswamy, M. and Basnyat, N. (eds.) *Founding Moments in Constitutionalism.* Oxford: Hart Publishing.
Bark, D.L. and Grees, D.R. (1989) *A History of West Germany: From Shadow to Substance 1945–1963,* Vol. 1. Oxford: Basil Blackwell.
Barnett, E.R. (2004) *Restoring the Lost Constitution: The Presumption of Liberty.* Princeton, NJ: Princeton University Press.
Bates, D. (2007) Constitutional Violence. *Journal of Law and in Society* 34(1): 14–30.
Batnitzky, L. (2016) Hans Kelsen and Hemann Cohen. From Theology to Law and Back. In: Bryan, I., Langford, P. and McGarry, J. (eds.) *The Foundation of the Juridico-Political: Concept Formation in Hans Kelsen.* Abingdon: Routledge.
Beard, Ch.A. (1964) *An Economic Interpretation of the Constitution of the United States.* New York: The Macmillan Company (1st edition 1913).
Beaud, O. (1994) *La puissance de l'état.* Paris: Presses Universitaires de France.
Beevor, A. (2007) *Berlin. The Downfall 1945.* London: Penguin Books (1st edition 2002).
Bellolio, C. (2016) Will the People of Chile Succeed in Rewriting Their "Dictatorship Constitution"? Available at https://www.fljs.org/content/will-people-chile-succeed-rewriting-their-Dictatorship-Constitution.
Benhabib, S. (1994) Democracy and Difference: Reflections on the Metapolitics of Lyotard and Derrida. *The Journal of Political Philosophy* 2(1): 1–23.
Benhabib, S. (1996) Toward a Deliberative Model of Democratic Legitimacy. In: Benhabib, S. (ed.) *Democracy and Difference: Contesting the Boundaries of the Political.* Princeton, NJ: Princeton University Press.
Benjamin, W. (1986) Critic of Violence. In: Benjamin, W. (ed.) *Reflections.* New York: Schocken Books.
Benjamin, W. (1989) Theses on the Philosophy of History. In: Benjamin, W. (ed.) *Illuminations.* New York: Schocken Books.
Benz, A. (1994) A Forum of Constitutional Deliberation? A Critical Analysis of the Joint Constitutional Commission. *German Politics* 3(3): 99–117.
Benz, W. (1984) *Von der Besatzungsherrschaft zur Bundesrepublik. Stationen einer Staatsgründung, 1946–1949.* Frankfurt am Main: Fischer.

Bergmann, E. (2016) Participatory Constitutional Deliberation in the Wake of Crises: The Case of Iceland. In: Reuchamps, M. and Suiter, J. (eds.) *Constitutional Deliberative Democracy in Europe*. Colchester: European Consortium of Political Research Press.

Bergsson, B.T. and Blokker, P. (2014) The Constitutional Experiment in Iceland. In: Boss, E. and Pócza, K. (eds.) *Verfassunggebung in konsolidierten Demokratien: Neubeginn oder Verfall eines politischen Systems?* Baden-Baden: Nomos/Andrássy Universität.

Berkin, C. (2002) *A Brilliant Solution: Inventing the American Constitution*. New York: Harcourt.

Berlin, I. (2004) American Slavery in History and Memory and the Search for Social Justice. *Journal of American History* 90(4): 1251–1268.

Beyme, K. von (1971) *Die Politische Elite in der Bundesrepublik*. München: Piper.

Bieber, R. (2009) An Association of Sovereign States. *European Constitutional Law Review* 5(3): 391–406.

Blank, B. (1995) *Die westdeutschen Länder und die Entstehung der Bundesrepublik*. München: Oldenburg.

Blokker, P. (2017) Constitutional Reform in Europe and Recourse to the People. In: Contiades, X. and Fotiadou, A. (eds.) *Participatory Constitutional Change. The People as Amenders of the Constitution*. London: Routledge.

Blount, J. (2011) Participation in Constitutional Design. In: Ginsburg, T. and Dixon, R. (eds.) *Comparative Constitutional Law*. Cheltenham: Edward Elgar Publishing.

Böckenförde, E.-W. (1992a) Die verfassungsgebende Gewalt Des Volkes-Ein Grenzbegriff Des Verfassungsrechts. In: Böckenförde, E.-W. (ed.) *Staat, Verfassung, Demokratie*. Frankfurt am Main. Suhrkamp Verlag.

Böckenförde, E.-W. (1992b) Demokratie als Verfassungsprinzip. In: Böckenförde, E.-W. (ed.) *Staat, Verfassung, Demokratie*. Frankfurt am Main. Suhrkamp Verlag.

Böckenförde, E.-W. (1999) Die Zukunft politischer Autonomie. In: Böckenförde, E.-W. (ed.) *Staat, Nation, Europa*. Frankfurt am Main: Suhrkamp Verlag.

Boggards, M. (2018) De-Democratization in Hungary: Diffusely Defective Democra cy.*Democratization* 25(8): 1481–1499.

Boix, C. (2008) Economic Roots of Civil Wars and Revolutions in the Contemporary World. *World Politics* 60(3): 390–437.

Bonnard, R. (1942) *Les actes constitutionnels de 1940*. Paris: R. Pichon et R. Durand-Auzias.

Bossacoma, P. (2017) *Secesión e integración en la Unión Europea. Cataluña ¿nuevo Estado de la Unión?* Barcelona: Institut d'Estudis d'Autogovern.

Bossacoma, P. (2020) *Morality and Legality of Secession. A Theory of National Self-Determination*. Cham: Palgrave Macmillan.

Bossacoma, P. and López Bofill, H. (2016) The Secession of Catalonia. Legal Strategies and Barriers. In: Cuadras-Morató, X. (ed.) *Catalonia: A New Independent State in Europe. A Debate on Secession within the European Union*. Abingdon: Routledge.

Bouton, T. (2007) *Taming Democracy "The People" the Founders, and the Troubled Ending of the American Revolution*. Oxford: Oxford University Press.

Bowen, C.D. (1986) *Miracle at Philadelphia: The Story of the Constitutional Convention, May to September 1787*. Boston, MA: Little Brown & Co.

Bowring, F. (2011) *Hannah Arendt: A Critical Introduction*. London: Pluto Press.

Bozóki, A. and Hegedűs, D. (2018) An Externally Constrained Hybrid Regime: Hungary in the European Union. *Democratization* 25(7): 1173–1189.

Brant, I. (1950) *James Madison: Father of the Constitution, 1787–1800*. Indianapolis, IN: Bobbs-Merill Company.

Breda, V. (2018) *Constitutional Law and Regionalism. A Comparative Analysis of Regionalist Negotiations.*Cheltenham: Edward Elgar.

Brewer-Carías, A. (2007) El Inicio del Proceso Constituyente en Ecuador en 2007 y las Lecciones de la Experiencia Venezolana de 1999. *Iuris Dictio* 7: 71–94.

Brogan, W. (2011) On Giorgio Agamben's Naked Life. *Epoché: A Journal for the History of Philosophy* 16(1): 113–124.

Brown, R.E. (1956) *Charles Beard and the Constitution: A Critical Analysis of an Economic Interpretation of the Constitution*. Princeton, NJ: Princeton University Press.

Buchanan, A.E. (1991) *Secession. The Morality of Political Divorce from Fort Sumter to Lithuania and Quebec*. Boulder, CO: Westview Press.

Buettner, E. (2016) *Europe after Empire. Decolonization, Society, and Culture*. Cambridge: Cambridge University Press.

Burchard, Ch. (2006) Interlinking the Domestic with the International: Carl Schmitt on Democracy and International Relations. *Leiden Journal of International Law* 19(1): 9–40.

Calhoun, R.M. (1983) *The Loyalists in Revolutionary America, 1760–1781*. New York: Harcourt Brace Jovanovich.

Carbonell, M. (2003) Nuevos tiempos para el constitucionalismo. In: Carbonell, M. (ed.) *Neoconstitucionalismo(s)*. Madrid: Trotta.

Carolan, E. (2015) Ireland's Constitutional Convention: Behind the Hype about Citizen-Led Constitutional Change. *International Journal of Comparative Constitutional Law* 13(3): 733–748.

Carré de Malberg, R. (2004) *Contribution à la générale Théorie de l'état. II*. Paris: Dalloz (1st edition 1922).

Carrillo, M. (2002) Las Hipotecas de la Constitución de Chile. *Revista de estudios políticos* 115: 81–98.

Chambers, S. (2004) Democracy, Popular Sovereignty, and Constitutional Legitimacy. *Constellations* 11(2): 153–173.

Chambers, S. (2019) Democracy and Constitutional Reform: Deliberative versus Populist Constitutionalism. *Philosophy and Social Criticism* 45(9–10): 1116–1131.

Choudhry, S. and Tushnet, M. (2020) Participatory Constitution-Making: Introduction. *International Journal of Comparative Constitutional Law* 18(1): 173–178.

Chryssogonos, K. (2008) Popular Involvement in Constitution Making. *Revue européenne de droit public* 20: 1299–1316.

Churchill, W. (1954) *The Second World War: Triumph and Tragedy*, Vol. 6. London: Educational Book Company.

Classen, C.D. (2009) Legitime Stärkung Des Bundestages oder verfassungsrechtliches Prokrustesbett? *Juristen zeitung* 18: 881–889.

Coddou McManus, A. (2016) The Chilean Constituent Process: A Long and Winding Road. *Blog of the International Journal of Constitutional Law*, May 4. Available at http://www.iconnectblog.com/2016/05/the-chilean-constituent-process-a-long-and-winding-road/.

Čolić, J. (2014) *Constitutional Reform in Ireland: Legal Memorandum*. Public International Law and Policy Group, 4. Available at https://www.mreza-mira.net/wp-content/uploads/Constitutional-Reform-in-Ireland-Feb-2014.pdf.

Collier, C. and Collier, J.L. (1986) *Decision in Philadelphia: The Constitutional Convention of 1787*. New York: Random House.
Colón-Ríos, J. (2012) *Weak Constitutionalism: Democratic Legitimacy and the Question of Constituent Power*. London: Routledge.
Colón-Ríos, J. (2014) Five Conceptions of Constituent Power. *Law Quarterly Review* 130: 306–336.
Colón-Ríos, J. (2015) Introduction: The Forms and Limits of Constitutional Amendments. *International Journal of Constitutional Law* 13(3): 567–574.
Colón-Ríos, J. (2016) Rousseau, Theorist of Constituent Power. *Oxford Journal of Legal Studies* 36(4): 885–908.
Colón-Ríos, J. (2020) *Constituent Power and the Law*. Oxford: Oxford University Press.
Contiades, X. and Fotiadou, A. (2017) The People as Amenders of the Constitution. In: Contiades, X. and Fotiadou, A. (eds.) *Participatory Constitutional Change. The People as Amenders of the Constitution*. London: Routledge.
Correa, R.P. (2020) Symposium on Chilean Referendum Part I: Drafting a Constitution on a Clean Slate. *Blog of the International Journal of Constitutional Law*, November 1. Available at http://www.iconnectblog.com/2020/11/symposium-on-chilean-referendum-part-i-drafting-a-new-constitution-on-a-clean-slate/.
Corwin, E.S. (1950) The Passing of Dual Federalism. *Virginia Law Review* 36(1): 1–24.
Couzens Hoy, D. (1998) Genealogy and the Scope of the Political. In: Moss, J. (ed.) *The Later Foucault. Politics and Philosophy*. London: SAGE Publications.
Craven, W.F. (1956) *The Legend of the Founding Fathers*. New York: New York University Press.
Cristi, R. (1997) Carl Schmitt on Sovereignty and Constituent Power. *Canadian Journal of Law and Jurisprudence* 10(1): 189–202.
Cronin, C. (2006) On the Possibility of a Democratic Constitutional Founding: Habermas and Michelman in Dialogue. *Ratio Juris* 19(3): 343–369.
Cusack, T.R. (2003) *A National Challenge at the Local Level: Citizens, Elites and Institutions in Reunified Germany*. Aldershot: Ashgate Publishing.
Dahl, R.A. (1979) *After the Revolution? Authority in a Good Society*. New Haven, CT: Yale University Press.
Dahl, R.A. (2002) *How Democratic Is the American Constitution?* New Haven, CT: Yale, University Press.
Dahrendorf, R. (1967) *Society and Democracy in Germany*. New York: Norton.
De Haan, W. (2009) Violence as an Essentially Contested Concept. In: Body-Gendrot, S. and Spierenburg, P. (eds.) *Violence in Europe. Historical and Contemporary*. New York: Springer.
De Londras, F. and Enright, M. (2018) *Repealing the 8th: Reforming Irish Abortion Law*. Bristol: Bristol University Press and Policy Press.
De Londras, F. and Morgan, D.G. (2013) Constitutional Amendment in Ireland. In: Contiades, X. (ed.) *Engineering Constitutional Change: A Comparative Perspective on Europe, Canada and the USA*. Abingdon: Routledge.
De Vattel, E. (2008) *The Law of Nations*. Indianapolis: Liberty Fund (1st edition 1758).
De Vega (1995) *La Reforma constitucional y la problemática del poder constituyente*. Madrid: Tecnos.

De Zayas, A. (2006) *A Terrible Revenge: The Ethnic Cleansing of the East European Germans*. New York: Palgrave Macmillan.

Dellinger, W.E. (1979) The Recurring Question of the "Limited" Constitutional Convention. *Yale Law Journal* 88(8): 1623–1640.

Derrida, J. (1986) Declarations of Independence 1. *New Political Science* 7(1): 7–15.

Derrida, J. (1990) Force of Law: The "Mystical Foundation of Authority". *Cardozo Law Review* 11: 919–1047.

Dietze, G. (1960) The Federal Republic of Germany: An Evaluation after Ten Years. *The Journal of Politics* 22(1): 112–147.

Dinan, J.J. (2006) *The American State Constitutional Tradition*. Lawrence, KS: University Press of Kansas.

Dixon, R. (2017) Populist Constitutionalism and the Democratic Minimum Core. *Verfassungsblog.de*, April 26. Available at https://verfassungsblog.de/populist-constitutionalism-and-the-democratic-minimum-core/.

Douglass, E.P. (1955) *Rebels and Democrats: The Struggle for Equal Political Rights and Majority Rule during the American Revolution*. Chapel Hill, NC: The University of North Carolina Press.

Doyle, M. (1983) Kant, Liberal Legacies and Foreign Affairs. *Philosophy and Public Affairs* 12: 205–235.

Doyle, O. (2013a) The Dynamics of Constitutional Change. *Studies: An Irish Quarterly Review* 102: 191–202.

Doyle, O. (2013b) Ireland Considers Move to Unicameral Parliament. *Blog of the International Journal of Constitutional Law*, July 7. Available at http://www.iconnectblog.com/2013/07/ireland-considers-move-to-unicameral-parliament/.

Doyle, O. (2017) Constitutional Change in Ireland: Political History and Balance of Power. *Dublin University Law Journal* 40: 3–18.

Doyle, W. (1989) *The Oxford History of the French Revolution*. Oxford: Oxford University Press.

Dunbar-Ortiz, R. (2014) *An Indigenous Peoples' History of the United States*. Boston, MA: Beacon Press.

Duong, K. (2017) The People as a Natural Disaster: Redemptive Violence in Jacobin Political Thought. *American Political Science Review* 111(4): 786–800.

Dyzenhaus, D. (2007) The Politics of the Question of Constituent Power. In: Loughlin, M. and Walker, N. (eds.) *The Paradox of Constitutionalism, Constituent Power and Constitutional Form*. Oxford: Oxford University Press.

Dyzenhaus, D. (2012) Constitutionalism in an Old Key: Legality and Constituent Power. *Global Constitutionalism* 1(2): 229–260.

Dyzenhaus, D. (2016) The Idea of a Constitution. A Plea for *Staatsrechtslehre*. In: Dyzenhaus, D. and Thorburn, M. (eds.) *Philosophical Foundations of Constitutional Law*. Oxford: Oxford University Press.

Dyzenhaus, D. (2019) The Concept of the Rule-of-Law State in Carl Schmitt's Verfassungslehre. In: Meierhenrich, J. and Simons, O. (eds.) *The Oxford Handbook of Carl Schmitt*. Oxford: Oxford University Press (1st edition 2016).

Eisenstadt, T.A., Carl LeVan, A. and Maboudi, T. (2015) When Talk Trumps Text: The Democratizing Effects of Deliberation during Constitution Making, 1974–2011. *American Political Science Review* 109(3): 592–612.

Eisenstadt, T.A., Carl LeVan, A. and Maboudi, T. (2017) *Constitutions before Assembly. Participation, Deliberation, and Representation in the Crafting of New Constitutions*. New York: Cambridge University Press.

Elster, J. (1994) Constitutional Bootstrapping in Philadelphia and Paris. In: Rosenfeld, M. (ed.) *Constitutionalism, Identity, Difference, and Legitimacy, Theoretical Perspectives.* Durham, NC: Duke University Press.

Elster, J. (1995) Forces and Mechanisms in the Constitution-Making Process. *Duke Law Journal* 45(2): 364–396.

Elster, J. (1998) Deliberation and Constitution Making. In: Elster, J. (ed.) *Deliberative Democracy.* Cambridge: Cambridge University Press.

Elster, J. (2000a) *Ulysses Unbound: Studies in Rationality, Precommitment, and Constraints.* Cambridge: Cambridge University Press.

Elster, J. (2000b) Arguing and Bargaining in Two Constituent Assemblies. *University of Pennsylvania Journal of Constitutional Law* 2: 345–421.

Elster, J. (2012a) Constitution-Making and Violence. *Journal of Legal Analysis* 4(1): 7–39.

Elster, J. (2012b) The Optimal Design of a Constituent Assembly. In: Elster, J. and Landemore, H. (eds.) *Collective Wisdom: Principles and Mechanisms.* New York: Cambridge University Press.

Elstub, S. and Pomatto, G. (2018) Mini-Publics and Deliberative Constitutionalism. In: Levy, R. et al. (eds.) *The Cambridge Handbook of Deliberative Constitutionalism.* Cambridge: Cambridge University Press.

Eschenburg, T. and Benz, W. (1983) Der Weg zum grundgesetz. In: Eschenburg, T. (ed.) *Geschichte der Bundesrepublik Deutschland Jahre der Besatzung, 1945–1949,* Vol. 1. Stuttgart: Deutsche Verlagsanstalt, F.A.Brockhaus.

Fait, B. (1985) "In einer Atmosphäre der Freiheit" Die Rolle der Amerikaner bei der Verfassungsgebung in den Ländern der US-Zone 1946. *Vierteljahrshefte für zeitgeschichte* 33: 420–455.

Fallon, R. (2005) Legitimacy and the Constitution. *Harvard Law Review* 118: 1787–1853.

Farrand, M. (1960) *The Framing of the Constitution of the United States.* New Haven, CT: Yale University Press (1st edition 1913).

Farrand, M. (1966) *The Records of the Federal Convention of 1787,* vol. I. New Haven, CT: Yale University Press (1st edition 1911).

Farrell, D.M. (2014) The Irish Constitutional Convention: A Bold Step or a Damp Squib? In: O'Dowd, J. and Ferrari, G. (eds.) *75 Years of the Constitution of Ireland: An Irish-Italian Dialogue.* Dublin: Clarus Press.

Farrell, D.M., Harris, C. and Suiter, J. (2016) The Irish Constitutional Convention. A Case of "High Legitimacy?" In: Reuchamps, M. and Suiter, J. (eds.) *Constitutional Deliberative Democracy in Europe.* Colchester: European Consortium of Political Research Press.

Farrell, D.M., Harris, C. and Suiter, J. (2017) Bringing People into the Heart of Constitutional Design. The Irish Constitutional Convention of 2012–14. In: Contiades, X. and Fotiadou, A. (eds.) *Participatory Constitutional Change. The People as Amenders of the Constitution.* London: Routledge.

Fassbender, B. (2008) We the Peoples of the United Nations: Constituent Power and Constitutional Form in International Law. In: Loughlin, M. and Walker, N. (eds.) *The Paradox of Constitutionalism, Constituent Power and Constitutional Form.* Oxford: Oxford University Press.

Feagin, J.R. (2014) *Racist America. Roots, Current Realities and Future Reparations.* London: Routledge.

Fearon, J.D. and Laitin, D. (2003) Ethnicity, Insurgency, and Civil War. *American Political Science Review* 97(1): 75–90.

Fehrenbacher, D.E. (2001) *The Slaveholding Republic: An Account of the United States Government's Relations to Slavery*. Oxford: Oxford University Press.
Feldkamp, M.F. (1998) *Der Parlamentarische Rat, 1948–1948. Die Entstehung des Grundgesetzes*. Göttingen: Vandenhoeck & Ruprecht.
Feldman, N. (2004–2005) Imposed Constitutionalism. *Connecticut Law Review* 37: 857–889.
Ferreres, V. (2018) Does *Brexit* Normalize Secession? *Texas International Law Journal* 53: 139–151.
Fischer, S.L. (1974) *The Minor Parties of the Federal Republic of Germany: Toward a Comparative Theory of Minor Parties*. The Hague: Martinus Nijhoff.
Fleiner, T. (2013) Constitutional Revision: The Case of Switzerland. In: Contiades, X. (ed.) *Engineering Constitutional Change. A Comparative Perspective on Europe, Canada and the USA*. London: Routledge.
Forsyth, M. (1987) *Reason and Revolution. The Political Thought of the Abbé Sieyès*. Leicester: Leicester University Press.
Foucault, M. (1976) *Historie de la sexualité I. La volonté de savoir*. Paris: Éditions Gallimard.
Foucault, M. (1994a) Cours du 7 janvier 1976. In: Foucault, M. (ed.) *Dits et écrits, 1954–1988*, vol. III. Paris: Éditions Gallimard.
Foucault, M. (1994b) Nietzsche, la généalogie, l'histoire. In: Foucault, M. (ed.) *Dits et écrits, 1954–1988*, vol. II. Paris : Éditions Gallimard.
Foucault, M. (1994c) Par-delà le bien et le mal. In: Foucault, M. (ed.) *Dits et écrits, 1954–1988*, vol. II. Paris: Éditions Gallimard.
Fox-Decent, E. (2016) Constitutional Legitimacy Unbound. In: Dyzenhaus, D. and Thorburn, M. (eds.) *Philosophical Foundations of Constitutional Law*. Oxford: Oxford University Press.
Friedrich, C.J. (1968) *Constitutional Government and Democracy: Theory and Practice in Europe and America*. Waltham, MA: Blaisdell Publishing Company.
Friedrich, C.J. (1949a) Rebuilding the German Constitution I. *American Political Science Review* 43(3): 461–482.
Friedrich, C.J. (1949b) Rebuilding the German Constitution II. *American Political Science Review* 44(4): 704–720.
Fritz, G. (2008) *American Sovereigns. The People and America's Constitutional Tradition before the Civil War*. New York: Cambridge University Press.
Frowein, J.A. (1992) The Reunification of Germany. *American Journal of International Law* 8(1): 152–163.
Garavini, G. (2012) *After Empires: European Integration, Decolonization, and the Challenge from Global South, 1957–1986*. New York: Oxford University Press.
Gardbaum, S. (2020) Uncharismatic Revolutionary Constitutionalism. In: Albert, R. (ed.) *Revolutionary Constitutionalism. Law, Legitimacy, Power*. Oxford: Hart Publishing.
Gargarella, R. (2010) *The Legal Foundations of Inequality. Constitutionalism in the Americas, 1776–1860*. New York: Cambridge University Press.
Gargarella, R. (2020) Bruce Ackerman's Theory of History. In: Albert, R. (ed.) *Revolutionary Constitutionalism. Law, Legitimacy, Power*. Oxford: Hart Publishing.
Gastil, J. (2000) *By Popular Demand: Revitalizing Representative Democracy through Deliberative Elections*. Berkeley, CA: University of California Press.
Gat, A. (2008) *War in Human Civilization*. Oxford: Oxford University Press (1st edition 2006).
Gildea, R. (2002) *France Since 1945*. Oxford: Oxford University Press.

Gilhooley, S. (2019) "And Then They Begin to Look after the History of Their Founders" (Re)Configurations of the Founding in the Early Republic. In: Albert, R., Guruswamy, M. and Basnyat, N. (eds.) *Founding Moments in Constitutionalism.* Oxford: Hart Publishing.
Gill, S. (2008) *Power and Resistance in the New World Order.* Houndmills: Palgrave Macmillan.
Gimbel, J. (1968) *The American Occupation of Germany: Politics and the Military, 1945–1949.* Stanford, CA: Stanford University Press.
Ginsburg, T., Blount, J. and Elkins, Z. (2008) The Citizen as Founder: Public Participation in Constitutional Approval. *Temple Law Review* 81: 361–382.
Ginsburg, T., Elkins, Z. and Blount, J. (2009) Does the Process of Constitution-Making Matter? *The Annual Review of Law and Social Science* 5(1): 201–223.
Golay, J.F. (1958) *The Founding of the Federal Republic of Germany.* Chicago, IL: University of Chicago Press.
Goldoni, M. (2019) Introduction to the Material Study of Global Constitutional Law. *Global Constitutionalism* 8(1): 71–93.
Gordon, R. and Nelson, W. (1988) An Exchange on Critical Legal Studies between Robert W.Gordon and William Nelson. *Law and History Review* 6(1): 139–186.
Görtemaker, M. (1999) *Geschichte der Bundesrepublik Deutschland: Von der Gründung bis zur Gegenwart.* München: C.H. Beck.
Gözler, K. (1999) *Pouvoir Constituant.* Bursa: Ekin Press.
Grabbe, H.J. (1978) Die deutsch-alliierte Kontroverse um den Grundgesetzentwurf im Frühjahr 1949. *Vierteljahrshefte für zeitgeschichte* 26: 393–418.
Graber, M.A. (2006) *Dred Scott and the Problem of Constitutional Evil.* Cambridge: Cambridge University Press.
Graml, H. (1983) Die Deutsche Frage. In: Eschenburg, T. (ed.) *Geschichte der Bundesrepublik Deutschland Jahre der Besatzung 1945–1949*, Vol. 1. Stuttgart/Wiesbaden: Deutsche Verlagsanstalt, F.A.Brockhaus.
Green, J.P. (1968). Introduction. In: Green, J.P. (ed.) *The Reinterpretation of the American Revolution 1763–1789.* New York: Harper & Row.
Grenier, J. (2005) *The First Way of War: American War Making on the Frontier.* New York: Cambridge University Press.
Grimm, D. (2010) The Achievement of Constitutionalism and Its Prospects in a Changed World. In: Dobner, P. and Loughlin, M. (eds.) *The Twilight of Constitutionalism.* Oxford: Oxford University Press.
Grimm, D. (2020) A Political, Not a Legal History of the Rise of Worldwide Constitutionalism. In: Albert, R. (ed.) *Revolutionary Constitutionalism. Law, Legitimacy, Power.* Oxford: Hart Publishing.
Gutmann, A. and Thompson, D. (2004) *Why Deliberative Democracy?* Princeton, NJ: Princeton University Press.
Häberle, P. (1996) *Verfassung als öffentlicher Prozeß: Materiallen zu einer Verfassungstheorie der offenen Gesellschaft.* Berlin: Duncker & Humblot.
Häberle, P. (2000) The Constitutional State and Its Reform Requirements. *Ratio Juris* 13(1): 77–94.
Habermas, J. (1977a) Über den doppelten Boden Des demokratischen Rechtsstaats. In: Habermas, J. (ed.) *Eine Art Schadensabwicklung. Kleine Politische Schriften VI.* Frankfurt am Main: Suhrkamp.
Habermas, J. (1977b) Hannah Arendt's Communications Concept of Power. *Social Research* 44: 3–24.

Habermas, J. (1996) *Between Facts and Norms: Contributions to a Discourse Theory of Law and Democracy.* Cambridge MA: MIT Press.
Habermas, J. (2001) Constitutional Democracy. A Paradoxical Union of Contradictory Principles? *Political Theory* 29(6): 766–781.
Hahm, Ch. and Kim, S.H. (2010) To Make "We the People": Constitutional Founding in Postwar Japan and South Korea. *International Journal of Comparative Constitutional Law* 8: 800–848.
Hahn, E.J. (1995) The Occupying Powers and the Constitutional Reconstruction of Germany (1945–1949). In: Hahn, E.J., Junker, D. et al. (eds.) *Cornerstone of Democracy. The West German Grundgesetz 1949–1989.* Occasional Paper number 13. Washington, DC. German Historical Institute.
Halberstam, D. (2020) How Europe Brought Judicial Review to France. A Response to Bruce Ackerman. In: Albert, R. (ed.) *Revolutionary Constitutionalism. Law, Legitimacy, Power.* Oxford: Hart Publishing.
Halberstam, D. and Möllers, C. (2009) The German Constitutional Court says "*Ja zu Deutschland*!" *German Law Journal* 10(8): 1241–1257.
Halmai, G. (2018) The Rise and Fall of Constitutionalism in Hungary. In: Blokker, P. (ed.) *Constitutional Acceleration Within the European Union and Beyond.* London: Routledge.
Halmai, G. (2019) Populism, Authoritarianism and Constitutionalism. *German Law Journal* 20(3): 296–313.
Hamilton, A. (1962) *The Papers of Alexander Hamilton*, Vol. 3. New York: Columbia University Press.
Hamilton, A., Madison, J., and Jay, J. (1989) *The Federalist.* Middletown, CT: Wesleyan University Press (1st edition 1787).
Harari, Y.N. (2014) *Sapiens. A Brief History of Humankind.* London: Vintage Books.
Hart, H.L.A. (1994) *The Concept of Law.* Oxford: Clarendon Press (1st edition 1961).
Hart, V. (2003) *Democratic Constitution Making.* Wahington, DC: United States Institute of Peace.
Hartmann, T. (2019) *The Hidden History of Guns and the Second Amendment.* Oakland, CA: Berrett-Koehler Publishers.
Hauriou, M. (1923) *Précis de droit constitutionel.* Paris: Sirey.
Hawk, D. (1961) *In the Midst of a Revolution.* Philadelphia, PA: University of Pennsylvania Press.
Hayek, F.A. (1976) *Law, Legislation and Liberty: The Mirage of Social Justice*, Vol. 2. London: Routledge.
Hayek, F.A. (1999) *The Constitution of Liberty.* London: Routledge (1st edition 1960).
Heckel, M. (1995) Die Legitimation des Grundgesetzes durch das Deutsche Volk. In: Isensee, J. and Kirchhof, P. (eds.) *Handbuch des Staatsrechts der Bundesrepublik Deutschland*, Vol. VII. Heidelberg: C.F. Müller.
Heckelman, J.C. and Dougherty, K.L. (2007) An Economic Interpretation of the Constitutional Convention of 1787 Revisited. *The Journal of Economic History* 67(4): 829–848.
Heiss, C. (2017) Legitimacy Crisis and the Constitutional Problem in Chile: A Legacy of Authoritarianism. *Constellations* 24(3): 470–479.
Helgadóttir, R. (2014) Which Citizens? – Participation in the Drafting of the Icelandic Constitutional Draft of 2011. *Blog of the International Journal of Constitutional Law*, October 7. Available at http://www.iconnectblog.com

/2014/10/which-citizens-participation-in-the-drafting-of-the-icelandic-constitutional-draft-of-2011/.
Helgadóttir, R. and Ingólfsdóttir, A.L. (2017) Developments in Icelandic Constitutional Law: The Year 2016. In review. *Blog of the International Journal of Constitutional Law*, November 28. Available at http://www.iconnectblog.com/2017/11/developments-in-icelandic-constitutional-law-the-year-2016-in-review/.
Heller, H. (1983) *Staatslehre.* Tübingen: J.C.B. Mohr (Paul Siebeck) (1st edition 1934).
Heller, H. (1992) Die Krise der Staatslehre. In: Borinski, F., Drath, M., Niemeyer, G. and Stammer, O. (eds.) *Gesammelte Schrifften.* Tübingen: J.C.B. Mohr.
Herbst, L. (1982) *Der Totale Krieg und die Ordnung der Wirtschaft.* Stuttgart: Deutsche Verlagsanstalt.
Hestermeyer, H. (2013) *Staatsvolk* and Homogeneity: From Weimar to the Maastricht Decision of the German Federal Constitutional Law and Beyond. In: Annoni, A. and Forlati, S. (eds.) *The Changing Role of Nationality in International Law.* Abingdon: Routledge.
Hilbink, L. (2019) "New Constitution or Nothing!" the Promise and Pitfalls of Chile's Constitutional Moment. *Blog of the International Journal of Constitutional Law*, November 24. Available at http://www.iconnectblog.com/2019/11/new-constitution-or-nothing-the-promise-and-pitfalls-of-chiles-constitutional-moment/.
Hirschl, R. (2007) *Towards Juristocracy. The Origins and Consequences of the New Constitutionalism.* Cambridge, MA: Harvard University Press.
Hobbes, Th. (1965) *Leviathan. Or the Matter, Form & Power of a Common-Wealth Ecclesiasticall and Civil.* Oxford: Clarendon Press (1st edition 1651).
Hobsbawm, E. (1996) *The Age of Extremes. A History of the World, 1914–1991.* New York: Vintage Books (1st edition 1994).
Hoffmann-Lange, U. (1991) West German Elites: Cartel of Anxiety, Power Elite, or Responsive Representatives? In: Hoffmann-Lange, U. (ed.) *Social and Political Structures in West Germany: From Authoritarianism to Postindustrial Democracy.* Boulder, CO: Westview.
Honig, B. (2007) Between Decision and Deliberation: Political Paradox in Democratic Theory. *American Political Science Review* 101: 1–17.
Hont, I. (1994) The Permanent Crises of a Divided Mankind: "Contemporary Crises of the Nation State" in Historical Perspective. *Political Studies* 42: 166–231.
Horowitz, D.L. (1985) *Ethnic Groups in Conflict.* Berkeley: University of California Press.
Horton, J.O. and Horton, L.E. (2005) *Slavery and the Making of America.* Oxford: Oxford University Press.
Huber, E.R. (1951) *Quellen zum Staatsrecht der Neuzeit (Deutsche Verfassungsdokumente der Gegenwart 1919–1951)*, Vol. 2. Tübingen: Matthiesen.
Hudson, A. (2018) Will Iceland Get a New Constitution? A New Revision Process Is Taking Shape. *Blog of the International Journal of Constitutional Law*, October 23. Available at http://www.iconnectblog.com/2018/10/will-iceland-get-a-new-constitution-a-new-revision-process-is-taking-shape/.
Hume, D. (1963) Of the Original Contract. In: Hume, D. (ed.) *Essays: Moral, Political and Literary.* Oxford: Oxford University Press (1st edition 1748).
Ingold, A. (2015) Die verfassungsrechtliche Identität der Bundesrepublik Deutschland. Karriere-Konzept-Kritik. *Archiv des öffentlichen Rechts* 140(1): 1–30.

Isensee, J. (1992) Schlußbestimmung Des Grundgesetzes: Art. 146. In: Isensee, J. and Kirchhof, P. (eds.) *Handbuch des Staatsrechts der Bundesrepublik Deutschland*, Vol. VII. Heidelberg: C.F. Müller.

Jäckel, E. (1983) Geschichtliche Grundlagen der Bundesrepublik Deutschland. In: Eschenburg, T. (ed.) *Geschichte der Bundesrepublik Deutschland Jahre der Besatzung 1945–1949*, Vol. 1. Stuttgart: Deutsche Verlagsanstalt, F.A. Brockhaus.

Jackson, V.C. (2008) What's in a Name? Reflections on Timing, Naming, and Constitution-Making. *William and Mary Law Review* 49: 1249–1305.

Jackson, V.C. (2015) The (Myth of Un)Amendability of the US Constitution and the Democratic Component of Constitutionalism. *International Journal of Constitutional Law* 13: 575–605.

Jacobsohn, G.J. (2014) Theorizing the Constitutional Revolution. *Journal of Law and Courts* 2(1): 1–32.

Jacobsohn, G.J. and Roznai, Y. (2020) *Constitutional Revolution*. New Haven: Yale University Press.

Jaggi, S. (2016a) Revolutionary Constitutional Lawmaking in Germany – Rediscovering the German 1989 Revolution. *German Law Journal* 17(4): 580–626.

Jaggi, S. (2016b) *The 1989 Revolution in East Germany and Its Impact on Unified Germany's Constitutional Law. The Forgotten Revolution?* Oxford: Hart and Nomos.

Jensen, M. (1964) *The Making of the American Constitution*. Princeton, NJ: Van Nostrand.

Jensen, M. (1967) *The New Nation. A History of the United States during the Confederation 1781–1789*. New York: A. Knopf.

Jensen, M. (1976) *The Articles of Confederation. An Interpretation of the Social-Constitutional History of the American Revolution 1774–1781*. Madison, WI: The University of Wisconsin Press (1st edition 1940).

Johnson, P. (1997) *A History of the American People*. London: Phoenix Giant.

Judt, T. (2000) The Past Is Another Country. Myth and Memory in Postwar Europe. In: Deák, I., Gross, J.T. and Judt, T. (eds.) *The Politics of Retribution in Europe. World War II and Its Aftermath*. Princeton, NJ: Princeton University Press.

Judt, T. (2005) *Postwar. A History of Europe Since 1945*. London: Penguin.

Kahn, P.W. (2011) *Political Theology. Four New Chapters on the Concept of Sovereignty*. New York: Columbia University Press.

Kalyvas, A. (2005) Popular Sovereignty, Democracy and the Constituent Power. *Constellations* 12(2): 223–244.

Kalyvas, A. (2006) The Basic Norm and Democracy in Hans Kelsen's Legal and Political Theory. *Philosophy and Social Criticism* 32: 572–599.

Kalyvas, A. (2008) *Democracy and the Politics of the Extraordinary. Max Weber, Carl Schmitt and Hannah Arendt*. New York: Cambridge University Press.

Kalyvas, S. (2006) *The Logic of Violence in Civil War*. New York: Cambridge University Press.

Kalyvas, St.N., Shapiro, I. and Masoud, T. (2008) Introduction: Integrating the Study of Order, Conflict, and Violence. In: Kalyvas, St.N., Shapiro, I. and Masoud, T. (eds.) *Order, Conflict and Violence*. Cambridge: Cambridge University Press.

Karl, T.L. (1990) Dilemmas of Democratization in Latin America. *Comparative Politics* 23(1): 1–21.

Karl, T.L. and Schmitter, P.C. (1991) Models of Transition in Latin America, Southern and Eastern Europe. *International Social Science Journal* 128: 269–284.

Kaufmann, E. (1927) Die Gleicheit vor dem Gesetz im Sinne des Art. 109 der Reichsverfassung. *Veröffentlichen der vereinigung der deutschen Staatsrechtslehrer* 3: 54–55.
Kay, R.S. (1984) The Creation of Constitutions in Canada and the United States. *Canada–United States Law Journal* 7: 111–163.
Kay, R.S. (1987) The Illegality of the Constitution. *Constitutional Commentary* 4: 57–80.
Kay, R.S. (1998) American Constitutionalism. In: Alexander, L. (ed.) *Constitutionalism: Philosophical Foundations*. Cambridge: Cambridge University Press.
Kay, R.S. (2011) Constituent Authority. *The American Journal of Comparative Law* 59: 715–761.
Keenan, A. (2003) *Democracy in Question: Democratic Openness in a Time of Political Closure*. Stanford, CA: Stanford University Press.
Kelsen, H. (1992) *Introduction to the Problems of Legal Theory: A Translation of the First Edition of the Reine Rechtslehre or Pure Theory of Law*. Oxford: Clarendon Press (1st German edition 1934).
Kelsen, H. (2005) *Pure Theory of Law*. Clark, NJ: The Lawbook Exchange (Translation from the 2nd German edition revised and enlarged, 1967).
Kenyon, C.M. (1955) Men of Little Faith: The Anti-Federalists on the Nature of Representative Government. *The William and Mary Quarterly* 12: 3–43.
Kershaw, I. (2018) *Roller-Coaster: Europe, 1950–2017*. London: Allen Lane: Penguin Books.
Keyssar, A. (2000) *The Right to Vote: The Contested History of Democracy in the United States*. New York: Basic Books.
Kilian, M. (2003) Der Vorgang der Deutschen Wiedervereinigung. In: Isensee, J. and Kirchhof, P. (eds.) *Handbuch Des Staatsrechts der Bundesrepublik Deutschland*, Vol. I. Heidelberg: C.F. Müller.
Kirchhof, P. (1992) Der Deutsche Staat im Prozeß der europäischen Integration. In: Isensee, J. and Kirchhof, P. (eds.) *Handbuch Des Staatsrechts der Bundesrepublik Deutschland*, Vol. VII. Heidelberg: C.F. Müller.
Kirchhof, P. (1994) Das Maastricht-Urteil des Bundesverfassungsgericht. In: Hommelhoff, P. and Kirchhof, P. (eds.) *Der Staatenverbund der Europäischen Union*. Heidelberg: C.F. Müller.
Kirchhof, P. (2004) Die Identität der Verfassung. In: Isensee, J. and Kirchhof, P. (eds.) *Handbuch des Staatsrechts der Bundesrepublik Deutschland*, Vol. II. Heidelberg: C.F. Müller.
Klein, C. (1996) *Théorie et pratique du pouvoir constituant*. Paris: Presses Universitaires de France.
Klein, C. and Sajó, A. (2012) Constitution-Making: Process and Substance. In: Rosenfeld, M. and Sajó, A. (eds.) *The Oxford Handbook of Comparative Constitutional Law*. Oxford: Oxford University Press.
Klein, H.H. (1995) Kontinuität des Grundgesetzes und seine Änderung im Zuge der Wiedervereinigung. In: Isensee, J. and Kirchhof, P. (eds.) *Handbuch des Staatsrechts der Bundesrepublik Deutschland*, Vol. VIII. Heidelberg: C.F. Müller.
Kloepfer, M. (1983) Zur historischen Legitimation Des Grundgesetzes. *Zeitschrift für Rechtspolitik* 3: 57–59.
Kohn, M. and McBride, K. (2011) *Political Theories of Decolonization: Postcolonialism and the Problem of Foundations*. Oxford: Oxford University Press.

Kokott, J. (1998) Report on Germany. In: Slaughter, A.-M., Stone Sweet, A. and Weiler, J.H.H. (eds.) *The European Court and National Courts: Doctrine and Jurisprudence; Legal Change in Its Social Context.* Oxford: Hart Publishing.

Kommers, D.P. (1997) *The Constitution of the Federal Republic of Germany.* Durham, NC: Duke University Press.

Kong, H.L. and Levy, R. (2018) Deliberative Constitutionalism. In: Bächtinger, A., Dryzek, J.S., Mansbridge, J. and Warren, M.E. (eds.) *The Oxford Handbook of Deliberative Democracy.* Oxford: Oxford University Press.

Kotzur, M. (2012) Constitutional Amendments and Constitutional Changes in Germany. In: Contiades, X. (ed.) *Engineering Constitutional Change: A Comparative Perspective on Europe, Canada and the USA.* London: Routledge.

Kovács, K. and Tóth, G.A. (2011) Hungary's Constitutional Transformation. *European Constitutional Law Review* 7(2): 183–203.

Kramer, D. (2004) *The People Themselves. Popular Constitutionalism and Judicial Review.* Oxford: Oxford University Press.

Krisch, N. (2010) *Beyond Constitutionalism: The Pluralist Structure of Postnational Law.* Oxford: Oxford University Press.

Krisch, N. (2016) Pouvoir Constituent and Pouvoir Irritant in the Postnational Order. *International Journal of Comparative Constitutional Law* 14: 657–679.

Kumm, M. (2008) The Cosmopolitan Turn in Constitutionalism: On the Relationship between Constitutionalism in and Beyond the State. In: Dunoff, J.L. and Trachtman, J.P. (eds.) *Ruling the World? Constitutionalism, International Law, and Global Governance.* New York: Cambridge University Press.

Kumm, M. (2016a) Constituent Power: Boundaries and Identity: On the Justificatory Depth of Constitutionalism – A Rejoinder to Neil Walker. *International Journal of Comparative Constitutional Law* 14(4): 914–924.

Kumm, M. (2016b) Constituent Power, Cosmopolitan Constitutionalism, and Post-Positivist Law. *International Journal of Comparative Constitutional Law* 14(3): 697–711.

Kundnani, H. (2015) *The Paradox of German Power.* Oxford: Oxford University Press.

Kuo, M.-S. (2019) Between Fact and Norm. Narrative and the Constitutionalisation of Founding Moments. In: Albert, R., Guruswamy, M. and Basnyat, N. (eds.) *Founding Moments in Constitutionalism.* Oxford: Hart Publishing.

Kymlicka, W. (2001a) Territorial Boundaries. A Liberal Egalitarian Perspective. In: Miller, D. and Hashmi, S.H. (eds.) *Boundaries and Justice. Diverse Ethical Perspectives.* Princeton, NJ: Princeton University Press.

Kymlicka, W. (2001b) *Politics in the Vernacular: Nationalism, Multiculturalism and Citizenship.* Oxford. Oxford University Press.

Laboulaye, E. (1993) *Questions constitutionnelles.* Caen: Centre de Philosophie politique et juridique (1st edition 1872).

Lafayette, L.G.d.M. (1838) *Mémoires Correspondance et manuscrits,* Vol. IV. Paris: H. Fournier Ainé.

Landau, D. (2013a) Constitution-Making Gone Wrong. *Alabama Law Review* 64: 923–980.

Landau, D. (2013b) Abusive Constitutionalism. *University of California, Davis Law Review* 47: 189–260.

Landemore, H. (2015) Inclusive Constitution-Making: The Icelandic Experiment. *Journal of Political Philosophy* 23(2): 166–191.

Landemore, H. (2020) When Public Participation Matters: The 2010–2013 Icelandic Constitutional Process. *International Journal of Comparative Constitutional Law* 18: 179–205.

Lange, E. (1993) *Die Würde Des Menschen ist unantastbar. Der parlamentarische Rat und das Grundgesetz.* Heidelberg: Decker & Müller.

Lassalle, F. (1993) *Über Verfassungswesen: Rede am 16 April 1862 in Berlin.* Hamburg: Europäische Verlagsanstalt Hamburg.

Lee, D. (2016) *Popular Sovereignty in Early Modern Constitutional Thought.* Oxford: Oxford University Press.

Lefort, C. (1988) *Democracy and Political Theory.* Minneapolis, MN: University of Minnesota Press.

Lerche, P. (1995) Der Beitritt de DDR – Voraussetzungen, Realisierung, Wirkungen. In: Isensee, J. and Kirchhof, P. (eds.) *Handbuch Des Staatsrechts der Bundesrepublik Deutschland*, vol. VIII. Heidelberg: C.F. Müller.

Levinson, S. (1996) The Political Implications of Amending Clauses. *Constitutional Commentary* 13: 107–124.

Levinson, S. (2001) Designing an Amendment Process. In: Ferejohn, John et al. (eds.) *Constitutional Culture and Democratic Rule.* Cambridge: Cambridge University Press.

Levinson, S. (2004) "Perpetual Union", "Free Love" and Secession: On the Limits to the "Consent of the Governed". *Tulsa Law Review* 39: 457–484.

Levinson, S. (2014) Popular Sovereignty and the United States Constitution: Tensions in the Ackermanian Program. *The Yale Law Journal* 123: 2644–2674.

Lewis, H.O. (1948) *New Constitutions in Occupied Germany.* Washington, DC: Foundation for Foreign Affairs.

Lindahl, H. (2003) Acquiring a Community: The *Acquis* and the Institution of European Legal Order. *European Law Journal* 9: 433–450.

Lindahl, H. (2007) Constituent Power and Reflexive Identity: Towards an Ontology of Collective Selfhood. In: Loughlin, M. and Walker, N. (eds.) *The Paradox of Constitutionalism, Constituent Power and Constitutional Form.* Oxford: Oxford University Press.

Lindahl, H. (2015) Possibility, Actuality, Rupture: Constituent Power and the Ontology of Change. *Constellations* 22(2): 163–174.

Locke, J. (2015) Second Treatise of Government. In: Locke, J. and Laslett, P. (eds.) *Two Treatises of Government.* Cambridge: Cambridge University Press (1st edition 1689).

López Bofill, H. (2014) The Limits of Constitutionalism: Politics, Economics, and Secessionism in Catalonia (2006–2013). In: Lluch, Jaime (ed.) *Constitutionalism and the Politics of Accomodation in Multinational Democracies.* Houndmills: Palgrave Macmillan.

López Bofill, H. (2019a) Hubris, Constitutionalism, and "the Indissoluble Unity of the Spanish Nation": The Repression of Catalan Secessionist Referenda in Spanish Constitutional Law. *International Journal of Constitutional Law* 17(3): 943–969.

López Bofill, H. (2019b) Hubris, Constitutionalism, and "the Indissoluble Unity of the Spanish Nation": A Rejoinder to Antonio Bar. *International Journal of Constitutional Law* 17(3): 984–991.

Loughlin, M. (2007) Constituent Power Subverted: From English Constitutional Argument to British Constitutional Practice. In: Loughlin, M. and Walker, N.

(eds.) *The Paradox of Constitutionalism, Constituent Power and Constitutional Form*. Oxford: Oxford University Press.

Loughlin, M. (2010) *Foundations of Public Law*. Oxford: Oxford University Press.

Loughlin, M. (2014) The Concept of Constituent Power. *European Journal of Political Theory* 13(2): 218–237.

Lowe, K. (2013) *Savage Continent. Europe in the Aftermath of World War II*. London: Penguin Books (1st edition 2012).

Lübbe, H. (2005) Der Nationalsozialismus im politischen Bewußtsein der Gegenwart. In: Broszat, M. et al. (ed.) *Deutschlands Weg in die Diktatur*. Berlin: Siedler.

Lutz, D. (1988) *The Origins of American Constitutionalism*. Baton Rouge: Louisiana State University Press.

Lynd, S. (1966) The Compromise of 1787. *Political Science Quarterly* 81: 225–250.

Lyotard, J.F. (1979) *La Condition Postmoderne. Rapport sur le savoir*. Paris: Les Editions de Minuit.

Lyotard, J.-F. (1983) *Le différend*. Paris: Les Éditions de Minuit.

Madison, J. (1979) *The Papers of James Madison*, Vol.9. Chicago, IL: University of Chicago Press.

Maier, P. (2010) *Ratification. The People Debate the Constitution, 1787–1788*. New York: Simon & Schuster.

Main, J.T. (1966) Government by the People: The American Revolution and the Democratization of the Legislatures. *William and Mary Quarterly* 23(3): 391–407.

Mann, M. (1986) *The Sources of Social Power. Volume I. A History of Power from the Beginning to A.D. 1760*. Cambridge: Cambridge University Press.

Mann, M. (2001) Democracy and Ethnic War. In: Barkawi, T. and Laffey, B. (eds.) *Demography, Liberalism and War*. Boulder, CO: Lynne Reiner.

Mann, M. (2005) *The Dark Side of Democracy. Explaining Ethnic Cleansing*. New York: Cambridge University Press.

Mansfield, E. and Snyder, J. (1995) Democratization and the Danger of War. *International Security* 20: 5–38.

Marchart, O. (2007) *Post-Foundational Political Thought. Political Difference in Nancy, Lefort, Badiou and Laclau*. Edinburgh: Edinburgh University Press.

Markovits, I. (2008) Constitution Making after National Catastrophes: Germany in 1948 and 1990. *William and Mary Law Review* 49: 1307–1346.

Marshall, T. (1987) The Constitution's Bicentennial: Commemorating the Wrong Document? *Vanderbilt Law Review* 40: 1337–1342.

Martí, D. and Cetrà, D. (2016) The 2015 Catalan Election: A De Facto Referendum on Independence? *Regional & Federal Studies* 26: 107–119.

Martínez Dalmau, R. (2009) El Proyecto de Constitución en Ecuador. Ejemplo del nuevo constitucionalismo. *IUS. Revista del Instituto de Ciencias Jurídicas de Puebla* 23: 264–274.

Marx, K. (1975) Contribution to the Critique of Hegel's Philosophy of Law: Introduction. In: Marx, K. and Engels, F., *Collected Works*, Vol.3. New York: International Publishers.

Mason, M. (2006) *Slavery and Politics in the Early American Republic*. Chapel Hill, NC: University of North Carolina Press.

Massüger Sánchez Sandoval, N. and Welp, Y. (2016) Legality and Legitimacy: Constituent Power in Venezuela, Bolivia and Ecuador. In: Wheatley, J. and

Mendez, F. (eds.) *Patterns of Constitutional Design: The Role of Citizens and Elites in Constitution-Making*. London: Routledge.
Mazower, M. (2000) *Dark Continent. Europe's Twentieth Century*. New York: Vintage Books.
Mazower, M. (2008) *Hitler's Empire. How the Nazis Ruled Europe*. New York: Penguin Books.
McDonald, F. (1958) *We the People: The Economic Origins of the Constitution*. Chicago, IL: Chicago University Press.
McDonald, F. (1968) *Confederation and Constitution 1781–1789*. New York: Harper Torchbooks.
McDonogh, G. (2009) *After the Reich, the Brutal History of the Allied Occupation*. New York: Basic Books.
McPherson, J. (1988) *Battle Cry of Freedom. The Civil War Era*. Oxford and New York: Oxford University Press.
McGuire, R.A. (2003) *To Form a More Perfect Union. A New Economic Interpretation of the United States Constitution*. Oxford: Oxford University Press.
McGuire, R.A. and Ohsfeldt, R.L. (1984) Economic Interests and the American Constitution: A Quantitative Rehabilitation of Charles A.Beard. *The Journal of Economic History* 44(2): 509–519.
McIlwain, C.H. (1923) *The American Revolution: A Constitutional Interpretation*. New York: The Macmillan Company.
McIlwain, C.H. (2007) *Constitutionalism Ancient and Modern*. Indianapolis, IN: Liberty Fund (1st edition 1940).
McLaughlin, A.C. (1932) *The Foundations of American Constitutionalism*. New York: The New York University Press.
Meehan, E. (2000) Britain's Irish Question: Britain's European Question? British-Irish Relations in the Context of European Union and the Belfast Agreement. *Review of International Studies* 26(1): 83–97.
Mendez, F. and Wheatley, J. (2013) The Constitution-Making Process: An Analytical Framework. In: Wheatley, J. and Mendez, F. (eds.) *Patterns of Constitutional Design. The Role of Citizens and Elites in Constitution-Making*. Farnham: Ashgate.
Merkl, P.H. (1963) *The Origins of the West German Republic*. New York: Oxford University Press.
Meuwese, A. (2013) Popular Constitution-Making: The Case of Iceland. In: Galligan, D.J. and Versteeg, M. (eds.) *Social and Political Foundations of Constitutions*. New York: Cambridge University Press.
Michelman, F.I. (1996) Jürgen Habermas' Between Facts and Norms. *The Journal of Philosophy* 93(6): 307–315.
Michelman, F.I. (1998) Constitutional Authorship. In: Alexander, L. (ed.) *Constitutionalism: Philosophical Foundations*. Cambridge: Cambridge University Press.
Michelman, F.I. (1999) *Brennan and Democracy*. Princeton, NJ: Princeton University Press.
Middlekauff, R. (2007) *The Glorious Cause. The American Revolution, 1763–1789*. Oxford: Oxford University Press.
Miliband, R. (1983) *The State in Capitalist Society*. London: Quartet Books.
Miller, J. (1979) The Pathos of Novelty: Hannah Arendt's Image of Freedom in the Modern World. In: Hill, M.A. (ed.) *Hannah Arendt: The Recovery of The Public World*. New York: St Martin's Press.

Mitchell, M.D. (1997) Stunde Null in German Politics? Confessional Culture, Realpolitik, and the Organization of Christian Democracy. In Giles, G.J. (ed.) *Stunde Null: The End and the Beginning. 50 Years Ago*. Occasional Paper Number 20. Washington, DC: German Historical Institute.

Möllers, C. (2007) We Are (Afraid of) the People: Constituent Power in German Constitutionalism. In: Loughlin, M. and Walker, N. (eds.) *The Paradox of Constitutionalism, Constituent Power and Constitutional Form*. Oxford: Oxford University Press.

Monaghan, H.P. (1981) Our Perfect Constitution. *New York University Law Review* 56: 353–396.

Morel, L. (2012) Referendum. In: Rosenfeld, M. and Sajó, A. (eds.) *The Oxford Handbook of Comparative Constitutional Law*. Oxford: Oxford University Press.

Morgan, E.S. (1975) *American Slavery, American Freedom. The Ordeal of Colonial Virginia*. New York: W.W. Norton & Company.

Mortati, C. (1998) *La Costituzione in senso materiale*. Milano: Giuffrè Editore (1st edition 1940).

Mosca, G. (1939) *The Ruling Class*. New York: McGraw-Hill.

Mouffe, Ch. (2000) *The Democratic Paradox (Radical Thinkers)*. London: Verso Books.

Mouffe, Ch. (2009) The Limits of John Rawls' Pluralism. *Theoria: A Journal of Social and Political Theory* 56(118): 1–14.

Mousseau, M. (2000) Market Prosperity, Democratic Consolidation, and Democratic Peace. *Journal of Conflict Resolution* 44: 472–507.

Murkens, J.E.K. (2010) We Want Our Identity Back: The Revival of National Sovereignty in the German Federal Court's Decision on the Lisbon Treaty. *Public Law* 3: 530–550.

Murswiek, D. (1978) *Die verfassunggebende Gewalt nach dem Grundgesetz für die Bundesrepublik Deutschland*. Berlin: Duncker & Humblot.

Mußgnung, R. (2003) Zustandenkommen Des Grundgesetzes und Entstehen der Bundesrepublik Deutschland. In: Isensee, J. and Kirchhof, P. (eds.) *Handbuch Des Staatsrechts*, Vol. I. Heidelberg: C.F. Müller.

Nash, G.B. (1976) Urban Wealth and Poverty in Pre-Revolutionary America. *The Journal of Interdisciplinary History* 6(4): 545–584.

Näsström, S. (2007) The Legitimacy of the People. *Political Theory* 35(5): 624–658.

Nedelsky, J. (1990) *Private Property and the Limits of American Constitutionalism. The Madisonian Framework and Its Legacy*. Chicago, IL: The University of Chicago Press.

Negretto, G. (2020) Constitution-Making and Liberal Democracy: The Role of Citizens and Representative Elites. *International Journal of Comparative Constitutional Law* 18(1): 206–232.

Negri, A. (2002) *Il potere costituente: Saggio sulle alternative del moderno*. Roma: Manifestolibri.

Nelson, E. (2014) *The Royalist Revolution. Monarchy and the American Founding*. Cambridge, MA: The Belknap Press of Harvard University Press.

Neuberg, R. (2001) *Die Ersten Landtagswahlen in Den Westzonen*. München: Grin Verlag. https://www.grin.com/document/100202.

Nevins, A. (1927) *The American States during and after the Revolution, 1775–1789*. New York: Macmillan.

Nietzsche, F. (1892) *Zur Genealogie der Moral*. Leipzig: C.G. Naumann.

Nootens, G. (2015) Constituent Power and People-as-the Governed: About the "Invisible" People of Political and Legal Theory. *Global Constitutionalism* 4(2): 137–156.
O'Donnell, G. and Schmitter, P.C. (1986) *Transitions from Authoritarian Rule: Tentative Conclusions about Uncertain Democracies.* Baltimore, MD: Johns Hopkins University Press.
O'Mahony, C. (2012) Principled Expediency. How the Irish Courts Can Compromise on Same-Sex Marriage. *Dublin University Law Journal* 35: 199–228.
O'Sullivan, S., Healy, A.E. and Breen, M.J. (2014) Political Legitimacy in Ireland during Economic Crisis: Insights from the European Social Survey. *Irish Political Studies* 29(4): 547–572.
Oakeshott, M. (1975) On the Character of a Modern European State. In: Oakeshott, M. (ed.) *On Human Conduct.* Oxford: Clarendon Press.
Oakeshott, M. (1999) *On History.* Carmel, IN: Liberty Fund (1st edition 1983).
Ohline, H.A. (1971) Republicanism and Slavery: Origins of the Three-Fifths Clause in the United States Constitution. *William and Mary Quarterly* 28(4): 563–584.
Ojanen, T. (2013) Constitutional Amendment in Finland. In: Contiades, X. (ed.) *Engineering Constitutional Change. A Comparative Perspective on Europe, Canada and the USA.* London: Routledge.
Oklopcic, Z. (2014) Three Arenas of Struggle: A Contextual Approach to the Constituent Power of "the People". *Global Constitutionalism* 3(2): 200–235.
Oklopcic, Z. (2018) *Beyond the People. Social Imaginary and Constituent Imaginary.* Oxford: Oxford University Press.
Okubasu, D. (2017) The Implication of Conflation of Normal and "Constitutional Politics" on Constitutional Change in Africa. In: Albert, R., Contiades, X. and Fotiadou, A. (eds.) *The Foundations and Traditions of Constitutional Law.* Oxford: Hart Publishing.
Ólafsson, J. (2021) Crowdsourcing the 2011 Proposal for a New Constitution: When Experts and the Crowd Disagree. In: Arnason, A. and Dupré, C. (eds.) *Icelandic Constitutional Reform. People, Processes, Politics.* Abingdon: Routledge.
Olson, K. (2007) Paradoxes of Constitutional Democracy. *American Journal of Political Science* 51(2): 330–343.
Ortega y Gasset, J. (1988) *España invertebrada. Bosquejo de algunos pensamientos históricos.* Madrid: Alianza Editorial (1st edition 1921).
Otake, H. (2001) Two Contrasting Constitutions in the Postwar World: The Making of the Japanese and West German Constitutions. In: Higuchi, Y. (ed.) *Five Decades of Constitutionalism in Japanese Society.* Tokyo: University of Tokyo Press.
Palmer, R.R. (1966) *The Age of Democratic Revolution. A Political History of Europe and America, 1760–1800.* Princeton, NJ: Princeton University Press.
Palmer, R.R. (1968) The American Revolution: The People as Constituent Power. In: Green, J.P. (ed.) *The Reinterpretation of the American Revolution 1763–1789.* New York: Harper & Row.
Partlett, W. (2012) The Dangers of Popular Constitution-Making. *Brooklyn Journal of International Law* 38: 193–238.
Partlett, W. (2017) The American Tradition of Constituent Power. *International Journal of Constitutional Law* 15(4): 955–987.
Pasquino, P. (1998) *Sieyès et l'invention de la constitution en France.* Paris: Editions Odile Jacob.

Pasquino, P. (2013) Classifying Constitutions: Preliminary Conceptual Analysis. *Cardozo Law Review* 34: 999–1019.

Patberg, M. (2017) Constituent Power: A Discourse-Theoretical Solution to the Conflict between Openness and Containment. *Constellations* 24(1): 51–62.

Pavković, A. (2011) *The Right to Secede: Do We Really Need It?* Ashgate: The Ashgate Research Companion to Secession.

Pettigrew, W. (2007) Free to Enslave: Politics and the Escalation of Britain's Transatlantic Slave Trade, 1688–1714. *William and Mary Quarterly*, Third Series, 64: 3–37.

Pfetsch, F.R. (1990) *Ursprünge der Zweiten Republik. Prozesse der Verfassungsgebung in den Westzonen und in der Bundesrepublik.* Opladen: Westdeutscher Verlag.

Pichl, M. (2019) Constitution of False Prophecies. The Illiberal Transformation of Hungary. In: Alviar Garcia, H. and Frankenberg, G. (eds.) *Authoritarian Constitutionalism. Comparative Analysis and Critique.* Cheltenham: Edward Elgar.

Polzin, M. (2016) Constitutional Identity, Unconstitutional Amendments and the Idea of Constituent Power: The Development of the Doctrine of Constitutional Identity in German Constitutional Law. *International Journal of Comparative Constitutional Law* 14(2): 411–438.

Pommerscheim, F. (2012) *Broken Landscape: Indians, Indian Tribes and the Constitution.* Oxford: Oxford University Press.

Preuss, U. (1992–1993) Constitutional Powermaking for the New Polity: Some Deliberations on the Relations between Constituent Power and the Constitution. *Cardozo Law Review* 14: 639–660.

Preuss, U. (1995) *Constitutional Revolution: The Link between Constitutionalism and Progress.* New Jersey: Humanities Press.

Preuss, U. (2006–2007) Perspectives on Post-Conflict Constitutionalism: Reflections on Regime Change through External Constitutionalization. *New York Law School Law Review* 51: 467–494.

Quaritsch, H. (1995) Wiedervereinigung in Selbstbestimmung – Recht, Realität, Legitimation. In: Isensee, J. and Kirchhof, P. (eds.) *Handbuch Des Staatsrechts der Bundesrepublik Deutschland*, Vol. VIII. Heidelberg: C.F. Müller.

Quiero, F. and Gajardo, J. (2016) *Por una Asamblea Constituyente: Mecanismos, procesos y contenidos para una nueva Constitución.* Santiago de Chile: Clacso/ICAL.

Quint, P.E. (1992–1993) Constitution-Making by Treaty in German Unification: A Comment on Arato, Elster, Preuss and Richards. *Cardozo Law Review* 14: 691–704.

Rakove, J.N. (1997) *Original Meanings: Political and Ideas in the Making of the Constitution.* New York: Vintage Books.

Rakove, J.N. and Adams, W.P. (1981) Review to *the First American Constitutions: Republican Ideology and the Making of the State Constitutions in the Revolutionary Era* by Willi Paul Adams. *The William and Mary Quarterly* 38(2): 297–301.

Rana, A. (2020) Constitutionalism and the Predicament of Postcolonial Independence. In: Albert, R. (ed.) *Revolutionary Constitutionalism. Law, Legitimacy, Power.* Oxford: Hart Publishing.

Rawls, J. (1971) *A Theory of Justice.* Cambridge, MA: The Belknap Press of Harvard University Press.

Rawls, J. (1996) *Political Liberalism: With a New Introduction and the "Reply to Habermas".* New York: Columbia University Press.

Rawls, J. (2001) Justice as Fairness: A Restatement. In: Kelly, E. (ed.) *Collected Papers*. Cambridge, MA: The Belknap Press of Harvard University Press.
Raz, J. (1974) Kelsen's Theory of the Basic Norm. *American Journal of Jurisprudence* 19(1): 94–111.
Raz, J. (1995) Authority, Law and Morality. In: Raz, J. (ed.) *Ethics in the Public Domain. Essays in the Morality of Public Domain*. Oxford: Clarendon Press.
Redfield, R. (1955) *The Little Community. View Points for the Study of a Human Whole*. Uppsala: Almqvist & Wiksells Boktryckeri.
Reid, J.Ph. (1986) *Constitutional History of the American Revolution*, Vol. 1. Madison, WI: University of Wisconsin Press.
Renan, E. (1961) Qu'est-ce qu'une Nation? In: Renan, E. (ed.) *Œuvres complètes*. Vol I. Paris: Calmann-Lévy (1st edition 1882).
Richards, D.A.J. (1989) *Foundations of American Constitutionalism*. Oxford: Oxford University Press.
Richards, D.A.J. (1992–1993) Revolution and Constitutionalism in America. *Cardozo Law Review* 14: 577–634.
Richards, L.L. (2000) *The Slave Power: The Free North and Southern Dominion, 1780–1860*. Baton Rouge: Louisiana State University Press.
Richards, L.L. (2002) *Shays' Rebellion. The American Revolution's Final Battle*. Philadelphia, PA: University of Pennsylvania Press.
Riker, W.H. (1964) *Federalism: Origin, Operation, Significance*. Boston: Little, Brown and Company.
Robertson, D.B. (2015) The Constitution from 1620 to the Early Republic. In: Tushnet, M., Graber, M.A. and Levinson, S. (eds.) *The Oxford Handbook of the U.S. Constitution*. New York: Oxford University Press.
Röhrich, W. (1997) Die "Stunde Null". In: Conze, E. and Metzler, G. (eds.) *Deutschland nach 1945. Ein Lesebuch zur Deutschen Geschichte von 1945 bis zur Gegenwart*. München: C.H. Beck.
Rosenfeld, M. (2005) The European Treaty-Constitution and Constitutional Identity: A View from America. *International Journal of Constitutional Law* 3(2–3): 316–331.
Rosenthal, I. (2019) Ontology and Political Theory: A Critical Encounter between Rawls and Foucault. *European Journal of Political Theory* 18(2): 238–258.
Rossi, E. (2016) Can Realism Move beyond a *Methodenstreit*? *Political Theory* 44: 410–420.
Rossi, E. and Sleat, M. (2014) Realism in Normative Political Theory. *Philosophy Compass* 9(10): 689–701.
Rousseau, J.-J. (1966) *Du Contrat Social*. Paris: Garnier-Flammarion (1st edition 1762).
Rowe, G. and Frewer, L.J. (2015) A Typology of Public Engagement Mechanisms. *Science, Technology and Human Values* 30(2): 251–290.
Roznai, Y. (2016) "We the Limited People", conference paper presented at the 2016 Annual Meeting of ICON-S, The International Society of Public Law, Humboldt University Berlin, 18 June 2016.
Roznai, Y. (2017) *Unconstitutional Constitutional Amendments. The Limits of Amendment Powers*. Oxford: Oxford University Press.
Rua Wall, I. (2012) *Human Rights and Constituent Power. Without Model or Warranty*. Abingdon: Routledge.
Rubenfeld, J. (2001) *Freedom and Time: A Theory of Constitutional Self-Government*. New Haven, CT: Yale University Press.

Rubinelli, L. (2019) How to Think beyond Sovereignty: On Sieyes and Constituent Power. *European Journal of Political Theory* 18(1): 47–67.

Rubinelli, L. (2020) *Constituent Power: A History*. Cambridge: Cambridge University Press.

Russell, P. H. (1993) *Constitutional Odyssey: Can Canadians Become Sovereign People?* Toronto, ON: University of Toronto Press.

Samahon, T. (2011–2012) Democracy, Violence and Constitutional Revision in the Shadow of Democratic Revolution Theory. *Denver University Law Review* 89: 735–745.

Samuels, K. (2006) Post-Conflict Peace-Building and Constitution-Making. *Chicago Journal of International Law* 6: 663–682.

Sánchez Agesta, L. (1959) *Lecciones de derecho político*. Granada: Libreria Prieto.

Sanjaume-Calvet, M. (2019) Moralism in Theories of Secession: A Realist Perspective. *Nations and Nationalism* 1–21, doi:10.1111/nana.12544.

Saunders, C. (2012) Constitution-Making in the 21st Century. *International Review of Law* 4: 3–13.

Scarry, E. (1991) War and the Social Contract: Nuclear Policy, Distribution and the Right to Bear Arms. *University of Pennsylvania Law Review* 139(5): 1257–1316.

Schäuble, W. (1991) Der Einigungsvertrag – Vollendung der Einheit Deutschlands in Freheit. In: Guggenberger, B. and Stein, T. (eds.) *Die Verfassungsdiskussion im Jahr der Deutschen Einheit*. München: Carl Hanser.

Schauer, F. (1993) Constitutional Positivism. *Connecticut Law Review* 25: 797–841.

Scheidel, W. (2017) *The Great Leveler. Violence and the History of Inequality from the Stone Age to Twenty-First Century*. Princeton, NJ: Princeton University Press.

Scheuerman, W.E. (1997) Revolutions and Constitutions: Hannah Arendt's Challenge to Carl Schmitt. *Canadian Journal of Law and Jurisprudence* 10(1): 141–161.

Schmitt, C. (1974) *Der Nomos der Erde: Im Völkerrecht de Jus Publicum Europaeum*. Berlin: Duncker & Humblot (1st edition 1950).

Schmitt, C. (1978) Die legale Weltrevolution: Politischer Mehrwert als Prämie auf juristische Legalität und Superlegalität. *Der Staat* 17: 321–339.

Schmitt, C. (1993) *Verfassungslehre*. Berlin: Duncker & Humblot (1st edition 1928).

Schmitt, C. (2003) *Der Leviathan in der Staatslehre Des Thomas Hobbes. Sinn und Fehlschlag eines politischen Symbols*. Stuttgart: Klett-Cotta (1st edition 1938).

Schmitt, C. (2004) *Politische Theologie. Vier Kapitel zur Lehre von der Souveränität*. Berlin: Duncker & Humblot (1st edition 1922).

Schmitt, C. (2018) *Der Begriff Des Politischen*. Berlin: Duncker & Humblot (1st edition 1932).

Schneider, H.-P. (1954) Fünf Jahre grundgesetz. *Neue juristische wochenschrift* 25: 937–941.

Schneider, H.-P. (1992) Die verfassunggebende Gewalt. In: Isensee, J. and Kirchhof, P. (eds.) *Handbuch des Staatsrechts der Bundesrepublik Deutschland*, Vol. VII. Heidelberg: C.F. Müller.

Schneider, K. (2014) Der Ultra-Vires-Maßtab im Außenverfassungsrecht Verfassungsrecht. *Archiv des öffentlichen Rechts* 139(2): 196–237.

Schneiderman, D. (2008) *Constitutionalizing Economic Globalization. Investment Rules and Democracy's Promise*. Cambridge: Cambridge University Press.

Schulz, P. (1984) *Ursprünge unserer Freiheit: Von de Amerikanische Revolution zum Bonner Grundgesetz*. Hamburg: Hoffmann & Canpe.

Schumpeter, J.A. (2010) *Capitalism, Socialism and Democracy*. Abingdon: Routledge (1st edition 1942).
Schupmann, B.A. (2017) *Carl Schmitt's State and Constitutional Theory. A Critical Analysis*. Oxford: Oxford University Press.
Schweber, H.H. (2012) *Democracy and Authenticity. Toward a Theory of Public Justification*. New York: Cambridge University Press.
Schweitzer, M. (1995) Die Verträge Deutschlands mit der Siegermächten. In: Isensee, J. and Kirchhof, P. (eds.) *Handbuch Des Staatsrechts der Bundesrepublik Deutschland*, Vol. VIII. Heidelberg: C.F. Müller.
Sebok, A.J. (1997) Is the Rule of Recognition a Rule? *Notre Dame Law Review* 72: 1539–1563.
Selsam, J.P. (1971) *The Pennsylvania Constitution of 1776: A Study in Revolutionary Democracy*. New York: Da Capo Press (1st edition 1936).
Setälä, M., Grönlund, K. and Herne, K. (2010) Citizen Deliberation on Nuclear Power: A Comparison of Two Decision-Making Methods. *Political Studies* 58(4): 688–714.
Shaw, J. (1999) Postnational Constitutionalism in the European Union. *Journal of European Public Policy* 6(4): 579–597.
Sieyès, E. (1985) Dire de l'abbé Sieyes sur la Question du Veto Royal, & C.A la séance du 7 septembre 1789. In: Sieyès, E. and Zapperi, R. (eds.) *Écrites politiques*. Paris: Editions des Archives Contemporaines.
Sieyès, E. (1988) *Qu'est-ce que le tiers-état?* Paris: Flammarion (1st edition 1789).
Sieyès, E. (2014) Reasoned Exposition of the Rights of Man and Citizen. In: Lembcke, O.W. and Weber, F. (eds.) *Emmanuel Joseph Sieyès: The Essential Political Writings*. Leiden: Brill (1st edition 1789).
Simmons, A.J. (2001) *Justification and Legitimacy. Essays on Rights and Obligations*. New York: Cambridge University Press.
Simons, H. (1952) The Bonn Constitution and Its Government. In: Morgenthau, H.J. (ed.) *Germany and the Future of Europe*. Chicago: The University of Chicago Press.
Sinnott, R. (2002) Cleavages, Parties and Referendums: Relationships between Representative and Direct Democracy in the Republic of Ireland. *European Journal of Political Research* 41(6): 811–826.
Skoutaris, N. (2020) What's in an Irish Border? *Brexit*, the Backstop(S) and the Constitutional Integrity of the UK. *DCU/Brexit Institute*. Working Paper 2.
Slobodian, Q. (2018) *Globalists. The End of the Empire and the Birth of Neoliberalism*. Cambridge, MA: Harvard University Press.
Snyder, J. (2000) *From Voting to Violence: Democratization and Nationalist Conflict*. New York: Norton.
Snyder, T. (2018) *The Road to Unfreedom*. London: Penguin Random House.
Solt, L.F. (1990) *Church and State in Early Modern England*. Oxford: Oxford University Press, 1509–1640.
Sólyom, L. (2015) Rise and Decline of Constitutional Culture in Hungary. In: Von Bogdandy, A. and Sonnevend, P. (eds.) *Constitutional Crises in the European Constitutional Area: Theory, Law and Politics in Hungary and Romania*. Oxford: Hart Publishing.
Somek, A. (2012) Constituent Power in National and Transnational Contexts. *Transnational Legal Theory* 3(1): 31–60.
Spalding, M. (2014) Slave Trade. In: Spalding, M. and Forte, D.F. (eds.) *The Heritage Guide to the Constitution*. Washington, DC: Regnery Publishing.

Spevack, E. (2001) *Allied Control and German Freedom. American Political and Ideological Influences on the Framing of the West German Basic Law*. Münster: Lit Verlag.

Stadelmann, M. (1995) Adenauer. In: Wilsford, D. (ed.) *Political Leaders of Contemporary Western Europe: A Biographical Dictionary*. Westport, CT: Greenwood Press.

Steinberg, H. (1990) Bemerkungen zu einer Synthese Des Einflusses ausländischer Verfassungsideen auf die Entstehung Des Grundgesetzes mit Deutschen verfassungsrechtlichen Traditionen. In: Stern, K. (ed.) *40 Jahre Grundgesetz Entstehung, Bewährung und internationale Ausstrahlung. Internationales Symposion vom 17. bis 20. Mai 1989*. München: Beck, Institut für öffentliches Recht und Verwaltungslehre der Universität zu Köln und der Fritz Thyssen Stiftung.

Steiner, U. (1966) *Verfassunggebung und verfassunggebende Gewalt Des Volkes*. Berlin: Duncker & Humblot.

Sternberger, D. (1977) The Sunken City: Hannah Arendt's Idea of Politics. *Social Research* 44: 132–146.

Sternberger, D. (1982) *Verfassungspatriotismus*. Hannover: Niedersächsische Landeszentrale für Politische Bildung.

Stolleis, M. (2003) Besatzung und Wiederaufbau deutscher Staatlichkeit. In: Isensee, J. and Kirchhof, P. (eds.) *Handbuch des Staatsrechts*, Vol. I. Heidelberg: C.F. Müller.

Suiter, J. and Reuchamps, M. (2016) A Constitutional Turn for Deliberative Democracy in Europe? In: Reuchamps, M. and Suiter, J. (eds.) *Constitutional Deliberative Democracy in Europe*. Colchester: European Consortium of Political Research Press.

Sunstein, C. (1988) Beyond the Republican Revival. *The Yale Law Journal* 97: 1539–1590.

Suteu, S. (2015) Constitutional Conventions in the Digital Era: Lessons from Iceland and Ireland. *Boston College International and Comparative Law Review* 38: 251–276.

Szatmary, D.P. (1980) *Shays' Rebellion: The Making of an Agrarian Insurrection*. Amherst, MA: The University of Massachusetts Press.

Tamir, Y. (1993) *Liberal Nationalism*. Princeton, NJ: Princeton University Press.

Tarr, G.A. (2006). Introduction. In: Tarr, G.A. and Williams, R.F. (eds.) *State Constitutions for the Twenty-First Century. The Politics of State Constitutional Reform*, Vol. 1. Albany, NY: State University of New York Press.

Taylor, Ch. (1992) *Multiculturalism and "The Politics of Recognition"*. Princeton, NJ: Princeton University Press.

Tekin, S. (2016) *Founding Acts. Constitutional Origins in a Democratic Age*. Philadelphia, PA: University of Pennsylvania Press.

Thayer, Th. (1953) *Pennsylvania Politics and the Growth of Democracy, 1740–1776*. Harrisburg, PA: Pennsylvania Historical and Museum Commission.

Thorarensen, B. (2017) The People's Contribution to Constitutional Changes. Writing, Advising or Approving? – Lessons from Iceland. In: Contiades, X. and Fotiadou, A. (eds.) *Participatory Constitutional Change. The People as Amenders of the Constitution*. London: Routledge.

Thornhill, C. (2012) Contemporary Constitutionalism and the Dialectic of Constituent Power. *Global Constitutionalism* 3: 369–404.

Tierney, S. (2012) *Constitutional Referendums: The Theory and Practice of Republican Deliberation*. Oxford: Oxford University Press.

Tierney, S. (2014) Europe Is Entering the "Age of the Referendum", but There Is Nothing to Fear for European Democracy if Referendums Are Properly Regulated. *Scottish Constitutional Futures Forum*, September 3. Available at http://blogs.lse.ac.uk/europpblog/2014/09/02/europe-is-now-entering-the-age-of-the-referendum-but-there-is-nothing-to-fear-for-european-democracy-if-referendums-are-properly-regulated/.

Tilly, C. (1975) Reflections on the History of European State-Making. In: Tilly, C. (ed.) *The Formation of National States in Western Europe*. Princeton, NJ: Princeton University Press.

Tilly, C. (1990) *Coercion, Capital, and European States.AD 990–1992*. Cambridge: Basil Blackwell.

Tobin, B. (2016) Marriage Equality in Ireland: The Politico-Legal Context. *International Journal of Law, Policy and the Family* 30(2): 115–130.

Tocqueville, A. (1955) *The Old Régime and the French Revolution*. Translation by Stuart Gilbert. Garden City, NY: Doubleday Anchor Books (1st edition 1856).

Tomuschat, C. (2009) The Ruling of the German Constitutional Court on the Treaty of Lisbon. *German Law Journal* 10(8): 1259–1262.

Tooze, A. (2018) *Crashed. How a Decade of Financial Crises Changed the World*. New York: Viking.

Topf, M.A. (2019) Foundation and Revolution. Hannah Arendt and the Problem of Legitimacy and Stability in Constitutional Consolidation. In: Albert, R., Guruswamy, M. and Basnyat, N. (eds.) *Founding Moments in Constitutionalism*. Oxford: Hart Publishing.

Torres, G. and Guinier, L. (2012) The Constitutional Imaginary: Just Stories about the People. *Maryland Law Review* 71: 1052–1072.

Tribe, L. (1995) Taking Text and Structure Seriously: Reflections on Free-Form Method in Constitutional Interpretation. *Harvard Law Review* 108(6): 1221–1303.

Tuck, R. (1999) *The Rights of War and Peace: Political Thought and the International Order from Grotius to Kant*. Oxford: Oxford University Press.

Tuck, R. (2016) *The Sleeping Sovereign: The Invention of Modern Democracy*. Cambridge: Cambridge University Press.

Tully, J. (1995) *Strange Multiplicity. Constitutionalism in an Age of Diversity*. Cambridge: Cambridge University Press.

Tully, J. (2002) The Unfreedom of the Moderns in Comparison to Their Ideals of Constitutional Democracy. *The Modern Law Review* 65(2): 204–228.

Turner Main, J. (1968) Government by the People: The American Revolution and the Democratization of the Legislatures. In: Green, J.P. (ed.) *The Reinterpretation of the American Revolution 1763–1789*. New York: Harper & Row.

Tushnet, M. (2009) *The Constitution of the United States of America. A Contextual Analysis*. Oxford: Hart Publishing.

Tushnet, M. (2013) Constitution-Making: An Introduction. *Texas Law Review* 91: 1983–2013.

Tushnet, M. (2015a) Authoritarian Constitutionalism. *Cornell Law Review* 100: 391–462.

Tushnet, M. (2015b) Peasants with Pitchforks, and Toilers with Twitter. Constitutional Revolutions and the Constituent Power. *International Journal of Comparative Constitutional Law* 13(3): 639–654.

Ugarte, S. (2013) El Nuevo Constitucionalismo latinoamericano (una Perspectiva Crítica). In: González Pérez, L.R. and Valadés, D. (eds.) *Constitucionalismo contemporáneo. Homenaje a Jorge Carpizo.* México City. Universidad Nacional Autónoma de México.

Uitz, R. (2015) Can You Tell When an Illiberal Democracy Is in the Making? An Appeal to Comparative Constitutional Scholarship from Hungary. *International Journal of Constitutional Law* 13(1): 279–300.

Van Middelaar, L. (2013) *The Passage to Europe: How a Continent Became a Union.* New Haven, CT: Yale University Press.

Verdugo, S. (2019a) On the Protests and Riots in Chile: Why Chile Should Modify Its Presidential System. *Blog of the International Journal of Constitutional Law*, October 29. Available at http://www.iconnectblog.com/2019/10/on-the-protests-and-riots-in-chile-why-chile-should-modify-its-presidential-system/.

Verdugo, S. (2019b) The Role of the Chilean Constitutional Court in Times of Change. In: Richard, A., Bernal, C. and Zaiden Benvindo, J. (eds.) *Constitutional Change and Transformation in Latin America.* Oxford: Hart Publishing.

Verdugo, S. and Contesse, J. (2018) The Rise and Fall of a Constitutional Moment: Lessons from the Chilean Experiment and the Failure of Bachelet's Project. *Blog of the International Journal of Constitutional Law*, March 13. Available at http://www.iconnectblog.com/2018/03/the-rise-and-fall-of-a-constitutional-moment-lessons-from-the-chilean-experiment-and-the-failure-of-bachelets-project/.

Versteeg, M. (2014) Unpopular Constitutionalism. *Indiana Law Journal* 89: 1133–1190.

Vogel, W. (1967) Die Ursprünge der Teilung Deutschlands in der Kriegszielpolitik der Alliierten. *Geschichte in Wissenschaft und Unterricht* 18: 193–211.

Von Bogdandy, A. (2010) Prinzipien der Rechtsfortbildung im europäischen Rechtsraum. Überlegungen zum Lissabon-Urteil Des BVerfG. *Neue juristische wochenschrift* 1–2: 1–5.

Wade, H.W.R. (1955) The Basis of Legal Sovereignty. *The Cambridge Law Journal* 13(2): 172–197.

Waldron, J. (1999) *Law and Disagreement.* Oxford: Oxford University Press.

Waldron, J. (2016) *Political Political Theory. Essays on Institutions.* Cambridge, MA: Harvard University Press.

Walker, N. (2008) Taking Constitutionalism Beyond the State. *Political Studies* 56(3): 519–543.

Walker, N. (2016) The Return of Constituent Power: A Reply to Mattias Kumm. *International Journal of Comparative Constitutional Law* 14(4): 906–913.

Walker, R.K. (2006) *The Hunger Strikes.* Belfast: Lagan Press.

Walzer, M. (1983) *Spheres of Justice. A Defense of Pluralism and Equality.* New York: Basic Books.

Weart, S. (1998) *Never at War: Why Democracies Will Not Fight One Another.* New Haven, CT: Yale University Press.

Weber, M. (1972) *Wirtschaft und gesellschaft.* Tübingen: J.C.B. Mohr (Paul Siebeck). (1st edition 1922).

Wehmer, G. (1994) *Die Westalliierten und das Grundgesetz, 1948–1949. Die Londoner Sechsmächtekonferenz.* Freiburg im Bresgau: Ronbach.

Weiler, J.H.H. (1999) To Be a European Citizen: Eros and Civilization. In: Weiler, J.H.H. (ed.) *The Constitution of Europe. "Do the New Clothes Have an Emperor?" and Other Essays on European Integration.* Cambridge: Cambridge University Press.

Weiler, J.H.H. (2003) In Defense of Status Quo: Europe's Constitutional *Sonderweg*. In: Weiler, J.H.H. and Wind, M. (eds.) *European Constitutionalism beyond the State*. Cambridge: Cambridge University Press.

Weingast, B.R. (1997) The Political Foundations of Democracy and the Rule of Law. *The American Political Science Review* 91(2): 245–263.

Werner, W. (1996). Introduction. In: Schick, R. and Kahlemberg, F.P. (eds.) *Der Parlamentarische Rat, 1948–1949: Akten und Protokolle*, Vol. 9. München: Harald Boldt Verlag im R. Oldenbourg Verlag.

Weyland, K. (2013) The Threat from Populist Left. *Journal of Democracy* 24(3): 18–32.

Widner, J. (2008) Constitution-Writing in Post-Conflict Settings: An Overview. *William and Mary Law Review* 49: 1513–1537.

Wiederin, E. (1992) Die Verfassunggebung im wiedervereinigten Deutschland. *Archiv des öffentlichen Rechts* 117: 410–448.

Wolin, Sh. (1983) Hannah Arendt: Democracy and the Political. *Salmagundi* 60: 3–19.

Wolin, Sh. (1989) *The Presence of the Past. Essays on the State and the Constitution.* Baltimore, MD: Johns Hopkins University Press.

Wolin, Sh. (1996) Fugitive Democracy. In: Benhabib, S. (ed.) *Democracy and Difference: Contesting the Boundaries of the Political.* Princeton, NJ: Princeton University Press.

Wolin, Sh. (2004) *Politics and Vision, Princeton.* NJ: Princeton University Press.

Wood, G.S. (1998) *The Creation of the American Republic, 1776–1787.* Chapell Hill, NC: The University of North Carolina Press (1st edition 1969).

Wood, G.S. (2002) *The American Revolution. A History.* New York: Random House.

Wright Mills, C. (2000) *The Power Elite.* Oxford: Oxford University Press (1st edition 1956).

Zacher, H.F. (1993) Deutsche. In: Nawiasky, Hans et al. (eds.) *Juristen jüdischer Herkunft.* München: Beck.

Zapf, W. (1965) *Wandlungen der Deutschen Elite.* München: Piper.

Žižek, S. (2008) *Violence. Six Sideways Reflections.* New York: Picador.

Zurn, C.H.F. (2010) The Logic of Legitimacy: Bootstrapping Paradoxes of Constitutional Democracy. *Legal Theory* 16(3): 191–227.

Zweig, E. (1909) *Die Lehre vom "pouvoir constituant". ein Beitrag zum Staatsrecht der französischen Revolution.* Tübingen: J.C.B. Mohr.

Index

For Product Safety Concerns and Information please contact our EU
representative GPSR@taylorandfrancis.com
Taylor & Francis Verlag GmbH, Kaufingerstraße 24, 80331 München, Germany

www.ingramcontent.com/pod-product-compliance
Ingram Content Group UK Ltd.
Pitfield, Milton Keynes, MK11 3LW, UK
UKHW020012200926
475702UK00014B/1839
* 9 7 8 0 3 6 7 5 1 6 7 3 4 *